STOCK
TRADER'S
ALMANAC
2017

Jeffrey A. Hirsch & Yale Hirsch

WILEY

www.stocktradersalmanac.com

This Fiftieth Anniversary Edition could be dedicated to none other than:

Yale Hirsch

If I have seen further, it is by standing upon the shoulders of giants.
—Sir Isaac Newton

Yale has been a giant to us all. We have proudly stood on his shoulders, magically ridden his coattails, and humbly attempted to build upon his genius. He created this masterpiece 50 years ago and its longevity is his legacy. His iconic thinking and thought leadership will live forever. At 92 and still rocking, he continues to test our intelligence, integrity, imagination, and mettle. Mensch, mentor, enduring source of inspiration, and loving father, thank you for teaching us to strive for excellence with a keen attention to detail and a nose for behavioral changes in finance, markets, economics, and sociology—not to mention a zest for wit.

Thank you to all those who helped us research and build the *Stock Trader's Almanac* legacy over the years and to those readers and colleagues that inspired, discussed and debated with us.
A special thanks and acknowledgement to those below who had a profound and direct impact on the evolution, improvement and production of the *Almanac*:
Scott Barrie (R.I.P.), George Brooks, Judd Brown, Bob Cardwell, Joseph Childrey, Sy Harding (R.I.P.), Davida Hirsch, Leslie Hirsch, Dave Kamm, Peter Lynch, Chris Mistal, Victor Niederhoffer, John Person, Betty Ross (R.I.P.), Daniel Turov, Pamela van Giessen, Larry Williams.

INTRODUCTION TO THE FIFTIETH ANNIVERSARY EDITION

We are pleased, proud, humbled, and amazed to introduce the Fiftieth Anniversary Edition of the *Stock Trader's Almanac*. The *Almanac* provides you with the necessary tools to invest successfully in the twenty-first century.

J. P. Morgan's classic retort, "Stocks will fluctuate," is often quoted with a wink-of-the-eye implication that the only prediction one can make about the stock market is that it will go up, down, or sideways. Many investors agree that no one ever really knows which way the market will move. Nothing could be further from the truth.

We discovered that while stocks do indeed fluctuate, they do so in well-defined, often predictable patterns. These patterns recur too frequently to be the result of chance or coincidence. How else do we explain that since 1950 all the gains in the market were made during November through April, compared to a loss May through October? (See page 52.)

The *Almanac* is a practical investment tool. It alerts you to those little-known market patterns and tendencies on which shrewd professionals enhance profit potential. You will be able to forecast market trends with accuracy and confidence when you use the *Almanac* to help you understand:

- How our presidential elections affect the economy and the stock market—just as the moon affects the tides. Many investors have made fortunes following the political cycle. You can be sure that money managers who control billions of dollars are also political cycle watchers. Astute people do not ignore a pattern that has been working effectively throughout most of our economic history.

- How the passage of the Twentieth Amendment to the Constitution fathered the January Barometer. This barometer has an outstanding record for predicting the general course of the stock market each year, with only eight major errors since 1950, for an 87.7% accuracy ratio. (See page 16.)

- Why there is a significant market bias at certain times of the day, week, month, and year.

Even if you are an investor who pays scant attention to cycles, indicators, and patterns, your investment survival could hinge on your interpretation of one of the recurring patterns found within these pages. One of the most intriguing and important patterns is the symbiotic relationship between Washington and Wall Street. Aside from the potential profitability in seasonal patterns, there's the pure joy of seeing the market very often do just what you expected.

The *Stock Trader's Almanac* is also an organizer. Its wealth of information is presented on a calendar basis. The *Almanac* puts investing in a business framework and makes investing easier because it:

- Updates investment knowledge and informs you of new techniques and tools.
- Is a monthly reminder and refresher course.
- Alerts you to both seasonal opportunities and dangers.
- Furnishes a historical viewpoint by providing pertinent statistics on past market performance.
- Supplies forms necessary for portfolio planning, record keeping, and tax preparation.

 The WITCH icon signifies THIRD FRIDAY OF THE MONTH on calendar pages and alerts you to extraordinary volatility due to the expiration of equity and index options and index futures contracts. Triple-witching days appear during March, June, September, and December.

 The BULL icon on calendar pages signifies favorable trading days based on the S&P 500 rising 60% or more of the time on a particular trading day during the 21-year period January 1995 to December 2015.

 A BEAR icon on calendar pages signifies unfavorable trading days based on the S&P falling 60% or more of the time for the same 21-year period.

Also, to give you even greater perspective, we have listed next to the date of every day that the market is open the Market Probability numbers for the same 21-year period for the Dow (D), S&P 500 (S), and NASDAQ (N). You will see a "D," "S," and "N" followed by a number signifying the actual Market Probability number for that trading day, based on the recent 21-year period. On pages 121–128, you will find complete Market Probability Calendars, both long-term and 21-year for the Dow, S&P, and NASDAQ, as well as for the Russell 1000 and Russell 2000 indices.

Other seasonalities near the ends, beginnings, and middles of months—options expirations, around holidays, and other significant times—as well as all FOMC Meeting dates are noted for *Almanac* investors' convenience on the weekly planner pages. All other important economic releases are provided in the Strategy Calendar every month in our e-newsletter, *Almanac Investor*, available at our website, *www.stocktradersalmanac.com*.

One-year seasonal pattern charts for Dow, S&P 500, NASDAQ, Russell 1000, and Russell 2000 appear on pages 171 to 173. There are three charts each for Dow and S&P 500 spanning our entire database starting in 1901 and one each for the younger indices. Since 2017 is a post-election year, each chart contains typical post-election year performance compared to all years.

The Notable Events on page 6 provides a handy list of major events of the past year that can be helpful when evaluating things that may have moved the market. Over the past few years, our research had been restructured to flow better with the rhythm of the year. This has also allowed us more room for added data. Again, we have included historical data on the Russell 1000 and Russell 2000 indices. The Russell 2K is an excellent proxy for small and mid-caps, which we have used over the years, and the Russell 1K provides a broader view of large caps. Annual highs and lows for all five indices covered in the *Almanac* appear on pages 149–151, and we've tweaked the Best & Worst section.

In order to cram in all this material, some of our Record Keeping section was cut. We have converted many of these paper forms into computer spreadsheets for our own internal use. As a service to our faithful readers, we are making these forms available at our website, *www.stocktradersalmanac.com*.

Post-election years have been the worst year of the four-year cycle and seventh years of decades have been the second worst, so 2017 has a troubled history behind it. You can find all the market charts of post-elections since the Depression on page 24, "Market Behavior Under New Presidents" on page 20, "Post-Election Year Performance by Party" on page 26, "Post-Election Years: Paying the Piper" on page 28, "Market Fares Better Under Democrats; Dollar Holds Up Better Under Republicans" on page 32, and "Republican Congress and Democratic President Best for the Market" on page 40. The last nine seventh years of decades appear on page 42. A Fifty-Year Retrospective appears on pages 34–36.

On page 76 is our Best Investment Book of the Year, *Juggling with Knives: Smart Investing in the Coming Age of Volatility*, by Jim Jubak (PublicAffairs, 2016), which should help you prepare for the next Super Boom. Other top books are listed on page 116. Sector seasonalities include several consistent shorting opportunities and appear on pages 94–98.

We are constantly searching for new insights and nuances about the stock market and welcome any suggestions from our readers.

Have a healthy and prosperous 2017!

NOTABLE EVENTS

2015

May 29	U.S. officially removes Cuba from state-sponsored terrorism list
Jun 6	American Pharaoh becomes the first winner of the Triple Crown since 1978
Jun 26	Islamic State gunman kills 38 tourists at Tunisian resort, second attack in three months
Jun 29	Greece misses 1.5 billion euro debt payment to IMF, exacerbating financial crisis
Jul 5–6	Greece votes no referendum to budget cuts in return for loans, banks closed 6 days
Jul 14	New Horizons spacecraft comes within 7,800 miles of Pluto, confirms nitrogen and methane ice
Jul 20	Cuba reopens U.S. embassy, restoring full diplomatic relations for first time since 1961
Sep 10	*Homo naledi*, previously unknown species of early human, discovered in South Africa
Sep 16	8.3 magnitude earthquake hits Chile, 1 million evacuate
Sep 18	Volkswagen worldwide rigging of diesel emissions tests on 11 million vehicles announced by EPA
Sep 28	NASA announces that liquid water has been found on Mars
Sep 28	Taliban seizes control over major city of Kunduz, Afghanistan
Sep 30	Russia begins air strikes in Syria in support of government against ISIL and rebels
Oct 10	Suicide bombs kill at least 100 at peace rally in Ankara, Turkey, injure more than 400
Oct 23	Hurricane Patricia most intense tropical cyclone ever, with 215 mph winds and 872 mbar pressure
Oct 26	7.5 magnitude earthquake strikes Hindu Kush region, causing 398 deaths
Oct 29	China ends one-child policy after decades to offset the country's aging workforce
Oct 31	ISIL bomb crashes Russian airliner in Egypt—all 224 people on board are killed
Nov 12	Several ISIL suicide bombings in Beirut kill 43 and injure 239
Nov 13	Three coordinated attacks by ISIS in Paris kill 130, hundreds wounded
Nov 20	Islamic extremists kill 27 in Mali hotel attack
Nov 24	Turkey shoots down Russian warplane—first NATO destruction of Russian warplane since Korean War
Dec 2	Terrorist couple kills 14, injures 22 in San Bernardino Social Services Center shooting
Dec 12	Global climate change pact at UN COP 21; first time all countries agree to reduce carbon emissions
Dec 16	U.S. Federal Reserve FOMC raises federal funds rate for first time in seven years, from 0.00–0.25% to 0.25–0.50%

2016

Jan 3	Following execution of Shia Sheikh Nimr, Iran ends diplomatic relations with Saudi Arabia
Jan 16	Landmark Iran nuclear deal goes into effect; inspections prove weapons dismantled; UN lifts sanctions
Jan 28	World Health Organization announces outbreak of the Zika virus
Feb 7	North Korea launches a long-range rocket into space, violating multiple UN treaties
Feb 11	Crude Oil WTI hits intraday low of $26.05
Mar 13	Car bomb explodes in Ankara, Turkey, killing at least 32
Mar 22	Three coordinated bombings in Brussels kill at least 32 and injure at least 250; ISIL claims responsibility
Mar 27	Suicide blast in Lahore targeting Christians celebrating Easter kills over 70, injures almost 300
Apr 2	Armenian and Azerbaijani military clashes kill at least 193 people, heaviest breach of the 1994 ceasefire

2017 OUTLOOK

Despite the impressive performance of Republican nominee Donald Trump, the market is leaning Democratic. The Dow up 2% the first five months of 2016 suggests that the Democrats will retain the White House. When the first five months are up in election years, the incumbent party usually wins and the market performs better for the full year. However, this presidential campaign resembling something of a daytime talk show is a threat to the bull.

If Trump gains traction, the market may falter. Trump has successfully run an unorthodox campaign so far, but he is an unknown with no track record in politics. As the general election campaign gets underway, his uncertainty and brash nature may be unsettling to Wall Street. Clinton's long, well-defined history and traditional campaign indicates she will not be a disruptive force and will continue many current policies.

Post-election years have been worse for the market under new Republican administrations, as they tend to come in hot and change things up fast. Midterm years have been worse for new Democrats, as they often hem and haw for a year and take little action until the midterm year. The party that rules the Oval Office next is likely to have a major impact on when the next major market bottom will occur.

Our Super Boom forecast that we first released in May 2010—for the market to make a 500+%-move by the year 2025, or DJIA 38,820, a six-fold gain from the intraday low on March 6, 2009, of 6470—is still firmly in play. Unfortunately, it does not call for much upside over the next couple years.

The next bear market, which could take the market 20–30% lower into 2017–2018, may already be underway or may commence sometime in late 2016 or early 2017. We expect this will be the last cyclical, garden-variety bear market, which will finally put an end to this secular bear that began in early 2000. After this next bear market, our Super Boom forecast should kick in.

Early signs of the end of the secular bear and coming Super Boom have already begun to materialize. The commodity secular bull market since 2000 has waned and the 30-year bull market in bonds that began near the end of the last secular bear for stocks in 1980–1982 looks to finally be fading.

In addition, new market leaders are rising to the top and we may get our next paradigm-shifting, culturally enabling technology from biotech or healthcare, or perhaps robotics or alternative energy. But that remains to be seen. Either way, continue to let your winners ride and enjoy the rally while it lasts. Just be prepared for gains to be less easy to come by over the next couple years while the stage is set for the Next Super Boom and secular bull market.

—*Jeffrey A. Hirsch, June 6, 2016*

6

THE 2017 STOCK TRADER'S ALMANAC

CONTENTS

DIRECTORY OF TRADING PATTERNS AND DATABANK

STRATEGY PLANNING AND RECORD SECTION

2017 STRATEGY CALENDAR

(Option expiration dates circled)

	MONDAY	TUESDAY	WEDNESDAY	THURSDAY	FRIDAY	SATURDAY	SUNDAY
JANUARY	26	27	28	29	30	31	1 JANUARY New Year's Day
	2	3	4	5	6	7	8
	9	10	11	12	13	14	15
	16 Martin Luther King Day	17	18	19	(20)	21	22
	23	24	25	26	27	28	29
FEBRUARY	30	31	1 FEBRUARY	2	3	4	5
	6	7	8	9	10	11	12
	13	14 ♥	15	16	(17)	18	19
	20 President's Day	21	22	23	24	25	26
MARCH	27	28	1 MARCH Ash Wednesday	2	3	4	5
	6	7	8	9	10	11	12 Daylight Saving Time Begins
	13	14	15	16	(17) ♣ St. Patrick's Day	18	19
	20	21	22	23	24	25	26
APRIL	27	28	29	30	31	1 APRIL	2
	3	4	5	6	7	8	9
	10	11 Passover	12	13	14 Good Friday	15	16 Easter
	17	18	19	20	(21)	22	23
	24	25	26	27	28	29	30
MAY	1 MAY	2	3	4	5	6	7
	8	9	10	11	12	13	14 Mother's Day
	15	16	17	18	(19)	20	21
	22	23	24	25	26	27	28
JUNE	29 Memorial Day	30	31	1 JUNE	2	3	4
	5	6	7	8	9	10	11
	12	13	14	15	(16)	17	18 Father's Day
	19	20	21	22	23	24	25
	26	27	28	29	30	1 JULY	2

10   *Market closed on shaded weekdays; closes early when half-shaded.*

2017 STRATEGY CALENDAR

(Option expiration dates circled)

MONDAY	TUESDAY	WEDNESDAY	THURSDAY	FRIDAY	SATURDAY	SUNDAY	
3	4 Independence Day	5	6	7	8	9	JULY
10	11	12	13	14	15	16	
17	18	19	20	(21)	22	23	
24	25	26	27	28	29	30	
31	1 AUGUST	2	3	4	5	6	
7	8	9	10	11	12	13	AUGUST
14	15	16	17	(18)	19	20	
21	22	23	24	25	26	27	
28	29	30	31	1 SEPTEMBER	2	3	
4 Labor Day	5	6	7	8	9	10	SEPTEMBER
11	12	13	14	(15)	16	17	
18	19	20	21 Rosh Hashanah	22	23	24	
25	26	27	28	29	30 Yom Kippur	1 OCTOBER	
2	3	4	5	6	7	8	OCTOBER
9 Columbus Day	10	11	12	13	14	15	
16	17	18	19	(20)	21	22	
23	24	25	26	27	28	29	
30	31	1 NOVEMBER	2	3	4	5 Daylight Saving Time Ends	
6	7 Election Day	8	9	10	11 Veterans' Day	12	NOVEMBER
13	14	15	16	(17)	18	19	
20	21	22	23 Thanksgiving Day	24	25	26	
27	28	29	30	1 DECEMBER	2	3	DECEMBER
4	5	6	7	8	9	10	
11	12	13 Chanukah	14	(15)	16	17	
18	19	20	21	22	23	24	
25 Christmas	26	27	28	29	30	31	

11

JANUARY ALMANAC

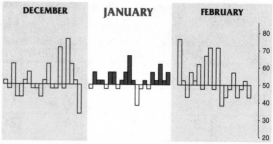

JANUARY							FEBRUARY						
S	M	T	W	T	F	S	S	M	T	W	T	F	S
1	2	3	4	5	6	7				1	2	3	4
8	9	10	11	12	13	14	5	6	7	8	9	10	11
15	16	17	18	19	20	21	12	13	14	15	16	17	18
22	23	24	25	26	27	28	19	20	21	22	23	24	25
29	30	31					26	27	28				

Market Probability Chart above is a graphic representation of the S&P 500 Recent Market Probability Calendar on page 124.

◆ January Barometer predicts year's course with .758 batting average (page 16) ◆ 13 of last 16 post-presidential election years followed January's direction ◆ Every down January on the S&P since 1950, *without exception,* preceded a new or extended bear market, a flat market, or a 10% correction (page 46) ◆ S&P gains in January's first five days preceded full-year gains 83.3% of the time, 12 of last 16 post-presidential election years followed first five days' direction (page 14) ◆ November, December, and January constitute the year's best three-month span, a 4.0% S&P gain (pages 50 & 147) ◆ January NASDAQ powerful 2.5% since 1971 (pages 58 & 148) ◆ "January Effect" now starts in mid-December and favors small-cap stocks (pages 106 & 110) ◆ 2009 has the dubious honor of the worst S&P 500 January on record.

January Vital Statistics

	DJIA		S&P 500		NASDAQ		Russell 1K		Russell 2K	
Rank	6		6		1		7		5	
Up	42		40		29		23		20	
Down	25		27		17		15		18	
Average % Change	0.9 %		0.9 %		2.5 %		0.9 %		1.4 %	
Post-Election Year	0.7 %		0.7 %		2.2 %		1.6 %		2.0 %	
Best & Worst January										
	% Change		% Change		% Change		% Change		% Change	
Best	1976	14.4	1987	13.2	1975	16.6	1987	12.7	1985	13.1
Worst	2009	−8.8	2009	−8.6	2008	−9.9	2009	−8.3	2009	−11.2
Best & Worst January Weeks										
Best	01/09/76	6.1	01/02/09	6.8	01/12/01	9.1	01/02/09	6.8	01/09/87	7.0
Worst	01/08/16	−6.2	01/08/16	−6.0	01/28/00	−8.2	01/08/16	−6.0	01/08/16	−7.9
Best & Worst January Days										
Best	01/17/91	4.6	01/03/01	5.0	01/03/01	14.2	1/3/01	5.3	01/21/09	5.3
Worst	01/08/88	−6.9	01/08/88	−6.8	01/02/01	−7.2	1/8/88	−6.1	01/20/09	−7.0
First Trading Day of Expiration Week: 1980–2016										
Record (#Up − #Down)	25–12		22–15		20–17		20–17		20–17	
Current streak	U1		U1		D4		D4		D4	
Avg % Change	0.10		0.07		0.09		0.05		0.09	
Options Expiration Day: 1980–2016										
Record (#Up − #Down)	20–17		20–17		20–17		20–17		21–16	
Current streak	U6		U2		U2		U2		U2	
Avg % Change	−0.02		−0.001		−0.04		−0.02		−0.001	
Options Expiration Week: 1980–2016										
Record (#Up − #Down)	20–17		16–21		21–16		16–21		20–17	
Current streak	U1		U1		U1		U1		U1	
Avg % Change	−0.16		−0.06		0.27		−0.07		0.25	
Week After Options Expiration: 1980–2016										
Record (#Up − #Down)	20–17		23–14		21–16		23–14		25–12	
Current streak	U2		U2		U2		U2		U2	
Avg % Change	0.03		0.22		0.13		0.20		0.21	
First Trading Day Performance										
% of Time Up	58.2		47.8		54.3		42.1		44.7	
Avg % Change	0.24		0.15		0.17		0.13		0.02	
Last Trading Day Performance										
% of Time Up	56.7		61.2		63.0		57.9		73.7	
Avg % Change	0.22		0.26		0.3		0.33		0.27	

Dow & S&P 1950–April 2016, NASDAQ 1971–April 2016, Russell 1K & 2K 1979–April 2016.

20th Amendment made "lame ducks" disappear.
Now, "As January goes, so goes the year."

Christmas Day *(observed) (Market Closed)*

Bad days are good days in disguise.
— Christopher Reeves (Actor, on Johnson & Johnson commercial)

TUESDAY

D 76.2
S 76.2
N 66.7 **27**

Writing a book is an adventure. To begin with it is a toy, an amusement; then it is a mistress, and then a master, and then a tyrant.
— Winston Churchill (British statesman, 1874–1965)

WEDNESDAY

D 52.4
S 61.9
N 52.4 **28**

In the twenty-two presidential elections from 1900 through 1984, Americans chose the most optimistic-sounding candidate eighteen times.
— Martin E. Seligman, PhD (Professor of psychology, University of Pennsylvania; *Learned Optimism*, 1990)

THURSDAY

D 42.9
S 52.4
N 38.1 **29**

Eighty percent of success is showing up.
— Woody Allen (Filmaker, b. 1935)

Last Trading Day of the Year, NASDAQ Down 14 of Last 16
NASDAQ Was Up 29 Years in a Row 1971–1999

FRIDAY

D 38.1
S 33.3
N 38.1 **30**

...those inquirers who desire an exact knowledge of the past as an aid to the interpretation of the future...
— Thucydides (Greek aristocrat and historian, *The Peloponnesian War*, 460–400 BC)

SATURDAY

31

New Years Day
January Almanac Investor Sector Seasonalities: See Pages 94, 96, and 98

SUNDAY

1

JANUARY'S FIRST FIVE DAYS: AN EARLY WARNING SYSTEM

The last 42 up First Five Days were followed by full-year gains 35 times for an 83.3% accuracy ratio and a 13.6% average gain in all 42 years. The seven exceptions include flat 1994, 2011, 2015 and four related to war. Vietnam military spending delayed the start of the 1966 bear market. Ceasefire imminence early in 1973 raised stocks temporarily. Saddam Hussein turned 1990 into a bear. The war on terrorism, instability in the Mideast, and corporate malfeasance shaped 2002 into one of the worst years on record. The 24 down First Five Days were followed by 13 up years and 11 down (45.8% accurate) and an average gain of 0.7%.

In post-election years this indicator has a solid record. In the last 16 post-presidential election years, 12 full years followed the direction of the First Five Days.

THE FIRST-FIVE-DAYS-IN-JANUARY INDICATOR

	Chronological Data					Ranked by Performance		
	Previous Year's Close	January 5th Day	5-Day Change	Year Change	Rank		5-Day Change	Year Change
1950	16.76	17.09	2.0%	21.8%	1	1987	6.2%	2.0%
1951	20.41	20.88	2.3	16.5	2	1976	4.9	19.1
1952	23.77	23.91	0.6	11.8	3	1999	3.7	19.5
1953	26.57	26.33	-0.9	-6.6	4	2003	3.4	26.4
1954	24.81	24.93	0.5	45.0	5	2006	3.4	13.6
1955	35.98	35.33	-1.8	26.4	6	1983	3.3	17.3
1956	45.48	44.51	-2.1	2.6	7	1967	3.1	20.1
1957	46.67	46.25	-0.9	-14.3	8	1979	2.8	12.3
1958	39.99	40.99	2.5	38.1	9	2010	2.7	12.8
1959	55.21	55.40	0.3	8.5	10	1963	2.6	18.9
1960	59.89	59.50	-0.7	-3.0	11	1958	2.5	38.1
1961	58.11	58.81	1.2	23.1	12	1984	2.4	1.4
1962	71.55	69.12	-3.4	-11.8	13	1951	2.3	16.5
1963	63.10	64.74	2.6	18.9	14	2013	2.2	29.6
1964	75.02	76.00	1.3	13.0	15	1975	2.2	31.5
1965	84.75	85.37	0.7	9.1	16	1950	2.0	21.8
1966	92.43	93.14	0.8	-13.1	17	2004	1.8	9.0
1967	80.33	82.81	3.1	20.1	18	2012	1.8	13.4
1968	96.47	96.62	0.2	7.7	19	1973	1.5	-17.4
1969	103.86	100.80	-2.9	-11.4	20	1972	1.4	15.6
1970	92.06	92.68	0.7	0.1	21	1964	1.3	13.0
1971	92.15	92.19	0.04	10.8	22	1961	1.2	23.1
1972	102.09	103.47	1.4	15.6	23	1989	1.2	27.3
1973	118.05	119.85	1.5	-17.4	24	2011	1.1	-0.003
1974	97.55	96.12	-1.5	-29.7	25	2002	1.1	-23.4
1975	68.56	70.04	2.2	31.5	26	1997	1.0	31.0
1976	90.19	94.58	4.9	19.1	27	1980	0.9	25.8
1977	107.46	105.01	-2.3	-11.5	28	1966	0.8	-13.1
1978	95.10	90.64	-4.7	1.1	29	1994	0.7	-1.5
1979	96.11	98.80	2.8	12.3	30	1965	0.7	9.1
1980	107.94	108.95	0.9	25.8	31	2009	0.7	23.5
1981	135.76	133.06	-2.0	-9.7	32	1970	0.7	0.1
1982	122.55	119.55	-2.4	14.8	33	1952	0.6	11.8
1983	140.64	145.23	3.3	17.3	34	1954	0.5	45.0
1984	164.93	168.90	2.4	1.4	35	1996	0.4	20.3
1985	167.24	163.99	-1.9	26.3	36	1959	0.3	8.5
1986	211.28	207.97	-1.6	14.6	37	1995	0.3	34.1
1987	242.17	257.28	6.2	2.0	38	1992	0.2	4.5
1988	247.08	243.40	-1.5	12.4	39	1968	0.2	7.7
1989	277.72	280.98	1.2	27.3	40	2015	0.2	-0.7
1990	353.40	353.79	0.1	-6.6	41	1990	0.1	-6.6
1991	330.22	314.90	-4.6	26.3	42	1971	0.04	10.8
1992	417.09	418.10	0.2	4.5	43	2007	-0.4	3.5
1993	435.71	429.05	-1.5	7.1	44	2014	-0.6	11.4
1994	466.45	469.90	0.7	-1.5	45	1960	-0.7	-3.0
1995	459.27	460.83	0.3	34.1	46	1957	-0.9	-14.3
1996	615.93	618.46	0.4	20.3	47	1953	-0.9	-6.6
1997	740.74	748.41	1.0	31.0	48	1974	-1.5	-29.7
1998	970.43	956.04	-1.5	26.7	49	1998	-1.5	26.7
1999	1229.23	1275.09	3.7	19.5	50	1988	-1.5	12.4
2000	1469.25	1441.46	-1.9	-10.1	51	1993	-1.5	7.1
2001	1320.28	1295.86	-1.8	-13.0	52	1986	-1.6	14.6
2002	1148.08	1160.71	1.1	-23.4	53	2001	-1.8	-13.0
2003	879.82	909.93	3.4	26.4	54	1955	-1.8	26.4
2004	1111.92	1131.91	1.8	9.0	55	2000	-1.9	-10.1
2005	1211.92	1186.19	-2.1	3.0	56	1985	-1.9	26.3
2006	1248.29	1290.15	3.4	13.6	57	1981	-2.0	-9.7
2007	1418.30	1412.11	-0.4	3.5	58	1956	-2.1	2.6
2008	1468.36	1390.19	-5.3	-38.5	59	2005	-2.1	3.0
2009	903.25	909.73	0.7	23.5	60	1977	-2.3	-11.5
2010	1115.10	1144.98	2.7	12.8	61	1982	-2.4	14.8
2011	1257.64	1271.50	1.1	-0.003	62	1969	-2.9	-11.4
2012	1257.60	1280.70	1.8	13.4	63	1962	-3.4	-11.8
2013	1426.19	1457.15	2.2	29.6	64	1991	-4.6	26.3
2014	1848.36	1837.49	-0.6	11.4	65	1978	-4.7	1.1
2015	2058.90	2062.14	0.2	-0.7	66	2008	-5.3	-38.5
2016	2043.94	1922.03	-6.0	??	67	2016	-6.0	??

Based on S&P 500

New Years Day *(observed) (Market Closed)*

MONDAY

2

The way a young man spends his evenings is a part of that thin area between success and failure.
— Robert R. Young (U.S. financier and railroad tycoon, 1897–1958)

Small Caps Punished First Trading Day of Year
Russell 2000 Down 16 of Last 27, But Up 5 of Last 8

D 66.7
S 47.6
N 66.7

TUESDAY

3

On [TV financial news programs], if the stock is near its high, 90% of the guests like it, if it is near its lows, 90% of the guests hate it.
— Michael L. Burke (*Investors Intelligence*, May 2002)

Second Trading Day of the Year, Dow Up 15 of Last 23
Santa Claus Rally Ends (Page 114)

D 66.7
S 57.1
N 52.4

WEDNESDAY

4

The task of leadership is not to put greatness into humanity, but to elicit it, for the greatness is already there.
— Sir John Buchan (Scottish author, Governor General of Canada 1935–1940; 1875–1940)

D 47.6
S 52.4
N 47.6

THURSDAY

5

Governments last as long as the under-taxed can defend themselves against the over-taxed.
— Bernard Berenson (American art critic, 1865–1959)

D 52.4
S 52.4
N 57.1

FRIDAY

6

When everyone starts downgrading a stock, it's usually time to buy.
— Meryl Witmer (General partner, Eagle Capital Partners; *Barron's*, 1/29/07)

SATURDAY

7

SUNDAY

8

THE INCREDIBLE JANUARY BAROMETER (DEVISED 1972): ONLY EIGHT SIGNIFICANT ERRORS IN 66 YEARS

Devised by Yale Hirsch in 1972, our January Barometer states that as the S&P 500 goes in January, so goes the year. The indicator has registered **only eight major errors since 1950 for an 87.9% accuracy ratio**. Vietnam affected 1966 and 1968; 1982 saw the start of a major bull market in August; two January rate cuts and 9/11 affected 2001; the anticipation of military action in Iraq held down the market in January 2003; 2009 was the beginning of a new bull market following the second worst bear market on record; the Fed saved 2010 with QE2; and QE3 likely staved off declines in 2014. (*Almanac Investor* newsletter subscribers receive full analysis of each reading as well as its potential implications for the full year.)

Including the eight flat-year errors (less than +/– 5%) yields a 75.8% accuracy ratio. A full comparison of all monthly barometers for the Dow, S&P, and NASDAQ can be seen in the January 21, 2016 Alert at *www.stocktradersalmanac.com*. Bear markets began or continued when Januarys suffered a loss (see page 46). Full years followed January's direction in 13 of the last 16 post-election years. See page 18 for more.

AS JANUARY GOES, SO GOES THE YEAR

	Market Performance in January					January Performance by Rank			
	Previous Year's Close	January Close	January Change	Year Change		Rank	Year	January Change	Year's Change
1950	16.76	17.05	1.7%	21.8%		1	1987	13.2%	2.0% flat
1951	20.41	21.66	6.1	16.5		2	1975	12.3	31.5
1952	23.77	24.14	1.6	11.8		3	1976	11.8	19.1
1953	26.57	26.38	-0.7	-6.6		4	1967	7.8	20.1
1954	24.81	26.08	5.1	45.0		5	1985	7.4	26.3
1955	35.98	36.63	1.8	26.4		6	1989	7.1	27.3
1956	45.48	43.82	-3.6	2.6 flat		7	1961	6.3	23.1
1957	46.67	44.72	-4.2	-14.3		8	1997	6.1	31.0
1958	39.99	41.70	4.3	38.1		9	1951	6.1	16.5
1959	55.21	55.42	0.4	8.5		10	1980	5.8	25.8
1960	59.89	55.61	-7.1	-3.0 flat		11	1954	5.1	45.0
1961	58.11	61.78	6.3	23.1		12	2013	5.0	29.6
1962	71.55	68.84	-3.8	-11.8		13	1963	4.9	18.9
1963	63.10	66.20	4.9	18.9		14	2012	4.4	13.4
1964	75.02	77.04	2.7	13.0		15	1958	4.3	38.1
1965	84.75	87.56	3.3	9.1		16	1991	4.2	26.3
1966	92.43	92.88	0.5	-13.1 X		17	1999	4.1	19.5
1967	80.33	86.61	7.8	20.1		18	1971	4.0	10.8
1968	96.47	92.24	-4.4	7.7 X		19	1988	4.0	12.4
1969	103.86	103.01	-0.8	-11.4		20	1979	4.0	12.3
1970	92.06	85.02	-7.6	0.1 flat		21	2001	3.5	-13.0 X
1971	92.15	95.88	4.0	10.8		22	1965	3.3	9.1
1972	102.09	103.94	1.8	15.6		23	1983	3.3	17.3
1973	118.05	116.03	-1.7	-17.4		24	1996	3.3	20.3
1974	97.55	96.57	-1.0	-29.7		25	1994	3.3	-1.5 flat
1975	68.56	76.98	12.3	31.5		26	1964	2.7	13.0
1976	90.19	100.86	11.8	19.1		27	2006	2.5	13.6
1977	107.46	102.03	-5.1	-11.5		28	1995	2.4	34.1
1978	95.10	89.25	-6.2	1.1 flat		29	2011	2.3	-0.003 flat
1979	96.11	99.93	4.0	12.3		30	1972	1.8	15.6
1980	107.94	114.16	5.8	25.8		31	1955	1.8	26.4
1981	135.76	129.55	-4.6	-9.7		32	1950	1.7	21.8
1982	122.55	120.40	-1.8	14.8 X		33	2004	1.7	9.0
1983	140.64	145.30	3.3	17.3		34	1952	1.6	11.8
1984	164.93	163.41	-0.9	1.4 flat		35	2007	1.4	3.5 flat
1985	167.24	179.63	7.4	26.3		36	1998	1.0	26.7
1986	211.28	211.78	0.2	14.6		37	1993	0.7	7.1
1987	242.17	274.08	13.2	2.0 flat		38	1966	0.5	-13.1 X
1988	247.08	257.07	4.0	12.4		39	1959	0.4	8.5
1989	277.72	297.47	7.1	27.3		40	1986	0.2	14.6
1990	353.40	329.08	-6.9	-6.6		41	1953	-0.7	-6.6
1991	330.22	343.93	4.2	26.3		42	1969	-0.8	-11.4
1992	417.09	408.79	-2.0	4.5 flat		43	1984	-0.9	1.4 flat
1993	435.71	438.78	0.7	7.1		44	1974	-1.0	-29.7
1994	466.45	481.61	3.3	-1.5 flat		45	2002	-1.6	-23.4
1995	459.27	470.42	2.4	34.1		46	1973	-1.7	-17.4
1996	615.93	636.02	3.3	20.3		47	1982	-1.8	14.8 X
1997	740.74	786.16	6.1	31.0		48	1992	-2.0	4.5 flat
1998	970.43	980.28	1.0	26.7		49	2005	-2.5	3.0 flat
1999	1229.23	1279.64	4.1	19.5		50	2003	-2.7	26.4 X
2000	1469.25	1394.46	-5.1	-10.1		51	2015	-3.1	-0.7
2001	1320.28	1366.01	3.5	-13.0 X		52	2014	-3.6	11.4 X
2002	1148.08	1130.20	-1.6	-23.4 X		53	1956	-3.6	2.6 flat
2003	879.82	855.70	-2.7	26.4 X		54	2010	-3.7	12.8 X
2004	1111.92	1131.13	1.7	9.0		55	1962	-3.8	-11.8
2005	1211.92	1181.27	-2.5	3.0 flat		56	1957	-4.2	-14.3
2006	1248.29	1280.08	2.5	13.6		57	1968	-4.4	7.7 X
2007	1418.30	1438.24	1.4	3.5 flat		58	1981	-4.6	-9.7
2008	1468.36	1378.55	-6.1	-38.5		59	1977	-5.1	-11.5
2009	903.25	825.88	-8.6	23.5 X		60	2000	-5.1	-10.1
2010	1115.10	1073.87	-3.7	12.8 X		61	2008	-6.1	-38.5
2011	1257.64	1286.12	2.3	-0.003 flat		62	2016	-5.1	??
2012	1257.60	1312.41	4.4	13.4		63	1978	-6.2	1.1 flat
2013	1426.19	1498.11	5.0	29.6		64	1990	-6.9	-6.6
2014	1848.36	1782.59	-3.6	11.4 X		65	1960	-7.1	-3.0 flat
2015	2058.90	1994.99	-3.1	-0.7		66	1970	-7.6	0.1 flat
2016	2043.94	1940.24	-5.1	??		67	2009	-8.6	23.5 X

X = major error   Based on S&P 500

JANUARY 2017

MONDAY

D 38.1
S 47.6
N 57.1

9

The average man desires to be told specifically which particular stock to buy or sell. He wants to get something for nothing. He does not wish to work.
— William LeFevre (Senior analyst, Ehrenkrantz King Nussbaum, 1928–1997)

TUESDAY

D 47.6
S 57.1
N 61.9

10

A good trader has to have three things: a chronic inability to accept things at face value, to feel continuously unsettled, and to have humility.
— Michael Steinhardt (Financier, philanthropist, political activist, chairman WisdomTree Investments, b. 1940)

WEDNESDAY

D 47.6
S 57.1
N 61.9

11

The average man is always waiting for something to happen to him instead of setting to work to make things happen. For one person who dreams of making 50,000 pounds, a hundred people dream of being left 50,000 pounds.
— A. A. Milne (British author, *Winnie-the-Pooh*, 1882–1956)

THURSDAY

D 57.1
S 47.6
N 52.4

12

It is the growth of total government spending as a percentage of gross national product—not the way it is financed—that crowds out the private sector.
— Paul Craig Roberts (*Business Week*, 1984)

FRIDAY

D 52.4
S 52.4
N 47.6

13

Analysts are supposed to be critics of corporations. They often end up being public relations spokesmen for them.
— Ralph Wanger (Chief investment officer, Acorn Fund)

SATURDAY

14

SUNDAY

15

JANUARY BAROMETER IN GRAPHIC FORM SINCE 1950

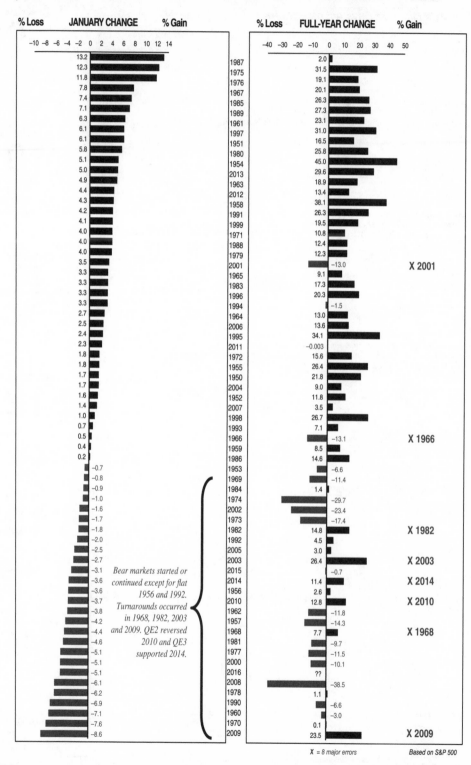

% Loss	JANUARY CHANGE	% Gain
	−10 −8 −6 −4 −2 0 2 4 6 8 10 12 14	

% Loss	FULL-YEAR CHANGE	% Gain
	−40 −30 −20 −10 0 10 20 30 40 50	

Year	January Change	Full-Year Change	Error
1987	13.2	2.0	
1975	12.3	31.5	
1976	11.8	19.1	
1967	7.8	20.1	
1985	7.4	26.3	
1989	7.1	27.3	
1961	6.3	23.1	
1997	6.1	31.0	
1951	6.1	16.5	
1980	5.8	25.8	
1954	5.1	45.0	
2013	5.0	29.6	
1963	4.9	18.9	
2012	4.4	13.4	
1958	4.3	38.1	
1991	4.2	26.3	
1999	4.1	19.5	
1971	4.0	10.8	
1988	4.0	12.4	
1979	4.0	12.3	
2001	3.5	−13.0	X 2001
1965	3.3	9.1	
1983	3.3	17.3	
1996	3.3	20.3	
1994	3.3	−1.5	
1964	2.7	13.0	
2006	2.5	13.6	
1995	2.4	34.1	
2011	2.3	−0.003	
1972	1.8	15.6	
1955	1.8	26.4	
1950	1.7	21.8	
2004	1.7	9.0	
1952	1.6	11.8	
2007	1.4	3.5	
1998	1.0	26.7	
1993	0.7	7.1	
1966	0.5	−13.1	X 1966
1959	0.4	8.5	
1986	0.2	14.6	
1953	−0.7	−6.6	
1969	−0.8	−11.4	
1984	−0.9	1.4	
1974	−1.0	−29.7	
2002	−1.6	−23.4	
1973	−1.7	−17.4	
1982	−1.8	14.8	X 1982
1992	−2.0	4.5	
2005	−2.5	3.0	
2003	−2.7	26.4	X 2003
2015	−3.1	−0.7	
2014	−3.6	11.4	X 2014
1956	−3.6	2.6	
2010	−3.7	12.8	X 2010
1962	−3.8	−11.8	
1957	−4.2	−14.3	
1968	−4.4	7.7	X 1968
1981	−4.6	−9.7	
1977	−5.1	−11.5	
2000	−5.1	−10.1	
2016	−5.1	??	
2008	−6.1	−38.5	
1978	−6.2	1.1	
1990	−6.9	−6.6	
1960	−7.1	−3.0	
1970	−7.6	0.1	
2009	−8.6	23.5	X 2009

Bear markets started or continued except for flat 1956 and 1992. Turnarounds occurred in 1968, 1982, 2003 and 2009. QE2 reversed 2010 and QE3 supported 2014.

X = 8 major errors   Based on S&P 500

18

Martin Luther King Jr. Day *(Market Closed)*

MONDAY

16

Man's mind, once stretched by a new idea, never regains its original dimensions.
— Oliver Wendell Holmes (American author, poet, and physician, 1809–1894)

First Trading Day of January Expiration Week, Dow Up 17 of Last 24

TUESDAY

D 57.1
S 57.1
N 42.9

17

Individualism, private property, the law of accumulation of wealth and the law of competition…are the highest result of human experience, the soil in which, so far, has produced the best fruit.
— Andrew Carnegie (Scottish-born U.S. industrialist, philanthropist, *The Gospel of Wealth*, 1835–1919)

January Expiration Week Horrible Since 1999, Dow Down 10 of Last 18
Average Dow loss: –1.2%

WEDNESDAY

D 52.4
S 66.7
N 76.2

18

Technology will gradually strengthen democracies in every country and at every level.
— William H. Gates (Microsoft founder)

THURSDAY

D 42.9
S 52.4
N 66.7

19

If you destroy a free market you create a black market. If you have ten thousand regulations you destroy all respect for the law.
— Winston Churchill (British statesman, 1874–1965)

January Expiration Day, Dow Down 10 of Last 18 With Big Losses
Off 2.1% in 2010, Off 2.0% in 2006, and 1.3% in 2003

FRIDAY

D 33.3
S 38.1
N 33.3

20

Get to the Point! Blurt it out! Tell me plainly what's in it for me!
— Roy H. Williams (*The Wizard of Ads*: a reader's mental response to a poorly constructed advertisement. Quoted in *Your Company*, 12/98)

SATURDAY

21

SUNDAY

22

MARKET BEHAVIOR UNDER NEW PRESIDENTS

For 50 annual editions of this *Almanac*, we have had to look ahead 6 to 18 months and try to anticipate what the stock market will do in the year to come. Predictable effects on the economy and stock market from quadrennial presidential and biennial congressional elections have steered us well over the years. Also, bear markets lasting about a year on average tended to consume the first year of Republican and second of Democratic terms (page 26).

Prognosticating was tougher in the 1990s during the greatest bull cycle in history. Being bullish and staying bullish was the best course. Bear markets were few and far between and, when they did come, were swift and over in a few months. Market timers and fundamentalists, as a result, did not keep pace with the momentum players. The market has come back to earth and many of these patterns have re-emerged.

POST-ELECTION MARKETS WHEN PARTY IN POWER IS OUSTED

New Democrats		Dow %	New Republicans		Dow %
Wilson	1913	−10.3%	Harding	1921	12.7%
Roosevelt	1933	66.7	Eisenhower	1953	−3.8
Kennedy	1961	18.7	Nixon	1969	−15.2
Carter	1977	−17.3	Reagan	1981	−9.2
Clinton	1993	13.7	G.W. Bush	2001	−7.1
Obama	2009	23.5			

WHEN INCUMBENT PARTY RETAINS POWER WITH NEW PRESIDENT

Succeeding Democrats			Succeeding Republicans		
Truman	1949	12.9%	Hoover	1929	−17.2%
			G.H.W. Bush	1989	27.0

Looking at the past, you can see that new and succeeding Democrats fared better in post-election years than Republicans. Democrats have tended to come to power following economic and market woes. Republicans often reclaimed the White House after Democratic-initiated foreign entanglements. Both have fallen to scandal and party division.

Wilson won after the Republican Party split in two, Carter after the Watergate scandal, and G.W. Bush after the Lewinsky affair. Roosevelt, Kennedy, Clinton, and Obama won elections during bad economies. Republicans took over after major wars were begun under Democrats, benefiting Harding, Eisenhower, and Nixon. Reagan ousted Carter following the late 1970s stagflation and the Iran hostage crisis.

Truman held the White House after 16 years of effective Democratic rule. Hoover and G.H.W. Bush were passed the torch after eight years of Republican-led peace and prosperity.

A struggling economy, ongoing foreign military operations, and a divided Republican party make handicapping this November's winner elusive at press time. Prospects for 2017 improve should the market decline further in 2016.

MONDAY

D 33.3
S 47.6
N 38.1
23

If you can buy all you want of a new issue, you do not want any; if you cannot obtain any, you want all you can buy.
— Rod Fadem (Stifel Nicolaus & Co., *Barron's*, 1989)

TUESDAY

D 33.3
S 47.6
N 57.1
24

Technology has no respect for tradition.
— Peter C. Lee (Merchants' Exchange CEO, quoted in *Stocks, Futures & Options Magazine*, May 2003)

January Ends "Best Three-Month Span" (Pages 50, 58, 147, and 148)

WEDNESDAY

D 61.9
S 57.1
N 47.6
25

Imagination is more important than knowledge.
— Albert Einstein (German/American physicist, 1921 Nobel Prize, 1879–1955)

THURSDAY

D 57.1
S 52.4
N 71.4
26

At the age of 24, I began setting clear, written goals for each area of my life. I accomplished more in the following year than I had in the previous 24.
— Brian Tracy (Motivational speaker)

FRIDAY

D 57.1
S 61.9
N 66.7
27

Don't fritter away your time. Create, act, take a place wherever you are and be somebody.
— Theodore Roosevelt (26th U.S. President, 1858–1919)

SATURDAY

28

February Almanac Investor Sector Seasonalities: See Pages 94, 96, and 98

SUNDAY

29

FEBRUARY ALMANAC

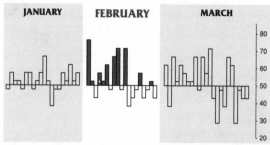

FEBRUARY							MARCH						
S	M	T	W	T	F	S	S	M	T	W	T	F	S
				1	2	3	4				1	2	3
5	6	7	8	9	10	11	5	6	7	8	9	10	11
12	13	14	15	16	17	18	12	13	14	15	16	17	18
19	20	21	22	23	24	25	19	20	21	22	23	24	25
26	27	28					26	27	28	29	30	31	

Market Probability Chart above is a graphic representation of the S&P 500 Recent Market Probability Calendar on page 124.

◆ February is the weak link in "Best Six Months" (pages 50, 52, & 147) ◆ RECENT RECORD: S&P up 9, down 6, average change –0.2% last 15 years ◆ Worst NASDAQ month in post-presidential election years, average loss 3.9%, up 3 down 8 (page 157), #11 Dow, up 7, down 9, and #12 S&P, up 7, down 9 (pages 153 & 155) ◆ Day before Presidents' Day weekend S&P down 17 of 25, 11 straight 1992–2002, day after up 6 of last 7 (see pages 88 & 133) ◆ Many technicians modify market predictions based on January's market.

February Vital Statistics

	DJIA	S&P 500	NASDAQ	Russell 1K	Russell 2K
Rank	8	9	9	9	7
Up	40	37	25	23	22
Down	27	30	21	15	16
Average % Change	0.2%	0.05%	0.7%	0.4%	1.2%
Post-Election Year	–1.4%	–1.8%	–3.9%	–1.9%	–2.0%

Best & Worst February

	% Change		% Change		% Change		% Change		% Change	
Best	1986	8.8	1986	7.1	2000	19.2	1986	7.2	2000	16.4
Worst	2009	–11.7	2009	–11.0	2001	–22.4	2009	–10.7	2009	–12.3

Best & Worst February Weeks

Best	02/01/08	4.4	02/06/09	5.2	02/04/00	9.2	02/06/09	5.3	02/01/91	6.6
Worst	02/20/09	–6.2	02/20/09	–6.9	02/09/01	–7.1	02/20/09	–6.9	02/20/09	–8.3

Best & Worst February Days

Best	02/24/09	3.3	02/24/09	4.0	02/11/99	4.2	02/24/09	4.1	02/24/09	4.5
Worst	02/10/09	–4.6	02/10/09	–4.9	02/16/01	–5.0	02/10/09	–4.8	02/10/09	–4.7

First Trading Day of Expiration Week: 1980–2016

Record (#Up – #Down)	22–15	26–11	21–16	26–11	22–15
Current streak	U2	U3	U3	U3	U3
Avg % Change	0.30	0.26	0.09	0.24	0.14

Options Expiration Day: 1980–2016

Record (#Up – #Down)	18–19	15–22	15–22	16–21	17–20
Current streak	D1	D1	U2	D1	U3
Avg % Change	–0.05	–0.12	–0.25	–0.12	–0.07

Options Expiration Week: 1980–2016

Record (#Up – #Down)	22–15	20–17	20–17	20–17	24–13
Current streak	U2	U2	U3	U7	U7
Avg % Change	0.39	0.20	0.11	0.20	0.30

Week After Options Expiration: 1980–2016

Record (#Up – #Down)	17–20	17–20	21–16	17–20	20–17
Current streak	U1	U1	U3	U1	U3
Avg % Change	–0.26	–0.19	–0.15	–0.14	–0.04

First Trading Day Performance

% of Time Up	61.2	61.2	71.7	65.8	65.8
Avg % Change	0.14	0.15	0.33	0.19	0.33

Last Trading Day Performance

% of Time Up	49.3	55.2	50.0	55.3	55.3
Avg % Change	–0.001	–0.02	–0.08	–0.07	0.08

Dow & S&P 1950–April 2016, NASDAQ 1971–April 2016, Russell 1K & 2K 1979–April 2016.

Either go short, or stay away the day before Presidents' Day.

JANUARY/FEBRUARY 2017

"January Barometer" 87.9% Accurate (Page 16)
Almanac Investor Subscribers E-mailed Official Results (See Insert)

MONDAY
D 47.6
S 52.4
N 47.6
30

In business, the competition will bite you if you keep running; if you stand still, they will swallow you.
— William Knudsen (Former president of GM)

FOMC Meeting (2 Days)

TUESDAY
D 52.4
S 57.1
N 52.4
31

When a falling stock becomes a screaming buy because it cannot conceivably drop further, try to buy it 30 percent lower.
— Al Rizzo (1986)

First Day Trading in February, Dow and S&P Up 11 of Last 14

WEDNESDAY
D 76.2
S 76.2
N 81.0
1

I have but one lamp by which my feet (or "investments") are guided, and that is the lamp of experience. I know of no way of judging the future but by the past.
— Patrick Henry (U.S. founding father, twice Governor of VA, 1736–1799; March 23, 1775 speech)

THURSDAY
D 47.6
S 52.4
N 57.1
2

I am glad that I paid so little attention to good advice; had I abided by it I might have been saved from my most valuable mistakes.
— Gene Fowler (Journalist, screenwriter, film director, biographer, 1890–1960)

FRIDAY
D 47.6
S 42.9
N 42.9
3

By the law of nature the father continues master of his child no longer than the child stands in need of his assistance; after that term they become equal, and then the son entirely independent of the father, owes him no obedience, but only respect.
— Jean-Jacques Rousseau (Swiss philosopher, *The Social Contract*, 1712–1778)

SATURDAY
4

SUNDAY
5

MARKET CHARTS OF POST-PRESIDENTIAL ELECTION YEARS

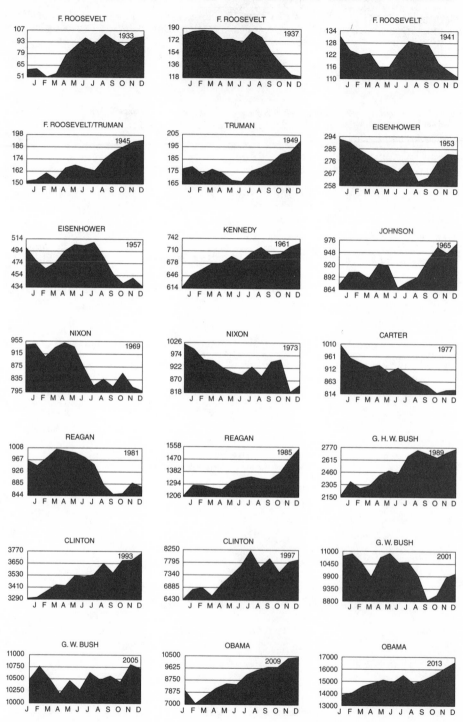

Based on Dow Jones Industial Average monthly closing prices.

MONDAY

D 57.1
S 57.1
N 57.1

6

If I have seen further, it is by standing upon the shoulders of giants.
— Sir Isaac Newton (English physicist, mathematician; Laws of Gravity, letter to Robert Hooke 2/15/1676; 1643–1727)

TUESDAY

D 52.4
S 52.4
N 57.1

7

What lies behind us and what lies before us are tiny matters, compared to what lies within us.
— Ralph Waldo Emerson (American author, poet, and philosopher, *Self-Reliance*, 1803–1882)

Week Before February Expiration Week, NASDAQ Down 10 of Last 16, 2010 Up 2.0%, 2011 Up 1.5%, 2014 Up 2.9%, 2015 Up 3.2%

WEDNESDAY

D 47.6
S 61.9
N 61.9

8

A foolish consistency is the hobgoblin of little minds.
— Ralph Waldo Emerson (American author, poet, and philosopher, *Self-Reliance*, 1803–1882)

THURSDAY

D 57.1
S 47.6
N 47.6

9

I've continued to recognize the power individuals have to change virtually anything and everything in their lives in an instant. I've learned that the resources we need to turn our dreams into reality are within us, merely waiting for the day when we decide to wake up and claim our birthright.
— Anthony Robbins (Motivator, advisor, consultant, author, entrepreneur, philanthropist, b. 1960)

FRIDAY

D 57.1
S 66.7
N 57.1

10

We go to the movies to be entertained, not see rape, ransacking, pillage and looting. We can get all that in the stock market.
— Kennedy Gammage (*The Richland Report*)

SATURDAY

11

SUNDAY

12

POST-ELECTION YEAR PERFORMANCE BY PARTY

From the table on page 130 it is clear that during the first two years of a president's term, market performance lags well behind the later two. After a president wins the election, the first two years are spent pushing through as much policy as possible. Frequently, the market, economy, and country experience bear markets, recessions, and war. Conversely, as presidents and their parties get anxious about holding on to power, they begin to prime the pump in the third year, fostering bull markets, prosperity, and peace.

There is a dramatic difference in market performance under the two parties in post-election and midterm years over the last 16 administrations. Since 1953, there have been 19 confirmed bull and 20 bear markets. Only 6 bear markets have bottomed in the pre-election or election year and 10 tops have occurred in these years, as the bulk of the declines were relegated to the post-election and midterm years. However, more bear markets and negative market action have plagued Republican administrations in the post-election year, whereas the midterm year has been worse under Democrats.

Republicans have mostly taken over after foreign entanglements and personal transgressions during boom times and administered tough action right away, knocking the market down: 1953 (Korea), 1969 (Vietnam), 1981 (Iran hostage crisis), and 2001 (Lewinsky affair). Democrats have usually reclaimed power after economic duress or political scandal during leaner times and addressed more favorable policy moves the first year, buoying the market: 1961 (recession), 1977 (Watergate), 1993 (recession), and 2009 (financial crisis).

MARKET ACTION UNDER REPUBLICANS & DEMOCRATS SINCE 1953
Annual % Change in Dow Jones Industrial Average[1]

4-Year Cycle Beginning		Post-Election Year	Midterm Year	Pre-Election Year	Election Year	Totals
REPUBLICANS						
1953*	Eisenhower (R)	−3.8	44.0	20.8	2.3	
1957	Eisenhower (R)	−12.8	34.0	16.4	−9.3	
1969*	Nixon (R)	−15.2	4.8	6.1	14.6	
1973	Nixon (R)***	−16.6	−27.6	38.3	17.9	
1981*	Reagan (R)	−9.2	19.6	20.3	−3.7	
1985	Reagan (R)	27.7	22.6	2.3	11.8	
1989	G. H. W. Bush (R)	27.0	−4.3	20.3	4.2	
2001*	G. W. Bush (R)	−7.1	−16.8	25.3	3.1	
2005	G. W. Bush (R)	−0.6	16.3	6.4	−33.8	
	Total % Gain	−10.6	92.6	156.2	7.1	245.3
	Average % Gain	−1.2	10.3	17.4	0.8	6.8
	# Up	2	6	9	6	23
	# Down	7	3	0	3	13
DEMOCRATS						
1961*	Kennedy (D)**	18.7	−10.8	17.0	14.6	
1965	Johnson (D)	10.9	−18.9	15.2	4.3	
1977*	Carter (D)	−17.3	−3.1	4.2	14.9	
1993*	Clinton (D)	13.7	2.1	33.5	26.0	
1997	Clinton (D)	22.6	16.1	25.2	−6.2	
2009*	Obama (D)	18.8	11.0	5.5	7.3	
2013	Obama (D)	26.5	7.5	−2.2		
	Total % Gain	93.9	3.9	98.4	60.9	257.1
	Average % Gain	13.4	0.6	14.1	10.2	9.5
	# Up	6	4	6	5	21
	# Down	1	3	1	1	6
BOTH PARTIES						
	Total % Gain	83.3	96.5	254.6	68.0	502.4
	Average % Gain	5.2	6.0	15.9	4.5	7.9
	# Up	8	10	15	11	44
	# Down	8	6	1	4	19

*Party in power ousted. **Death in office. ***Resigned. D—Democrat, R—Republican. [1]Based on annual close.

First Trading Day of February Expiration Week Dow Down 7 of Last 12

MONDAY
D 66.7
S 71.4
N 66.7
13

Setting a goal is not the main thing. It is deciding how you will go about achieving it and staying with that plan.
— Tom Landry (Dallas Cowboys head coach 1960–1988)

Valentine's Day ♥

TUESDAY
D 47.6
S 47.6
N 66.7
14

Most people can stay excited for two or three months. A few people can stay excited for two or three years. But a winner will stay excited for 20 to 30 years—or as long as it takes to win.
— A.L. Williams (Motivational speaker)

WEDNESDAY
D 66.7
S 71.4
N 57.1
15

Ignorance is not knowing something; stupidity is not admitting your ignorance.
— Daniel Turov (*Turov on Timing*)

THURSDAY
D 42.9
S 38.1
N 42.9
16

If there's anything duller than being on a board in Corporate America, I haven't found it.
— H. Ross Perot (American businessman, *NY Times*, 10/28/92, two-time presidential candidate 1992 & 1996, b. 1930)

February Expiration Day, NASDAQ Down 12 of Last 17
Day Before Presidents' Day Weekend, S&P Down 17 of Last 25

FRIDAY
D 38.1
S 42.9
N 47.6
17

Since 1950, the S&P 500 has enjoyed total returns averaging 33.18% annually during periods when the S&P 500 price/peak earnings ratio was below 15 and both 3-month T-bill yields and 10-year Treasury yields were below their levels of 6 months earlier.
— John P. Hussman, PhD (Hussman Funds, 5/22/06)

SATURDAY
18

SUNDAY
19

POST-ELECTION YEARS: PAYING THE PIPER

Politics being what it is, incumbent administrations during election years try to make the economy look good to impress the electorate and tend to put off unpopular decisions until the votes are counted. This produces an American phenomenon: the Post-Election Year Syndrome. The year begins with an Inaugural Ball, after which the piper must be paid, and we Americans have often paid dearly in the past 103 years.

Victorious candidates rarely succeed in fulfilling campaign promises of "peace and prosperity." In the past 26 post-election years, three major wars began: World War I (1917), World War II (1941), and Vietnam (1965); four drastic bear markets started, in 1929, 1937, 1969, and 1973; 9/11, recession, and continuing bear markets in 2001 and 2009; less severe bear markets occurred or were in progress in 1913, 1917, 1921, 1941, 1949, 1953, 1957, 1977, and 1981. Only in 1925, 1985, 1989, 1993, 1997, and 2013 were Americans blessed with peace and prosperity.

THE RECORD SINCE 1913

1913	Wilson (D)	Minor bear market.
1917	Wilson (D)	World War I and a bear market.
1921	Harding (R)	Post-war depression and bear market.
1925	Coolidge (R)	Peace and prosperity. Hallelujah!
1929	Hoover (R)	Worst market crash in history until 1987.
1933	Roosevelt (D)	Devaluation, bank failures, Depression still on but market strong.
1937	Roosevelt (D)	Another crash, 20% unemployment rate.
1941	Roosevelt (D)	World War II and a continuing bear.
1945	Roosevelt (D)	Post-war industrial contraction, strong market precedes 1946 crash.
1949	Truman (D)	Minor bear market.
1953	Eisenhower (R)	Minor post-war (Korea) bear market.
1957	Eisenhower (R)	Major bear market.
1961	Kennedy (D)	Bay of Pigs fiasco, strong market precedes 1962 crash.
1965	Johnson (D)	Vietnam escalation. Bear came in 1966.
1969	Nixon (R)	Start of worst bear market since 1937.
1973	Nixon, Ford (R)	Start of worst bear market since 1929.
1977	Carter (D)	Bear market in blue chip stocks.
1981	Reagan (R)	Bear strikes again.
1985	Reagan (R)	No bear in sight.
1989	Bush (R)	Effect of 1987 Crash wears off.
1993	Clinton (D)	S&P up 7.1%, next year off 1.5%.
1997	Clinton (D)	S&P up 31.0%, next year up 26.7%.
2001	Bush, GW (R)	9/11, recession, bear market intensifies.
2005	Bush, GW (R)	Flat year, narrowest range, Dow off –0.6%.
2009	Obama (D)	Financial crisis, bear market bottom, Dow +18.8%.
2013	Obama (D)	Fed QE, Dow up, 26.5%.

Republicans took back the White House following foreign involvements under Democrats in 1921 (WWI), 1953 (Korea), 1969 (Vietnam), and 1981 (Iran); and scandal in 2001. Bear markets occurred in these post-election years. Democrats recaptured power after domestic problems under Republicans in 1913 (GOP split), 1933 (Crash and Depression), 1961 (recession), 1977 (Watergate), 1993 (sluggish economy), and 2009 (financial crisis). Post-election years have been better under Democrats (page 26).

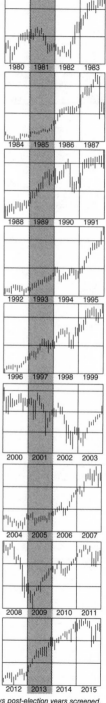

Graph shows post-election years screened.
Based on Dow Jones industial average monthly ranges.

Presidents' Day *(Market Closed)*

Nothing gives one person so much advantage over another as to remain always cool and unruffled under all circumstances.
— Thomas Jefferson (3rd U.S. President, 1743–7/4/1826)

Day After Presidents Day, NASDAQ Down 14 of Last 22

D 52.4
S 47.6
N 38.1

It is tact that is golden, not silence.
— Samuel Butler (English writer, 1600–1680)

Week After February Expiration Week, Dow Down 11 of Last 18

D 52.4
S 57.1
N 66.7

In the course of evolution and a higher civilization we might be able to get along comfortably without Congress, but without Wall Street, never.
— Henry Clews (1900)

D 38.1
S 42.9
N 57.1

In order to be great writer (or "investor") a person must have a built-in, shockproof crap detector.
— Ernest Hemingway (American writer, 1954 Nobel Prize, 1899–1961)

End of February Miserable in Recent Years, (Page 22 and 133)

D 47.6
S 47.6
N 52.4

Of 120 companies from 1987 to 1992 that relied primarily on cost cutting to improve the bottom line, 68 percent failed to achieve profitable growth during the next five years.
— Mercer Management Consulting (*Smart Money Magazine*, August 2001)

March Almanac Investor Sector Seasonalities: See Pages 94, 96, and 98

MARCH ALMANAC

MARCH							APRIL						
S	M	T	W	T	F	S	S	M	T	W	T	F	S
				1	2	3	4		30						1
5	6	7	8	9	10	11	2	3	4	5	6	7	8
12	13	14	15	16	17	18	9	10	11	12	13	14	15
19	20	21	22	23	24	25	16	17	18	19	20	21	22
26	27	28	29	30	31		23	24	25	26	27	28	29

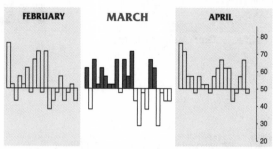

Market Probability Chart above is a graphic representation of the S&P 500 Recent Market Probability Calendar on page 124.

◆ Mid-month strength and late-month weakness are most evident above ◆ RECENT RECORD: S&P 14 up, 7 down, average gain 1.8%, third best ◆ Rather turbulent in recent years with wild fluctuations and large gains and losses ◆ March has been taking some mean end-of-quarter hits (page 134), down 1469 Dow points March 9–22, 2001 ◆ Last three or four days Dow a net loser 17 out of last 27 years ◆ NASDAQ hard hit in 2001, down 14.5% after 22.4% drop in February ◆ Fourth worst NASDAQ month during post-presidential election years, average loss 0.3%, up 5, down 6 ◆ Third Dow month to gain more than 1000 points in 2016.

March Vital Statistics

	DJIA		S&P 500		NASDAQ		Russell 1K		Russell 2K	
Rank	4		4		5		4		3	
Up	44		44		29		26		28	
Down	23		23		17		12		10	
Average % Change	1.2%		1.2%		0.9%		1.2%		1.5%	
Post-Election Year	0.4%		0.6%		-0.3%		0.8%		1.2%	
Best & Worst March										
	% Change		% Change		% Change		% Change		% Change	
Best	2000	7.8	2000	9.7	2009	10.9	2000	8.9	1979	9.7
Worst	1980	-9.0	1980	-10.2	1980	-17.1	1980	-11.5	1980	-18.5
Best & Worst March Weeks										
Best	03/13/09	9.0	03/13/09	10.7	03/13/09	10.6	03/13/09	10.7	03/13/09	12.0
Worst	03/16/01	-7.7	03/06/09	-7.0	03/16/01	-7.9	03/06/09	-7.1	03/06/09	-9.8
Best & Worst March Days										
Best	03/23/09	6.8	03/23/09	7.1	03/10/09	7.1	03/23/09	7.0	03/23/09	8.4
Worst	03/02/09	-4.2	03/02/09	-4.7	03/12/01	-6.3	03/02/09	-4.8	03/27/80	-6.0
First Trading Day of Expiration Week: 1980–2016										
Record (#Up – #Down)	25–12		24–13		18–19		22–15		19–18	
Current streak	U5		D1		U4		D1		D1	
Avg % Change	0.20		0.07		-0.26		0.02		-0.32	
Options Expiration Day: 1980–2016										
Record (#Up – #Down)	20–17		22–15		18–19		20–17		17–19	
Current streak	U2		U2		U2		U2		U2	
Avg % Change	0.09		0.03		-0.03		0.03		-0.01	
Options Expiration Week: 1980–2016										
Record (#Up – #Down)	26–10		25–12		23–14		24–13		21–16	
Current streak	U5		U5		U5		U5		U5	
Avg % Change	0.95		0.79		0.09		0.72		0.25	
Week After Options Expiration: 1980–2016										
Record (#Up – #Down)	16–21		12–25		18–19		12–25		17–20	
Current streak	D2		D5		D4		D5		D5	
Avg % Change	-0.26		-0.17		-0.01		-0.18		-0.09	
First Trading Day Performance										
% of Time Up	67.2		64.2		63.0		60.5		65.8	
Avg % Change	0.17		0.18		0.27		0.16		0.23	
Last Trading Day Performance										
% of Time Up	41.8		40.3		65.2		47.4		81.6	
Avg % Change	-0.10		-0.01		0.17		0.08		0.39	

Dow & S&P 1950–April 2016, NASDAQ 1971–April 2016, Russell 1K & 2K 1979–April 2016.

March has Ides and St. Patrick's Day;
Begins bullishly, then fades away.

MONDAY

D 47.6
S 52.4
N 52.4

27

Methodology is the last refuge of a sterile mind.
— Marianne L. Simmel (Psychologist)

TUESDAY

D 42.9
S 42.9
N 28.6

28

[Look for companies] where the executives have a good ownership position—not only options, but outright ownership—so that they will ride up and down with the shareholder.
— George Roche (Chairman, T. Rowe Price, *Barron's* 12/18/06)

Ash Wednesday
First Trading Day in March Mixed, Dow Down 5 of Last 10, –4.2% in 2009, 1996–2006 Up 9 of 11

WEDNESDAY

D 61.9
S 61.9
N 57.1

1

Develop interest in life as you see it; in people, things, literature, music—the world is so rich, simply throbbing with rich treasures, beautiful souls and interesting people. Forget yourself.
— Henry Miller (American writer, *Tropic of Cancer, Tropic of Capricorn*, 1891–1980)

THURSDAY

D 42.9
S 38.1
N 38.1

2

The first human being to live to 150 years of age is alive today, but will he get Social Security for 85 years of his longer life span, more than twice the number of years he worked?
— John Mauldin (Millennium Wave Advisors, 2000wave.com, 2/2/07)

March Historically Strong Early in the Month (Pages 30 and 134)

FRIDAY

D 57.1
S 66.7
N 66.7

3

Never lend money to someone who must borrow money to pay interest [on other money owed].
— (A Swiss Banker's First Rule, quoted by Lester Thurow)

SATURDAY

4

SUNDAY

5

MARKET FARES BETTER UNDER DEMOCRATS; DOLLAR HOLDS UP BETTER UNDER REPUBLICANS

Does the market perform better under Republicans or Democrats? The market surge under Reagan and Bush I after Vietnam, OPEC and Iran inflation helped Republicans even up the score in the 20th Century vs. the Democrats, who benefited when Roosevelt came in following an 89.2% drop by the Dow. However, under Clinton, the Democrats took the lead again. Both Parties were more evenly matched in the last half of the 20th Century. Under Bush II, the Dow lost 12.1% while the dollar has lost 20.0%. Under Obama, the Dow has gained 81.7% while the dollar has lost 9.9%.

THE STOCK MARKET UNDER REPUBLICANS AND DEMOCRATS

Republican Eras		% Change	Democratic Eras		% Change
1901-1912	12 Years	48.3%	1913-1920	8 Years	29.2%
1921-1932	12 Years	−24.5%	1933-1952	20 Years	318.4%
1953-1960	8 Years	121.2%	1961-1968	8 Years	58.3%
1969-1976	8 Years	2.1%	1977-1980	4 Years	−3.0%
1981-1992	12 Years	247.0%	1993-2000	8 Years	236.7%
2001-2008	8 Years	−12.1%	2009-2016*	8 Years	81.7%
Totals	60 Years	382.1%	Totals	56 Years*	721.5%
Average Annual Change		6.4%	Average Annual Change		13.0%

Based on Dow Jones Industrial Average on previous year's Election Day or day before when closed.
*Through May 23, 2016.

A $10,000 investment compounded during Democratic eras would have grown to $508,335 in 56* years. The same investment during 60 Republican years would have appreciated to $77,175. After lagging for many years, performance under the Republicans improved under Reagan and Bush. Under Clinton Democratic performance surged ahead. Under Bush II Republicans lost ground.

DECLINE OF THE DOLLAR UNDER REPUBLICANS AND DEMOCRATS

Republican Eras		Loss in Purch. Power	Value of Dollar	Democratic Eras		Loss in Purch. Power	Value of Dollar
1901-1912	12 Years	−23.6%	$0.76	1913-1920	8 Years	−51.4%	$0.49
1921-1932	12 Years	+46.9%	$1.12	1933-1952	20 Years	−48.6%	$0.25
1953-1960	8 Years	−10.2%	$1.01	1961-1968	8 Years	−15.0%	$0.21
1969-1976	8 Years	−38.9%	$0.62	1977-1980	4 Years	−30.9%	$0.15
1981-1992	12 Years	−41.3%	$0.36	1993-2000	8 Years	−18.5%	$0.12
2001-2008	8 Years	−20.0%	$0.29	2009-2016*	8 Years	−9.9%	$0.11

The Republican Dollar declined to $0.29 in 60 years.   **The Democratic Dollar declined to $0.11 in 56 years.**

Based on average annual Consumer Price Index 1982-1984 = 100.
*Through May 23, 2016.

Adjusting stock market performance for loss of purchasing power reduced the Democrats '$508,335 to $54,740 and the Republicans' $77,175 to $22,344. Republicans may point out that all four major wars of the 20th century began while the Democrats were in power. Democrats can counter that the 46.7 percent increase in purchasing power occurred during the Depression and was not very meaningful to the 25 percent who were unemployed.

For the record, there have been 14 recessions and 18 bear markets under the Republicans and 7 recessions and 17 bear markets under the Democrats.

Happy 50ᵗʰ Anniversary
Stock Trader's Almanac

Cumulative Growth Chart

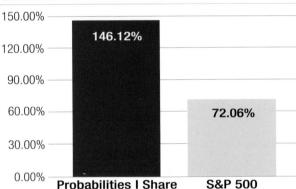

Past Performance is no indication of future returns. Since inception, January 1, 2008 to present.

Using historical trends and patterns to obtain dynamic exposure to the US stock market.

Statistical Analysis vs S&P 500

	Probabilities I Share	S&P 500
Cumulative Performance	146.12%	72.06%
Annualized Alpha	8.59%	0.00%
Beta	0.48	1.00
Sharpe Ratio	0.69	0.46
Standard Deviation	17.07%	16.18%
Maximum Drawdown	-22.29%	-48.45%
Correlation	0.45	1.00
Up Capture of S&P 500	83.61%	100%
Down Capture of S&P 500	56.19%	100%

Performance
As of 06/30/2016 (Greater than one year, annualized)

	YTD	1 Year	3 Years	5 Years	Since Inception*
Probabilities Fund (Class I)	2.37%	1.18%	1.98%	8.26%	11.18%
Probabilities Fund A at NAV	2.28%	0.89%	N/A	N/A	0.86%
Probabilities Fund A at ML**	-3.64%	-4.89%	N/A	N/A	-1.55%

*A share since inception 1/16/14 to present. I share since inception 12/12/13 to present.
**ML refers to maximum load.

Disclosures

Historical Performance

	Jan	Feb	Mar	Apr	May	Jun	Jul	Aug	Sep	Oct	Nov	Dec	YTD	S&P 500
2016	-6.02%	-1.36%	9.89%	0.19%	-0.48%	0.78%							2.37%	3.84%
2015	-7.56%	7.58%	-1.95%	-1.14%	0.29%	-0.95%	1.35%	-3.61%	0.39%	3.83%	1.04%	-3.93%	-5.35%	1.38%
2014	-4.46%	2.98%	1.35%	0.19%	0.10%	-0.47%	0.00%	1.62%	-0.66%	2.27%	1.85%	0.61%	5.30%	13.69%
2013	5.91%	0.53%	6.57%	-0.24%	0.62%	0.28%	0.71%	-2.23%	-0.35%	0.71%	2.53%	2.61%	18.73%	32.39%
2012	6.19%	5.83%	2.04%	2.38%	-2.80%	0.18%	4.19%	1.77%	-0.26%	0.70%	5.13%	0.07%	28.07%	16.00%
2011	4.16%	7.75%	2.12%	6.09%	0.81%	-3.26%	-0.49%	-8.86%	-6.67%	5.79%	4.38%	2.54%	13.65%	2.11%
2010	-6.75%	10.41%	4.41%	2.16%	-3.56%	0.62%	-2.97%	1.22%	1.70%	0.62%	3.09%	5.45%	16.43%	15.06%
2009	-0.94%	-15.90%	1.44%	10.98%	15.15%	0.75%	3.01%	-1.84%	-1.82%	-7.96%	8.31%	5.76%	13.88%	26.46%
2008	1.68%	-15.28%	-8.28%	5.59%	6.07%	-0.61%	-0.07%	-2.56%	-2.33%	10.19%	11.65%	2.30%	5.27%	-37.00%

Important Disclosures

MONDAY
D 47.6
S 52.4
N 38.1
6

I want the whole of Europe to have one currency; it will make trading much easier.
— Napoleon Bonaparte (Emperor of France 1804–1815; 1769–1821)

TUESDAY
D 61.9
S 61.9
N 42.9
7

All you need to succeed is a yellow pad and a pencil.
— Andre Meyer (Top deal maker at Lazard Freres)

WEDNESDAY
D 52.4
S 57.1
N 52.4
8

The test of success is not what you do when you are on top. Success is how high you bounce when you hit bottom.
— General George S. Patton, Jr. (U.S. Army field commander WWII, 1885–1945)

Dow Down 1469 Points March 9–22 in 2001

THURSDAY
D 57.1
S 52.4
N 42.9
9

Become more humble as the market goes your way.
— Bernard Baruch (Financier, speculator, statesman, presidential advisor, 1870–1965)

FRIDAY
D 61.9
S 52.4
N 47.6
10

Whenever you see a successful business, someone once made a courageous decision.
— Peter Drucker (Austrian-born pioneer management theorist, 1909–2005)

SATURDAY
11

Daylight Saving Time Begins

SUNDAY
12

FIFTY-YEAR RETROSPECTIVE

In February 1966, three months before Jeff was born, Yale Hirsch set out on his own. With his wife Davida six months pregnant, Yale incorporated the Hirsch Organization and began work on his new brainchild, *The Stock Trader's Almanac*. After spending the previous five years running operations for the renowned *Indicator Digest* newsletter founded by his cousin Samson Coslow, to whom the first edition and three others were dedicated, Yale had the ingenious idea to organize all the research and analysis on market cycles, patterns, seasonality, and indicators into a calendar format so he and his readers could track the market's schedule along with their own.

For the next two years, Yale toiled away the hours, and he released the first edition of *The Stock Trader's Almanac & Record 1968* in the fall of 1967. Brokers, advisors, money managers, and individuals alike endorsed the book and clamored for more. Over the next five decades, we solidified our position as thought leaders in behavioral finance and market analysis. Yale discovered or created some of the most iconic cycles, patterns, strategies, and indicators on Wall Street. Here is a look at some of the major milestones, discoveries, research, and analysis from the past 50 editions. Please pardon any omissions and feel free to send us anything worthy we may have overlooked.

1968–1969: Lays groundwork for 50 years. First two editions distill years of painstaking research and evaluation and a world of facts and figures, revealing a new awareness of market patterns, seasonal trends, and other market data, plus trading tools and tactics and record keeping forms never before available. Many of these consistently recurring patterns related to hours of the day, days of the week, months of the year, fiscal quarters, sector and market seasonality, trading around holidays, and the presidential election cycle. The first study of the major shift in market seasonality post-WWII, precursor to our Best Six Months. George Lindsay's Three Peaks and a Domed House Top Pattern revealed. Our proprietary Market Probability Calendar was first introduced in 1968; it has been honed and improved a great deal in the past several years. *Mutual Funds Almanac* created in 1969 and edited and published for 11 years until it was sold.

1970: Major overhaul. "Record" is dropped from the title. Snazzier binding and printing. Reorganized into three sections with separate seasonal trading patterns and strategy, planning, and record-keeping sections. Decennial pattern introduced. Best short-term buying times: market performance in all one-, two-, three-, and six-month periods. More sector seasonality. Lindsay's amazing 12-year forecast. December "Free Lunch" bargain stock strategy unveiled. **1971:** Labor Day week indicator revealed. **1973:** The January Barometer devised (page 16) and the Santa Claus Rally discovered (page 114). Mid-year rally. *Smart Money* companion monthly newsletter to the *Almanac* launched June 1973.

1974: January's First Five Days "Early Warning" System (page 14). "Lame Duck" 20th Amendment to the Constitution gave birth to the January Barometer. Pre-Easter Rally strongest two days of the year. May–June Disaster Area. October 1, 1974, Dow 605, we printed "BUY! BUY! BUY!" 18 times across the front of our *Smart Money* two days before the S&P 500 low. December 11, 1974, two days after the Dow intraday low of 570 and three days after its closing low of 577.60, *Smart Money* front page headlines read: "The Darkness before The Dawn" and "Dow 800 by April 1975."

1976: Last + First Four "prime five days" of the month formulated. First half of April outperforms second half. April 1976 *Smart Money* 500% move forecast, projecting Dow 3420 by 1990, a 500% gain from the 570 December 1974 low: based on in-depth research into how inflationary periods following major wars have triggered subsequent 500% moves in the stock market. **1977:** January 1977 *Smart Money* Special Report "Invitation to a Super Boom" reaffirms 500% move forecast. **1978:** Yale appears in April on *Wall $treet Week* with Louis Rukeyser. **1979:** Bullish last three days before Labor Day, up 17 straight. Gold stocks bullish fourth quarter.

1980: June 1980 first *Smart Money* seminar, Tarrytown, New York Hilton, themed "Getting Ready for the First Bull Market of the Eighties." Headlined by keynote speaker Louis Rukeyser. Navy blue t-shirts with big bold white lettering "DOW 3420!" were given to attendees. **1981:** Yale appears in December on *Wall $treet Week* with Louis Rukeyser. *Ground Floor* newsletter launched in October 1981, focusing on early-stage undervalued dynamic growth stocks.

1982: Dedicated to "The Next Thousand Points" in the Dow "during the mid-1980s." Unable since 1966 to clear Dow 1000 and hovering around 1000 at press-time, the Dow closes above 2000 January 8, 1987. Contrary indicators: magazine cover stories and cartoons about Wall Street; special presidential meeting with economic experts as stocks plunge; record-sized Barron's packed with ads and investment newsletters advertises superior records on strong rising market. *Directory of Exceptional Stockholders* published.

1983: Composite indicator of Santa Claus Rally, First Five Days, and January Barometer. **1985:** A Rally for All Seasons; summer rally weakest. **1986:** Thanksgiving bullish day before and after. *Don't Sell Stocks on Monday* first edition published. **1987:** Weekly planner pages switched to right side, study pages to the left. Bullish Bonanza week after expiration. New "Best Six Months" Switching Strategy invented.

Monday Before March Triple Witching, Dow Up 22 of Last 29

MONDAY

D 52.4
S 66.7
N 66.7

13

The world has changed! You can't be an 800-pound gorilla; you need to be an economic gazelle. You've got to be able to change directions quickly.
— Mark Breier (*The 10-Second Internet Manager*)

TUESDAY

D 61.9
S 47.6
N 47.6

14

In Washington people tell the truth off the record and lie on the record. In the Middle East they lie off the record and tell the truth on the record.
— Thomas L. Friedman (*NY Times* Foreign Affairs columnist, "Meet the Press" 12/17/06)

WEDNESDAY

D 66.7
S 66.7
N 47.6

15

I've learned that only through focus can you do world-class things, no matter how capable you are.
— William H. Gates (Microsoft founder, *Fortune*, July 8, 2002)

THURSDAY

D 52.4
S 57.1
N 57.1

16

The most valuable executive is one who is training somebody to be a better man than he is.
— Robert G. Ingersoll (American lawyer and orator, "The Great Agnostic," 1833–1899)

St. Patrick's Day

FRIDAY

D 66.7
S 71.4
N 61.9

17

March Triple Witching Day Mixed Last 28 Years, but Dow Down 5 of Last 8

I'm a great believer in luck, and I find the harder I work the more I have of it.
— Thomas Jefferson (3rd U.S. President, 1743–7/4/1826)

SATURDAY

18

SUNDAY

19

"Skull and crossbones" added to weekly calendar pages signifying third Friday of the month options/futures expiration with three on Triple Witching. **1989:** Half-hourly trading patterns.

1990: Jeff joins Yale full-time in the business. **1991:** Dow gains 50% from midterm low to pre-election year high. **1992:** 25th anniversary. Concealed wire-o hardcover binding. **1993:** "Happy bulls" added to weekly calendar pages on favorable market days. A Correction for All Seasons; fall correction worst. Market behavior three days before and after holidays. **1995:** Monday now best day of the week. New seasonality Memorial-Day-week up 11 years in a row.

1996: No Losses Last Seven Months of Election Years. Change in seasonality: now, First 3 Days, week before Labor Day, are Best. **1997:** Expanded from 160 to 192 pages. Market behavior when presidents are reelected. Largest daily, weekly, monthly, and yearly gains and losses. **1998:** Profit Day before St. Patrick's Day. **1999:** Super Six Days Last 4 + First 2 Days of the Month. First Month of First 3 Quarters is Most Bullish.

2000: "Best Six Months" Results Doubled with MACD Timing (Hat tip to Sy Harding, R.I.P.). Small Cap "January Effect" Starts in Mid-December. **2001:** Witch icon replaces skull and crossbones on third Friday of the month options/futures expiration with three on Triple Witching weekly calendar pages. First Days of the Month Sizzle. Monthly Bullish Seasonality Shifting; mid-month strength appears. "Free Lunch" Bargain Stocks Served Later in December. NASDAQ Market Probability Calendar. July 2001 *Smart Money* and *Ground Floor* merged into *Almanac Investor*.

2002: How Crises Impact the Market. Down Triple Witching Weeks Trigger Weakness Week After. Sector Seasonality, Selected Percentage Plays. October 16, 2002 *Almanac Investor* headline "BUY! BUY! BUY!" 18 times across the top. **2003:** Down Januarys a Remarkable Record. Super 8 Days of the Month. Down Friday/Down Monday Warning. Dow Market Probability Calendar and Recent 21-Year S&P 500 Market Probability Calendar. "Bull Symbol" signifying S&P 500 up 60% of the time on a trading day and other seasonalities noted on weekly calendar pages. **2004:** December Low Indicator. NASDAQ "Best 8 Months" Strategy + MACD Timing. Jeff takes the reins as Editor-in-Chief. Online Almanac Research Tool launched.

2005: Market Behavior When White House Changes Hands. Democratic President/Republican Congress Best for Market. Aura of the Triple Witch Q1/Q4 Bullish, Weeks After Q2/Q3 Bearish. **2006:** New "Bull Symbol." "Bear Symbol" signifying S&P 500 down 60% of the time on a trading day. Next 500% Move setting up. NASDAQ Mid-Year Rally: Christmas in July. Sector Index Strategy Calendar. *The Almanac Investor: Profit from Market History and Seasonal Trends* 525-page book published (now in 3rd printing).

2007: 40th edition, major restructuring. Russell 1000 and 2000 data added. Market probability numbers for the most recent 21 years for every trading day for Dow, S&P, and NASDAQ noted on weekly calendar pages. Vital Stats on Monthly Almanac pages. Ten years Daily Dow Point Changes moved to Databank. Notable Events. Sell Rosh Hashanah, Buy Yom Kippur, Sell Passover. Best & Worst section tweaked, quarters added. S&P and NASDAQ Bull & Bear Markets. *Commodity Trader's Almanac* created in 2007 with the help of Scott Barrie (R.I.P.) and published for seven years.

2008: Free Lunch Bargain Stocks picked December Triple Witching Friday before Christmas. When *Evidence-Based Technical Analysis* Best Investment Book of the year, author David Aronson back-tested our Best Six Months Switching Strategy using the scientific method to 1987. The year after it was first published it generated an annualized return of 16.3% versus 3.9% for the Worst Six Months 1987-April 2006. They also found it to be sound, valuable, and to have predictive power. The returns were considered to be statistically significant, unlike any of the 6,402 rules tested for the book. 2008 *Almanac Investor* headlines: January 16 "Long-Hibernating Bear Awakes in Bull's Season, Steepest Correction Since 2003, Looming Recession, Negative Early Readings Portend More Carnage"; February 13 "Negative January Barometer Points to Further Declines, Don't Get Snared by the Bear Market Rally"; December 12 "Bottom May Be In and a New Bull Market Underway…"

2009: Best Six Months + 4-Year Cycle, triple returns less trades. Market Behavior Under New Presidents. 4th Quarter Market Magic. John Person helps revamp, improve, and expand the *Commodity Trader's Almanac* as contributing editor. **2011:** Next Super Boom: Dow 38820 by 2025 forecast, first revealed at Dow 10,783 in May 13, 2010 *Almanac Investor*. What to Trade During Best and Worst Months. *Super Boom* book released in April 2011 at Dow 12,320. **2012:** Fifteen Year Projection based on Super Boom forecast for Dow 38820 by 2025. *Little Book of Stock Market Cycles*. **2013:** Market Behavior after Sitting President Wins & Losses. Post-Election Performance by Party.

2014: Switched back to old school spiral binding with foil-stamped soft cover. One-year seasonality charts for Dow, S&P 500, NASDAQ, Russell 1000, and Russell 2000 with midterm year versus all years. **2015:** Outlooks from 18 of our favorite minds on Wall Street. **2016:** Eighth Year of Presidential Terms charts.

It has been a privilege and an honor to present our analysis these past 50 years. We intend to endure for many more and hope the next generation carries the torch.

MONDAY

D 57.1
S 42.9
N 61.9

20

...the most successful positions I've taken have been those about which I've been most nervous (and ignored that emotion anyway). Courage is not about being fearless; courage is about acting appropriately even when you are fearful.
— Daniel Turov (*Turov on Timing*)

Week After Triple Witching, Dow Down 19 of Last 29, 2000 Up 4.9%, 2007 Up 3.1%, 2009 Up 6.8%, 2011 Up 3.1%, Down 4 of Last 5

TUESDAY

D 33.3
S 28.6
N 33.3

21

Each day is a building block to the future. Who I am today is dependent on who I was yesterday.
— Matthew McConaughey (Actor; *Parade Magazine*)

WEDNESDAY

D 47.6
S 47.6
N 42.9

22

In this game, the market has to keep pitching, but you don't have to swing. You can stand there with the bat on your shoulder for six months until you get a fat pitch.
— Warren Buffett (CEO Berkshire Hathaway, investor and philanthropist, b. 1930)

March Historically Weak Later in the Month (Pages 30 and 134)

THURSDAY

D 42.9
S 38.1
N 52.4

23

For a country, everything will be lost when the jobs of an economist and a banker become highly respected professions.
— Montesquieu

FRIDAY

D 42.9
S 66.7
N 61.9

24

The average bottom-of-the-ladder person is potentially as creative as the top executive who sits in the big office. The problem is that the person on the bottom of the ladder doesn't trust his own brilliance and doesn't, therefore, believe in his own ideas.
— Robert Schuller (Minister)

SATURDAY

25

SUNDAY

26

APRIL ALMANAC

APRIL						
S	M	T	W	T	F	S
30						
2	3	4	5	6	7	8
9	10	11	12	13	14	15
16	17	18	19	20	21	22
23	24	25	26	27	28	29

MAY						
S	M	T	W	T	F	S
	1	2	3	4	5	6
7	8	9	10	11	12	13
14	15	16	17	18	19	20
21	22	23	24	25	26	27
28	29	30	31			

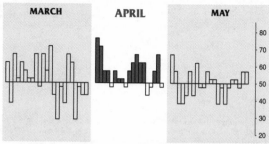

Market Probability Chart above is a graphic representation of the S&P 500 Recent Market Probability Calendar on page 124.

◆ April is still the best Dow month (average 1.9%) since 1950 (page 50) ◆ April 1999, first month ever to gain 1000 Dow points, 856 in 2001, knocked off its high horse in 2002, down 458, 2003 up 488 ◆ Up ten straight, average gain 2.6% ◆ Prone to weakness after mid-month tax deadline ◆ Stocks anticipate great first-quarter earnings by rising sharply before earnings are reported, rather than after ◆ Rarely a dangerous month, recent exceptions are 2002, 2004, and 2005 ◆ "Best Six Months" of the year end with April (page 52) ◆ Post-presidential election year Aprils solid since 1950 (Dow 1.9%, S&P 1.6%, NASDAQ 2.4%) ◆ End of April NASDAQ strength (pages 125 & 126).

April Vital Statistics

	DJIA		S&P 500		NASDAQ		Russell 1K		Russell 2K	
Rank	1		3		4		2		4	
Up	45		47		29		26		23	
Down	22		20		17		12		15	
Average % Change	1.9%		1.5%		1.3%		1.5%		1.5%	
Post-Election Year	1.9%		1.6%		2.4%		2.5%		2.2%	
Best & Worst April										
	% Change		% Change		% Change		% Change		% Change	
Best	1978	10.6	2009	9.4	2001	15.0	2009	10.0	2009	15.3
Worst	1970	−6.3	1970	−9.0	2000	−15.6	2002	−5.8	2000	−6.1
Best & Worst April Weeks										
Best	04/11/75	5.7	04/20/00	5.8	04/12/01	14.0	04/20/00	5.9	04/03/09	6.3
Worst	04/14/00	−7.3	04/14/00	−10.5	04/14/00	−25.3	04/14/00	−11.2	04/14/00	−16.4
Best & Worst April Days										
Best	04/05/01	4.2	04/05/01	4.4	04/05/01	8.9	04/05/01	4.6	04/09/09	5.9
Worst	04/14/00	−5.7	04/14/00	−5.8	04/14/00	−9.7	04/14/00	−6.0	04/14/00	−7.3
First Trading Day of Expiration Week: 1980–2016										
Record (#Up – #Down)	22–15		20–17		19–18		19–18		16–21	
Current streak	D2		D2		D2		D2		D1	
Avg % Change	0.18		0.10		0.09		0.09		−0.04	
Options Expiration Day: 1980–2016										
Record (#Up – #Down)	24–13		24–13		21–16		24–13		24–13	
Current streak	D3		D2		D2		D2		U1	
Avg % Change	0.17		0.17		−0.04		0.16		0.20	
Options Expiration Week: 1980–2016										
Record (#Up – #Down)	29–8		26–11		24–13		24–13		27–10	
Current streak	U1		U1		U1		U1		U1	
Avg % Change	1.07		0.87		0.90		0.85		0.80	
Week After Options Expiration: 1980–2016										
Record (#Up – #Down)	25–12		25–12		26–11		25–12		25–12	
Current streak	U2		U2		D1		U2		U2	
Avg % Change	0.44		0.43		0.68		0.44		0.86	
First Trading Day Performance										
% of Time Up	59.7		62.7		47.8		60.5		50.0	
Avg % Change	0.18		0.15		−0.08		0.18		−0.05	
Last Trading Day Performance										
% of Time Up	50.7		55.2		65.2		55.3		65.8	
Avg % Change	0.08		0.07		0.13		0.05		0.06	

Dow & S&P 1950–April 2016, NASDAQ 1971–April 2016, Russell 1K & 2K 1979–April 2016.

April "Best Month" for Dow since 1950;
Day-before-Good Friday gains are nifty.

MARCH/APRIL 2017

MONDAY
D 61.9
S 61.9
N 66.7
27

A bank is a place where they lend you an umbrella in fair weather and ask for it back again when it begins to rain.
— Robert Frost (American poet, 1874–1963)

TUESDAY
D 23.8
S 28.6
N 33.3
28

Those who are of the opinion that money will do everything may very well be suspected to do everything for money.
— Sir George Savile (British statesman and author, 1633–1695)

Start Looking for the Dow and S&P MACD SELL Signal (Pages 52 and 54)
Almanac Investor Subscribers E-mailed When It Triggers (See Insert)

WEDNESDAY
D 52.4
S 47.6
N 47.6
29

Liberal institutions straightaway cease from being liberal the moment they are firmly established.
— Friedrich Nietzsche (German philosopher, 1844–1900)

THURSDAY
D 57.1
S 42.9
N 52.4
30

Only buy stocks when the market declines 10% from that date a year ago, which happens once or twice a decade.
— Eugene D. Brody (Oppenheimer Capital)

Last Trading Day of March, Dow Down 17 of Last 27
Russell 2000 Up 16 of Last 23

FRIDAY
D 38.1
S 42.9
N 57.1
31

Ideas are easy; it's execution that's hard.
— Jeff Bezos (Amazon.com)

SATURDAY
1

SUNDAY
2

REPUBLICAN CONGRESS & DEMOCRATIC PRESIDENT IS BEST FOR THE MARKET

Six possible political alignments exist in Washington: a Republican president with a Republican Congress, Democratic Congress, or split Congress; and a Democratic president with a Democratic Congress, Republican Congress, or split Congress. Data presented in the chart below begin in 1949 with the first full presidential term following WWII. Lopsided market moves during the first half of the 20th Century prior to latter-day improvements to financial systems, including the Depression, have been omitted to focus on the modern era.

First, looking at just the historical performance of the Dow under Democratic and Republican Presidents, we see a pattern that is contrary to popular belief. Under a Democrat, the Dow has performed better than under a Republican. The Dow has historically returned 10.0% under Democrats, compared to 6.8% under a Republican executive. Congressional results are the opposite and are much more dramatic. Republican Congresses since 1949 have yielded an average 15.3% gain in the Dow, compared to a 6.1% return when Democrats have controlled the Hill.

With total Republican control of Washington, the Dow has been up, on average, 14.1%. Democrats in power of the two branches have produced an average Dow gain of 7.4%. When power is split with a Republican president and a Democratic Congress or a split Congress, the Dow has not done well, averaging only a 5.4% gain. With a Democratic president and a Republican Congress or a split Congress, the Dow has performed well, averaging an 14.7% gain. The best scenario for all investors has been a Democrat in the White House and Republican control of Congress, with average gains of 16.4%.

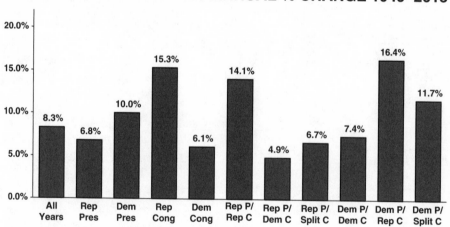

DOW JONES INDUSTRIALS ANNUAL % CHANGE 1949–2015

APRIL 2017

First Trading Day in April, Dow Up 17 of Last 22

MONDAY
D 76.2
S 76.2
N 66.7

3

Chance favors the informed mind.
— Louis Pasteur (French chemist, founder of microbiology, 1822–1895)

TUESDAY
D 71.4
S 71.4
N 61.9

4

"Be yourself!" is about the worst advice you can give to some people.
— Tom Masson

April is the Best Month for the Dow, Average 1.9% Gain Since 1950

WEDNESDAY
D 42.9
S 57.1
N 71.4

5

Brazil is the country of the future and always will be.
— (Brazilian joke)

THURSDAY
D 61.9
S 57.1
N 52.4

6

A small debt produces a debtor, a large one, an enemy.
— Publilius Syrus (Syrian-born Roman mime and former slave, 83–43 B.C.)

April is 3rd Best Month for S&P, 4th Best for NASDAQ (Since 1971)

FRIDAY
D 42.9
S 47.6
N 38.1

7

It's a lot of fun finding a country nobody knows about. The only thing better is finding a country everybody's bullish on and shorting it.
— Jim Rogers (Financier, *Investment Biker*, b. 1942)

SATURDAY

8

SUNDAY

9

THE SEVENTH YEAR OF DECADES

Only three of the nine "seven" years below were sizable winners; two were Pre-Election Years 1927 and 1967. Post-Election Year 1997 benefited from the 5-year millennial bull-run. Other post-election "seven" years, 1937, 1957, and 1977, were nasty, with an average loss of 21.0%. If a meaningful election-year decline is avoided in 2016, 2017 could prove to be a challenging year for the market.

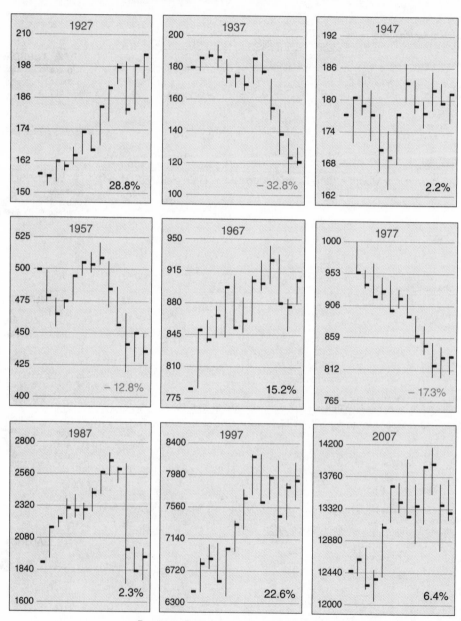

Based on Dow Jones Industrial Average monthly ranges and closing.

42

April 1999 First Month Ever to Gain 1000 Dow Points

MONDAY

D 52.4
S 57.1
N 66.7

10

Anytime there is change there is opportunity. So it is paramount that an organization get energized rather than paralyzed.
— Jack Welch (GE CEO, *Fortune*)

Passover

TUESDAY

D 57.1
S 52.4
N 52.4

11

Success isn't measured by the position you reach in life; it's measured by the obstacles you overcome.
— Booker T. Washington (Founder of Tuskegee Institute, 1856–1915)

WEDNESDAY

D 61.9
S 52.4
N 61.9

12

In politics as in chess, or in the military or in business, when you have the advantage you must press it quickly—or lose it. For the first time in history, we are in a position to checkmate tyranny. Momentum is largely on the side of democracy.
— Garry Kasparov (World chess champion 1985–2000)

NASDAQ Up 16 Straight Days Before Good Friday

THURSDAY

D 52.4
S 47.6
N 42.9

13

The choice of starting a war this [pre-election] spring was made for political as well as military reasons…
[The president] cleary does not want to have a war raging on the eve of his presumed reelection campaign.
— Senior European diplomat (*NY Times* 3/14/03)

Good Friday *(Market Closed)*

FRIDAY

14

Whoso would be a man, must be a non-conformist… Nothing is at last sacred but the integrity of your own mind.
— Ralph Waldo Emerson (American author, poet, and philosopher, *Self-Reliance*, 1803–1882)

SATURDAY

15

Easter
April Almanac Investor Sector Seasonalities: See Pages 94, 96, and 98

SUNDAY

16

THE DECEMBER LOW INDICATOR: A USEFUL PROGNOSTICATING TOOL

When the Dow closes below its December closing low in the first quarter, it is frequently an excellent warning sign. Jeffrey Saut, Managing Director, Chief Investment Strategist at Raymond James, brought this to our attention a few years ago. The December Low Indicator was originated by Lucien Hooper, a *Forbes* columnist and Wall Street analyst back in the 1970s. Hooper dismissed the importance of January and January's first week as reliable indicators. He noted that the trend could be random or even manipulated during a holiday-shortened week. Instead, said Hooper, "Pay much more attention to the December low. If that low is violated during the first quarter of the New Year, watch out!"

Nineteen of the 33 occurrences were followed by gains for the rest of the year—and 16 full-year gains—after the low for the year was reached. For perspective, we've included the January Barometer readings for the selected years. Hooper's "Watch Out" warning was absolutely correct, though. All but two of the instances since 1952 experienced further declines, as the Dow fell an additional 10.5% on average when December's low was breached in Q1.

Only three significant drops occurred (not shown) when December's low was not breached in Q1 (1974, 1981, and 1987). Both indicators were wrong only six times, and nine years ended flat. If the December low is not crossed, turn to our January Barometer for guidance. It has been virtually perfect, right nearly 100% of these times (view the complete results at *www.stocktradersalmanac.com*).

YEARS DOW FELL BELOW DECEMBER LOW IN FIRST QUARTER

Year	Previous Dec Low	Date Crossed	Crossing Price	Subseq. Low	% Change Cross-Low	Rest of Year % Change	Full Year % Change	Jan Bar
1952	262.29	2/19/52	261.37	256.35	−1.9%	11.7%	8.4%	1.6%[2]
1953	281.63	2/11/53	281.57	255.49	−9.3	−0.2	−3.8	−0.7[3]
1956	480.72	1/9/56	479.74	462.35	−3.6	4.1	2.3	−3.6[1, 2, 3]
1957	480.61	1/18/57	477.46	419.79	−12.1	−8.7	−12.8	−4.2
1960	661.29	1/12/60	660.43	566.05	−14.3	−6.7	−9.3	−7.1
1962	720.10	1/5/62	714.84	535.76	−25.1	−8.8	−10.8	−3.8
1966	939.53	3/1/66	938.19	744.32	−20.7	−16.3	−18.9	0.5[1]
1968	879.16	1/22/68	871.71	825.13	−5.3	8.3	4.3	−4.4[1, 2, 3]
1969	943.75	1/6/69	936.66	769.93	−17.8	−14.6	−15.2	−0.8
1970	769.93	1/26/70	768.88	631.16	−17.9	9.1	4.8	−7.6[2, 3]
1973	1000.00	1/29/73	996.46	788.31	−20.9	−14.6	−16.6	−1.7
1977	946.64	2/7/77	946.31	800.85	−15.4	−12.2	−17.3	−5.1
1978	806.22	1/5/78	804.92	742.12	−7.8	0.01	−3.1	−6.2[3]
1980	819.62	3/10/80	818.94	759.13	−7.3	17.7	14.9	5.8[2]
1982	868.25	1/5/82	865.30	776.92	−10.2	20.9	19.6	−1.8[1, 2]
1984	1236.79	1/25/84	1231.89	1086.57	−11.8	−1.6	−3.7	−0.9[3]
1990	2687.93	1/15/90	2669.37	2365.10	−11.4	−1.3	−4.3	−6.9[3]
1991	2565.59	1/7/91	2522.77	2470.30	−2.1	25.6	20.3	4.2[2]
1993	3255.18	1/8/93	3251.67	3241.95	−0.3	15.5	13.7	0.7[2]
1994	3697.08	3/30/94	3626.75	3593.35	−0.9	5.7	2.1	3.3[2, 3]
1996	5059.32	1/10/96	5032.94	5032.94	NC	28.1	26.0	3.3[2]
1998	7660.13	1/9/98	7580.42	7539.07	−0.5	21.1	16.1	1.0[2]
2000	10998.39	1/4/00	10997.93	9796.03	−10.9	−1.9	−6.2	−5.1
2001	10318.93	3/12/01	10208.25	8235.81	−19.3	−1.8	−7.1	3.5[1]
2002	9763.96	1/16/02	9712.27	7286.27	−25.0	−14.1	−16.8	−1.6
2003	8303.78	1/24/03	8131.01	7524.06	−7.5	28.6	25.3	−2.7[1, 2]
2005	10440.58	1/21/05	10392.99	10012.36	−3.7	3.1	−0.6	−2.5[3]
2006	10717.50	1/20/06	10667.39	10667.39	NC	16.8	16.3	2.5
2007	12194.13	3/2/07	12114.10	12050.41	−0.5	9.5	6.4	1.4[2]
2008	13167.20	1/2/08	13043.96	7552.29	−42.1	−32.7	−33.8	−6.1
2009	8149.09	1/20/09	7949.09	6547.05	−17.6	31.2	18.8	−8.6[1, 2]
2010	10285.97	1/22/10	10172.98	9686.48	−4.8	13.8	11.0	−3.7[1, 2]
2014	15739.43	1/31/14	15698.85	15372.80	−2.1	13.5	7.5	−3.6[1, 2]
2016	17128.55	1/6/2016	16906.51	15660.18	−7.4	??	??	−5.1
				Average Drop	**−10.6%**			

[1]January Barometer wrong. [2]December Low Indicator wrong. [3]Year Flat.

Income Tax Deadline, *Day After Easter, Second Worst Post-Holiday (Page 88)*
Monday Before Expiration, Dow Up 18 of Last 28, Mixed Last 12 Years

MONDAY

D 71.4
S 57.1
N 52.4

17

Small volume is usually accompanied by a fall in price; large volume by a rise in price.
— Charles C. Ying ("Stock Market Prices and Volumes of Sales," *Econometrica*, July 1966)

TUESDAY

D 66.7
S 61.9
N 47.6

18

Big money is made in the stock market by being on the right side of major moves. I don't believe in swimming against the tide.
— Martin Zweig (Fund manager, *Winning on Wall Street*, 1943–2013)

April Prone to Weakness After Tax Deadline (Pages 38 and 134)

WEDNESDAY

D 61.9
S 66.7
N 57.1

19

You have powers you never dreamed of. You can do things you never thought you could do. There are no limitations in what you can do except the limitations in your own mind.
— Darwin P. Kingsley (President New York Life, 1857–1932)

THURSDAY

D 57.1
S 61.9
N 57.1

20

If a battered stock refuses to sink any lower no matter how many negative articles appear in the papers, that stock is worth a close look.
— James L. Fraser (*Contrary Investor*)

April Expiration Day Dow Up 14 of Last 20

FRIDAY

D 66.7
S 61.9
N 61.9

21

The ability to foretell what is going to happen tomorrow, next week, next month, and next year. And to have the ability afterwards to explain why it didn't happen.
— Winston Churchill (British statesman, 1874–1965; when asked what qualities a politician required)

SATURDAY

22

SUNDAY

23

DOWN JANUARYS: A REMARKABLE RECORD

In the first third of the twentieth century, there was no correlation between January markets and the year as a whole. Then, in 1972, Yale Hirsch discovered that the 1933 "lame duck" Amendment to the Constitution changed the political calendar, and the January Barometer was born—its record has been quite accurate (page 16).

Down Januarys are harbingers of trouble ahead, in the economic, political, or military arenas. Eisenhower's heart attack in 1955 cast doubt on whether he could run in 1956—a flat year. Two other election years with down Januarys were also flat (1984 and 1992). Twelve bear markets began, and ten continued into second years with poor Januarys. 1968 started down, as we were mired in Vietnam, but Johnson's "bombing halt" changed the climate. Imminent military action in Iraq held January 2003 down before the market triple-bottomed in March. After Baghdad fell, pre-election and recovery forces fueled 2003 into a banner year. 2005 was flat, registering the narrowest Dow trading range on record. 2008 was the worst January on record and preceded the worst bear market since the Great Depression. A negative reading in 2015 and 2016 preceded an official Dow bear market declaration in February 2016.

Unfortunately, bull and bear markets do not start conveniently at the beginnings and ends of months or years. Though some years ended higher, **every down January since 1950 was followed by a new or continuing bear market, a 10% correction, or a flat year. Down Januarys were followed by substantial declines averaging** *minus* **13.2%,** providing excellent buying opportunities later in most years.

FROM DOWN JANUARY S&P CLOSES TO LOW NEXT 11 MONTHS

Year	January Close	% Change	11-Month Low	Date of Low	Jan Close to Low %	% Feb to Dec	Year % Change	
1953	26.38	−0.7%	22.71	14-Sep	−13.9%	−6.0%	−6.6%	bear
1956	43.82	−3.6	43.42	14-Feb	−0.9	6.5	2.6	FLAT/bear
1957	44.72	−4.2	38.98	22-Oct	−12.8	−10.6	−14.3	Cont. bear
1960	55.61	−7.1	52.30	25-Oct	−6.0	4.5	−3.0	bear
1962	68.84	−3.8	52.32	26-Jun	−24.0	−8.3	−11.8	bear
1968	92.24	−4.4	87.72	5-Mar	−4.9	12.6	7.7	−10%/bear
1969	103.01	−0.8	89.20	17-Dec	−13.4	−10.6	−11.4	Cont. bear
1970	85.02	−7.6	69.20	26-May	−18.6	8.4	0.1	Cont. bear/FLAT
1973	116.03	−1.7	92.16	5-Dec	−20.6	−15.9	−17.4	bear
1974	96.57	−1.0	62.28	3-Oct	−35.5	−29.0	−29.7	Cont. bear
1977	102.03	−5.1	90.71	2-Nov	−11.1	−6.8	−11.5	bear
1978	89.25	−6.2	86.90	6-Mar	−2.6	7.7	1.1	Cont. bear/bear
1981	129.55	−4.6	112.77	25-Sep	−13.0	−5.4	−9.7	bear
1982	120.40	−1.8	102.42	12-Aug	−14.9	16.8	14.8	Cont. bear
1984	163.42	−0.9	147.82	24-Jul	−9.5	2.3	1.4	Cont. bear/FLAT
1990	329.07	−6.9	295.46	11-Oct	−10.2	0.4	−6.6	bear
1992	408.79	−2.0	394.50	8-Apr	−3.5	6.6	4.5	FLAT
2000	1394.46	−5.1	1264.74	20-Dec	−9.3	−5.3	−10.1	bear
2002	1130.20	−1.6	776.76	9-Oct	−31.3	−22.2	−23.4	bear
2003	855.70	−2.7	800.73	11-Mar	−6.4	29.9	26.4	Cont. bear
2005	1181.27	−2.5	1137.50	20-Apr	−3.7	5.7	3.0	FLAT
2008	1378.55	−6.1	752.44	20-Nov	−45.4	−34.5	−38.5	Cont. bear
2009	825.88	−8.6	676.53	9-Mar	−18.1	35.0	23.5	Cont. bear
2010	1073.87	−3.7	1022.58	2-Jul	−4.8	17.1	12.8	−10%
2014	1782.59	−3.6	1741.89	3-Feb	−2.3	15.5	11.4	−10% intraday
2015	1994.99	−3.1	1867.61	25-Aug	−6.4	2.5	−0.7	bear
Totals		**−343.1%**				**16.9%**	**−85.5%**	
Average		**−13.2%**				**0.7%**	**−3.3%**	

MONDAY

D 47.6
S 42.9
N 57.1

24

Resentment is like taking poison and waiting for the other person to die.
— Malachy McCourt (*A Monk Swimming: A Memoir*)

TUESDAY

D 52.4
S 47.6
N 42.9

25

All free governments are managed by the combined wisdom and folly of the people.
— James A. Garfield (20th U.S. President, 1831–1881)

WEDNESDAY

D 66.7
S 57.1
N 57.1

26

America, this brash and noble container of dreams, this muse to artists and inventors and entrepreneurs, this beacon of optimism, this dynamo of energy, this trumpet blare of liberty.
— Peter Jennings (Canadian-born anchor, *ABC World News Tonight*, July 2003 after gaining U.S. citizenship in May; 1938–2005)

THURSDAY

D 71.4
S 66.7
N 76.2

27

I have a simple philosophy. Fill what's empty. Empty what's full. And scratch where it itches.
— Alice Roosevelt Longworth

End of "Best Six Months" of the Year (Pages 50, 52, 54, and 147)

FRIDAY

D 38.1
S 47.6
N 61.9

28

You are your own Promised Land, your own new frontier.
— Julia Margaret Cameron (19th century English photographer)

SATURDAY

29

May Almanac Investor Sector Seasonalities: See Pages 94, 96, and 98

SUNDAY

30

MAY ALMANAC

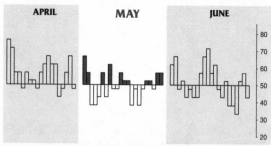

MAY							JUNE						
S	M	T	W	T	F	S	S	M	T	W	T	F	S
	1	2	3	4	5	6						1	2	3
7	8	9	10	11	12	13	4	5	6	7	8	9	10
14	15	16	17	18	19	20	11	12	13	14	15	16	17
21	22	23	24	25	26	27	18	19	20	21	22	23	24
28	29	30	31				25	26	27	28	29	30	

Market Probability Chart above is a graphic representation of the S&P 500 Recent Market Probability Calendar on page 124.

◆ "May/June disaster area" between 1965 and 1984 with S&P down 15 out of 20 Mays ◆ Between 1985 and 1997 May was the best month with 13 straight gains, gaining 3.3% per year on average, up 10, down 8 since ◆ Worst six months of the year begin with May (page 52) ◆ A $10,000 investment compounded to $843,577 for November–April in 66 years compared to a $319 loss for May–October ◆ Dow Memorial Day week record: up 12 years in a row (1984–1995), down 12 of the last 20 years ◆ Since 1950, post-presidential election year Mays rank well: #4 Dow, #3 S&P, and #1 NASDAQ.

May Vital Statistics

	DJIA		S&P 500		NASDAQ		Russell 1K		Russell 2K	
Rank	9		8		6		6		6	
Up	34		38		27		25		24	
Down	32		28		18		12		13	
Average % Change	−0.02%		0.2%		0.9%		1.0%		1.3%	
Post-Election Year	1.3%		1.7%		3.4%		3.2%		4.6%	
Best & Worst May										
		% Change		% Change		% Change		% Change		% Change
Best	1990	8.3	1990	9.2	1997	11.1	1990	8.9	1997	11.0
Worst	2010	−7.9	1962	−8.6	2000	−11.9	2010	−8.1	2010	−7.7
Best & Worst May Weeks										
Best	05/29/70	5.8	05/02/97	6.2	05/17/02	8.8	05/02/97	6.4	05/14/10	6.3
Worst	05/25/62	−6.0	05/25/62	−6.8	05/07/10	−8.0	05/07/10	−6.6	05/07/10	−8.9
Best & Worst May Days										
Best	05/27/70	5.1	05/27/70	5.0	05/30/00	7.9	05/10/10	4.4	05/10/10	5.6
Worst	05/28/62	−5.7	05/28/62	−6.7	05/23/00	−5.9	05/20/10	−3.9	05/20/10	−5.1
First Trading Day of Expiration Week: 1980–2015										
Record (#Up – #Down)	23–14		24–13		20–17		22–15		19–18	
Current streak	U1		U1		U1		U1		U3	
Avg % Change	0.19		0.18		0.17		0.15		0.02	
Options Expiration Day: 1980–2015										
Record (#Up – #Down)	18–19		21–16		18–19		21–16		18–19	
Current streak	U4		U4		U1		U4		U1	
Avg % Change	−0.09		−0.09		−0.09		−0.07		0.03	
Options Expiration Week: 1980–2015										
Record (#Up – #Down)	19–18		19–18		20–17		18–19		20–17	
Current streak	D1		U2		U4		U2		U2	
Avg % Change	0.06		0.04		0.20		0.04		−0.11	
Week After Options Expiration: 1980–2015										
Record (#Up – #Down)	19–17		22–14		24–12		22–14		26–10	
Current streak	D1		U2		U2		U1		U2	
Avg % Change	−0.04		0.11		0.16		0.13		0.29	
First Trading Day Performance										
% of Time Up	58.2		58.2		63.0		56.8		59.5	
Avg % Change	0.22		0.24		0.33		0.26		0.25	
Last Trading Day Performance										
% of Time Up	60.6		62.1		66.7		56.8		64.9	
Avg % Change	0.19		0.26		0.19		0.21		0.32	

Dow & S&P 1950–April 2016, NASDAQ 19711–April 2016, Russell 1K & 2K 19791–April 2016.

May's new pattern, a smile or a frown,
Odd years UP and even years DOWN.

First Trading Day in May, Dow Up 14 of Last 19

MONDAY

D 66.7
S 66.7
N 71.4

1

What technology does is make people more productive. It doesn't replace them.
— Michael Bloomberg (Founder Bloomberg L.P., philanthropist, New York mayor 2002–2013, b. 1942)

TUESDAY

D 66.7
S 57.1
N 61.9

2

People who can take a risk, who believe in themselves enough to walk away [from a company] are generally people who bring about change.
— Cynthia Danaher (Exiting GM of Hewlett-Packard's Medical Products Group, *Newsweek*)

WEDNESDAY

D 33.3
S 38.1
N 47.6

3

If buying equities seem the most hazardous and foolish thing you could possibly do, then you are near the bottom that will end the bear market.
— Joseph E. Granville

THURSDAY

D 33.3
S 38.1
N 42.9

4

New issues: The closest thing to a "Sure Thing" Wall Street has to offer.
— Norm Fosback (*Stock Market Logic, Fosback's Fund Forecaster, New Issues Newsletter*)

FRIDAY

D 47.6
S 42.9
N 38.1

5

Some people are so boring they make you waste an entire day in five minutes.
— Jules Renard (French author, 1864–1910)

SATURDAY

6

SUNDAY

7

TOP PERFORMING MONTHS PAST 66⅓ YEARS: STANDARD & POOR'S 500 AND DOW JONES INDUSTRIALS

Monthly performance of the S&P and the Dow are ranked over the past 66⅓ years. NASDAQ monthly performance is shown on page 58.

April, November, and December still hold the top three positions in both the Dow and the S&P. March has reclaimed the fourth spot on the S&P. Two disastrous Januarys in 2008 and 2009 knocked January into fifth. This, in part, led to our discovery in 1986 of the market's most consistent seasonal pattern. You can divide the year into two sections and have practically all the gains in one six-month section and very little in the other. September is the worst month on both lists. (See "Best Six Months" on page 52.)

MONTHLY % CHANGES (JANUARY 1950–APRIL 2016)

Standard & Poor's 500					Dow Jones Industrials				
Month	Total % Change	Avg. % Change	# Up	# Down	Month	Total % Change	Avg. % Change	# Up	# Down
Jan	62.8%	0.9%	40	27	Jan	57.7	0.9	42	25
Feb	3.1	0.05	37	30	Feb	14.1	0.2	40	27
Mar	83.4	1.2	44	23	Mar	77.7	1.2	44	23
Apr	98.8	1.5	47	20	Apr	127.6	1.9	45	22
May	13.0	0.2	38	28	May	−1.5	−0.02	34	32
Jun	−2.2	−0.03	34	32	Jun	−21.9	−0.3	30	36
Jul	64.5	1.0	36	30	Jul	75.9	1.2	41	25
Aug	−6.0	−0.09	36	30	Aug	−12.0	−0.2	37	29
Sep*	−34.2	−0.5	29	36	Sep	−50.1	−0.8	26	40
Oct	62.3	0.9	40	26	Oct	43.3	0.7	40	26
Nov	99.0	1.5	44	22	Nov	99.1	1.5	44	22
Dec	106.7	1.6	49	17	Dec	107.8	1.6	46	20
% Rank					**% Rank**				
Dec	106.7%	1.6%	49	17	Apr	127.6	1.9	45	22
Nov	99.0	1.5	44	22	Dec	107.8	1.6	46	20
Apr	98.8	1.5	47	20	Nov	99.1	1.5	44	22
Mar	83.4	1.2	44	23	Mar	77.7	1.2	44	23
Jul	64.5	1.0	36	30	Jul	75.9	1.2	41	25
Jan	62.8	0.9	40	27	Jan	57.7	0.9	42	25
Oct	62.3	0.9	40	26	Oct	43.3	0.7	40	26
May	13.0	0.2	38	28	Feb	14.1	0.2	40	27
Feb	3.1	0.1	37	30	May	−1.5	−0.02	34	32
Jun	−2.2	−0.03	34	32	Aug	−12.0	−0.2	37	29
Aug	−6.0	−0.09	36	30	Jun	−21.9	−0.3	30	36
Sep*	−34.2	−0.5	29	36	Sep	−50.1	−0.8	26	40
Totals	551.2%	8.2%			**Totals**	517.7%	7.9%		
Average		0.69%			**Average**		0.66%		

*No change 1979.

Anticipators, shifts in cultural behavior, and faster information flow have altered seasonality in recent years. Here is how the months ranked over the past 15⅓ years (184 months) using total percentage gains on the S&P 500: April 32.8, October 28.9, March 22.9, November 21.7, December 14.3, July 8.0, May 4.8, February −5.9, August −11.0, September −15.4, January −16.2, and June −22.1.

During the last 15⅓ years front-runners of our Best Six Months may have helped push October into the number-two spot. January has declined in 10 of the last 17 years. Sizeable turnarounds in "bear killing" October were a common occurrence from 1999 to 2007. Recent big Dow losses in the period were: September 2001 (9/11 attack), off 11.1%; September 2002 (Iraq war drums), off 12.4%; June 2008, off 10.2%; October 2008, off 14.1%; and February 2009 (financial crisis), off 11.7%.

MONDAY

D 71.4
S 57.1
N 76.2

8

While one person hesitates because he feels inferior, the other is busy making mistakes and becoming superior.
— Henry C. Link (Industrial psychologist, author, Psychological Corporation, 1889–1952)

TUESDAY

D 52.4
S 42.9
N 42.9

9

I just wait until the fourth year, when the business cycle bottoms, and buy whatever I think will have the biggest bounce.
— Larry Tisch's investment style

WEDNESDAY

D 71.4
S 61.9
N 47.6

10

If you bet on a horse, that's gambling. If you bet you can make three spades, that's entertainment. If you bet cotton will go up three points, that's business. See the difference?
— Blackie Sherrod (Sportswriter, b. 1919)

THURSDAY

D 42.9
S 47.6
N 57.1

11

The greatest discovery of my generation is that human beings can alter their lives by altering their attitudes.
— William James (Philosopher, psychologist, 1842–1910)

Friday Before Mother's Day, Dow Up 15 of Last 22

FRIDAY

D 57.1
S 47.6
N 47.6

12

Selling a soybean contract short is worth two years at the Harvard Business School.
— Robert Stovall (Managing director, Wood Asset Management, b. 1926)

SATURDAY

13

Mother's Day

SUNDAY

14

"BEST SIX MONTHS": STILL AN EYE-POPPING STRATEGY

Our Best Six Months Switching Strategy consistently delivers. Investing in the Dow Jones Industrial Average between November 1st and April 30th each year and then switching into fixed income for the other six months has produced reliable returns with reduced risk since 1950.

The chart on page 147 shows November, December, January, March, and April to be the top months since 1950. Add February, and an excellent strategy is born! These six consecutive months gained 17992.80 Dow points in 66 years, while the remaining May-through-October months lost 433.49 points. The S&P gained 1843.77 points in the same best six months versus 203.46 points in the worst six.

Percentage changes are shown along with a compounding $10,000 investment. The November–April $843,577 gain overshadows May–October's $319 loss. (S&P results $623,805 to $8,036.) Just three November–April losses were double-digit: April 1970 (Cambodian invasion), 1973 (OPEC oil embargo), and 2008 (financial crisis). Similarly, Iraq muted the Best Six and inflated the Worst Six in 2003. When we discovered this strategy in 1986, November–April outperformed May–October by $88,163 to minus $1,522. Results improved substantially these past 29 years, $755,414 to $1,203. A simple timing indicator triples results (page 54).

SIX-MONTH SWITCHING STRATEGY

	DJIA % Change May 1–Oct 31	Investing $10,000	DJIA % Change Nov 1–Apr 30	Investing $10,000
1950	5.0%	$10,500	15.2%	$11,520
1951	1.2	10,626	−1.8	11,313
1952	4.5	11,104	2.1	11,551
1953	0.4	11,148	15.8	13,376
1954	10.3	12,296	20.9	16,172
1955	6.9	13,144	13.5	18,355
1956	−7.0	12,224	3.0	18,906
1957	−10.8	10,904	3.4	19,549
1958	19.2	12,998	14.8	22,442
1959	3.7	13,479	−6.9	20,894
1960	−3.5	13,007	16.9	24,425
1961	3.7	13,488	−5.5	23,082
1962	−11.4	11,950	21.7	28,091
1963	5.2	12,571	7.4	30,170
1964	7.7	13,539	5.6	31,860
1965	4.2	14,108	−2.8	30,968
1966	−13.6	12,189	11.1	34,405
1967	−1.9	11,957	3.7	35,678
1968	4.4	12,483	−0.2	35,607
1969	−9.9	11,247	−14.0	30,622
1970	2.7	11,551	24.6	38,155
1971	−10.9	10,292	13.7	43,382
1972	0.1	10,302	−3.6	41,820
1973	3.8	10,693	−12.5	36,593
1974	−20.5	8,501	23.4	45,156
1975	1.8	8,654	19.2	53,826
1976	−3.2	8,377	−3.9	51,727
1977	−11.7	7,397	2.3	52,917
1978	−5.4	6,998	7.9	57,097
1979	−4.6	6,676	0.2	57,211
1980	13.1	7,551	7.9	61,731
1981	−14.6	6,449	−0.5	61,422
1982	16.9	7,539	23.6	75,918
1983	−0.1	7,531	−4.4	72,578
1984	3.1	7,764	4.2	75,626
1985	9.2	8,478	29.8	98,163
1986	5.3	8,927	21.8	119,563
1987	−12.8	7,784	1.9	121,835
1988	5.7	8,228	12.6	137,186
1989	9.4	9,001	0.4	137,735
1990	−8.1	8,272	18.2	162,803
1991	6.3	8,793	9.4	178,106
1992	−4.0	8,441	6.2	189,149
1993	7.4	9,066	0.03	189,206
1994	6.2	9,628	10.6	209,262
1995	10.0	10,591	17.1	245,046
1996	8.3	11,470	16.2	284,743
1997	6.2	12,181	21.8	346,817
1998	−5.2	11,548	25.6	435,602
1999	−0.5	11,490	0.04	435,776
2000	2.2	11,743	−2.2	426,189
2001	−15.5	9,923	9.6	467,103
2002	−15.6	8,375	1.0	471,774
2003	15.6	9,682	4.3	492,060
2004	−1.9	9,498	1.6	499,933
2005	2.4	9,726	8.9	544,427
2006	6.3	10,339	8.1	588,526
2007	6.6	11,021	−8.0	541,444
2008	−27.3	8,012	−12.4	474,305
2009	18.9	9,526	13.3	537,388
2010	1.0	9,621	15.2	619,071
2011	−6.7	8,976	10.5	684,073
2012	−0.9	8,895	13.3	775,055
2013	4.8	9,322	6.7	826,984
2014	4.9	$9,779	2.6	$848,486
2015	−1.0	$9,681	0.6	$853,577
Average/Gain	**0.4%**	**($319)**	**7.4%**	**$843,577**
# Up/Down	**39/27**		**52/14**	

Monday After Mother's Day, Dow Up 15 of Last 22
Monday Before May Expiration, Dow Up 22 of Last 29, Average Gain 0.4%

MONDAY

D 57.1
S 57.1
N 52.4

15

I really do inhabit a system in which words are capable of shaking the entire structure of government, where words can prove mightier than ten military divisions.
— Vaclav Havel (Czech dramatist, essayist, political leader, and president, 1936–2011)

TUESDAY

D 47.6
S 52.4
N 57.1

16

There is only one corner of the universe you can be certain of improving, and that's yourself.
— Aldous Huxley (English author, *Brave New World*, 1894–1963)

WEDNESDAY

D 57.1
S 52.4
N 61.9

17

Three passions, simple but overwhelmingly strong, have governed my life: the longing for love, the search for knowledge, and unbearable pity for the suffering of mankind.
— Bertrand Russell (British mathematician and philosopher, 1872–1970)

THURSDAY

D 38.1
S 38.1
N 33.3

18

It's a buy when the 10-week moving average crosses the 30-week moving average and the slope of both averages is up.
— Victor Sperandeo (*Trader Vic—Methods of a Wall Street Master*)

May Expiration Day Mixed, Dow Down 14 of Last 27

FRIDAY

D 52.4
S 47.6
N 61.9

19

The whole problem with the world is that fools and fanatics are always so certain of themselves, but wiser people so full of doubts.
— Bertrand Russell (British mathematician and philosopher, 1872–1970)

SATURDAY

20

SUNDAY

21

MACD-TIMING TRIPLES "BEST SIX MONTHS" RESULTS

Using the simple MACD (Moving Average Convergence Divergence) indicator developed by our friend Gerald Appel to better time entries and exits into and out of the Best Six Months (page 52) period nearly triples the results. Several years ago, Sy Harding (R.I.P.) enhanced our Best Six Months Switching Strategy with MACD triggers, dubbing it the "best mechanical system ever." In 2006, we improved it even more, achieving similar results with just four trades every four years (page 62).

Our *Almanac Investor eNewsletter* (see ad insert) implements this system with quite a degree of success. Starting October 1, we look to catch the market's first hint of an uptrend after the summer doldrums, and beginning April 1, we prepare to exit these seasonal positions as soon as the market falters.

In up-trending markets, MACD signals get you in earlier and keep you in longer. But if the market is trending down, entries are delayed until the market turns up, and exit points can come a month earlier.

The results are astounding, applying the simple MACD signals. Instead of $10,000 gaining $843,577 over the 66 recent years when invested only during the Best Six Months (page 52), the gain nearly tripled to $2,496,640. The $319 loss during the Worst Six Months expanded to a loss of $6,709.

Impressive results for being invested during only 6.3 months of the year on average! For the rest of the year consider money markets, bonds, puts, bear funds, covered calls, or credit call spreads.

Updated signals are e-mailed to our *Almanac Investor eNewsletter* subscribers as soon as they are triggered. Visit *www.stocktradersalmanac.com*, or see the ad insert for details and a special offer for new subscribers.

BEST SIX-MONTH SWITCHING STRATEGY+TIMING

	DJIA % Change May 1–Oct 31*	DJIA Investing $10,000	DJIA % Change Nov 1–Apr 30*	DJIA Investing $10,000
1950	7.3%	$10,730	13.3%	$11,330
1951	0.1	10,741	1.9	11,545
1952	1.4	10,891	2.1	11,787
1953	0.2	10,913	17.1	13,803
1954	13.5	12,386	16.3	16,053
1955	7.7	13,340	13.1	18,156
1956	−6.8	12,433	2.8	18,664
1957	−12.3	10,904	4.9	19,579
1958	17.3	12,790	16.7	22,849
1959	1.6	12,995	−3.1	22,141
1960	−4.9	12,358	16.9	25,883
1961	2.9	12,716	−1.5	25,495
1962	−15.3	10,770	22.4	31,206
1963	4.3	11,233	9.6	34,202
1964	6.7	11,986	6.2	36,323
1965	2.6	12,298	−2.5	35,415
1966	−16.4	10,281	14.3	40,479
1967	−2.1	10,065	5.5	42,705
1968	3.4	10,407	0.2	42,790
1969	−11.9	9,169	−6.7	39,923
1970	−1.4	9,041	20.8	48,227
1971	−11.0	8,046	15.4	55,654
1972	−0.6	7,998	−1.4	54,875
1973	−11.0	7,118	0.1	54,930
1974	−22.4	5,524	28.2	70,420
1975	0.1	5,530	18.5	83,448
1976	−3.4	5,342	−3.0	80,945
1977	−11.4	4,733	0.5	81,350
1978	−4.5	4,520	9.3	88,916
1979	−5.3	4,280	7.0	95,140
1980	9.3	4,678	4.7	99,612
1981	−14.6	3,995	0.4	100,010
1982	15.5	4,614	23.5	123,512
1983	2.5	4,729	−7.3	114,496
1984	3.3	4,885	3.9	118,961
1985	7.0	5,227	38.1	164,285
1986	−2.8	5,081	28.2	210,613
1987	−14.9	4,324	3.0	216,931
1988	6.1	4,588	11.8	242,529
1989	9.8	5,038	3.3	250,532
1990	−6.7	4,700	15.8	290,116
1991	4.8	4,926	11.3	322,899
1992	−6.2	4,621	6.6	344,210
1993	5.5	4,875	5.6	363,486
1994	3.7	5,055	13.1	411,103
1995	7.2	5,419	16.7	479,757
1996	9.2	5,918	21.9	584,824
1997	3.6	6,131	18.5	693,016
1998	−12.4	5,371	39.9	969,529
1999	−6.4	5,027	5.1	1,018,975
2000	−6.0	4,725	5.4	1,074,000
2001	−17.3	3,908	15.8	1,243,692
2002	−25.2	2,923	6.0	1,318,314
2003	16.4	3,402	7.8	1,421,142
2004	−0.9	3,371	1.8	1,446,723
2005	−0.5	3,354	7.7	1,558,121
2006	4.7	3,512	14.4	1,782,490
2007	5.6	3,709	−12.7	1,556,114
2008	−24.7	2,793	−14.0	1,338,258
2009	23.8	3,458	10.8	1,482,790
2010	4.6	3,617	7.3	1,591,034
2011	−9.4	3,277	18.7	1,888,557
2012	0.3	3,287	10.0	2,077,413
2013	4.1	3,422	7.1	2,224,909
2014	2.3	3,501	7.4	2,389,552
2015	−6.0	3,291	4.9	2,506,640
Average	**−1.2%**		**9.2%**	
# Up	**35**		**57**	
# Down	**31**		**9**	
66-Year Gain (Loss)		**($6,709)**		**$2,496,640**

*MACD generated entry and exit points (earlier or later) can lengthen or shorten six-month periods.

🐻 **MONDAY**

D 28.6
S 38.1
N 42.9

22

The difference between life and the movies is that a script has to make sense, and life doesn't.
— Joseph L. Mankiewicz (Film director, writer, producer, 1909–1993)

TUESDAY

D 42.9
S 47.6
N 52.4

23

An inventor fails 999 times, and if he succeeds once, he's in. He treats his failures simply as practice shots.
— Charles Kettering (Inventor of electric ignition, founded Delco in 1909, 1876–1958)

WEDNESDAY

D 47.6
S 52.4
N 38.1

24

If the models are telling you to sell, sell, sell, but only buyers are out there, don't be a jerk. Buy!
— William Silber, PhD (New York University, *Newsweek*, 1986)

THURSDAY

D 47.6
S 52.4
N 47.6

25

We are handicapped by policies based on old myths rather than current realities.
— James William Fulbright (U.S. Senator Arkansas 1944–1974, 1905–1995)

Friday Before Memorial Day Tends to Be Lackluster with Light Trading,
Dow Down 9 of Last 16, Average -0.3%

FRIDAY

D 47.6
S 47.6
N 57.1

26

I've never been poor, only broke. Being poor is a frame of mind. Being broke is only a temporary situation.
— Mike Todd (Movie producer, 1903–1958)

SATURDAY

27

June Almanac Investor Sector Seasonalities: See Pages 94, 96, and 98

SUNDAY

28

JUNE ALMANAC

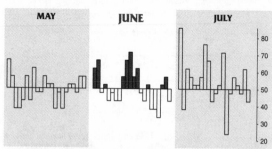

| | MAY | JUNE | JULY | |

Market Probability Chart above is a graphic representation of the S&P 500 Recent Market Probability Calendar on page 124.

◆ The "summer rally" in most years is the weakest rally of all four seasons (page 72) ◆ Week after June Triple-Witching Day Dow down 23 of last 26 (page 78) ◆ RECENT RECORD: S&P up 12, down 9, average loss 0.2%, ranks tenth ◆ Stronger for NASDAQ, average gain 1.2% last 21 years ◆ Watch out for end-of-quarter "portfolio pumping" on last day of June, Dow down 17 of last 25, NASDAQ down 6 of last 11 ◆ Post-presidential election year Junes: #10 S&P and Dow, #8 NASDAQ ◆ June ends NASDAQ's Best Eight Months.

June Vital Statistics

	DJIA		S&P 500		NASDAQ		Russell 1K		Russell 2K	
Rank	11		10		8		11		8	
Up	30		34		25		21		23	
Down	36		32		20		16		14	
Average % Change	−0.3%		−0.03%		0.7%		0.2%		0.6%	
Post-Election Year	−1.2%		−0.7%		0.5%		0.1%		0.9%	
Best & Worst June										
		% Change		% Change		% Change		% Change		% Change
Best	1955	6.2	1955	8.2	2000	16.6	1999	5.1	2000	8.6
Worst	2008	−10.2	2008	−8.6	2002	−9.4	2008	−8.5	2010	−7.9
Best & Worst June Weeks										
Best	06/07/74	6.4	06/02/00	7.2	06/02/00	19.0	06/02/00	8.0	06/02/00	12.2
Worst	06/30/50	−6.8	06/30/50	−7.6	06/15/01	−8.4	06/15/01	−4.2	06/09/06	−4.9
Best & Worst June Days										
Best	06/28/62	3.8	06/28/62	3.4	06/02/00	6.4	06/10/10	3.0	06/02/00	4.2
Worst	06/26/50	−4.7	06/26/50	−5.4	06/29/10	−3.9	06/04/10	−3.5	06/04/10	−5.0
First Trading Day of Expiration Week: 1980–2015										
Record (#Up – #Down)	19–17		21–15		16–20		19–17		14–21	
Current streak	D1		D1		D1		D1		D1	
Avg % Change	−0.02		−0.09		−0.25		−0.11		−0.33	
Options Expiration Day: 1980–2015										
Record (#Up – #Down)	22–14		23–13		20–16		23–13		21–15	
Current streak	D1		D1		D1		D1		D1	
Avg % Change	−0.04		0.03		−0.001		0.001		0.02	
Options Expiration Week: 1980–2015										
Record (#Up – #Down)	21–15		19–17		16–20		17–19		17–19	
Current streak	U2		U2		U2		U2		U2	
Avg % Change	−0.05		−0.08		−0.27		−0.14		−0.22	
Week After Options Expiration: 1980–2015										
Record (#Up – #Down)	11–25		17–19		21–15		17–19		18–18	
Current streak	D2		D2		D1		D2		D1	
Avg % Change	−0.44		−0.16		0.15		−0.13		−0.07	
First Trading Day Performance										
% of Time Up	54.5		53.0		57.8		59.5		62.2	
Avg % Change	0.14		0.11		0.11		0.06		0.11	
Last Trading Day Performance										
% of Time Up	53.0		50.0		68.9		51.4		67.6	
Avg % Change	0.04		0.09		0.31		0.02		0.39	

Dow & S&P 1950–April 2016, NASDAQ 1971–April 2016, Russell 1K & 2K 1979–April 2016.

◆

Last Day of June not hot for the Dow;
Down 17 of 25, WOW!

Memorial Day *(Market Closed)*

Give me a stock clerk with a goal and I will give you a man who will make history. Give me a man without a goal, and I will give you a stock clerk.
— James Cash Penney (JCPenney founder)

Day After Memorial Day, Dow Up 21 of Last 30
Memorial Day Week Dow Down 12 of Last 20, Up 12 Straight 1984–1995

D 61.9
S 57.1
N 66.7

Every time everyone's talking about something, that's the time to sell.
— George Lindemann (Billionaire, *Forbes*)

D 47.6
S 57.1
N 52.4

The words "I am…" are potent words; be careful what you hitch them to. The thing you're claiming has a way of reaching back and claiming you.
— A. L. Kitselman (Author, math teacher)

First Trading Day in June, Dow Up 21 of Last 28
Down 2008/2010 –1.1%, 2011/12 –2.2%

D 66.7
S 61.9
N 52.4

Iron rusts from disuse; stagnant water loses its purity and in cold weather becomes frozen; even so does inaction sap the vigor of the mind.
— Leonardo da Vinci (Italian Renaissance polymath, 1452–1519)

Start Looking for NASDAQ MACD Sell Signal on June 1 (Page 60)
Almanac Investor Subscribers E-mailed When It Triggers (See Insert)

D 47.6
S 66.7
N 66.7

One only gets to the top rung on the ladder by steadily climbing up one at a time, and suddenly all sorts of powers, all sorts of abilities, which you thought never belonged to you, suddenly become within your own possibility….
— Margaret Thatcher (British prime minister, 1979–1990, b. 1925)

TOP PERFORMING NASDAQ MONTHS PAST 45⅓ YEARS

NASDAQ stocks continue to run away during three consecutive months, November, December, and January, with an average gain of 6.0% despite the slaughter of November 2000, −22.9%, December 2000, −4.9%, December 2002, −9.7%, November 2007, −6.9%, January 2008, −9.9%, November 2008, −10.8%, January 2009, −6.4%, January 2010, −5.4%, and January 2016, −7.9%. Solid gains in November and December 2004 offset January 2005's 5.2% Iraq-turmoil-fueled drop.

You can see the months graphically on page 148. January by itself is impressive, up 2.5% on average. April, May, and June also shine, creating our NASDAQ Best Eight Months strategy. What appears as a Death Valley abyss occurs during NASDAQ's bleakest months: July, August, and September. NASDAQ's Best Eight Months seasonal strategy using MACD timing is displayed on page 60.

MONTHLY % CHANGES (JANUARY 1971–APRIL 2016)

NASDAQ Composite*					Dow Jones Industrials				
Month	Total % Change	Avg. % Change	# Up	# Down	Month	Total % Change	Avg. % Change	# Up	# Down
Jan	115.6%	2.5%	29	17	Jan	48.0%	1.0%	28	18
Feb	30.6	0.7	25	21	Feb	19.7	0.4	28	18
Mar	41.2	0.9	29	17	Mar	56.5	1.2	31	15
Apr	61.9	1.3	29	17	Apr	96.6	2.1	30	16
May	39.8	0.9	27	18	May	11.9	0.3	24	21
Jun	33.2	0.7	25	20	Jun	−4.7	−0.1	22	23
Jul	9.5	0.2	23	22	Jul	32.4	0.7	25	20
Aug	4.4	0.1	24	21	Aug	−14.7	−0.3	25	20
Sep	−26.2	−0.6	24	21	Sep	−46.2	−1.0	16	29
Oct	36.7	0.8	25	20	Oct	31.9	0.7	28	17
Nov	71.9	1.6	30	15	Nov	55.1	1.2	30	15
Dec	83.7	1.9	26	19	Dec	71.5	1.6	31	14
% Rank					**% Rank**				
Jan	115.6%	2.5%	29	17	Apr	96.6%	2.1%	30	16
Dec	83.7	1.9	26	19	Dec	71.5	1.6	31	14
Nov	71.9	1.6	30	15	Mar	56.5	1.2	31	15
Apr	61.9	1.3	29	17	Nov	55.1	1.2	30	15
Mar	41.2	0.9	29	17	Jan	48.0	1.0	28	18
May	39.8	0.9	27	18	Jul	32.4	0.7	25	20
Oct	36.7	0.8	25	20	Oct	31.9	0.7	28	17
Jun	33.2	0.7	25	20	Feb	19.7	0.4	28	18
Feb	30.6	0.7	25	21	May	11.9	0.3	24	21
Jul	9.5	0.2	23	22	Jun	−4.7	−0.1	22	23
Aug	4.4	0.1	24	21	Aug	−14.7	−0.3	25	20
Sep	−26.2	−0.6	24	21	Sep	−46.2	−1.0	16	29
Totals	**502.3%**	**11.0%**			**Totals**	**358.0%**	**7.8%**		
Average		**0.92%**			**Average**		**0.65%**		

*Based on NASDAQ composite; prior to Feb. 5, 1971 based on National Quotation Bureau indices.

For comparison, Dow figures are shown. During this period, NASDAQ averaged a 0.92% gain per month, 41.5 percent more than the Dow's 0.65% per month. Between January 1971 and January 1982, NASDAQ's composite index doubled in 12 years, while the Dow stayed flat. But while NASDAQ plummeted 77.9% from its 2000 highs to the 2002 bottom, the Dow only lost 37.8%. The Great Recession and bear market of 2007–2009 spread its carnage equally across Dow and NASDAQ. Recent market moves are increasingly more correlated.

MONDAY
5

D 52.4
S 47.6
N 52.4

Some men see things as they are and say "why?" I dream things that never were and say "why not?"
— George Bernard Shaw (Irish dramatist, 1856–1950)

June Ends NASDAQ's "Best Eight Months" (Pages 58, 60, and 148)

TUESDAY
6

D 57.1
S 52.4
N 52.4

If you don't know who you are, the stock market is an expensive place to find out.
— George Goodman (Author, financial commentator, *New York Magazine's* "Adam Smith," *The Money Game*, 1930–2014)

WEDNESDAY
7

D 61.9
S 42.9
N 47.6

I had an unshakable faith. I had it in my head that if I had to, I'd crawl over broken glass. I'd live in a tent—it was gonna happen. And I think when you have that kind of steely determination…people get out of the way.
— Rick Newcombe (Syndicator, *Investor's Business Daily*)

2008 Second Worst June Ever, Dow −10.2%, S&P −8.6%,
Only 1930 Was Worse, NASDAQ −9.1%, June 2002 −9.4%

THURSDAY
8

D 52.4
S 47.6
N 42.9

Whoso neglects learning in his youth, loses the past and is dead for the future.
— Euripides (Greek tragedian, *Medea*, 485–406 BC)

FRIDAY
9

D 33.3
S 42.9
N 42.9

Pullbacks near the 30-week moving average are often good times to take action.
— Michael L. Burke (*Investors Intelligence*)

SATURDAY
10

SUNDAY
11

GET MORE OUT OF NASDAQ'S "BEST EIGHT MONTHS" WITH MACD TIMING

NASDAQ's amazing eight-month run from November through June is hard to miss on pages 58 and 148. A $10,000 investment in these eight months since 1971 gained $523,518 versus a loss of $1,547 during the void that is the four-month period July–October (as of May 25, 2016).

Using the same MACD timing indicators on the NASDAQ as is done for the Dow (page 54) has enabled us to capture much of October's improved performance, pumping up NASDAQ's results considerably. Over the 45 years since NASDAQ began, the gain on the same $10,000 more than doubles to $1,391,205 and the loss during the four-month void increases to $6,899. Only four sizeable losses occurred during the favorable period, and the bulk of NASDAQ's bear markets were avoided including the worst of the 2000–2002 bear.

Updated signals are e-mailed to our monthly newsletter subscribers as soon as they are triggered. Visit *www.stocktradersalmanac.com,* or see ad insert for details and a special offer for new subscribers.

BEST EIGHT MONTHS STRATEGY + TIMING

MACD Signal Date	Worst 4 Months July 1–Oct 31* NASDAQ	% Change	Investing $10,000	MACD Signal Date	Best 8 Months Nov 1–June 30* NASDAQ	% Change	Investing $10,000
22-Jul-71	109.54	−3.6	$9,640	4-Nov-71	105.56	24.1	$12,410
7-Jun-72	131.00	−1.8	9,466	23-Oct-72	128.66	−22.7	9,593
25-Jun-73	99.43	−7.2	8,784	7-Dec-73	92.32	−20.2	7,655
3-Jul-74	73.66	−23.2	6,746	7-Oct-74	56.57	47.8	11,314
11-Jun-75	83.60	−9.2	6,125	7-Oct-75	75.88	20.8	13,667
22-Jul-76	91.66	−2.4	5,978	19-Oct-76	89.45	13.2	15,471
27-Jul-77	101.25	−4.0	5,739	4-Nov-77	97.21	26.6	19,586
7-Jun-78	123.10	−6.5	5,366	6-Nov-78	115.08	19.1	23,327
3-Jul-79	137.03	−1.1	5,307	30-Oct-79	135.48	15.5	26,943
20-Jun-80	156.51	26.2	6,697	9-Oct-80	197.53	11.2	29,961
4-Jun-81	219.68	−17.6	5,518	1-Oct-81	181.09	−4.0	28,763
7-Jun-82	173.84	12.5	6,208	7-Oct-82	195.59	57.4	45,273
1-Jun-83	307.95	−10.7	5,544	3-Nov-83	274.86	−14.2	38,844
1-Jun-84	235.90	5.0	5,821	15-Oct-84	247.67	17.3	45,564
3-Jun-85	290.59	−3.0	5,646	1-Oct-85	281.77	39.4	63,516
10-Jun-86	392.83	−10.3	5,064	1-Oct-86	352.34	20.5	76,537
30-Jun-87	424.67	−22.7	3,914	2-Nov-87	328.33	20.1	91,921
8-Jul-88	394.33	−6.6	3,656	29-Nov-88	368.15	22.4	112,511
13-Jun-89	450.73	0.7	3,682	9-Nov-89	454.07	1.9	114,649
11-Jun-90	462.79	−23.0	2,835	2-Oct-90	356.39	39.3	159,706
11-Jun-91	496.62	6.4	3,016	1-Oct-91	528.51	7.4	171,524
11-Jun-92	567.68	1.5	3,061	14-Oct-92	576.22	20.5	206,686
7-Jun-93	694.61	9.9	3,364	1-Oct-93	763.23	−4.4	197,592
17-Jun-94	729.35	5.0	3,532	11-Oct-94	765.57	13.5	224,267
1-Jun-95	868.82	17.2	4,140	13-Oct-95	1018.38	21.6	272,709
3-Jun-96	1238.73	1.0	4,181	7-Oct-96	1250.87	10.3	300,798
4-Jun-97	1379.67	24.4	5,201	3-Oct-97	1715.87	1.8	306,212
1-Jun-98	1746.82	−7.8	4,795	15-Oct-98	1611.01	49.7	458,399
1-Jun-99	2412.03	18.5	5,682	6-Oct-99	2857.21	35.7	622,047
29-Jun-00	3877.23	−18.2	4,648	18-Oct-00	3171.56	−32.2	421,748
1-Jun-01	2149.44	−31.1	3,202	1-Oct-01	1480.46	5.5	444,944
3-Jun-02	1562.56	−24.0	2,434	2-Oct-02	1187.30	38.5	616,247
20-Jun-03	1644.72	15.1	2,802	6-Oct-03	1893.46	4.3	642,746
21-Jun-04	1974.38	−1.6	2,757	1-Oct-04	1942.20	6.1	681,954
8-Jun-05	2060.18	1.5	2,798	19-Oct-05	2091.76	6.1	723,553
1-Jun-06	2219.86	3.9	2,907	5-Oct-06	2306.34	9.5	792,291
7-Jun-07	2541.38	7.9	3,137	1-Oct-07	2740.99	−9.1	724,796
2-Jun-08	2491.53	−31.3	2,155	17-Oct-08	1711.29	6.1	769,009
15-Jun-09	1816.38	17.8	2,539	9-Oct-09	2139.28	1.6	781,313
7-Jun-10	2173.90	18.6	3,011	4-Nov-10	2577.34	7.4	839,130
1-Jun-11	2769.19	−10.5	2,695	7-Oct-11	2479.35	10.8	929,756
1-Jun-12	2747.48	9.6	2,954	6-Nov-12	3011.93	16.2	1,080,376
4-Jun-13	3445.26	10.1	3,252	15-Oct-13	3794.01	15.4	1,227,442
26-Jun-14	4379.05	0.9	3,281	21-Oct-14	4419.48	14.5	1,405,421
4-Jun-15	5059.12	−5.5	3,101	5-Oct-15	4781.26	−0.3	1,401,205
23-May-16	4765.78						

As of 5/23/2016, MACD Sell Signal not triggered at press time

45-Year Loss ($6,899)   **45-Year Gain $1,391,205**

* MACD-generated entry and exit points (earlier or later) can lengthen or shorten eight-month periods.

JUNE 2017

Monday of Triple Witching Week, Dow Down 11 of Last 19

MONDAY

D 47.6
S 42.9
N 42.9

12

Life is an illusion. You are what you think you are.
— Yale Hirsch (Creator of *Stock Trader's Almanac*, b. 1923)

TUESDAY

D 57.1
S 57.1
N 52.4

13

Get inside information from the president and you will probably lose half your money. If you get it from the chairman of the board, you will lose all your money.
— Jim Rogers (Financier, b. 1942)

Triple Witching Week Often Up in Bull Markets and Down in Bears (Page 78) WEDNESDAY

D 66.7
S 66.7
N 57.1

14

I measure what's going on, and I adapt to it. I try to get my ego out of the way. The market is smarter than I am so I bend.
— Martin Zweig (Fund manager, *Winning on Wall Street*, 1943–2013)

THURSDAY

D 61.9
S 71.4
N 71.4

15

Intense concentration hour after hour can bring out resources in people they didn't know they had.
— Edwin Land (Polaroid inventor and founder, 1909–1991)

June Triple Witching Day, Dow Up 9 of Last 13
However, Average Loss 0.3%

FRIDAY

D 57.1
S 57.1
N 57.1

16

Of the S&P 500 companies in 1957, only 74 were still on the list in 1998 and only 12 outperformed the index itself over that period. By 2020, more than 375 companies in the S&P 500 will consist of companies we don't know today.
— Richard Foster and Sarah Kaplan (*Creative Destruction*)

SATURDAY

17

Father's Day

SUNDAY

18

TRIPLE RETURNS, LESS TRADES: BEST 6 + 4-YEAR CYCLE

We first introduced this strategy to *Almanac Investor* newsletter subscribers in October 2006. Recurring seasonal stock market patterns and the four-year Presidential Election/Stock Market Cycle (page 130) have been integral to our research since the first Almanac 49 years ago. Yale Hirsch discovered the Best Six Months in 1986 (page 52), and it has been a cornerstone of our seasonal investment analysis and strategies ever since.

Most of the market's gains have occurred during the Best Six Months, and the market generally hits a low point every four years in the first (post-election) or second (midterm) year and exhibits the greatest gains in the third (pre-election) year. This strategy combines the best of these two market phenomena, the Best Six Months and the four-year cycle, timing entries and exits with MACD (pages 54 and 60).

We've gone back to 1949 to include the full four-year cycle that began with post-election year 1949. Only four trades every four years are needed to nearly triple the results of the Best Six Months. Buy and sell during the post-election and midterm years and then hold from the mid-term MACD seasonal buy signal sometime after October 1 until the post-election MACD seasonal sell signal sometime after April 1, approximately 2.5 years: better returns, less effort, lower transaction fees, and fewer taxable events.

FOUR TRADES EVERY FOUR YEARS		
	Worst	Best
	Six Months	Six Months
Year	May–Oct	Nov–April
Post-election	Sell	Buy
Midterm	Sell	Buy
Pre-election	Hold	Hold
Election	Hold	Hold

BEST SIX MONTHS+TIMING+4-YEAR CYCLE STRATEGY

	DJIA % Change May 1–Oct 31*	DJIA Investing $10,000	DJIA % Change Nov 1–Apr 30*	DJIA Investing $10,000
1949	3.0%	$10,300	17.5%	$11,750
1950	7.3	11,052	19.7	14,065
1951		11,052		14,065
1952		11,052		14,065
1953	0.2	11,074	17.1	16,470
1954	13.5	12,569	35.7	22,350
1955		12,569		22,350
1956		12,569		22,350
1957	−12.3	11,023	4.9	23,445
1958	17.3	12,930	27.8	29,963
1959		12,930		29,963
1960		12,930		29,963
1961	2.9	13,305	−1.5	29,514
1962	−15.3	11,269	58.5	46,780
1963		11,269		46,780
1964		11,269		46,780
1965	2.6	11,562	−2.5	45,611
1966	−16.4	9,666	22.2	55,737
1967		9,666		55,737
1968		9,666		55,737
1969	−11.9	8,516	−6.7	52,003
1970	−1.4	8,397	21.5	63,184
1971		8,397		63,184
1972		8,397		63,184
1973	−11.0	7,473	0.1	63,247
1974	−22.4	5,799	42.5	90,127
1975		5,799		90,127
1976		5,799		90,127
1977	−11.4	5,138	0.5	90,578
1978	−4.5	4,907	26.8	114,853
1979		4,907		114,853
1980		4,907		114,853
1981	−14.6	4,191	0.4	115,312
1982	15.5	4,841	25.9	145,178
1983		4,841		145,178
1984		4,841		145,178
1985	7.0	5,180	38.1	200,491
1986	−2.8	5,035	33.2	267,054
1987		5,035		267,054
1988		5,035		267,054
1989	9.8	5,528	3.3	275,867
1990	−6.7	5,158	35.1	372,696
1991		5,158		372,696
1992		5,158		372,696
1993	5.5	5,442	5.6	393,455
1994	3.7	5,643	88.2	740,482
1995		5,643		740,482
1996		5,643		740,482
1997	3.6	5,846	18.5	877,471
1998	−12.4	5,121	36.3	1,195,993
1999		5,121		1,195,993
2000		5,121		1,195,993
2001	−17.3	4,235	15.8	1,384,960
2002	−25.2	3,168	34.2	1,858,616
2003		3,168		1,858,616
2004		3,168		1,858,616
2005	−0.5	3,152	7.7	2,001,729
2006	4.7	3,300	−31.7	1,367,181
2007		3,300		1,367,181
2008		3,300		1,367,181
2009	23.8	4,085	10.8	1,514,738
2010	4.6	4,273	27.4	1,929,777
2011		4,273		1,929,777
2012		4,273		1,929,777
2013	4.1	4,448	7.1	2,066,791
2014	2.3	4,550	5.3**	2,176,331
2015		$4,550		$2,176,331
Average	−0.8%		9.6%	
# Up	18		30	
# Down	16		4	
67-Year Gain (Loss)		($5,450)		$2,166,331

* MACD and 2.5-year hold lengthen and shorten six-month periods.
** As of 5/23/2016.

MONDAY

D 61.9
S 61.9
N 66.7

19

Around the world, red tape is being cut. Whether it's telecom in Europe, water in South America, or power in Illinois, governments are stepping back, and competition is thriving where regulated monopolies once dominated.
— (Fortune, 12/20/99)

TUESDAY

D 52.4
S 47.6
N 47.6

20

The incestuous relationship between government and big business thrives in the dark.
— Jack Anderson (Washington journalist and author, Peace, War and Politics, 1922–2005)

Week After June Triple Witching, Dow Down 23 of Last 26
Average Loss Since 1990, 1.1%

WEDNESDAY

D 38.1
S 42.9
N 52.4

21

People's spending habits depend more on how wealthy they feel than with the actual amount of their current income.
— A.C. Pigou (English economist, The Theory of Unemployment, 1877–1959)

THURSDAY

D 42.9
S 52.4
N 38.1

22

When I have to depend upon hope in a trade, I get out of it.
— Jesse Livermore (Early 20th century stock trader and speculator, How to Trade in Stocks, 1877–1940)

FRIDAY

D 38.1
S 38.1
N 38.1

23

Our philosophy here is identifying change, anticipating change. Change is what drives earnings growth, and if you identify the underlying change, you recognize the growth before the market, and the deceleration of that growth.
— Peter Vermilye (Baring America Asset Management, 1987)

SATURDAY

24

July Almanac Investor Sector Seasonalities: See Pages 94, 96, and 98

SUNDAY

25

JULY ALMANAC

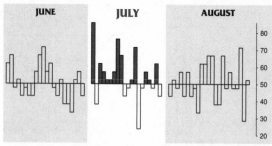

JULY							AUGUST						
S	M	T	W	T	F	S	S	M	T	W	T	F	S
30	31					1			1	2	3	4	5
2	3	4	5	6	7	8	6	7	8	9	10	11	12
9	10	11	12	13	14	15	13	14	15	16	17	18	19
16	17	18	19	20	21	22	20	21	22	23	24	25	26
23	24	25	26	27	28	29	27	28	29	30	31		

Market Probability Chart above is a graphic representation of the S&P 500 Recent Market Probability Calendar on page 124.

◆ July is the best month of the third quarter (page 66) ◆ Start of 2nd half brings an inflow of retirement funds ◆ First trading day Dow up 22 of last 27 ◆ Graph above shows strength in the first half of July ◆ Huge gain in July usually provides better buying opportunity over next 4 months ◆ Start of NASDAQ's worst four months of the year (page 60) ◆ Post-presidential election year Julys are ranked #1 Dow (up 13, down 3) and S&P (up 10, down 6) and #2 NASDAQ (up 9, down 2).

July Vital Statistics

	DJIA		S&P 500		NASDAQ		Russell 1K		Russell 2K	
Rank	5		5		10		8		11	
Up	41		36		23		17		17	
Down	25		30		22		20		20	
Average % Change	1.2%		1.0%		0.2%		0.6%		−0.5%	
Post-Election Year	2.2%		2.2%		3.4%		3.3%		3.1%	
	Best & Worst July									
	% Change		% Change		% Change		% Change		% Change	
Best	1989	9.0	1989	8.8	1997	10.5	1989	8.2	1980	11.0
Worst	1969	−6.6	2002	−7.9	2002	−9.2	2002	−7.5	2002	−15.2
	Best & Worst July Weeks									
Best	07/17/09	7.3	07/17/09	7.0	07/17/09	7.4	07/17/09	7.0	07/17/09	8.0
Worst	07/19/02	−7.7	07/19/02	−8.0	07/28/00	−10.5	07/19/02	−7.4	07/02/10	−7.2
	Best & Worst July Days									
Best	07/24/02	6.4	07/24/02	5.7	07/29/02	5.8	07/24/02	5.6	07/29/02	4.9
Worst	07/19/02	−4.6	07/19/02	−3.8	07/28/00	−4.7	07/19/02	−3.6	07/23/02	−4.1
	First Trading Day of Expiration Week: 1980–2015									
Record (#Up – #Down)	22–14		23–13		24–12		22–14		20–16	
Current streak	U3		U3		U3		U3		U3	
Avg % Change	0.12		0.05		0.06		0.02		−0.05	
	Options Expiration Day: 1980–2015									
Record (#Up – #Down)	16–18		19–17		16–20		19–17		14–22	
Current streak	D1		U3		U2		U3		D1	
Avg % Change	−0.25		−0.28		−0.42		−0.30		−0.46	
	Options Expiration Week: 1980–2015									
Record (#Up – #Down)	23–13		20–16		19–17		20–16		19–17	
Current streak	U4		U4		U2		U4		U1	
Avg % Change	0.46		0.16		0.09		0.10		−0.12	
	Week After Options Expiration: 1980–2015									
Record (#Up – #Down)	18–18		17–19		16–20		18–18		13–23	
Current streak	D2		D1		D1		D1		D3	
Avg % Change	−0.07		−0.19		−0.46		−0.21		−0.40	
	First Trading Day Performance									
% of Time Up	65.2		71.2		62.2		73.0		64.9	
Avg % Change	0.27		0.26		0.13		0.32		0.10	
	Last Trading Day Performance									
% of Time Up	50.0		60.6		48.9		56.8		64.9	
Avg % Change	0.02		0.06		−0.04		−0.03		−0.02	

Dow & S&P 1950–April 2016, NASDAQ 1971–April 2016, Russell 1K & 2K 1979–April 2016.

When Dow and S&P in July are inferior,
NASDAQ days tend to be even drearier.

Those who study market history are bound to profit from it!

"I gladly subscribe because it has made me a very successful trader. In October of 2014 the email newsletter gave me a signal to buy the QQQ index at about 98. Then I patiently waited for the signal to sell which came in early June of 2015. The sell price of about 108 gave me an 11 per cent return or $170,000 profit in just eight months!" – Rick from Arizona

Almanac Investor Ranked Top 5 Market Timer by Hulbert 10 Years 2004-2014

What's even more gratifying is that the independent newsletter watchdog, the *Hulbert Financial Digest*, ranked my *Almanac Investor* among the Top 5 Market Timers in 2014 for the past decade.

Now you can find out which seasonal trends are on schedule and which are not, and how to take advantage of them. You will be kept abreast of upcoming market-moving events and what our indicators are saying about the next major market move. Every week you will receive timely dispatches about bullish and bearish seasonal patterns.

Our digital subscription service, *Almanac Investor*, provides all this plus unusual investing opportunities – exciting small-, mid- and large-cap stocks; seasoned, undervalued equities; timely sector ETF trades and more. Our **Data-Rich and Data-Driven Market Cycle Analysis** is the only investment tool of its kind that helps traders and investors forecast market trends with accuracy and confidence.

YOU RECEIVE 2 EMAIL ALERTS WEEKLY CONTAINING:

- ▶ Opportune ETF and Stock Trading Ideas with Specific Buy and Sell Price Limits
- ▶ Timely Data-Rich and Data-Driven Market Analysis
- ▶ Access to Webinars, Videos, Tools and Resources
- ▶ Market-Tested and Time-Proven Short- and Long-term Trading Strategies
- ▶ Best Six-Months Switching Strategy MACD Timing Signals.

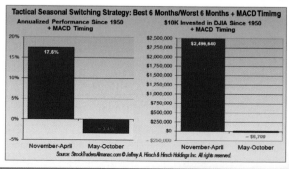

JUNE/JULY 2017

MONDAY
D 33.3
S 38.1
N 38.1
26

The measure of success is not whether you have a tough problem to deal with, but whether it's the same problem you had last year.
— John Foster Dulles (Secretary of State under Eisenhower, 1888–1959)

TUESDAY
D 42.9
S 33.3
N 42.9
27

In nature there are no rewards or punishments; there are consequences.
— Horace Annesley Vachell (English writer, *The Face of Clay*, 1861–1955)

WEDNESDAY
D 57.1
S 52.4
N 66.7
28

A gold mine is a hole in the ground with a liar on top.
— Mark Twain (pen name of Samuel Longhorne Clemens, American novelist and satirist, 1835–1910)

THURSDAY
D 52.4
S 57.1
N 66.7
29

The advice of the elders to young men is very apt to be as unreal as a list of the best books.
— Oliver Wendell Holmes Jr. (U.S. Supreme Court Justice 1902–1932, *The Mind and Faith of Justice Holmes*, edited by Max Lerner, 1841–1935)

Last Day of Q2 Bearish for Dow, Down 17 of Last 25
But Bullish for NASDAQ, Up 17 of 24

FRIDAY
D 38.1
S 42.9
N 66.7
30

If we hire people bigger than ourselves, we will become a company of giants—smaller than ourselves, a company of midgets.
— David Oglivy (*Forbes ASAP*)

SATURDAY
1

SUNDAY
2

FIRST MONTH OF QUARTERS IS THE MOST BULLISH

We have observed over the years that the investment calendar reflects the annual, semiannual, and quarterly operations of institutions during January, April, and July. The opening month of the first three quarters produces the greatest gains in the Dow Jones Industrials and the S&P 500. NASDAQ's record differs slightly.

The fourth quarter had behaved quite differently, since it is affected by year-end portfolio adjustments and presidential and congressional elections in even-numbered years. Since 1991, major turnarounds have helped October join the ranks of bullish first months of quarters. October transformed into a bear-killing-turnaround month, posting some mighty gains in 13 of the last 18 years; 2008 was a significant exception. (See pages 152–160.)

After experiencing the most powerful bull market of all time during the 1990s, followed by two ferocious bear markets early in the millennium, we divided the monthly average percentage changes into two groups: before 1991 and after. Comparing the month-by-month quarterly behavior of the three major U.S. averages in the table, you'll see that first months of the first three quarters perform best overall. Nasty sell-offs in April 2000, 2002, 2004, and 2005, and July 2000–2002 and 2004 hit the NASDAQ hardest. The bear market of October 2007–March 2009, which more than cut the markets in half, took a toll on every first month except April. October 2008 was the worst month in a decade. January was also a difficult month in six of the last nine years, pulling its performance lower. (See pages 152–160.)

Between 1950 and 1990, the S&P 500 gained 1.3% (Dow, 1.4%) on average in first months of the first three quarters. Second months barely eked out any gain, while third months, thanks to March, moved up 0.23% (Dow, 0.07%) on average. NASDAQ's first month of the first three quarters averages 1.67% from 1971–1990, with July being a negative drag.

DOW JONES INDUSTRIALS, S&P 500, AND NASDAQ
AVERAGE MONTHLY % CHANGES BY QUARTER

	DJIA 1950–1990			S&P 500 1950–1990			NASDAQ 1971–1990		
	1st Mo	2nd Mo	3rd Mo	1st Mo	2nd Mo	3rd Mo	1st Mo	2nd Mo	3rd Mo
1Q	1.5%	−0.01%	1.0%	1.5%	−0.1%	1.1%	3.8%	1.2%	0.9%
2Q	1.6	−0.4	0.1	1.3	−0.1	0.3	1.7	0.8	1.1
3Q	1.1	0.3	−0.9	1.1	0.3	−0.7	−0.5	0.1	−1.6
Tot	4.2%	−0.1%	0.2%	3.9%	0.1%	0.7%	5.0%	2.1%	0.4%
Avg	1.40%	−0.04%	0.07%	1.30%	0.03%	0.23%	1.67%	0.70%	0.13%
4Q	−0.1%	1.4%	1.7%	0.4%	1.7%	1.6%	−1.4%	1.6%	1.4%
	DJIA 1991-April 2016			S&P 500 1991-April 2016			NASDAQ 1991-April 2016		
1Q	−0.1%	0.6%	1.3%	0.1%	0.3%	1.5%	1.5%	0.2%	0.9%
2Q	2.3	0.6	−1.0	1.8	0.7	−0.5	1.1	0.9	0.5
3Q	1.2	−1.0	−0.6	0.8	−0.7	−0.3	0.8	0.1	0.2
Tot	3.4%	0.2%	−0.3%	2.7%	0.3%	0.7%	3.4%	1.2%	1.6%
Avg	1.13%	0.05%	−0.10%	0.90%	0.10%	0.23%	1.13%	0.41%	0.53%
4Q	1.9%	1.6%	1.6%	1.9%	1.2%	1.7%	2.5%	1.6%	2.2%
	DJIA 1950-April 2016			S&P 500 1950-April 2016			NASDAQ 1971-April 2016		
1Q	0.9%	0.21%	1.2%	0.9%	0.1%	1.2%	2.5%	0.7%	0.9%
2Q	1.9	−0.02	−0.3	1.5	0.2	−0.03	1.3	0.9	0.7
3Q	1.2	−0.2	−0.8	1.0	−0.09	−0.5	0.2	0.1	−0.6
Tot	4.0%	−0.01%	0.1%	3.4%	0.16%	0.7%	4.0%	1.7%	1.0%
Avg	1.33%	−0.003%	0.03%	1.13%	0.05%	0.22%	1.34%	0.57%	0.33%
4Q	0.7%	1.5%	1.6%	0.9%	1.5%	1.6%	0.8%	1.6%	1.9%

JULY 2017

First Trading Day in July, Dow Up 22 of Last 27, Average Gain 0.6%
(Shortened Trading Day)

🐂 **MONDAY**

D 81.0
S 85.7
N 76.2

3

Buy a stock the way you would buy a house. Understand and like it such that you'd be content to own it in the absence of any market.
— Warren Buffett (CEO Berkshire Hathaway, investor and philanthropist, b. 1930)

Independence Day *(Market Closed)*

TUESDAY

4

Friendship renders prosperity more brilliant, while it lightens adversity by sharing it and making its burden common.
— Marcus Tullius Cicero (Great Roman orator, politician, 106–43 BC)

Market Subject to Elevated Volatility After July 4th

🐻 **WEDNESDAY**

D 38.1
S 38.1
N 38.1

5

Marx's great achievement was to place the system of capitalism on the defensive.
— Charles A. Madison (1977)

July Begins NASDAQ's "Worst Four Months" (Pages 58, 60, and 148)

🐂 **THURSDAY**

D 52.4
S 61.9
N 57.1

6

All the features and achievements of modern civilization are, directly or indirectly, the products of the capitalist process.
— Joseph A. Schumpeter (Austrian-American economist, *Theory of Economic Development*, 1883–1950)

FRIDAY

D 57.1
S 57.1
N 61.9

7

If I had eight hours to chop down a tree, I'd spend six sharpening my axe.
— Abraham Lincoln (16th U.S. President, 1809–1865)

SATURDAY

8

SUNDAY

9

2015 DAILY DOW POINT CHANGES
(DOW JONES INDUSTRIAL AVERAGE)

Week #		Monday**	Tuesday	Wednsday	Thursday	Friday**	Weekly Dow Close	Net Point Change
						2014 Close	17823.07	
1					Holiday	9.92	17832.99	9.92
2	J	−331.34	−130.01	212.88	323.35	−170.50	17737.37	−95.62
3	A	−96.53	−27.16	−186.59	−106.38	190.86	17511.57	−225.80
4	N	Holiday	3.66	39.05	259.70	−141.38	17672.60	161.03
5		6.10	−291.49	−195.84	225.48	−251.90	17164.95	−507.65
6	F	196.09	305.36	6.62	211.86	−60.59	17824.29	659.34
7	E	−95.08	139.55	−6.62	110.24	46.97	18019.35	195.06
8	B	Holiday	28.23	−17.73	−44.08	154.67	18140.44	121.09
9		−23.60	92.35	15.38	−10.15	−81.72	18132.70	−7.74
10	M	155.93	−85.26	−106.47	38.82	−278.94	17856.78	−275.92
11	M	138.94	−332.78	−27.55	259.83	−145.91	17749.31	−107.47
12	A	228.11	−128.34	227.11	−117.16	168.62	18127.65	378.34
13	R	−11.61	−104.90	−292.60	−40.31	34.43	17712.66	−414.99
14		263.65	−200.19	−77.94	65.06	Holiday	17763.24	50.58
15	A	117.61	−5.43	27.09	56.22	98.92	18057.65	294.41
16	P	−80.61	59.66	75.91	−6.84	−279.47	17826.30	−231.35
17	R	208.63	−85.34	88.68	20.42	21.45	18080.14	253.84
18		−42.17	72.17	−74.61	−195.01	183.54	18024.06	−56.08
19	M	46.34	−142.20	−86.22	82.08	267.05	18191.11	167.05
20	A	−85.94	−36.94	−7.74	191.75	20.32	18272.56	81.45
21	Y	26.32	13.51	−26.99	0.34	−53.72	18232.02	−40.54
22		Holiday	−190.48	121.45	−36.87	−115.44	18010.68	−221.34
23		29.69	−28.43	64.33	−170.69	−56.12	17849.46	−161.22
24	J	−82.91	−2.51	236.36	38.97	−140.53	17898.84	49.38
25	U	−107.67	113.31	31.26	180.10	−99.89	18015.95	117.11
26	N	103.83	24.29	−178.00	−75.71	56.32	17946.68	−69.27
27		−350.33	23.16	138.40	−27.80	Holiday	17730.11	−216.57
28	J	−46.53	93.33	−261.49	33.20	211.79	17760.41	30.30
29	U	217.27	75.90	−3.41	70.08	−33.80	18086.45	326.04
30	L	13.96	−181.12	−68.25	−119.12	−163.39	17568.53	−517.92
31		−127.94	189.68	121.12	−5.41	−56.12	17689.86	121.33
32		−91.66	−47.51	−10.22	−120.72	−46.37	17373.38	−316.48
33	A	241.79	−212.33	−0.33	5.74	69.15	17477.40	104.02
34	U	67.78	−33.84	−162.61	−358.04	−530.94	16459.75	−1017.65
35	G	−588.40	−204.91	619.07	369.26	−11.76	16643.01	183.26
36		−114.98	−469.68	293.03	23.38	−272.38	16102.38	−540.63
37	S	Holiday	390.30	−239.11	76.83	102.69	16433.09	330.71
38	E	−62.13	228.89	140.10	−65.21	−290.16	16384.58	−48.51
39	P	125.61	−179.72	−50.58	−78.57	113.35	16314.67	−69.91
40		−312.78	47.24	234.87	−11.99	200.36	16472.37	157.70
41	O	304.06	13.76	122.10	138.46	33.74	17084.49	612.12
42	C	47.37	−49.97	−157.14	217.00	74.22	17215.97	131.48
43	T	14.57	−13.43	−48.50	320.55	157.54	17646.70	430.73
44		−23.65	−41.62	198.09	−23.72	−92.26	17663.54	16.84
45		165.22	89.39	−50.57	−4.15	46.90	17910.33	246.79
46	N	−179.85	27.73	−55.99	−254.15	−202.83	17245.24	−665.09
47	O	237.77	6.49	247.66	−4.41	91.06	17823.81	578.57
48	V	−31.13	19.51	1.20	Holiday	−14.90*	17798.49	−25.32
49		−78.57	168.43	−158.67	−252.01	369.96	17847.63	49.14
50	D	−117.12	−162.51	−75.70	82.45	−309.54	17265.21	−582.42
51	E	103.29	156.41	224.18	−253.25	−367.29	17128.55	−136.66
52	C	123.07	165.65	185.34	−50.44*	Holiday	17552.17	423.62
53		−23.90	192.71	−117.11	−178.84	Year's Close	17425.03	−127.14
TOTALS		**308.28**	**−879.14**	**926.70**	**982.16**	**−1736.04**		**−398.04**

Bold Color: Down Friday, Down Monday
** Monday denotes first trading day of week, Friday denotes last trading day of week

* Shortened trading day: Nov 27, Dec 24

MONDAY

D 57.1
S 52.4
N 57.1

10

Stocks are super-attractive when the Fed is loosening and interest rates are falling. In sum: Don't fight the Fed!
— Martin Zweig (Fund manager, *Winning on Wall Street*, 1943–2013)

TUESDAY

D 52.4
S 52.4
N 61.9

11

To an imagination of any scope the most far-reaching form of power is not money, it is the command of ideas.
— Oliver Wendell Holmes Jr. (U.S. Supreme Court Justice 1902–1932, *The Mind and Faith of Justice Holmes*, edited by Max Lerner, 1841–1935)

July is the Best Performing Dow and S&P Month of the Third Quarter

WEDNESDAY

D 57.1
S 57.1
N 57.1

12

The man who can master his time can master nearly anything.
— Winston Churchill (British statesman, 1874–1965)

THURSDAY

D 66.7
S 76.2
N 71.4

13

Life is what happens, while you're busy making other plans.
— John Lennon (Beatle, 1940–1980)

FRIDAY

D 61.9
S 66.7
N 71.4

14

Bill Gates' One-Minus Staffing: *For every project, figure out the bare minimum of people needed to staff it. Cut to the absolute muscle and bones, then take out one more. When you understaff, people jump on the loose ball. You find out who the real performers are. Not so when you're overstaffed. People sit around waiting for somebody else to do it.*
— Quoted by Rich Karlgaard (Publisher, *Forbes* December 25, 2000)

SATURDAY

15

SUNDAY

16

DON'T SELL STOCKS ON MONDAY OR FRIDAY

Since 1989, Monday* and Tuesday have been the most consistently bullish days of the week for the Dow, Thursday and Friday* the most bearish, as traders have become reluctant to stay long going into the weekend. Since 1989 Mondays and Tuesdays gained 13131.72 Dow points, while Thursday and Friday combined for a total gain of 123.64 points. Also broken out are the last 15 and a third years to illustrate Monday's and Friday's poor performance in bear market years 2001–2002 and 2008–2009. During uncertain market times traders often sell before the weekend and are reluctant to jump in on Monday. See pages 68, 80, and 141–144 for more.

ANNUAL DOW POINT CHANGES FOR DAYS OF THE WEEK SINCE 1953

Year	Monday*	Tuesday	Wednesday	Thursday	Friday*	Year's DJIA Closing	Year's Point Change
1953	−36.16	−7.93	19.63	5.76	7.70	280.90	−11.00
1954	15.68	3.27	24.31	33.96	46.27	404.39	123.49
1955	−48.36	26.38	46.03	−0.66	60.62	488.40	84.01
1956	−27.15	−9.36	−15.41	8.43	64.56	499.47	11.07
1957	−109.50	−7.71	64.12	3.32	−14.01	435.69	−63.78
1958	17.50	23.59	29.10	22.67	55.10	583.65	147.96
1959	−44.48	29.04	4.11	13.60	93.44	679.36	95.71
1960	−111.04	−3.75	−5.62	6.74	50.20	615.89	−63.47
1961	−23.65	10.18	87.51	−5.96	47.17	731.14	115.25
1962	−101.60	26.19	9.97	−7.70	−5.90	652.10	−79.04
1963	−8.88	47.12	16.23	22.39	33.99	762.95	110.85
1964	−0.29	−17.94	39.84	5.52	84.05	874.13	111.18
1965	−73.23	39.65	57.03	3.20	68.48	969.26	95.13
1966	−153.24	−27.73	56.13	−46.19	−12.54	785.69	−183.57
1967	−68.65	31.50	25.42	92.25	38.90	905.11	119.42
1968†	6.41	34.94	25.16	−72.06	44.19	943.75	38.64
1969	−164.17	−36.70	18.33	23.79	15.36	800.36	−143.39
1970	−100.05	−46.09	116.07	−3.48	72.11	838.92	38.56
1971	−2.99	9.56	13.66	8.04	23.01	890.20	51.28
1972	−87.40	−1.23	65.24	8.46	144.75	1020.02	129.82
1973	−174.11	10.52	−5.94	36.67	−36.30	850.86	−169.16
1974	−149.37	47.51	−20.31	−13.70	−98.75	616.24	−234.62
1975	39.46	−109.62	56.93	124.00	125.40	852.41	236.17
1976	70.72	71.76	50.88	−33.70	−7.42	1004.65	152.24
1977	−65.15	−44.89	−79.61	−5.62	21.79	831.17	−173.48
1978	−31.29	−70.84	71.33	−64.67	69.31	805.01	−26.16
1979	−32.52	9.52	−18.84	75.18	0.39	838.74	33.73
1980	−86.51	135.13	137.67	−122.00	60.96	963.99	125.25
1981	−45.68	−49.51	−13.95	−14.67	34.82	875.00	−88.99
1982	5.71	86.20	28.37	−1.47	52.73	1046.54	171.54
1983	30.51	−30.92	149.68	61.16	1.67	1258.64	212.10
1984	−73.80	78.02	−139.24	92.79	−4.84	1211.57	−47.07
1985	80.36	52.70	51.26	46.32	104.46	1546.67	335.10
1986	−39.94	97.63	178.65	29.31	83.63	1895.95	349.28
1987	−559.15	235.83	392.03	139.73	−165.56	1938.83	42.88
1988	268.12	166.44	−60.48	−230.84	86.50	2168.57	229.74
1989	−53.31	143.33	233.25	90.25	171.11	2753.20	584.63
SubTotal	*−1937.20*	*941.79*	*1708.54*	*330.82*	*1417.35*		*2461.30*
1990	219.90	−25.22	47.96	−352.55	−9.63	2633.66	−119.54
1991	191.13	47.97	174.53	254.79	−133.25	3168.83	535.17
1992	237.80	−49.67	3.12	108.74	−167.71	3301.11	132.28
1993	322.82	−37.03	243.87	4.97	−81.65	3754.09	452.98
1994	206.41	−95.33	29.98	−168.87	108.16	3834.44	80.35
1995	262.97	210.06	357.02	140.07	312.56	5117.12	1282.68
1996	626.41	155.55	−34.24	268.52	314.91	6448.27	1331.15
1997	1136.04	1989.17	−590.17	−949.80	−125.26	7908.25	1459.98
1998	649.10	679.95	591.63	−1579.43	931.93	9181.43	1273.18
1999	980.49	−1587.23	826.68	735.94	1359.81	11497.12	2315.69
2000	2265.45	306.47	−1978.34	238.21	−1542.06	10786.85	−710.27
SubTotal	*7098.52*	*1594.69*	*−327.96*	*−1299.41*	*967.81*		*8033.65*
2001	−389.33	336.86	−396.53	976.41	−1292.76	10021.50	−765.35
2002	−1404.94	−823.76	1443.69	−428.12	−466.74	8341.63	−1679.87
2003	978.87	482.11	−425.46	566.22	510.55	10453.92	2112.29
2004	201.12	523.28	358.76	−409.72	−344.35	10783.01	329.09
2005	316.23	−305.62	27.67	−128.75	24.96	10717.50	−65.51
2006	95.74	573.98	1283.87	193.34	−401.28	12463.15	1745.65
2007	278.23	−157.93	1316.74	−766.63	131.26	13264.82	801.67
2008	−1387.20	1704.51	−3073.72	−940.88	−791.14	8776.39	−4488.43
2009	−45.22	161.76	617.56	932.68	−15.12	10428.05	1651.66
2010	1236.88	−421.80	1019.66	−76.73	−608.55	11577.51	1149.46
2011	−571.02	1423.66	−776.05	246.27	317.19	12217.56	640.05
2012	254.59	−49.28	−456.37	847.34	299.30	13104.14	886.58
2013	−79.63	1091.75	170.93	653.64	1635.83	16576.66	3472.52
2014	−171.63	817.56	265.07	−337.48	672.89	17823.07	1246.41
2015	308.28	−879.14	926.70	982.16	−1736.04	17425.03	−398.04
2016 ‡	114.72	224.88	−473.18	−315.75	525.24		
Subtotal	*−264.31*	*4702.82*	*1829.34*	*1994.00*	*−1538.76*		*6638.18*
Totals	**4897.01**	**7239.30**	**3209.92**	**1025.41**	**846.40**		**17133.13**

* Monday denotes first trading day of week, Friday denotes last trading day of week
† Most Wednesdays closed last 7 months of 1968 ‡ Partial year through May 20, 2016

Monday Before July Expiration, Dow Up 10 of Last 13

MONDAY
D 47.6
S 42.9
N 57.1
17

It has been said that politics is the second oldest profession. I have learned that it bears a striking resemblance to the first.
— Ronald Reagan (40th U.S. President, 1911–2004)

TUESDAY
D 57.1
S 47.6
N 52.4
18

Economics is a very difficult subject. I've compared it to trying to learn how to repair a car when the engine is running.
— Ben Bernanke (Fed chairman 2006–2014, June 2004 *Region* interview as Fed governor)

WEDNESDAY
D 52.4
S 52.4
N 61.9
19

The generally accepted view is that markets are always right—that is, market prices tend to discount future developments accurately even when it is unclear what those developments are. I start with the opposite point of view. I believe that market prices are always wrong in the sense that they present a biased view of the future.
— George Soros (Financier, philanthropist, political activist, author, and philosopher, b. 1930)

THURSDAY
D 71.4
S 71.4
N 71.4
20

Whenever a well-known bearish analyst is interviewed [Cover story] in the financial press, it usually coincides with an important near-term market bottom.
— Clif Droke (Clifdroke.com, 11/15/04)

July Expiration Day, Dow Down 10 of Last 16, –4.6% 2002, –2.5% 2010

FRIDAY
D 19.0
S 23.8
N 19.0
21

I don't believe in intuition. When you get sudden flashes of perception, it is just the brain working faster than usual.
— Katherine Anne Porter (American author, 1890–1980)

SATURDAY
22

SUNDAY
23

A RALLY FOR ALL SEASONS

Most years, especially when the market sells off during the first half, prospects for the perennial summer rally become the buzz on the street. Parameters for this "rally" were defined by the late Ralph Rotnem as the lowest close in the Dow Jones Industrials in May or June to the highest close in July, August, or September. Such a big deal is made of the "summer rally" that one might get the impression the market puts on its best performance in the summertime. Nothing could be further from the truth! Not only does the market "rally" in every season of the year, but it does so with more gusto in the winter, spring, and fall than in the summer.

Winters in 53 years averaged a 12.7% gain as measured from the low in November or December to the first quarter closing high. Spring rose 11.4% followed by fall with 11.0%. Last and least was the average 9.1% "summer rally." Even 2009's impressive 19.7% "summer rally" was outmatched by spring. Nevertheless, no matter how thick the gloom or grim the outlook, don't despair! There's always a rally for all seasons, statistically.

SEASONAL GAINS IN DOW JONES INDUSTRIALS

	WINTER RALLY Nov/Dec Low to Q1 High	SPRING RALLY Feb/Mar Low to Q2 High	SUMMER RALLY May/Jun Low to Q3 High	FALL RALLY Aug/Sep Low to Q4 High
1964	15.3%	6.2%	9.4%	8.3%
1965	5.7	6.6	11.6	10.3
1966	5.9	4.8	3.5	7.0
1967	11.6	8.7	11.2	4.4
1968	7.0	11.5	5.2	13.3
1969	0.9	7.7	1.9	6.7
1970	5.4	6.2	22.5	19.0
1971	21.6	9.4	5.5	7.4
1972	19.1	7.7	5.2	11.4
1973	8.6	4.8	9.7	15.9
1974	13.1	8.2	1.4	11.0
1975	36.2	24.2	8.2	8.7
1976	23.3	6.4	5.9	4.6
1977	8.2	3.1	2.8	2.1
1978	2.1	16.8	11.8	5.2
1979	11.0	8.9	8.9	6.1
1980	13.5	16.8	21.0	8.5
1981	11.8	9.9	0.4	8.3
1982	4.6	9.3	18.5	37.8
1983	15.7	17.8	6.3	10.7
1984	5.9	4.6	14.1	9.7
1985	11.7	7.1	9.5	19.7
1986	31.1	18.8	9.2	11.4
1987	30.6	13.6	22.9	5.9
1988	18.1	13.5	11.2	9.8
1989	15.1	12.9	16.1	5.7
1990	8.8	14.5	12.4	8.6
1991	21.8	11.2	6.6	9.3
1992	14.9	6.4	3.7	3.3
1993	8.9	7.7	6.3	7.3
1994	9.7	5.2	9.1	5.0
1995	13.6	19.3	11.3	13.9
1996	19.2	7.5	8.7	17.3
1997	17.7	18.4	18.4	7.3
1998	20.3	13.6	8.2	24.3
1999	15.1	21.6	8.2	12.6
2000	10.8	15.2	9.8	3.5
2001	6.4	20.8	1.7	23.1
2002	14.8	7.9	2.8	17.6
2003	6.5	23.9	14.3	15.7
2004	11.6	5.2	4.4	10.6
2005	9.0	2.1	5.6	5.3
2006	8.8	8.3	9.5	13.0
2007	6.7	13.5	6.6	10.3
2008	2.5	11.2	3.8	4.5
2009	19.6	34.4	19.7	15.5
2010	11.6	13.1	11.1	16.0
2011	12.6	10.3	7.0	14.7
2012	18.0	4.5	12.4	5.7
2013	16.2	11.8	6.9	12.2
2014	6.0	10.2	5.5	10.3
2015	7.1	5.5	3.0	14.4
2016	3.4	15.6*		
Totals	**674.7%**	**604.4%**	**470.9%**	**570.2%**
Average	**12.7%**	**11.4%**	**9.1%**	**11.0%**

As of 5/20/2016

MONDAY
D 42.9
S 47.6
N 42.9
24

When a company reports higher earnings for its first quarter (over its previous year's first quarter), chances are almost five to one it will also have increased earnings in its second quarter.
— Niederhoffer, Cross & Zeckhauser

Week After July Expiration Prone to Wild Swings, Dow Up 9 of Last 14 1998
–4.3%, 2002 +3.1%, 2006 +3.2%, 2007 –4.2%, 2009 +4.0%, 2010 +3.2

TUESDAY
D 61.9
S 57.1
N 61.9
25

Everyone wants to make the same three things: money, a name, and a difference. What creates diversity in the human race is how we prioritize the three.
— Roy H. Williams (*The Wizard of Ads*)

WEDNESDAY
D 52.4
S 52.4
N 57.1
26

In most admired companies, key priorities are teamwork, customer focus, fair treatment of employees, initiative, and innovation. In average companies the top priorities are minimizing risk, respecting the chain of command, supporting the boss, and making budget.
— Bruce Pfau (*Fortune*)

Beware the "Summer Rally" Hype
Historically the Weakest Rally of All Seasons (Page 72)

THURSDAY
D 42.9
S 47.6
N 42.9
27

If you live each day as if it was your last, someday you'll most certainly be right.
— Favorite quote of Steve Jobs (CEO Apple & Pixar, Stanford University commencement address, 6/15/05)

FRIDAY
D 42.9
S 61.9
N 66.7
28

I'm always turned off by an overly optimistic letter from the president in the annual report. If his letter is mildly pessimistic to me, that's a good sign.
— Philip Carret (Centenarian, founded Pioneer Fund in 1928, 1896–1998)

SATURDAY
29

August Almanac Investor Sector Seasonalities: See Pages 94, 96, and 98

SUNDAY
30

AUGUST ALMANAC

AUGUST							SEPTEMBER					
S	M	T	W	T	F	S	S	M	T	W	T	F	S
		1	2	3	4	5						1	2
6	7	8	9	10	11	12	3	4	5	6	7	8	9
13	14	15	16	17	18	19	10	11	12	13	14	15	16
20	21	22	23	24	25	26	17	18	19	20	21	22	23
27	28	29	30	31			24	25	26	27	28	29	30

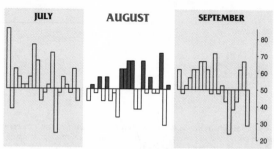

Market Probability Chart above is a graphic representation of the S&P 500 Recent Market Probability Calendar on page 124.

◆ Harvesting made August the best stock market month 1901–1951 ◆ Now that about 2% farm, August is the worst Dow, S&P, and NASDAQ (2000 up 11.7%, 2001 down 10.9) month since 1987 ◆ Shortest bear in history (45 days) caused by turmoil in Russia, currency crisis and hedge fund debacle ended here in 1998, 1344.22-point drop in the Dow, second worst behind October 2008, off 15.1% ◆ Saddam Hussein triggered a 10.0% slide in 1990 ◆ Best Dow gains: 1982 (11.5%) and 1984 (9.8%) as bear markets ended ◆ Next-to-last day S&P up only five times last 20 years ◆ Post-presidential election year Augusts' rankings: #11 S&P and NASDAQ, #12 Dow.

August Vital Statistics

	DJIA		S&P 500		NASDAQ		Russell 1K		Russell 2K	
Rank	10		11		11		10		9	
Up	37		36		24		23		21	
Down	29		30		21		14		16	
Average % Change	−0.2%		−0.1%		0.1%		0.2%		0.2%	
Post-Election Year	0.8%		1.0%		2.9%		2.2%		3.5%	
Best & Worst August										
	% Change		% Change		% Change		% Change		% Change	
Best	1982	11.5	1982	11.6	2000	11.7	1982	11.3	1984	11.5
Worst	1998	−15.1	1998	−14.6	1998	−19.9	1998	−15.1	1998	−19.5
Best & Worst August Weeks										
Best	08/20/82	10.3	08/20/82	8.8	08/03/84	7.4	08/20/82	8.5	08/03/84	7.0
Worst	08/23/74	−6.1	08/05/11	−7.2	08/28/98	−8.8	08/05/11	−7.7	08/05/11	−10.3
Best & Worst August Days										
Best	08/17/82	4.9	08/17/82	4.8	08/09/11	5.3	08/09/11	5.0	08/09/11	6.9
Worst	08/31/98	−6.4	08/31/98	−6.8	08/31/98	−8.6	08/08/11	−6.9	08/08/11	−8.9
First Trading Day of Expiration Week: 1980–2015										
Record (#Up – #Down)	23–13		26–10		27–9		26–10		23–13	
Current streak	U2		U2		U6		U2		U3	
Avg % Change	0.27		0.28		0.33		0.26		0.28	
Options Expiration Day: 1980–2015										
Record (#Up – #Down)	18–18		19–17		20–16		20–16		21–15	
Current streak	D3		D3		D1		D1		D3	
Avg % Change	−0.14		−0.09		−0.16		−0.09		0.07	
Options Expiration Week: 1980–2015										
Record (#Up – #Down)	18–18		21–15		20–16		21–15		22–14	
Current streak	D1		D1		D1		D1		D1	
Avg % Change	0.03		0.22		0.38		0.24		0.47	
Week After Options Expiration: 1980–2015										
Record (#Up – #Down)	22–14		24–12		23–13		24–12		23–13	
Current streak	U2		U3		U3		U3		U3	
Avg % Change	0.31		0.35		0.55		0.35		0.10	
First Trading Day Performance										
% of Time Up	47.0		50.0		51.1		45.9		48.6	
Avg % Change	0.02		0.05		−0.07		0.11		−0.01	
Last Trading Day Performance										
% of Time Up	60.6		63.6		66.7		59.5		70.3	
Avg % Change	0.12		0.12		0.03		−0.05		0.05	

Dow & S&P 1950–April 2016, NASDAQ 1971–April 2016, Russell 1K & 2K 1979–April 2016.

August's a good month to go on vacation;
Trading stocks will likely lead to frustration.

JULY/AUGUST 2017

Last Trading Day in July, NASDAQ Down 9 of Last 11

MONDAY

D 33.3
S 42.9
N 38.1

31

Behold, my son, with what little wisdom the world is ruled.
— Count Axel Gustafsson Oxenstierna (1648 letter to his son at conclusion of Thirty Years War; 1583–1654)

First Trading Day in August, Dow Down 13 of Last 19
Russell 2000 Up 7 of Last 12

TUESDAY

D 33.3
S 42.9
N 42.9

1

Love your enemies, for they tell you your faults.
— Benjamin Franklin (U.S. founding father, diplomat, inventor, 1706–1790)

WEDNESDAY

D 57.1
S 52.4
N 42.9

2

The inherent vice of capitalism is the unequal sharing of blessings; the inherent virtue of socialism is the equal sharing of miseries.
— Winston Churchill (British statesman, 1874–1965)

First Nine Trading Days of August Are Historically Weak (Pages 74 and 124)

THURSDAY

D 47.6
S 47.6
N 47.6

3

The price of a stock varies inversely with the thickness of its research file.
— Martin Sosnoff (Atalanta Sosnoff Capital, *Silent Investor, Silent Loser*)

FRIDAY

D 52.4
S 57.1
N 52.4

4

Successful innovation is not a feat of intellect, but of will.
— Joseph A. Schumpeter (Austrian-American economist, *Theory of Economic Development*, 1883–1950)

SATURDAY

5

SUNDAY

6

BEST INVESTMENT BOOK OF THE YEAR

Juggling with Knives: Smart Investing in the Coming Age of Volatility

By Jim Jubak

Luckily, we crossed paths with Jim Jubak at the Thirty-Fifth Anniversary MoneyShow in Las Vegas early in May 2016. It was humbling to find out that Jim is a devout *Almanac* reader. When we offered him a complimentary copy of the *2016 Almanac*, he happily proclaimed he already had a copy and dutifully buys one every year. Instead, he bestowed us with a copy of his latest opus, *Juggling with Knives: Smart Investing in the Coming Age of Volatility*. In honor of our 50-year milestone, Jim autographed his book: "To Jeff, 50 Years!!"

Once we dug into *Juggling with Knives*, Jim's wit, wisdom, and over 30 years of financial market experience sped off the pages. From the outset, Jim thrills readers with a fresh look at the history of market volatility cycles. This is not a dogmatic rehash of past crises and bull and bear markets. Jim imparts fresh insights and original thinking into what brought us into this new "Age of Volatility," how long it will last, how it will manifest, and how to invest for it.

Well-organized into three sections, the book first lays out the cycle of low volatility we enjoyed from about 1981 to 1997, the transition period from 1997 to 2008, and the period of high volatility we have experienced since the Global Financial Crisis took shape in 2008. Jim goes through some rather clear and concise data points and history that support his analysis of this new and different age of volatility that is upon us, what created it, what is likely to fuel it going forward, and how to position your portfolio for it.

Part II focuses on ten major secular, "real-life" trends that promise to shape and drive the roller coaster ride of volatility Jim expects over the next decade or so. He contends that China presents the "greatest pending source of global risk" to financial markets and the global economy. It's not a gloom and doom forecast—China will work things out—but it has the potential to create big volatility. For now, Jim contends that China's phase of easy growth is over.

The real meat of this book is in Part III, where Jim lays out a host of practical strategies that individuals and advisors can implement with relative ease. These are not get-rich-quick schemes or one-dimensional methods. Jim covers several stock selection strategies, including his "improved" dividend stock strategy. His "improved" bond strategy is based upon the conclusion that we have entered a period of "long-term downward volatility in bond prices as interest rates and yields rise in a reversal of the 1981–2014 trend" and "shorter-term volatility in credit quality."

This is only a taste of what Jim lays on the table. He serves up a buffet of in-depth analysis and detailed recommendations and strategies. We may have entered a new "Age of Volatility," but with Jim Jubak's *Juggling with Knives*, at least we can enjoy and profit from the ride.

PublicAffairs, $28.99, http://jubakpicks.com/. **2017 Best Investment Book of the Year.**

MONDAY

D 52.4
S 42.9
N 38.1

7

I cannot give you a formula for success but I can give you a formula for failure: Try to please everybody.
— Herbert Swope (American Journalist, 1882–1958)

August Worst Dow and S&P Month 1988–2015
Harvesting Made August Best Dow Month 1901–1951

TUESDAY

D 47.6
S 57.1
N 38.1

8

You must automate, emigrate, or evaporate.
— James A. Baker (General Electric)

WEDNESDAY

D 42.9
S 42.9
N 42.9

9

A statistician is someone who can draw a straight line from an unwarranted assumption to a foregone conclusion.
— Anonymous

Mid-August Stronger Than Beginning and End

THURSDAY

D 42.9
S 47.6
N 47.6

10

Sell stocks whenever the market is 30% higher over a year ago.
— Eugene D. Brody (Oppenheimer Capital)

FRIDAY

D 38.1
S 33.3
N 47.6

11

Good luck is what happens when preparation meets opportunity, bad luck is what happens when lack of preparation meets a challenge.
— Paul Krugman (Economist, *NY Times* 3/3/2006)

SATURDAY

12

SUNDAY

13

AURA OF THE TRIPLE WITCH—4TH QUARTER MOST BULLISH: DOWN WEEKS TRIGGER MORE WEAKNESS WEEK AFTER

Standard options expire the third Friday of every month, but in March, June, September, and December, a powerful coven gathers. Since the S&P index futures began trading on April 21, 1982, stock options, index options, as well as index futures all expire at the same time four times each year—known as Triple Witching. Traders have long sought to understand and master the magic of this quarterly phenomenon.

The market for single-stock and ETF futures and weekly options continues to grow. However, their impact on the market has thus far been subdued. As their availability continues to expand, trading volumes and market influence are also likely to broaden. Until such time, we do not believe the term "quadruple witching" is applicable just yet.

We have analyzed what the market does prior, during, and following Triple Witching expirations in search of consistent trading patterns. Here are some of our findings of how the Dow Jones Industrials perform around Triple-Witching Week (TWW).

- TWWs have become more bullish since 1990, except in the second quarter.
- Following weeks have become more bearish. Since Q1 2000, only 22 of 64 were up, and 10 occurred in December, 7 in March, 3 in September, 1 in June.
- TWWs have tended to be down in flat periods and dramatically so during bear markets.
- DOWN WEEKS TEND TO FOLLOW DOWN TWWs is a most interesting pattern. Since 1991, of 33 down TWWs, 23 following weeks were also down. This is surprising, inasmuch as the previous decade had an exactly opposite pattern: There were 13 down TWWs then, but 12 up weeks followed them.
- TWWs in the second and third quarter (Worst Six Months May through October) are much weaker, and the weeks following, horrendous. But in the first and fourth quarter (Best Six Months period November through April), only the week after Q1 expiration is negative.

Throughout the *Almanac* you will also see notations on the performance of Mondays and Fridays of TWW, as we place considerable significance on the beginnings and ends of weeks (pages 68, 70, and 141–144).

TRIPLE WITCHING WEEK AND WEEK AFTER DOW POINT CHANGES

	Expiration Week Q1	Week After	Expiration Week Q2	Week After	Expiration Week Q3	Week After	Expiration Week Q4	Week After
1991	−6.93	−89.36	−34.98	−58.81	33.54	−13.19	20.12	167.04
1992	40.48	−44.95	−69.01	−2.94	21.35	−76.73	9.19	12.97
1993	43.76	−31.60	−10.24	−3.88	−8.38	−70.14	10.90	6.15
1994	32.95	−120.92	3.33	−139.84	58.54	−101.60	116.08	26.24
1995	38.04	65.02	86.80	75.05	96.85	−33.42	19.87	−78.76
1996	114.52	51.67	55.78	−50.60	49.94	−15.54	179.53	76.51
1997	−130.67	−64.20	14.47	−108.79	174.30	4.91	−82.01	−76.98
1998	303.91	−110.35	−122.07	231.67	100.16	133.11	81.87	314.36
1999	27.20	−81.31	365.05	−303.00	−224.80	−524.30	32.73	148.33
2000	666.41	517.49	−164.76	−44.55	−293.65	−79.63	−277.95	200.60
2001	−821.21	−318.63	−353.36	−19.05	−1369.70	611.75	224.19	101.65
2002	34.74	−179.56	−220.42	−10.53	−326.67	−284.57	77.61	−207.54
2003	662.26	−376.20	83.63	−211.70	173.27	−331.74	236.06	46.45
2004	−53.48	26.37	6.31	−44.57	−28.61	−237.22	106.70	177.20
2005	−144.69	−186.80	110.44	−325.23	—36.62	−222.35	97.01	7.68
2006	203.31	0.32	122.63	−25.46	168.66	−52.67	138.03	−102.30
2007	−165.91	370.60	215.09	−279.22	377.67	75.44	110.80	−84.78
2008	410.23	−144.92	−464.66	−496.18	−33.55	−245.31	−50.57	−63.56
2009	54.40	497.80	−259.53	−101.34	214.79	−155.01	−142.61	191.21
2010	117.29	108.38	239.57	−306.83	145.08	252.41	81.59	81.58
2011	−185.88	362.07	52.45	−69.78	516.96	−737.61	−317.87	427.61
2012	310.60	−151.89	212.97	−126.39	−13.90	−142.34	55.83	−252.73
2013	117.04	−2.08	−270.78	110.20	75.03	−192.85	465.78	257.27
2014	237.10	20.29	171.34	−95.24	292.23	−166.59	523.97	248.91
2015	378.34	−414.99	117.11	−69.27	−48.51	−69.91	−136.66	423.62
2016	388.99	−86.57						
Up	19	10	15	3	15	5	19	18
Down	7	16	10	22	10	20	6	7

Monday Before August Expiration, Dow Up 14 of Last 21, Average Gain 0.4%

MONDAY
D 66.7
S 61.9
N 61.9
14

More people and increased income cause resources to become scarcer in the short run. Heightened scarcity causes prices to rise. The higher prices present opportunity and prompt investors to search for solutions. These solutions eventually lead to prices dropping lower than before the scarcity occurred.
— Julian Simon (Businessman, professor of business administration; *The Ultimate Resource*, 1996; 1932–1998)

TUESDAY
D 47.6
S 61.9
N 66.7
15

A realist believes that what is done or left undone in the short run determines the long run.
— Sydney J. Harris (American journalist and author, 1917–1986)

WEDNESDAY
D 57.1
S 66.7
N 66.7
16

I keep hearing "Should I buy? Should I buy?" When I start hearing "Should I sell?" that's the bottom.
— Nick Moore (portfolio manager, Jurika & Voyles, TheStreet.com March 12, 2001)

THURSDAY
D 66.7
S 66.7
N 61.9
17

I am not a member of any organized party—I am a Democrat.
— Will Rogers (American humorist and showman, 1879–1935)

August Expiration Day Less Bullish Lately, Dow Down 5 of Last 6 Down 531 Points (3.1%) in 2015

FRIDAY
D 42.9
S 38.1
N 38.1
18

There's a lot of talk about self-esteem these days. It seems pretty basic to me. If you want to feel good about yourself, you've got to do things that you can be proud of.
— Oseola McCarty (American author, *Simple Wisdom for Rich Living*, 1908–1999)

SATURDAY
19

SUNDAY
20

TAKE ADVANTAGE OF DOWN FRIDAY/ DOWN MONDAY WARNING

Fridays and Mondays are the most important days of the week. Friday is the day for squaring positions—trimming longs or covering shorts before taking off for the weekend. Traders want to limit their exposure (particularly to stocks that are not acting well) since there could be unfavorable developments before trading resumes two or more days later.

Monday is important because the market then has the chance to reflect any weekend news, plus what traders think after digesting the previous week's action and the many Monday morning research and strategy comments.

For over 30 years, a down Friday followed by down Monday has frequently corresponded to important market inflection points that exhibit a clearly negative bias, often coinciding with market tops and, on a few climactic occasions, such as in October 2002 and March 2009, near major market bottoms.

One simple way to get a quick reading on which way the market may be heading is to keep track of the performance of the Dow Jones Industrial Average on Fridays and the following Mondays. Since 1995, there have been 213 occurrences of Down Friday/ Down Monday (DF/DM), with 72 falling in the bear market years of 2001, 2002, 2008, 2011, 2015, and 2016, producing an average decline of 10.7%.

To illustrate how Down Friday/Down Monday can telegraph market inflection points we created the chart below of the Dow Jones Industrials from November 2014 to May 20, 2016 with arrows pointing to occurrences of DF/DM. Use DF/DM as a warning to examine market conditions carefully. Unprecedented central bank liquidity has tempered subsequent pullbacks, but has not eliminated them.

DOWN FRIDAY/DOWN MONDAY

Year	Total Number Down Friday/ Down Monday	Subsequent Average % Dow Loss*	Average Number of Days it took
1995	8	−1.2%	18
1996	9	−3.0%	28
1997	6	−5.1%	45
1998	9	−6.4%	47
1999	9	−6.4%	39
2000	11	−6.6%	32
2001	13	−13.5%	53
2002	18	−11.9%	54
2003	9	−3.0%	17
2004	9	−3.7%	51
2005	10	−3.0%	37
2006	11	−2.0%	14
2007	8	−6.0%	33
2008	15	−17.0%	53
2009	10	−8.7%	15
2010	7	−3.1%	10
2011	11	−9.0%	53
2012	11	−4.0%	38
2013	7	−2.4%	15
2014	7	−2.5%	8
2015	12	−9.2%	44
2016	3	−3.9%	14
Average	**10**	**−6.0%**	**33**

* Over next 3 months, ** Ending May 20, 2016

DOW JONES INDUSTRIALS (NOVEMBER 2014–MAY 20, 2016)

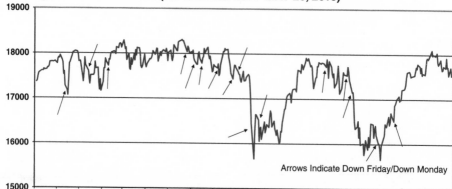

Arrows Indicate Down Friday/Down Monday

80

MONDAY
D 33.3
S 38.1
N 33.3
21

Big Business breeds bureaucracy and bureaucrats exactly as big government does.
— T.K. Quinn

TUESDAY
D 61.9
S 66.7
N 76.2
22

Make money and the whole nation will conspire to call you a gentleman.
— George Bernard Shaw (Irish dramatist, 1856–1950)

Week After August Expiration Mixed, Dow Down 6 of Last 11

WEDNESDAY
D 47.6
S 47.6
N 52.4
23

What is it that attracts me to the young? When I am with mature people I feel their rigidities, their tight crystallizations. They have become…like the statues of the famous. Achieved. Final.
— Anaïs Nin (*The Diaries of Anaïs Nin, Vol. IV*, 1903–1977)

THURSDAY
D 52.4
S 57.1
N 47.6
24

No other wisdom is better than the financial markets themselves. They incorporate the total wisdom of everyone that has money that is willing to vote their wisdom every second of every day.
— Don R. Hays (Hays Advisory, 3/14/07)

FRIDAY
D 47.6
S 47.6
N 52.4
25

Learn from the mistakes of others; you can't live long enough to make them all yourself.
— Eleanor Roosevelt (First Lady, 1884–1962)

SATURDAY
26

September Almanac Investor Sector Seasonalities: See Pages 94, 96, and 98

SUNDAY
27

SEPTEMBER ALMANAC

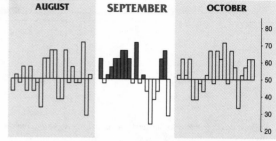

SEPTEMBER							OCTOBER						
S	M	T	W	T	F	S	S	M	T	W	T	F	S
					1	2				1	2	3	4
3	4	5	6	7	8	9	5	6	7	8	9	10	11
10	11	12	13	14	15	16	12	13	14	15	16	17	18
17	18	19	20	21	22	23	19	20	21	22	23	24	25
24	25	26	27	28	29	30	26	27	28	29	30	31	

Market Probability Chart above is a graphic representation of the S&P 500 Recent Market Probability Calendar on page 124.

◆ Start of business year, end of vacations, and back to school made September a leading barometer month in first 60 years of 20th century, now portfolio managers back after Labor Day tend to clean house ◆ Biggest % loser on the S&P, Dow, and NASDAQ since 1950 (pages 50 & 58) ◆ Streak of four great Dow Septembers averaging 4.2% gains ended in 1999 with six losers in a row averaging –5.9% (see page 152), up three straight 2005–2007, down 6% in 2008 and 2011 ◆ Day after Labor Day Dow up 15 of last 22 ◆ S&P opened strong 13 of last 21 years but tends to close weak due to end-of-quarter mutual fund portfolio restructuring, last trading day: S&P down 16 of past 23 ◆ September Triple-Witching Week can be dangerous, week after is pitiful (see page 78).

September Vital Statistics

	DJIA		S&P 500		NASDAQ		Russell 1K		Russell 2K	
Rank	12		12		12		12		12	
Up	26		29		24		18		20	
Down	40		36		21		19		17	
Average % Change	–0.8%		–0.5%		–0.6%		–0.7%		–0.6%	
Post-Election Year	–0.7%		–0.6%		–0.3%		–0.7%		–0.7%	
Best & Worst September										
	% Change		% Change		% Change		% Change		% Change	
Best	2010	7.7	2010	8.8	1998	13.0	2010	9.0	2010	12.3
Worst	2002	–12.4	1974	–11.9	2001	–17.0	2002	–10.9	2001	–13.6
Best & Worst September Weeks										
Best	09/28/01	7.4	09/28/01	7.8	09/16/11	6.3	09/28/01	7.6	09/28/01	6.9
Worst	09/21/01	–14.3	09/21/01	–11.6	09/21/01	–16.1	09/21/01	–11.7	09/21/01	–14.0
Best & Worst September Days										
Best	09/08/98	5.0	09/30/08	5.4	09/08/98	6.0	09/30/08	5.3	09/18/08	7.0
Worst	09/17/01	–7.1	09/29/08	–8.8	09/29/08	–9.1	09/29/08	–8.7	09/29/08	–6.7
First Trading Day of Expiration Week: 1980–2015										
Record (#Up – #Down)	23–13		19–17		12–23		19–17		14–22	
Current streak	D1		D2		D4		D2		D2	
Avg % Change	–0.08		–0.13		–0.34		–0.16		–0.25	
Options Expiration Day: 1980–2015										
Record (#Up – #Down)	18–18		19–17		23–13		20–16		23–13	
Current streak	D1		D4		D3		D3		D3	
Avg % Change	–0.04		0.09		0.11		0.08		0.12	
Options Expiration Week: 1980–2015										
Record (#Up – #Down)	19–17		21–15		21–15		21–15		19–17	
Current streak	D1		D1		U3		D1		U1	
Avg % Change	–0.22		0.03		0.05		0.02		0.12	
Week After Options Expiration: 1980–2015										
Record (#Up – #Down)	12–24		10–26		15–21		10–25		12–24	
Current streak	D5		D5		D2		D5		D2	
Avg % Change	–0.74		–0.81		–0.93		–0.82		–1.42	
First Trading Day Performance										
% of Time Up	59.1		60.6		55.6		51.4		51.4	
Avg % Change	–0.01		–0.02		–0.05		–0.09		–0.01	
Last Trading Day Performance										
% of Time Up	37.9		40.9		46.7		45.9		59.5	
Avg % Change	–0.12		–0.06		–0.01		0.03		0.24	

Dow & S&P 1950–April 2016, NASDAQ 1971–April 2016, Russell 1K & 2K 1979–April 2016.

September is when leaves and stocks tend to fall;
On Wall Street it's the worst month of all.

AUGUST/SEPTEMBER 2017

MONDAY
D 42.9
S 47.6
N 42.9
28

Patriotism is when love of your own people comes first. Nationalism is when hate for people other than your own comes first.
— Charles De Gaulle (WWII General, French president, 1890–1970, May 1969)

TUESDAY
D 71.4
S 71.4
N 71.4
29

I have seen it repeatedly throughout the world: politicians get a country in trouble but swear everything is okay in the face of overwhelming evidence to the contrary.
— Jim Rogers (Financier, *Adventure Capitalist*, b. 1942)

August's Next-to-Last Trading Day, S&P Down 15 of Last 20 Years

WEDNESDAY
D 23.8
S 28.6
N 52.4
30

The common denominator: Something that matters! Something that counts! Something that defines! Something that is imbued with soul. And with life!
— Tom Peters (*Reinventing Work*, 1999, referring to projects, b. 1942)

THURSDAY
D 52.4
S 52.4
N 57.1
31

The investor who concentrated on the 50 stocks in the S&P 500 that are followed by the fewest Wall Street analysts wound up with a rousing 24.6% gain in [2006 versus] 13.6% [for] the S&P 500.
— Rich Bernstein (Chief investment strategist, Merrill Lynch, *Barron's* 1/8/07)

First Trading Day in September, S&P Up 13 of Last 21, But Down 6 of Last 8

FRIDAY
D 57.1
S 61.9
N 61.9
1

The finest thought runs the risk of being irrevocably forgotten if we do not write it down.
— Arthur Schopenhauer (German philosopher, 1788–1860)

SATURDAY
2

SUNDAY
3

A CORRECTION FOR ALL SEASONS

While there's a rally for every season (page 72), almost always there's a decline or correction, too. Fortunately, corrections tend to be smaller than rallies, and that's what gives the stock market its long-term upward bias. In each season the average bounce outdoes the average setback. On average, the net gain between the rally and the correction is smallest in summer and fall.

The summer setback tends to be slightly outdone by the average correction in the fall. Tax selling and portfolio cleaning are the usual explanations—individuals sell to register a tax loss, and institutions like to get rid of their losers before preparing year-end statements. The October jinx also plays a major part. Since 1964, there have been 18 fall declines of over 10%, and in 10 of them (1966, 1974, 1978, 1979, 1987, 1990, 1997, 2000, 2002, and 2008) much damage was done in October, where so many bear markets end. Recent October lows were also seen in 1998, 1999, 2004, 2005, and 2011. Most often, it has paid to buy after fourth quarter or late third quarter "waterfall declines" for a rally that may continue into January or even beyond. Anticipation of war in Iraq put the market down in 2003 Q1. Quick success rallied stocks through Q3. Financial crisis affected the pattern in 2008–2009, producing the worst winter decline since 1932. Easy monetary policy and strong corporate earnings spared Q1 2011 and 2012 from a seasonal slump.

SEASONAL CORRECTIONS IN DOW JONES INDUSTRIALS

	WINTER SLUMP Nov/Dec High to Q1 Low	SPRING SLUMP Feb/Mar High to Q2 Low	SUMMER SLUMP May/Jun High to Q3 Low	FALL SLUMP Aug/Sep High to Q4 Low
1964	−0.1%	−2.4%	−1.0%	−2.1%
1965	−2.5	−7.3	−8.3	−0.9
1966	−6.0	−13.2	−17.7	−12.7
1967	−4.2	−3.9	−5.5	−9.9
1968	−8.8	−0.3	−5.5	+0.4
1969	−8.7	−8.7	−17.2	−8.1
1970	−13.8	−20.2	−8.8	−2.5
1971	−1.4	−4.8	−10.7	−13.4
1972	−0.5	−2.6	−6.3	−5.3
1973	−11.0	−12.8	−10.9	−17.3
1974	−15.3	−10.8	−29.8	−27.6
1975	−6.3	−5.5	−9.9	−6.7
1976	−0.2	−5.1	−4.7	−8.9
1977	−8.5	−7.2	−11.5	−10.2
1978	−12.3	−4.0	−7.0	−13.5
1979	−2.5	−5.8	−3.7	−10.9
1980	−10.0	−16.0	−1.7	−6.8
1981	−6.9	−5.1	−18.6	−12.9
1982	−10.9	−7.5	−10.6	−3.3
1983	−4.1	−2.8	−6.8	−3.6
1984	−11.9	−10.5	−8.4	−6.2
1985	−4.8	−4.4	−2.8	−2.3
1986	−3.3	−4.7	−7.3	−7.6
1987	−1.4	−6.6	−1.7	−36.1
1988	−6.7	−7.0	−7.6	−4.5
1989	−1.7	−2.4	−3.1	−6.6
1990	−7.9	−4.0	−17.3	−18.4
1991	−6.3	−3.6	−4.5	−6.3
1992	+0.1	−3.3	−5.4	−7.6
1993	−2.7	−3.1	−3.0	−2.0
1994	−4.4	−9.6	−4.4	−7.1
1995	−0.8	−0.1	−0.2	−2.0
1996	−3.5	−4.6	−7.5	+0.2
1997	−1.8	−9.8	−2.2	−13.3
1998	−7.0	−3.1	−18.2	−13.1
1999	−2.7	−1.7	−8.0	−11.5
2000	−14.8	−7.4	−4.1	−11.8
2001	−14.5	−13.6	−27.4	−16.2
2002	−5.1	−14.2	−26.7	−19.5
2003	−15.8	−5.3	−3.1	−2.1
2004	−3.9	−7.7	−6.3	−5.7
2005	−4.5	−8.5	−3.3	−4.5
2006	−2.4	−5.4	−7.8	−0.4
2007	−3.7	−3.2	−6.1	−8.4
2008	−14.5	−11.0	−20.6	−35.9
2009	−32.0	−6.3	−7.4	−3.5
2010	−6.1	−10.4	−13.1	−1.0
2011	+0.2	−4.0	−16.3	−12.2
2012	+0.5	−8.7	−5.3	−7.8
2013	−0.2	−0.3	−4.1	−5.7
2014	−7.3	−2.6	−3.4	−6.7
2015	−4.9	−3.8	−14.4	−7.6
2016	−12.6	−1.6*		
Totals	**−342.4%**	**−338.5%**	**−467.2%**	**−469.5 %**
Average	**−6.5%**	**−6.4%**	**−9.0%**	**−9.0 %**

* As of 5/20/2015

Labor Day *(Market Closed)*   MONDAY

4

The symbol of all relationships among such men, the moral symbol of respect for human beings, is the trader.
— Ayn Rand (Russian-born American novelist and philosopher, from Galt's Speech, *Atlas Shrugged*, 1957; 1905–1982)

Day After Labor Day, Dow Up 15 of Last 22, 1997 Up 3.4%, 1998 Up 5.0%,   TUESDAY
2015 Up 2.4%

D 71.4
S 47.6
N 52.4

5

A committee is a cul de sac down which ideas are lured and then quietly strangled.
— Sir Barnett Cocks (Member of Parliament, 1907–1989)

WEDNESDAY

D 52.4
S 52.4
N 47.6

6

Every man with a new idea is a crank until the idea succeeds.
— Mark Twain (American novelist and satirist, pen name of Samuel Longhorne Clemens, 1835–1910)

THURSDAY

D 42.9
S 57.1
N 57.1

7

When everybody starts looking really smart, and not realizing that a lot of it was luck, I get scared.
— Raphael Yavneh (President Forbes Investors Advisory Institute, 1930–1990)

FRIDAY

D 66.7
S 61.9
N 66.7

8

Unless you love EVERYBODY, you can't sell ANYBODY.
— (From *Jerry Maguire*, 1996)

SATURDAY

9

SUNDAY

10

FIRST-TRADING-DAY-OF-THE-MONTH PHENOMENON: DOW GAINS MORE ONE DAY THAN ALL OTHER DAYS

Over the last 19 years the Dow Jones Industrial Average has gained more points on the first trading days of all months than all other days combined. While the Dow has gained 9878.52 points between September 2, 1997 (7622.42) and May 20, 2016 (17500.94), it is incredible that 5885.92 points were gained on the first trading days of these 225 months. The remaining 4486 trading days combined gained 3992.6 points during the period. This averages out to gains of 26.16 points on first days, in contrast to just 0.89 points on all others.

Note September 1997 through October 2000 racked up a total gain of 2632.39 Dow points on the first trading days of these 38 months (winners except for seven occasions). But between November 2000 and September 2002, when the 2000–2002 bear markets did the bulk of their damage, frightened investors switched from pouring money into the market on that day to pulling it out, fourteen months out of twenty-three, netting a 404.80 Dow point loss. The 2007–2009 bear market lopped off 964.14 Dow points on first days in 17 months November 2007–March 2009. First days had their worst year in 2014, declining eight times for a total loss of 820.86 Dow points.

First days of June have performed worst. Triple-digit declines in four of the last eight years have resulted in the biggest net losses. Due to persistent weakness, August is a net loser as well. In rising market trends, first days tend to perform much better, as institutions are likely anticipating strong performance at each month's outset. S&P 500 first days differ slightly from Dow's pattern as October is a loser. NASDAQ first days are not as strong, with weakness in April, August, and October.

DOW POINTS GAINED FIRST DAY OF MONTH
SEPTEMBER 1997–MAY 20, 2016

	Jan	Feb	Mar	Apr	May	Jun	Jul	Aug	Sep	Oct	Nov	Dec	Totals
1997									257.36	70.24	232.31	189.98	749.89
1998	56.79	201.28	4.73	68.51	83.70	22.42	96.65	−96.55	288.36	−210.09	114.05	16.99	646.84
1999	2.84	−13.13	18.20	46.35	225.65	36.52	95.62	−9.19	108.60	−63.95	−81.35	120.58	486.74
2000	−139.61	100.52	9.62	300.01	77.87	129.87	112.78	84.97	23.68	49.21	−71.67	−40.95	636.30
2001	−140.70	96.27	−45.14	−100.85	163.37	78.47	91.32	−12.80	47.74	−10.73	188.76	−87.60	268.11
2002	51.90	−12.74	262.73	−41.24	113.41	−215.46	−133.47	−229.97	−355.45	346.86	120.61	−33.52	−126.34
2003	265.89	56.01	−53.22	77.73	−25.84	47.55	55.51	−79.83	107.45	194.14	57.34	116.59	819.32
2004	−44.07	11.11	94.22	15.63	88.43	14.20	−101.32	39.45	−5.46	112.38	26.92	162.20	413.69
2005	−53.58	62.00	63.77	−99.46	59.19	82.39	28.47	−17.76	−21.97	−33.22	−33.30	106.70	143.23
2006	129.91	89.09	60.12	35.62	−23.85	91.97	77.80	−59.95	83.00	−8.72	−49.71	−27.80	397.48
2007	11.37	51.99	−34.29	27.95	73.23	40.47	126.81	150.38	91.12	191.92	−362.14	−57.15	311.66
2008	−220.86	92.83	−7.49	391.47	189.87	−134.50	32.25	−51.70	−26.63	−19.59	−5.18	−679.95	−439.48
2009	258.30	−64.03	−299.64	152.68	44.29	221.11	57.06	114.95	−185.68	−203.00	76.71	126.74	299.49
2010	155.91	118.20	78.53	70.44	143.22	−112.61	−41.49	208.44	254.75	41.63	6.13	249.76	1172.91
2011	93.24	148.23	−168.32	56.99	−3.18	−279.65	168.43	−10.75	−119.96	−258.08	−297.05	−25.65	−695.75
2012	179.82	83.55	28.23	52.45	65.69	−274.88	−8.70	−37.62	−54.90	77.98	136.16	−59.98	187.80
2013	308.41	149.21	35.17	−5.69	−138.85	138.46	65.36	128.48	23.65	62.03	69.80	−77.64	758.39
2014	−135.31	−326.05	−153.68	74.95	−21.97	26.46	129.47	−69.93	−30.89	−238.19	−24.28	−51.44	−820.86
2015	9.92	196.09	155.93	−77.94	185.54	29.69	138.40	−91.66	−469.68	−11.99	165.22	168.43	395.95
2016	−276.09	−17.12	348.58	107.66	117.52								280.55
Totals	514.08	1023.31	398.05	1153.26	1415.29	−57.52	990.95	−41.04	15.09	88.83	269.33	116.29	5885.92

SUMMARY FIRST DAYS VS. OTHER DAYS OF MONTH

	# of Days	Total Points Gained	Average Daily Point Gain
First days	225	5885.92	26.16
Other days	4486	3992.60	0.89

2001 4-Day Closing, Longest Since 9-Day Banking Moratorium March 1933
Monday Before September Triple Witching, Russell 2000 Down 11 of Last 17

 MONDAY

D 52.4
S 61.9
N 61.9

11

"In Memory"

Let's roll!
— Todd Beamer (Passenger on United Airlines Flight 93 just before foiling the hijackers, September 11, 2001)

TUESDAY

D 66.7
S 66.7
N 57.1

12

What's going on… is the end of Silicon Valley as we know it. The next big thing ain't computers… it's biotechnology.
— Larry Ellison (Oracle CEO, quoted in *The Wall Street Journal*, April 8, 2003)

Expiration Week 2001, Dow Lost 1370 Points (14.3%)
2nd Worst Weekly Point Loss Ever, 5th Worst Week Overall

WEDNESDAY

D 61.9
S 66.7
N 71.4

13

Don't be overly concerned about your heirs. Usually, unearned funds do them more harm than good.
— Gerald M. Loeb (E.F. Hutton, author, *The Battle for Investment Survival*, predicted 1929 Crash; 1900–1974)

THURSDAY

D 52.4
S 61.9
N 76.2

14

The critical ingredient is getting off your butt and doing something. It's as simple as that. A lot of people have ideas, but there are few who decide to do something about them now. Not tomorrow. Not next week. But today. The true entrepreneur is a doer, not a dreamer.
— Nolan Bushnell (Founder, Atari and Chuck E. Cheese's, b. 1943)

September Triple Witching, Dow Up 10 of Last 14

FRIDAY

D 52.4
S 47.6
N 33.3

15

When someone told me "We're going with you guys because no one ever got fired for buying Cisco (products)." That's what they used to say in IBM's golden age.
— Mark Dickey (Former Cisco sales exec, then at SmartPipes, *Fortune* 5/15/00).

SATURDAY

16

SUNDAY

17

MARKET BEHAVIOR THREE DAYS BEFORE AND THREE DAYS AFTER HOLIDAYS

The *Stock Trader's Almanac* has tracked holiday seasonality annually since the first edition in 1968. Stocks used to rise on the day before holidays and sell off the day after, but nowadays, each holiday moves to its own rhythm. Eight holidays are separated into seven groups. Average percentage changes for the Dow, S&P 500, NASDAQ, and Russell 2000 are shown.

The Dow and S&P consist of blue chips and the largest cap stocks, whereas NASDAQ and the Russell 2000 would be more representative of smaller-cap stocks. This is evident on the last day of the year with NASDAQ and the Russell 2000 having a field day, while their larger brethren in the Dow and S&P are showing losses on average.

Thanks to the Santa Claus Rally, the three days before and after New Year's Day and Christmas are best. NASDAQ and the Russell 2000 average gains of 1.3% to 1.7% over the six-day spans. However, trading around the first day of the year has been mixed. Traders have been selling more the first trading day of the year recently, pushing gains and losses into the New Year.

Bullishness before Labor Day and after Memorial Day is affected by strength the first day of September and June. The second worst day after a holiday is the day after Easter. Surprisingly, the following day is one of the best second days after a holiday, right up there with the second day after New Year's Day.

Presidents' Day is the least bullish of all the holidays, bearish the day before and three days after. NASDAQ has dropped 19 of the last 27 days before Presidents' Day (Dow, 16 of 27; S&P, 18 of 27; Russell 2000, 14 of 27).

HOLIDAYS: 3 DAYS BEFORE, 3 DAYS AFTER (Average % change 1980–April 2016)

	−3	−2	−1	Mixed	+1	+2	+3
S&P 500	0.05	0.20	−0.12	**New Year's**	0.18	0.28	−0.01
DJIA	0.01	0.15	−0.19	**Day**	0.29	0.28	0.10
NASDAQ	0.12	0.24	0.17	*1/1/17*	0.17	0.55	0.12
Russell 2K	0.10	0.35	0.41		0.001	0.19	0.05
S&P 500	0.33	0.02	−0.15	**Negative Before & After**	−0.16	−0.04	−0.13
DJIA	0.30	0.004	−0.07	**Presidents'**	−0.09	−0.07	−0.15
NASDAQ	0.53	0.29	−0.29	**Day**	−0.46	−0.02	−0.08
Russell 2K	0.40	0.19	−0.04	*2/20/17*	−0.32	−0.15	−0.05
S&P 500	0.18	−0.05	0.38	**Positive Before &**	−0.19	0.32	0.11
DJIA	0.14	−0.08	0.29	**Negative After**	−0.12	0.31	0.11
NASDAQ	0.40	0.21	0.48	**Good Friday**	−0.31	0.37	0.20
Russell 2K	0.20	0.06	0.52	*4/14/17*	−0.31	0.26	0.13
S&P 500	0.03	0.06	−0.01	**Positive After**	0.32	0.12	0.25
DJIA	0.02	0.01	−0.06	**Memorial**	0.38	0.11	0.15
NASDAQ	0.09	0.24	0.03	**Day**	0.26	−0.01	0.47
Russell 2K	−0.05	0.32	0.10	*5/29/17*	0.28	0.03	0.41
S&P 500	0.15	0.10	0.07	**Negative After**	−0.14	0.05	0.03
DJIA	0.11	0.09	0.07	**Independence**	−0.08	0.08	0.02
NASDAQ	0.29	0.11	0.07	**Day**	−0.16	−0.11	0.17
Russell 2K	0.29	0.003	−0.03	*7/4/17*	−0.23	−0.03	0.003
S&P 500	0.21	−0.21	0.13	**Positive Before & After**	0.11	0.06	−0.07
DJIA	0.19	−0.26	0.13	**Labor**	0.14	0.12	−0.15
NASDAQ	0.43	−0.01	0.15	**Day**	0.05	−0.07	0.09
Russell 2K	0.54	0.04	0.09	*9/4/17*	0.12	0.11	0.04
S&P 500	0.14	0.01	0.26	**Thanksgiving**	0.19	−0.43	0.31
DJIA	0.14	0.02	0.26	*11/23/17*	0.15	−0.37	0.32
NASDAQ	0.09	−0.21	0.41		0.45	−0.44	0.13
Russell 2K	0.16	−0.08	0.39		0.30	−0.51	0.28
S&P 500	0.20	0.22	0.21	**Christmas**	0.14	0.02	0.26
DJIA	0.29	0.25	0.26	*12/25/17*	0.18	0.02	0.23
NASDAQ	−0.04	0.43	0.40		0.12	0.07	0.31
Russell 2K	0.27	0.39	0.36		0.18	0.08	0.43

MONDAY

D 71.4
S 71.4
N 76.2

18

When an old man dies, a library burns down.
— African proverb

Week After Sepetmber Triple Witching Dow Down 21 of Last 26
Average Loss Since 1990, 1.2%

TUESDAY

D 38.1
S 47.6
N 57.1

19

Investors operate with limited funds and limited intelligence, they don't need to know everything. As long as they understand something better than others, they have an edge.
— George Soros (Financier, philanthropist, political activist, author, and philosopher, b. 1930)

WEDNESDAY

D 57.1
S 52.4
N 61.9

20

There are very few instances in history when any government has ever paid off debt.
— Walter Wriston (Retired CEO of Citicorp and Citibank)

Rosh Hashanah

THURSDAY

D 52.4
S 42.9
N 47.6

21

Any human anywhere will blossom in a hundred unexpected talents and capacities simply by being given the opportunity to do so.
— Doris Lessing (British writer, 2007 Nobel Prize in Literature, born in Iran, 1919–2013)

End of September Prone to Weakness
From End-of-Q3 Institutional Portfolio Restructuring

FRIDAY

D 28.6
S 23.8
N 38.1

22

Pretending to know everything closes the door to finding out what's really there.
— Neil deGrasse Tyson (American astrophysicist, cosmologist, director Hayden Planetarium, *Cosmos: A Spacetime Odyssey*, b. 1958)

SATURDAY

23

SUNDAY

24

OCTOBER ALMANAC

OCTOBER							NOVEMBER					
S	M	T	W	T	F	S	S	M	T	W	T	F	S
1	2	3	4	5	6	7				1	2	3	4
8	9	10	11	12	13	14	5	6	7	8	9	10	11
15	16	17	18	19	20	21	12	13	14	15	16	17	18
22	23	24	25	26	27	28	19	20	21	22	23	24	25
29	30	31					26	27	28	29	30		

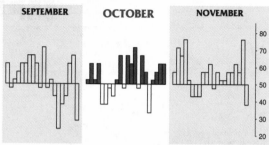

Market Probability Chart above is a graphic representation of the S&P 500 Recent Market Probability Calendar on page 124.

◆ Known as the jinx month because of crashes in 1929 and 1987, the 554-point drop on October 27, 1997, back-to-back massacres in 1978 and 1979, Friday the 13th in 1989, and the meltdown in 2008 ◆ Yet October is a "bear killer" and turned the tide in 12 post–WWII bear markets: 1946, 1957, 1960, 1962, 1966, 1974, 1987, 1990, 1998, 2001, 2002, and 2011 ◆ First October Dow top in 2007, 20-year 1987 Crash anniversary –2.6% ◆ Worst six months of the year ends with October (page 52) ◆ No longer worst month (pages 50 & 58) ◆ Best Dow, S&P, and NASDAQ month from 1993 to 2007 ◆ Post-presidential election year Octobers since 1950: #6 Dow (0.7%), #5 S&P (0.9%) and #6 NASDAQ (1.2%) ◆ October is a great time to buy ◆ Big October gains five years 1999–2003 after atrocious Septembers ◆ Can get into Best Six Months earlier using MACD (page 52) ◆ October 2011, second month to gain 1000 Dow points, and again in 2015.

October Vital Statistics

	DJIA	S&P 500	NASDAQ	Russell 1K	Russell 2K
Rank	7	7	7	5	10
Up	40	40	25	24	21
Down	26	26	20	13	16
Average % Change	0.7%	0.9%	0.8%	1.1	–0.2%
Post-Election Year	0.7%	0.9%	1.2%	0.8%	0.2%

	Best & Worst October				
	% Change	% Change	% Change	% Change	% Change
Best	1982	10.7	1974	16.3	1974	17.2	1982	11.3	2011	15.0
Worst	1987	–23.2	1987	–21.8	1987	–27.2	1987	–21.9	1987	–30.8

	Best & Worst October Weeks				
Best	10/11/74	12.6	10/11/74	14.1	10/31/08	10.9	10/31/08	10.8	10/31/08	14.1
Worst	10/10/08	–18.2	10/10/08	–18.2	10/23/87	–19.2	10/10/08	–18.2	10/23/87	–20.4

	Best & Worst October Days				
Best	10/13/08	11.1	10/13/08	11.6	10/13/08	11.8	10/13/08	11.7	10/13/08	9.3
Worst	10/19/87	–22.6	10/19/87	–20.5	10/19/87	–11.4	10/19/87	–19.0	10/19/87	–12.5

	First Trading Day of Expiration Week: 1980–2015				
Record (#Up – #Down)	29–7	27–9	25–11	28–8	26–10
Current streak	U1	U1	U1	U1	D2
Avg % Change	0.74	0.70	0.56	0.67	0.40

	Options Expiration Day: 1980–2015				
Record (#Up – #Down)	17–19	19–17	20–16	19–17	15–21
Current streak	U3	U3	U3	U3	D2
Avg % Change	–0.15	–0.22	–0.11	–0.21	–0.18

	Options Expiration Week: 1980–2015				
Record (#Up – #Down)	25–11	25–11	20–16	25–11	21–15
Current streak	U1	U1	U1	U1	D1
Avg % Change	0.61	0.66	0.71	0.65	0.41

	Week After Options Expiration: 1980–2015				
Record (#Up – #Down)	17–19	16–20	19–17	16–20	17–19
Current streak	U3	U3	U3	U3	U3
Avg % Change	–0.31	–0.31	–0.30	–0.34	–0.56

	First Trading Day Performance				
% of Time Up	48.5	50.0	48.9	54.1	48.6
Avg % Change	0.06	0.05	–0.15	0.22	–0.25

	Last Trading Day Performance				
% of Time Up	53.0	54.5	64.4	62.2	70.3
Avg % Change	0.07	0.14	0.49	0.34	0.60

Dow & S&P 1950–April 2016, NASDAQ 1971–April 2016, Russell 1K & 2K 1979–April 2016.

October has killed many a bear,
Buy techs and small caps and soon wear a grin ear to ear.

MONDAY
D 38.1
S 38.1
N 42.9
25

When you get to the end of your rope, tie a knot and hang on.
— Franklin D. Roosevelt (32nd U.S. President, 1882–1945)

TUESDAY
D 52.4
S 42.9
N 42.9
26

The men who can manage men manage the men who manage only things, and the men who can manage money manage all.
— Will Durant

Start Looking for MACD BUY Signals on October 1 (Pages 54, 60, and 62) **WEDNESDAY**
Almanac Investor Subscribers E-mailed When It Triggers (See Insert)
D 57.1
S 61.9
N 42.9
27

The very purpose of existence is to reconcile the glowing opinion we hold of ourselves with the appalling things that other people think about us.
— Quentin Crisp (Author, performer, 1908–1999)

THURSDAY
D 61.9
S 66.7
N 47.6
28

New indicator: CFO Magazine gave Excellence awards to WorldCom's Scott Sullivan (1998), Enron's Andrew Fastow (1999), and to Tyco's Mark Swartz (2000). All were subsequently indicted.
— Roger Lowenstein (Financial journalist and author, *Origins of the Crash*, b. 1954)

Last Day of Q3, Dow Down 14 of Last 19, Massive 4.7% Rally in 2008 **FRIDAY**
D 33.3
S 28.6
N 28.6
29

The only thing that saves us from the bureaucracy is its inefficiency.
— Eugene McCarthy (U.S. congressman and senator, 1949–1971; 3-time presidential candidate; 1916–2005)

Yom Kippur
SATURDAY
30

October Almanac Investor Sector Seasonalities: See Pages 94, 96, and 98 **SUNDAY**
1

MARKET GAINS MORE ON SUPER-8 DAYS EACH MONTH THAN ON ALL 13 REMAINING DAYS COMBINED

For many years, the last day plus the first four days were the best days of the month. The market currently exhibits greater bullish bias from the last three trading days of the previous month through the first two days of the current month, and now shows significant bullishness during the middle three trading days, 9 to 11, due to 401(k) cash inflows (see pages 145 and 146). This pattern was not as pronounced during the boom years of the 1990s, with market strength all month long. It returned in 2000 with monthly bullishness at the ends, beginnings, and middles of months versus weakness during the rest of the month. "Super Eight" performance in 2016 is back on track after a rough start in January.

SUPER-8 DAYS* DOW % CHANGES VS. REST OF MONTH

	Super 8 Days	Rest of Month		Super 8 Days	Rest of Month		Super 8 Days	Rest of Month
	2008			**2009**			**2010**	
Jan	−4.76%	−4.11%		3.16%	−6.92%		0.66%	−3.92%
Feb	1.83	0.65		−6.05	−4.39		3.31	−2.38
Mar	−4.85	2.92		−4.37	12.84		1.91	3.51
Apr	−0.27	4.09		1.52	−0.24		1.13	0.18
May	2.19	−4.81		2.64	2.98		−3.08	−5.75
Jun	0.37	−6.30		1.71	−1.64		4.33	−3.26
Jul	−3.80	−1.99		2.30	5.03		−7.07	11.34
Aug	1.53	1.06		0.04	4.91		0.20	−5.49
Sep	−2.23	−1.19		−0.81	2.21		3.83	4.22
Oct	−3.39	−13.70		−0.05	2.40		−0.18	3.47
Nov	6.07	−11.90		0.00	5.57		−1.20	1.37
Dec	−2.54	3.49		0.62	0.46		1.98	1.45
Totals	**−9.85%**	**−31.79%**		**0.71%**	**23.21%**		**5.82%**	**4.74%**
Average	**−0.82%**	**−2.65%**		**0.06%**	**1.93%**		**0.49%**	**0.40%**
	2011			**2012**			**2013**	
Jan	1.70%	1.80%		1.90%	1.66%		2.28%	3.47%
Feb	0.45	0.57		−0.39	2.33		−0.27	−0.41
Mar	−1.40	2.21		2.22	−0.55		2.93	1.82
Apr	2.30	0.95		1.00	−1.80		0.11	1.65
May	1.03	−2.61		−0.38	−4.52		1.93	2.81
Jun	−1.64	−1.19		−1.30	2.08		−0.27	−3.96
Jul	3.52	0.31		5.11	−2.22		1.11	4.23
Aug	2.04	−11.39		−0.40	2.09		−1.35	−3.75
Sep	3.24	−3.96		−0.24	2.98		2.55	0.83
Oct	−4.47	10.71		0.77	−3.60		−0.64	2.60
Nov	1.42	−6.66		−2.01	0.55		1.79	1.41
Dec	5.74	3.58		0.49	1.35		−0.72	3.30
Totals	**13.93%**	**−5.68%**		**6.77%**	**0.35%**		**9.45%**	**14.00%**
Average	**1.16%**	**−0.47%**		**0.56%**	**0.03%**		**0.79%**	**1.17%**
	2014			**2015**			**2016**	
Jan	0.92%	−4.26%		−3.64%	−0.07%		−2.95%	−4.93%
Feb	−1.99	3.66		2.65	2.00		1.69	0.30
Mar	0.77	−0.21		1.91	−4.78		4.02	2.21
Apr	2.44	−1.82		1.20	0.83		2.14	0.43
May	−0.56	2.50		1.31	−1.28			
Jun	−0.09	1.24		−1.32	0.49			
Jul	1.79	−1.10		−0.11	−1.31			
Aug	−1.81	2.61		0.37	−8.02			
Sep	0.32	−1.26		2.27	−2.04			
Oct	−3.28	3.82		1.03	6.57			
Nov	2.42	2.28		0.68	0.68			
Dec	−1.66	3.14		−0.74	−0.86			
Totals	**−0.73%**	**10.60%**		**5.61%**	**−7.79%**		**4.90%**	**−1.99%**
Average	**−0.06%**	**0.88%**		**0.47%**	**−0.65%**		**1.23%**	**−0.50%**

	Super Eight Days		Rest of Month (13 days)	
100	Net % Changes	36.61%	Net % Changes	5.65%
Month	Average Period	0.37%	Average Period	0.06%
Totals	Average Day	0.05%	Average Day	0.004%

* Super-8 Days = Last 3 + First 2 + Middle 3

OCTOBER 2017

First Trading Day in October, Dow Down 7 of Last 11, Off 2.4% in 2011

MONDAY

D 47.6
S 52.4
N 42.9

2

In the stock market those who expect history to repeat itself exactly are doomed to failure.
— Yale Hirsch (Creator of *Stock Trader's Almanac*, b. 1923)

TUESDAY

D 52.4
S 61.9
N 61.9

3

A day will come when all nations on our continent will form a European brotherhood…A day will come when we shall see…the United States of Europe…reaching out for each other across the seas.
— Victor Hugo (French novelist, playwright, *Hunchback of Notre Dame* and *Les Misérables*, 1802–1885)

October Ends Dow and S&P "Worst Six Months" (Pages 50, 52, 54, and 147)
And NASDAQ "Worst Four Months" (Pages 58, 60, and 148)

WEDNESDAY

D 52.4
S 52.4
N 61.9

4

Bull markets are born on pessimism, grow on skepticism, mature on optimism, and die on euphoria.
— Sir John Templeton (Founder Templeton Funds, philanthropist, 1912–2008)

THURSDAY

D 71.4
S 61.9
N 61.9

5

Age is a question of mind over matter. If you don't mind, it doesn't matter.
— Leroy Robert "Satchel" Paige (Negro League and Hall of Fame Pitcher, 1906–1982)

Dow Lost 1874 Points (18.2%) on the Week Ending 10/10/08
Worst Dow Week in the History of Wall Street

FRIDAY

D 38.1
S 38.1
N 47.6

6

The power to tax involves the power to destroy.
— John Marshall (U. S. Supreme Court, 1819)

SATURDAY

7

SUNDAY

8

SECTOR SEASONALITY: SELECTED PERCENTAGE PLAYS

Sector seasonality was featured in the first 1968 *Almanac*. A Merrill Lynch study showed that buying seven sectors around September or October and selling in the first few months of 1954–1964 tripled the gains of holding them for 10 years. Over the years we have honed this strategy significantly and now devote a large portion of our time and resources to investing and trading during positive and negative seasonal periods for different sectors with Exchange Traded Funds (ETFs).

Updated seasonalities appear in the table below. We specify whether the seasonality starts or finishes in the beginning third (B), middle third (M), or last third (E) of the month. These selected percentage plays are geared to take advantage of the bulk of seasonal sector strength or weakness.

By design, entry points are in advance of the major seasonal moves, providing traders ample opportunity to accumulate positions at favorable prices. Conversely, exit points have been selected to capture the majority of the move.

From the major seasonalities in the table below, we created the Sector Index Seasonality Strategy Calendar on pages 96 and 98. Note the concentration of bullish sector seasonalities during the Best Six Months, November to April, and bearish sector seasonalities during the Worst Six Months, May to October.

Almanac Investor eNewsletter subscribers receive specific entry and exit points for highly correlated ETFs and detailed analysis in ETF Trades Alerts. Visit *www.stocktradersalmanac.com,* or see the ad insert for additional details and a special offer for new subscribers.

SECTOR INDEX SEASONALITY TABLE

Ticker	Sector Index	Type	Seasonality Start		Finish		Average % Return[†] 15-Year	10-Year	5-Year
XCI	Computer Tech	Short	January	B	March	B	−6.3	−4.5	1.4
XNG	Natural Gas	Long	February	E	June	B	10.8	11.1	3.8
MSH	High-Tech	Long	March	M	July	B	6.9	6.3	2.5
UTY	Utilities	Long	March	M	October	B	6.1	6.6	4.8
XCI	Computer Tech	Long	April	M	July	M	6.2	5.9	7.2
BKX	Banking	Short	May	B	July	B	−7.5	−10.0	−2.0
XAU	Gold & Silver	Short	May	M	June	E	−7.2	−8.8	−7.5
S5MATR	Materials	Short	May	M	October	M	−6.3	−6.0	−6.5
XNG	Natural Gas	Short	June	M	July	E	−7.9	−6.0	−3.7
XAU	Gold & Silver	Long	July	E	December	E	11.6	2.6	−7.3
DJT	Transports	Short	July	M	October	M	−5.6	−4.8	−6.1
BTK	Biotech	Long	August	B	March	B	14.7	15.0	22.2
MSH	High-Tech	Long	August	M	January	M	11.9	8.1	9.1
SOX	Semiconductor	Short	August	M	October	E	−7.5	−6.0	−1.9
XOI	Oil	Short	September	B	November	E	−4.7	−4.4	−3.7
BKX	Banking	Long	October	B	May	B	12.3	11.6	18.9
XBD	Broker/Dealer	Long	October	B	April	M	16.4	11.5	22.8
XCI	Computer Tech	Long	October	B	January	B	13.7	8.3	7.7
S5COND	Consumer Discretionary	Long	October	B	June	B	14.1	13.4	21.0
S5CONS	Consumer Staples	Long	October	B	June	B	8.4	9.0	12.3
S5HLTH	Healthcare	Long	October	B	May	B	8.9	10.5	18.3
S5MATR	Materials	Long	October	B	May	B	18.1	17.7	18.1
DRG	Pharmaceutical	Long	October	M	January	B	6.4	6.5	7.7
RMZ	Real Estate	Long	October	E	May	B	13.2	12.5	13.0
SOX	Semiconductor	Long	October	E	December	B	12.9	7.3	7.5
XTC	Telecom	Long	October	M	December	E	8.1	4.0	3.1
DJT	Transports	Long	October	B	May	B	19.3	20.5	23.1
XOI	Oil	Long	December	M	July	B	11.9	11.6	7.5

[†] *Average % Return based on full seasonality completion through April 29, 2016.*

Columbus Day *(Bond Market Closed)*

MONDAY
D 38.1
S 38.1
N 52.4
9

Fortune favors the brave.
— Virgil (Roman poet, *Aeneid*, 70–19 BC)

TUESDAY
D 47.6
S 47.6
N 52.4
10

You try to be greedy when others are fearful, and fearful when others are greedy.
— Warren Buffett (CEO Berkshire Hathaway, investor, and philanthropist, b. 1930)

WEDNESDAY
D 42.9
S 42.9
N 52.4
11

The best minds are not in government. If any were, business would hire them away.
— Ronald Reagan (40th U.S. President, 1911–2004)

THURSDAY
D 47.6
S 52.4
N 61.9
12

With enough inside information and a million dollars, you can go broke in a year.
— Warren Buffett (CEO Berkshire Hathaway, investor, and philanthropist, b. 1930)

FRIDAY
D 71.4
S 66.7
N 71.4
13

First-rate people hire first-rate people; second-rate people hire third-rate people.
— Leo Rosten (American author, 1908–1997)

SATURDAY
14

SUNDAY
15

SECTOR INDEX SEASONALITY STRATEGY CALENDAR*

* Graphic representation of the Sector Index Seasonality Percentage Plays on page 94.
L = Long Trade, S = Short Trade, ⟶ = Start of Trade

(continued on page 98)

Monday Before October Expiration, Dow Up 29 of 36

MONDAY
D 47.6
S 47.6
N 47.6
16

It is a funny thing about life; if you refuse to accept anything but the best, you very often get it.
— W. Somerset Maugham

TUESDAY
D 57.1
S 66.7
N 57.1
17

There is a vitality, a life force, an energy, a quickening, that is translated through you into action, and because there is only one of you in all time, this expression is unique. And if you block it, it will never exist through any other medium and will be lost.
— Martha Graham (American choreographer, dancer, teacher)

October 2011, Second Dow Month to Gain 1000 Points

WEDNESDAY
D 47.6
S 61.9
N 47.6
18

If you develop the absolute sense of certainty that powerful beliefs provide, then you can get yourself to accomplish virtually anything, including those things that other people are certain are impossible.
— Anthony Robbins (Motivator, advisor, consultant, author, entrepreneur, philanthropist, b. 1960)

Crash of October 19, 1987, Dow down 22.6% in One Day

THURSDAY
D 66.7
S 71.4
N 71.4
19

Every man who knows how to read has it in his power to magnify himself, to multiply the ways in which he exists, to make his life full, significant and interesting.
— Aldous Huxley (English author, *Brave New World*, 1894–1963)

October Expiration Day, Dow Down 6 Straight 2005–2010 and 8 of Last 13

FRIDAY
D 38.1
S 47.6
N 42.9
20

Things may come to those who wait, but only the things left by those who hustle.
— Abraham Lincoln (16th U.S. President, 1809–1865)

SATURDAY
21

SUNDAY
22

(continued from page 96)

SECTOR INDEX SEASONALITY STRATEGY CALENDAR*

* Graphic representation of the Sector Index Seasonality Percentage Plays on page 94.
L = Long Trade, S = Short Trade, ⟶ = Start of Trade

98

You know a country is falling apart when even the government will not accept its own currency.
— Jim Rogers (Financier, *Adventure Capitalist*, b. 1942)

Late October is Time to Buy Depressed Stocks
Especially Techs and Small Caps

TUESDAY

D 52.4
S 57.1
N 47.6

24

The first rule is not to lose. The second rule is not to forget the first rule.
— Warren Buffett (CEO Berkshire Hathaway, investor, and philanthropist, b. 1930)

🐻 **WEDNESDAY**

D 38.1
S 33.3
N 42.9

25

The worst bankrupt in the world is the person who has lost his enthusiasm.
— H.W. Arnold

THURSDAY

D 57.1
S 52.4
N 47.6

26

Marketing is our No. 1 priority… A marketing campaign isn't worth doing unless it serves three purposes.
It must grow the business, create news, and enhance our image.
— James Robinson III (American Express)

FRIDAY

D 66.7
S 57.1
N 57.1

27

The single best predictor of overall excellence is a company's ability to attract, motivate, and retain talented people.
— Bruce Pfau (Vice chair human resources KPMG, *Fortune* 1998)

88th Anniversary of 1929 Crash, Dow Down 23.0% in Two Days, October 28–29

SATURDAY

28

November Almanac Investor Sector Seasonalities: See Pages 94, 96, and 98

SUNDAY

29

NOVEMBER ALMANAC

NOVEMBER						
S	M	T	W	T	F	S
				1	2	3	4
5	6	7	8	9	10	11
12	13	14	15	16	17	18
19	20	21	22	23	24	25
26	27	28	29	30		

DECEMBER						
S	M	T	W	T	F	S
31					1	2
3	4	5	6	7	8	9
10	11	12	13	14	15	16
17	18	19	20	21	22	23
24	25	26	27	28	29	30

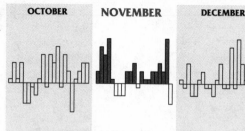

Market Probability Chart above is a graphic representation of the S&P 500 Recent Market Probability Calendar on page 124.

◆ #2 S&P and #3 Dow month since 1950, #3 on NASDAQ since 1971 (pages 50 & 58) ◆ Start of the "Best Six Months" of the year (page 52), NASDAQ's Best Eight Months and Best Three (pages 147 & 148) ◆ Simple timing indicator almost triples "Best Six Months" strategy (page 54), doubles NASDAQ's Best Eight (page 60) ◆ Day before and after Thanksgiving Day combined, only 14 losses in 64 years (page 104) ◆ Week before Thanksgiving Dow up 18 of last 23 ◆ Post-presidential election year Novembers rank #3 Dow, #2 S&P, and #3 NASDAQ.

November Vital Statistics

	DJIA		S&P 500		NASDAQ		Russell 1K		Russell 2K	
Rank	3		2		3		1		2	
Up	44		44		30		27		24	
Down	22		22		15		10		13	
Average % Change	1.5%		1.5%		1.6%		1.6%		1.8%	
Post-Election Year	1.8%		1.7%		2.4%		3.7%		2.8%	
Best & Worst November										
	% Change		% Change		% Change		% Change		% Change	
Best	1962	10.1	1980	10.2	2001	14.2	1980	10.1	2002	8.8
Worst	1973	−14.0	1973	−11.4	2000	−22.9	2000	−9.3	2008	−12.0
Best & Worst November Weeks										
Best	11/28/08	9.7	11/28/08	12.0	11/28/08	10.9	11/28/08	12.5	11/28/08	16.4
Worst	11/21/08	−5.3	11/21/08	−8.4	11/10/00	−12.2	11/21/08	−8.8	11/21/08	−11.0
Best & Worst November Days										
Best	11/13/08	6.7	11/13/08	6.9	11/13/08	6.5	11/13/08	7.0	11/13/08	8.5
Worst	11/20/08	−5.6	11/20/08	−6.7	11/19/08	−6.5	11/20/08	−6.9	11/19/08	−7.9
First Trading Day of Expiration Week: 1980–2015										
Record (#Up – #Down)	19–17		17–19		14–22		18–18		16–20	
Current streak	U3		U4		U1		U4		U1	
Avg % Change	−0.01		−0.04		−0.12		−0.05		−0.09	
Options Expiration Day: 1980–2015										
Record (#Up – #Down)	24–12		22–14		20–16		22–14		19–16	
Current streak	U6		U4		U4		U4		U6	
Avg % Change	0.25		0.18		0.05		0.17		0.14	
Options Expiration Week: 1980–2015										
Record (#Up – #Down)	24–12		22–14		19–17		21–15		18–18	
Current streak	U3		U3		U3		U3		U1	
Avg % Change	0.36		0.12		0.06		0.09		−0.23	
Week After Options Expiration: 1980–2015										
Record (#Up – #Down)	21–15		23–13		24–12		23–13		22–14	
Current streak	D1		U4		U4		U4		U4	
Avg % Change	0.67		0.66		0.78		0.66		0.81	
First Trading Day Performance										
% of Time Up	63.6		63.6		66.7		73.0		62.2	
Avg % Change	0.28		0.30		0.31		0.40		0.23	
Last Trading Day Performance										
% of Time Up	54.5		53.0		64.4		45.9		67.6	
Avg % Change	0.10		0.13		−0.07		0.01		0.15	

Dow & S&P 1950–April 2016, NASDAQ 1971–April 2016, Russell 1K & 2K 1979–April 2016.

*Astute investors always smile and remember,
When stocks seasonally start soaring, and salute November.*

MONDAY
D 61.9
S 61.9
N 61.9
30

Corporate guidance has become something of an art. The CFO has refined and perfected his art, gracefully leading on the bulls with the calculating grace and cunning of a great matador.
— Joe Kalinowski (I/B/E/S)

Halloween

TUESDAY
D 57.1
S 61.9
N 61.9
31

Capitalism without bankruptcy is like Christianity without hell.
— Frank Borman (CEO Eastern Airlines, April 1986)

First Trading Day in November, Dow Up 5 of Last 7

WEDNESDAY
D 57.1
S 57.1
N 71.4
1

It is not how right or how wrong you are that matters, but how much money you make when right and how much you do not lose when wrong.
— George Soros (Financier, philanthropist, political activist, author, and philosopher, b. 1930)

THURSDAY
D 61.9
S 71.4
N 66.7
2

Liberties voluntarily forfeited are not easily retrieved. All the more so for those that are removed surreptitiously.
— Ted Koppel (Newsman, *Nightline*, N Y Times 11/6/06, b. 1940)

November Begins Dow and S&P "Best Six Months" (Pages 50, 52, 54, and 147) And NASDAQ "Best Eight Months" (Pages 58, 60, and 148)

FRIDAY
D 66.7
S 66.7
N 71.4
3

The higher a people's intelligence and moral strength, the lower will be the prevailing rate of interest.
— Eugen von Bohm-Bawerk (Austrian economist, *Capital and Interest*, 1851–1914)

SATURDAY
4

Daylight Saving Time Ends

SUNDAY
5

FOURTH QUARTER MARKET MAGIC

Examining market performance on a quarterly basis reveals several intriguing and helpful patterns. Fourth-quarter market gains have been magical, providing the greatest and most consistent gains over the years. First-quarter performance runs a respectable second. This should not be surprising, as cash inflows, trading volume, and buying bias are generally elevated during these two quarters.

Positive market psychology hits a fever pitch as the holiday season approaches, and does not begin to wane until spring. Professionals drive the market higher, as they make portfolio adjustments to maximize year-end numbers. Bonuses are paid and invested around the turn of the year.

The market's sweet spot of the four-year cycle begins in the fourth quarter of the midterm year. The best two-quarter span runs from the fourth quarter of the midterm year through the first quarter of the pre-election year, averaging 14.6% for the Dow, 15.4% for the S&P 500, and an amazing 22.0% for NASDAQ. Pre-election Q2 is smoking, too, the third best quarter of the cycle, creating a three-quarter sweet spot from midterm Q4 to pre-election Q2.

Quarterly strength fades in the latter half of the pre-election year, but stays impressively positive through the election year. Losses dominate the first quarter of post-election years and the second and third quarters of midterm years.

QUARTERLY % CHANGES

	Q1	Q2	Q3	Q4	Year	Q2–Q3	Q4–Q1
Dow Jones Industrials (1949-March 2016)							
Average	2.2%	1.5%	0.4%	3.9%	8.3%	1.9%	6.4%
Post-election	−0.4%	1.6%	0.3%	3.8%	5.7%	2.0%	5.4%
Midterm	1.4%	−1.5%	−0.4%	7.1%	6.7%	−1.8%	14.6%
Pre-election	7.1%	4.9%	1.0%	2.6%	15.8%	5.9%	3.5%
Election	0.8%	1.0%	0.6%	2.0%	4.8%	1.7%	1.7%
S&P 500 (1949-March 2016)							
Average	2.2%	1.6%	0.6%	4.2%	8.9%	2.3%	6.7%
Post-election	−0.6%	2.2%	0.7%	3.5%	6.2%	3.0%	4.7%
Midterm	1.0%	−2.4%	0.1%	7.8%	6.7%	−2.2%	15.4%
Pre-election	7.1%	4.9%	0.6%	3.2%	16.1%	5.5%	4.7%
Election	1.3%	1.8%	0.9%	1.9%	6.6%	2.8%	1.6%
NASDAQ Composite (1971-March 2016)							
Average	4.2%	3.1%	−0.1%	4.5%	12.5%	3.3%	8.9%
Post-election	−2.2%	6.6%	2.2%	4.8%	11.1%	8.7%	6.7%
Midterm	2.0%	−2.7%	−4.5%	8.6%	2.8%	−6.7%	22.0%
Pre-election	12.9%	7.5%	0.9%	5.4%	28.8%	8.5%	9.3%
Election	3.4%	0.8%	1.1%	−0.8%	5.8%	2.2%	−2.4%

MONDAY
6

D 76.2
S 76.2
N 66.7

Show me a good phone receptionist and I'll show you a good company.
— Harvey Mackay (*Pushing the Envelope*, 1999)

Election Day

TUESDAY
7

D 57.1
S 52.4
N 57.1

I have a love affair with America, because there are no built-in barriers to anyone in America. I come from a country where there were barriers upon barriers.
— Michael Caine (British actor, quoted in *Parade Magazine*, 2/16/03)

WEDNESDAY
8

D 47.6
S 42.9
N 52.4

Anyone who has achieved excellence knows that it comes as a result of ceaseless concentration.
— Louise Brooks (Actress, 1906–1985)

THURSDAY
9

D 47.6
S 42.9
N 42.9

For want of a nail, the shoe was lost. For want of a shoe, the horse was lost. For want of a horse, the rider was lost. For want of a rider, the battle was lost. For want of a battle, the kingdom was lost. And all for the want of a nail!
— English proverb

FRIDAY
10

D 42.9
S 42.9
N 52.4

Press on. Nothing in the world can take the place of persistence. Talent will not: nothing is more common than unrewarded talent. Education alone will not: the world is full of educated failures. Persistence alone is omnipotent.
— Calvin Coolidge (30th U.S. President, 1872–1933)

Veterans' Day

SATURDAY
11

SUNDAY
12

TRADING THE THANKSGIVING MARKET

For 35 years, the "holiday spirit" gave the Wednesday before Thanksgiving and the Friday after a great track record, except for two occasions. Publishing it in the 1987 *Almanac* was the kiss of death. Wednesday, Friday, and Monday were all crushed, down 6.6% over the three days in 1987. Since 1988, Wednesday–Friday gained 17 of 28 times, with a total Dow point gain of 685.58 versus Monday's total Dow point loss of 869.03, down 13 of 18 since 1998. The best strategy appears to be coming into the week long and exiting into strength Friday.

DOW JONES INDUSTRIALS BEFORE AND AFTER THANKSGIVING

	Tuesday Before	Wednesday Before		Friday After	Total Gain Dow Points	Dow Close	Next Monday
1952	-0.18	1.54		1.22	2.76	283.66	0.04
1953	1.71	0.65		2.45	3.10	280.23	1.14
1954	3.27	1.89		3.16	5.05	387.79	0.72
1955	4.61	0.71		0.26	0.97	482.88	-1.92
1956	-4.49	-2.16		4.65	2.49	472.56	-2.27
1957	-9.04	10.69		3.84	14.53	449.87	-2.96
1958	-4.37	8.63		8.31	16.94	557.46	2.61
1959	2.94	1.41		1.42	2.83	652.52	6.66
1960	-3.44	1.37		4.00	5.37	606.47	-1.04
1961	-0.77	1.10		2.18	3.28	732.60	-0.61
1962	6.73	4.31		7.62	11.93	644.87	-2.81
1963	32.03	-2.52		9.52	7.00	750.52	1.39
1964	-1.68	-5.21	T	-0.28	-5.49	882.12	-6.69
1965	2.56	N/C		-0.78	-0.78	948.16	-1.23
1966	-3.18	1.84	H	6.52	8.36	803.34	-2.18
1967	13.17	3.07		3.58	6.65	877.60	4.51
1968	8.14	-3.17	A	8.76	5.59	985.08	-1.74
1969	-5.61	3.23		1.78	5.01	812.30	-7.26
1970	5.21	1.98	N	6.64	8.62	781.35	12.74
1971	-5.18	0.66		17.96	18.62	816.59	13.14
1972	8.21	7.29	K	4.67	11.96	1025.21	-7.45
1973	-17.76	10.08		-0.98	9.10	854.00	-29.05
1974	5.32	2.03	S	-0.63	1.40	618.66	-15.64
1975	9.76	3.15		2.12	5.27	860.67	-4.33
1976	-6.57	1.66	G	5.66	7.32	956.62	-6.57
1977	6.41	0.78		1.12	1.90	844.42	-4.85
1978	-1.56	2.95	I	3.12	6.07	810.12	3.72
1979	-6.05	-1.80		4.35	2.55	811.77	16.98
1980	3.93	7.00	V	3.66	10.66	993.34	-23.89
1981	18.45	7.90		7.80	15.70	885.94	3.04
1982	-9.01	9.01	I	7.36	16.37	1007.36	-4.51
1983	7.01	-0.20		1.83	1.63	1277.44	-7.62
1984	9.83	6.40	N	18.78	25.18	1220.30	-7.95
1985	0.12	18.92		-3.56	15.36	1472.13	-14.22
1986	6.05	4.64	G	-2.53	2.11	1914.23	-1.55
1987	40.45	-16.58		-36.47	-53.05	1910.48	-76.93
1988	11.73	14.58		-17.60	-3.02	2074.68	6.76
1989	7.25	17.49		18.77	36.26	2675.55	19.42
1990	-35.15	9.16	G	-12.13	-2.97	2527.23	5.94
1991	14.08	-16.10		-5.36	-21.46	2894.68	40.70
1992	25.66	17.56		15.94	33.50	3282.20	22.96
1993	3.92	13.41		-3.63	9.78	3683.95	-6.15
1994	-91.52	-3.36		33.64	30.28	3708.27	31.29
1995	40.46	18.06		7.23*	25.29	5048.84	22.04
1996	-19.38	-29.07	D	22.36*	-6.71	6521.70	N/C
1997	41.03	-14.17		28.35*	14.18	7823.13	189.98
1998	-73.12	13.13	A	18.80*	31.93	9333.08	-216.53
1999	-93.89	12.54		-19.26*	-6.72	10988.91	-40.99
2000	31.85	-95.18	Y	70.91*	-24.27	10470.23	75.84
2001	-75.08	-66.70		125.03*	58.33	9959.71	23.04
2002	-172.98	255.26		-35.59*	219.67	8896.09	-33.52
2003	16.15	15.63		2.89*	18.52	9782.46	116.59
2004	3.18	27.71		1.92*	29.63	10522.23	-46.33
2005	51.15	44.66		15.53*	60.19	10931.62	-40.90
2006	5.05	5.36		-46.78*	-41.42	12280.17	-158.46
2007	51.70	-211.10		181.84*	-29.26	12980.88	-237.44
2008	36.08	247.14		102.43*	349.57	8829.04	-679.95
2009	-17.24	30.69		-154.48*	-123.79	10309.92	34.92
2010	-142.21	150.91		-95.28*	55.63	11092.00	-39.51
2011	-53.59	-236.17		-25.77*	-261.94	11231.78	291.23
2012	-7.45	48.38		172.79*	221.17	13009.68	-42.31
2013	0.26	24.53		-10.92*	13.61	16086.41	-77.64
2014	-2.96	-2.69		15.99*	13.30	17828.24	-51.44
2015	19.51	1.20		-14.90*	-13.70	17798.49	-78.57

*Shortened trading day

104

Monday Before November Expiration, Dow Up 8 of Last 12

MONDAY
D 66.7
S 57.1
N 61.9
13

A generation from now, Americans may marvel at the complacency that assumed the dollar's dominance would never end.
— Floyd Norris (Chief financial correspondent, *NY Times*, 2/2/07)

TUESDAY
D 57.1
S 57.1
N 52.4
14

In a bear market everyone loses. And the winner is the one who loses the least.
— Richard Russell (*Dow Theory Letters*)

Week Before Thanksgiving, Dow Up 18 of Last 23,
2003 –1.4%, 2004 –0.8%, 2008 –5.3%, 2011 –2.9%, 2012 –1.8%

WEDNESDAY
D 71.4
S 61.9
N 47.6
15

Regret for the things we did can be tempered by time; it is regret for the things we did not do that is inconsolable.
— Sydney J. Harris (American journalist and author, 1917–1986)

THURSDAY
D 47.6
S 47.6
N 52.4
16

If you create an act, you create a habit. If you create a habit, you create a character. If you create a character, you create a destiny.
— André Maurois (Novelist, biographer, essayist, 1885–1967)

November Expiration Day, Dow Up 12 of Last 14
Dow Surged in 2008, Up 494 Points (6.5%)

FRIDAY
D 52.4
S 57.1
N 52.4
17

Tell me and I'll forget; show me and I may remember; involve me and I'll understand.
— Confucius (Chinese philosopher, 551–478 BC)

SATURDAY
18

SUNDAY
19

MOST OF THE SO-CALLED "JANUARY EFFECT" TAKES PLACE IN THE LAST HALF OF DECEMBER

Over the years we have reported annually on the fascinating January Effect, showing that small-cap stocks handily outperformed large-cap stocks during January 40 out of 43 years between 1953 and 1995. Readers saw that "Cats and Dogs" on average quadrupled the returns of blue chips in this period. Then, the January Effect disappeared over the next four years.

Looking at the graph on page 110, comparing the Russell 1000 index of large-capitalization stocks to the Russell 2000 smaller-capitalization stocks, shows small-cap stocks beginning to outperform the blue chips in mid-December. Narrowing the comparison down to half-month segments was an inspiration and proved to be quite revealing, as you can see in the table below.

29-YEAR AVERAGE RATES OF RETURN (DEC 1987–FEB 2016)

From	Russell 1000		Russell 2000	
mid-Dec*	Change	Annualized	Change	Annualized
12/15–12/31	1.8%	50.5%	3.4%	115.1%
12/15–01/15	1.9	24.1	3.5	48.3
12/15–01/31	2.1	18.4	3.7	34.4
12/15–02/15	3.1	20.1	5.2	35.5
12/15–02/28	2.6	13.8	5.2	29.1
end-Dec*				
12/31–01/15	0.1	2.1	0.1	2.1
12/31–01/31	0.3	3.7	0.3	3.7
12/31–02/15	1.2	9.8	1.8	15.1
12/31–02/28	0.7	4.5	1.7	11.2

36-YEAR AVERAGE RATES OF RETURN (DEC 1979–FEB 2015)

From	Russell 1000		Russell 2000	
mid-Dec*	Change	Annualized	Change	Annualized
12/15–12/31	1.7%	47.1%	3.0%	96.8%
12/15–01/15	2.1	26.9	3.9	55.0
12/15–01/31	2.4	21.3	4.2	39.7
12/15–02/15	3.3	21.5	5.7	39.5
12/15–02/28	2.9	15.2	5.7	31.5
end-Dec*				
12/31–01/15	0.5	11.0	0.9	20.7
12/31–01/31	0.8	10.0	1.2	15.4
12/31–02/15	1.6	13.3	2.6	22.4
12/31–02/28	1.3	8.5	2.6	17.6

* Mid-month dates are the 11th trading day of the month; month end dates are monthly closes.

Small-cap strength in the last half of December became even more magnified after the 1987 market crash. Note the dramatic shift in gains in the last half of December during the 29-year period starting in 1987, versus the 37 years from 1979 to 2016. With all the beaten-down small stocks being dumped for tax-loss purposes, it generally pays to get a head start on the January Effect in mid-December. You don't have to wait until December either; the small-cap sector often begins to turn around toward the end of November.

MONDAY

D 52.4
S 52.4
N 57.1

20

You may not have started out life in the best of circumstances. But if you can find a mission in life worth working for and believe in yourself, nothing can stop you from achieving success.
— Kemmons Wilson (Holiday Inn founder)

Trading Thanksgiving Market: Long into Weakness Prior,
Exit into Strength After (Page 104)

TUESDAY

D 52.4
S 52.4
N 47.6

21

If you don't keep [your employees] happy, they're not going to keep the [customers] happy.
— David Longest (Red Lobster VP, *NY Times* 4/23/89)

WEDNESDAY

D 66.7
S 57.1
N 66.7

22

[The Fed] is very smart, but [it] doesn't run the markets. In the end, the markets will run [the Fed]. The markets are bigger than any man or any group of men. The markets can even break a president…
— Richard Russell (*Dow Theory Letters*, 8/4/04)

Thanksgiving *(Market Closed)*

THURSDAY

23

Never doubt that a small group of thoughtful, committed citizens can change the world: indeed it's the only thing that ever has.
— Margaret Mead (American anthropologist)

(Shortened Trading Day)

FRIDAY

D 61.9
S 57.1
N 61.9

24

The pursuit of gain is the only way in which people can serve the needs of others whom they do not know.
— Friedrich von Hayek (*Counterrevolution of Science*)

SATURDAY

25

December Almanac Investor Sector Seasonalities: See Pages 94, 96, and 98

SUNDAY

26

DECEMBER ALMANAC

DECEMBER							JANUARY						
S	M	T	W	T	F	S	S	M	T	W	T	F	S
31					1	2		1	2	3	4	5	6
3	4	5	6	7	8	9	7	8	9	10	11	12	13
10	11	12	13	14	15	16	14	15	16	17	18	19	20
17	18	19	20	21	22	23	21	22	23	24	25	26	27
24	25	26	27	28	29	30	28	29	30	31			

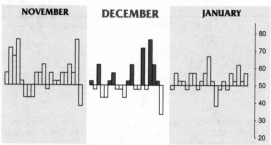

Market Probability Chart above is a graphic representation of the S&P 500 Recent Market Probability Calendar on page 124.

◆ #1 S&P (+1.6%) and #2 Dow (+1.6%) month since 1950 (page 50), #2 NASDAQ 1.9% since 1971 ◆ 2002 worst December since 1931, down over 6% Dow and S&P, –9.7% on NASDAQ (pages 152, 155, & 157) ◆ "Free lunch" served on Wall Street before Christmas (page 112) ◆ Small caps start to outperform larger caps near middle of month (pages 106 & 110) ◆ "Santa Claus Rally" visible in graph above and on page 114 ◆ In 1998 was part of best fourth quarter since 1928 (page 167) ◆ Fourth quarter expiration week most bullish triple witching week, Dow up 19 of last 25 (page 78) ◆ Post-presidential election year Decembers rankings: #5 Dow, #8 S&P, and #7 NASDAQ.

December Vital Statistics

	DJIA		S&P 500		NASDAQ		Russell 1K		Russell 2K	
Rank	2		1		2		3		1	
Up	46		49		26		28		29	
Down	20		17		19		9		8	
Average % Change	1.6%		1.6%		1.9%		1.5%		2.6%	
Post-Election Year	1.0%		0.5%		1.0%		1.3%		2.5%	
Best & Worst December										
	% Change		% Change		% Change		% Change		% Change	
Best	1991	9.5	1991	11.2	1999	22.0	1991	11.2	1999	11.2
Worst	2002	–6.2	2002	–6.0	2002	–9.7	2002	–5.8	2002	–5.7
Best & Worst December Weeks										
Best	12/02/11	7.0	12/02/11	7.4	12/08/00	10.3	12/02/11	7.4	12/02/11	10.3
Worst	12/04/87	–7.5	12/06/74	–7.1	12/15/00	–9.1	12/04/87	–7.0	12/12/80	–6.5
Best & Worst December Days										
Best	12/16/08	4.2	12/16/08	5.1	12/05/00	10.5	12/16/08	5.2	12/16/08	6.7
Worst	12/01/08	–7.7	12/01/08	–8.9	12/01/08	–9.0	12/01/08	–9.1	12/01/08	–11.9
First Trading Day of Expiration Week: 1980–2015										
Record (#Up – #Down)	21–15		22–14		16–20		22–14		16–20	
Current streak	U1		U1		U1		U1		D2	
Avg % Change	0.18		0.14		–0.05		0.10		–0.17	
Options Expiration Day: 1980–2015										
Record (#Up – #Down)	23–13		26–10		25–11		26–10		23–13	
Current streak	D1		D1		D1		D1		D1	
Avg % Change	0.26		0.33		0.31		0.32		0.41	
Options Expiration Week: 1980–2015										
Record (#Up – #Down)	27–9		26–10		21–15		25–11		19–17	
Current streak	D1		D1		D1		D1		D1	
Avg % Change	0.74		0.77		0.28		0.72		0.68	
Week After Options Expiration: 1980–2015										
Record (#Up – #Down)	25–10		22–14		23–13		22–14		25–11	
Current streak	U3		U3		U3		U3		U3	
Avg % Change	0.80		0.54		0.70		0.57		0.88	
First Trading Day Performance										
% of Time Up	47.0		50.0		60.0		51.4		51.4	
Avg % Change	–0.05		–0.03		0.13		–0.04		–0.14	
Last Trading Day Performance										
% of Time Up	53.0		60.6		71.1		51.4		67.6	
Avg % Change	0.06		0.09		0.32		–0.08		0.41	

Dow & S&P 1950–April 2016, NASDAQ 1971–April 2016, Russell 1K & 2K 1979–April 2016.

If Santa Claus should fail to call,
Bears may come to Broad and Wall.

NOVEMBER/DECEMBER 2017

MONDAY
D 66.7
S 61.9
N 57.1
27

If I owe a million dollars I am lost. But if I owe $50 billion the bankers are lost.
— Celso Ming (Brazilian journalist)

TUESDAY
D 61.9
S 57.1
N 61.9
28

One thing John Chambers (Cisco CEO) does well is stretch people's responsibilities and change the boxes they are in. It makes our jobs new all the time.
— Mike Volpi (Senior VP of business development and alliances at Cisco, Fortune)

WEDNESDAY
D 57.1
S 76.2
N 71.4
29

To know values is to know the meaning of the market.
— Charles Dow (Co-founder Dow Jones & Co, 1851–1902)

Last Trading Day of November, S&P Up 6 of Last 10

THURSDAY
D 47.6
S 38.1
N 47.6
30

Live beyond your means; then you're forced to work hard, you have to succeed.
— Edward G. Robinson (American actor)

First Trading Day in December, NASDAQ Up 20 of 29, Down 6 of Last 10

FRIDAY
D 47.6
S 52.4
N 61.9
1

Great spirits have always encountered violent opposition from mediocre minds.
— Albert Einstein (German/American physicist, 1921 Nobel Prize, 1879–1955)

SATURDAY
2

SUNDAY
3

JANUARY EFFECT NOW STARTS IN MID-DECEMBER

Small-cap stocks tend to outperform big caps in January. Known as the "January Effect," the tendency is clearly revealed by the graph below. Thirty-six years of daily data for the Russell 2000 index of smaller companies are divided by the Russell 1000 index of largest companies, and then compressed into a single year to show an idealized yearly pattern. When the graph is descending, big blue chips are outperforming smaller companies; when the graph is rising, smaller companies are moving up faster than their larger brethren.

In a typical year, the smaller fry stay on the sidelines while the big boys are on the field. Then, around late November, small stocks begin to wake up, and in mid-December they take off. Anticipated year-end dividends, payouts, and bonuses could be a factor. Other major moves are quite evident just before Labor Day—possibly because individual investors are back from vacations. Small caps hold the lead through the beginning of June, though the bulk of the move is complete by early March.

RUSSELL 2000/RUSSELL 1000 ONE-YEAR SEASONAL PATTERN

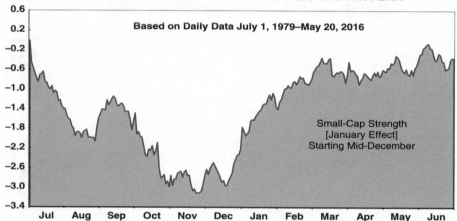

The bottom graph shows the actual ratio of the Russell 2000 divided by the Russell 1000 from 1979. Smaller companies had the upper hand for five years into 1983, as the last major bear trend wound to a close and the nascent bull market logged its first year. After falling behind for about eight years, they came back after the Persian Gulf War bottom in 1990, moving up until 1994, when big caps ruled the latter stages of the millennial bull. For six years, the picture was bleak for small fry, as the blue chips and tech stocks moved to stratospheric PE ratios. Small caps spiked in late 1999 and early 2000 and reached a peak in early 2006, as the four-year-old bull entered its final year. Note how the small-cap advantage has waned during major bull moves and intensified during weak market times.

RUSSELL 2000/RUSSELL 1000 (1979–APRIL 2016)

MONDAY

D 42.9
S 47.6
N 57.1

4

Mankind is divided into three classes: Those that are immovable, those that are movable, and those that move.
— Arabian proverb (also attributed to Benjamin Franklin)

TUESDAY

D 66.7
S 61.9
N 57.1

5

The only way to even begin to manage this new world is by focusing on...nation building—helping others restructure their economies and put in place decent non-corrupt government.
— Thomas L. Friedman (*NY Times* Foreign Affairs columnist)

Small Cap Strength Starts in Mid-December (Page 106)

WEDNESDAY

D 52.4
S 42.9
N 57.1

6

You don't learn to hold your own in the world by standing on guard, but by attacking and getting well hammered yourself.
— George Bernard Shaw (Irish dramatist, 1856–1950)

THURSDAY

D 47.6
S 42.9
N 38.1

7

The usual bull market successfully weathers a number of tests until it is considered invulnerable, whereupon it is ripe for a bust.
— George Soros (Financier, philanthropist, political activist, author, and philosopher, b. 1930)

FRIDAY

D 47.6
S 52.4
N 57.1

8

If the winds of fortune are temporarily blowing against you, remember that you can harness them and make them carry you toward your definite purpose, through the use of your imagination.
— Napoleon Hill (Author, *Think and Grow Rich*, 1883–1970)

SATURDAY

9

SUNDAY

10

WALL STREET'S ONLY "FREE LUNCH"
SERVED BEFORE CHRISTMAS

Investors tend to get rid of their losers near year-end for tax purposes, often hammering these stocks down to bargain levels. Over the years, the *Almanac* has shown that NYSE stocks selling at their lows on December 15 will usually outperform the market by February 15 in the following year. Preferred stocks, closed-end funds, splits, and new issues are eliminated. When there are a huge number of new lows, stocks down the most are selected, even though there are usually good reasons why some stocks have been battered.

BARGAIN STOCKS VS. THE MARKET*

Short Span* Late Dec–Jan/Feb	New Lows Late Dec	% Change Jan/Feb	% Change NYSE Composite	Bargain Stocks Advantage
1974–75	112	48.9%	22.1%	26.8%
1975–76	21	34.9	14.9	20.0
1976–77	2	1.3	−3.3	4.6
1977–78	15	2.8	−4.5	7.3
1978–79	43	11.8	3.9	7.9
1979–80	5	9.3	6.1	3.2
1980–81	14	7.1	−2.0	9.1
1981–82	21	−2.6	−7.4	4.8
1982–83	4	33.0	9.7	23.3
1983–84	13	−3.2	−3.8	0.6
1984–85	32	19.0	12.1	6.9
1985–86	4	−22.5	3.9	−26.4
1986–87	22	9.3	12.5	−3.2
1987–88	23	13.2	6.8	6.4
1988–89	14	30.0	6.4	23.6
1989–90	25	−3.1	−4.8	1.7
1990–91	18	18.8	12.6	6.2
1991–92	23	51.1	7.7	43.4
1992–93	9	8.7	0.6	8.1
1993–94	10	−1.4	2.0	−3.4
1994–95	25	14.6	5.7	8.9
1995–96	5	−11.3	4.5	−15.8
1996–97	16	13.9	11.2	2.7
1997–98	29	9.9	5.7	4.2
1998–99	40	−2.8	4.3	−7.1
1999–00	26	8.9	−5.4	14.3
2000–01	51	44.4	0.1	44.3
2001–02	12	31.4	−2.3	33.7
2002–03	33	28.7	3.9	24.8
2003–04	15	16.7	2.3	14.4
2004–05	36	6.8	−2.8	9.6
2005–06	71	12.0	2.6	9.4
2006–07	43	5.1	−0.5	5.6
2007–08	71	−3.2	−9.4	6.2
2008–09	88	11.4	−2.4	13.8
2009–10	25	1.8	−3.0	4.8
2010–11	20	8.3	3.4	4.9
2011–12	65	18.1	6.1	12.0
2012–13	17	20.9	3.4	17.5
2013–14	18	25.7	1.7	24.0
2014–15	17	0.2%	−0.4%	0.6%
2015–16	38	−9.2%	5.6%	−14.8%
42–Year Totals		**518.7%**	**129.8%**	**388.9%**
Average		**12.4%**	**3.1%**	**9.3%**

* Dec 15–Feb 15 (1974–1999), Dec 1999–2016 based on actual newsletter portfolio.

In response to changing market conditions, we tweaked the strategy the last 17 years, adding selections from NASDAQ and AMEX, and selling in mid-January some years. We e-mail the list of stocks to our *Almanac Investor eNewsletter* subscribers. Visit *www.stocktradersalmanac.com,* or see the ad insert for additional details and a special offer for new subscribers.

We have come to the conclusion that the most prudent course of action is to compile our list from the stocks making new lows on Triple-Witching Friday before Christmas, capitalizing on the Santa Claus Rally (page 114). This also gives us the weekend to evaluate the issues in greater depth and weed out any glaringly problematic stocks. Subscribers will receive the list of stocks selected from the new lows made on December 16, 2016 and December 15, 2017, via e-mail.

This "Free Lunch" strategy is an extremely short-term strategy reserved for the nimblest traders. It has performed better after market corrections and when there are more new lows to choose from. The object is to buy bargain stocks near their 52-week lows and sell any quick, generous gains, as these issues can often be real dogs.

Monday Before December Triple Witching S&P Up 11 of Last 16

MONDAY

D 52.4
S 57.1
N 61.9

11

I was in search of a one-armed economist so that the guy could never make a statement and then say: "on the other hand."
— Harry S. Truman (33rd U.S. President, 1884–1972)

TUESDAY

D 42.9
S 47.6
N 42.9

12

One determined person can make a significant difference; a small group of determined people can change the course of history.
— Sonia Johnson (author, lecturer)

Chanukah
December Triple Witching Week, S&P Up 25 of Last 32

WEDNESDAY

D 47.6
S 47.6
N 42.9

13

Moses Shapiro (of General Instrument) told me, "Son, this is Talmudic wisdom. Always ask the question 'If not?' Few people have good strategies for when their assumptions are wrong." That's the best business advice I ever got.
— John Malone (CEO of cable giant TCI, Fortune 2/16/98)

THURSDAY

D 52.4
S 42.9
N 42.9

14

I believe in the exceptional man—the entrepreneur who is always out of money, not the bureaucrat who generates cash flow and pays dividends.
— Armand Erpf (Investment banker, partner Loeb Rhoades, 1897–1971)

December Triple Witching, S&P Up 24 of 34, Average Gain 0.3%

FRIDAY

D 52.4
S 52.4
N 47.6

15

The worst crime against working people is a company that fails to make a profit.
— Samuel Gompers

SATURDAY

16

SUNDAY

17

IF SANTA CLAUS SHOULD FAIL TO CALL, BEARS MAY COME TO BROAD AND WALL

Santa Claus tends to come to Wall Street nearly every year, bringing a short, sweet, respectable rally within the last five days of the year and the first two in January. This has been good for an average 1.4% gain since 1969 (1.4% since 1950 as well). Santa's failure to show tends to precede bear markets, or times stocks could be purchased later in the year at much lower prices. We discovered this phenomenon in 1972.

DAILY % CHANGE IN S&P 500 AT YEAR END

	Trading Days Before Year End						First Days in January			Rally %
	6	5	4	3	2	1	1	2	3	Change
1969	−0.4	1.1	0.8	−0.7	0.4	0.5	1.0	0.5	−0.7	3.6
1970	0.1	0.6	0.5	1.1	0.2	−0.1	−1.1	0.7	0.6	1.9
1971	−0.4	0.2	1.0	0.3	−0.4	0.3	−0.4	0.4	1.0	1.3
1972	−0.3	−0.7	0.6	0.4	0.5	1.0	0.9	0.4	−0.1	3.1
1973	−1.1	−0.7	3.1	2.1	−0.2	0.01	0.1	2.2	−0.9	6.7
1974	−1.4	1.4	0.8	−0.4	0.03	2.1	2.4	0.7	0.5	7.2
1975	0.7	0.8	0.9	−0.1	−0.4	0.5	0.8	1.8	1.0	4.3
1976	0.1	1.2	0.7	−0.4	0.5	0.5	−0.4	−1.2	−0.9	0.8
1977	0.8	0.9	N/C	0.1	0.2	0.2	−1.3	−0.3	−0.8	−0.3
1978	0.03	1.7	1.3	−0.9	−0.4	−0.2	0.6	1.1	0.8	3.3
1979	−0.6	0.1	0.1	0.2	−0.1	0.1	−2.0	−0.5	1.2	−2.2
1980	−0.4	0.4	0.5	−1.1	0.2	0.3	0.4	1.2	0.1	2.0
1981	−0.5	0.2	−0.2	−0.5	0.5	0.2	0.2	−2.2	−0.7	−1.8
1982	0.6	1.8	−1.0	0.3	−0.7	0.2	−1.6	2.2	0.4	1.2
1983	−0.2	−0.03	0.9	0.3	−0.2	0.05	−0.5	1.7	1.2	2.1
1984	−0.5	0.8	−0.2	−0.4	0.3	0.6	−1.1	−0.5	−0.5	−0.6
1985	−1.1	−0.7	0.2	0.9	0.5	0.3	−0.8	0.6	−0.1	1.1
1986	−1.0	0.2	0.1	−0.9	−0.5	−0.5	1.8	2.3	0.2	2.4
1987	1.3	−0.5	−2.6	−0.4	1.3	−0.3	3.6	1.1	0.1	2.2
1988	−0.2	0.3	−0.4	0.1	0.8	−0.6	−0.9	1.5	0.2	0.9
1989	0.6	0.8	−0.2	0.6	0.5	0.8	1.8	−0.3	−0.9	4.1
1990	0.5	−0.6	0.3	−0.8	0.1	0.5	−1.1	−1.4	−0.3	−3.0
1991	2.5	0.6	1.4	0.4	2.1	0.5	0.04	0.5	−0.3	5.7
1992	−0.3	0.2	−0.1	−0.3	0.2	−0.7	−0.1	−0.2	0.04	−1.1
1993	0.01	0.7	0.1	−0.1	−0.4	−0.5	−0.2	0.3	0.1	−0.1
1994	0.01	0.2	0.4	−0.3	0.1	−0.4	−0.03	0.3	−0.1	0.2
1995	0.8	0.2	0.4	0.04	−0.1	0.3	0.8	0.1	−0.6	1.8
1996	−0.3	0.5	0.6	0.1	−0.4	−1.7	−0.5	1.5	−0.1	0.1
1997	−1.5	−0.7	0.4	1.8	1.8	−0.04	0.5	0.2	−1.1	4.0
1998	2.1	−0.2	−0.1	1.3	−0.8	−0.2	−0.1	1.4	2.2	1.3
1999	1.6	−0.1	0.04	0.4	0.1	0.3	−1.0	−3.8	0.2	−4.0
2000	0.8	2.4	0.7	1.0	0.4	−1.0	−2.8	5.0	−1.1	5.7
2001	0.4	−0.02	0.4	0.7	0.3	−1.1	0.6	0.9	0.6	1.8
2002	0.2	−0.5	−0.3	−1.6	0.5	0.05	3.3	−0.05	2.2	1.2
2003	0.3	−0.2	0.2	1.2	0.01	0.2	−0.3	1.2	0.1	2.4
2004	0.1	−0.4	0.7	−0.01	0.01	−0.1	−0.8	−1.2	−0.4	−1.8
2005	0.4	0.04	−1.0	0.1	−0.3	−0.5	1.6	0.4	0.002	0.4
2006	−0.4	−0.5	0.4	0.7	−0.1	−0.5	−0.1	0.1	−0.6	0.003
2007	1.7	0.8	0.1	−1.4	0.1	−0.7	−1.4	N/C	−2.5	−2.5
2008	−1.0	0.6	0.5	−0.4	2.4	1.4	3.2	−0.5	0.8	7.4
2009	0.2	0.5	0.1	−0.1	0.02	−1.0	1.6	0.3	0.05	1.4
2010	−0.2	0.1	0.1	0.1	−0.2	−0.02	1.1	−0.1	0.5	1.1
2011	0.8	0.9	0.01	−1.3	1.1	−0.4	1.6	0.02	0.3	1.9
2012	−0.9	−0.2	−0.5	−0.1	−1.1	1.7	2.5	−0.2	0.5	2.0
2013	0.5	0.3	0.5	−0.03	−0.02	0.4	−0.9	−0.03	−0.3	0.2
2014	0.2	−0.01	0.3	0.1	−0.5	−1.0	−0.03	−1.8	−0.9	−3.0
2015	1.2	−0.2	−0.2	1.1	−0.7	−0.9	−1.5	0.2	−1.3	−2.3
Avg	0.13	0.30	0.26	0.07	0.16	0.01	0.20	0.35	−0.01	1.4

The couplet above was certainly on the mark in 1999, as the period suffered a horrendous 4.0% loss. On January 14, 2000, the Dow started its 33-month 37.8% slide to the October 2002 midterm election year bottom. NASDAQ cracked eight weeks later, falling 37.3% in 10 weeks, eventually dropping 77.9% by October 2002. Saddam Hussein canceled Christmas by invading Kuwait in 1990. Energy prices and Middle East terror woes may have grounded Santa in 2004. In 2007, the third worst reading since 1950 was recorded, as a full-blown financial crisis led to the second worst bear market in history. In 2016, the period was hit again as global growth concerns escalated and the market digested the first interest rate hike in nearly a decade.

The Only FREE LUNCH on Wall Street is Served (Page 112)
Almanac Investors E-mailed Alert Before the Open, Monday (See Insert)

MONDAY
D 57.1
S 61.9
N 57.1
18

Bankruptcy was designed to forgive stupidity, not reward criminality.
— William P. Barr (Verizon general counsel, calling for government liquidation of MCI-WorldCom in Chapter 7 bankruptcy, 4/14/2003)

TUESDAY
D 42.9
S 47.6
N 38.1
19

The heights by great men reached and kept, were not attained by sudden flight, but they, while their companions slept, were toiling upward in the night.
— Henry Wadsworth Longfellow

WEDNESDAY
D 47.6
S 47.6
N 47.6
20

The fear of capitalism has compelled socialism to widen freedom, and the fear of socialism has compelled capitalism to increase equality.
— Will and Ariel Durant

Watch for the Santa Claus Rally (Page 114)

THURSDAY
D 76.2
S 71.4
N 66.7
21

Only those who will risk going too far can possibly find out how far one can go.
— T.S. Eliot (English poet, essayist, and critic, *The Wasteland*, 1888–1965)

Last Trading Day Before Christmas, Dow Up 7 of Last 9 Years

FRIDAY
D 47.6
S 47.6
N 61.9
22

Almost any insider purchase is worth investigating for a possible lead to a superior speculation. But very few insider sales justify concern.
— William Chidester (*Scientific Investing*)

SATURDAY
23

SUNDAY
24

YEAR'S TOP INVESTMENT BOOKS

Juggling with Knives: Smart Investing in the Coming Age of Volatility, Jim Jubak, PublicAffairs, $28.99. <u>2017 Best Investment Book of the Year. See page 76.</u>

The Seven Pillars of Statistical Wisdom, Stephen M. Stigler, Harvard University Press, $22.95. Our old friend Victor Niederhoffer says, "Stigler provides an illuminating and entertaining foundation for statistical activity....Every page contains something fascinating and instructive. It is at once an adventure story, a history lesson, a textbook on the foundations of statistics, and a tour de force with ingenious extensions of the works of the greats in each field in Stigler's own inimitable hand....The layman and the expert will both gain from it."

Winning with Commercial Real Estate: Today's Best Low-Risk, High-Return Investment, Harmel S. Rayat, CreateSpace (self-published), $19.95. Jeff had the pleasure of introducing Harmel as MC of The MoneyShow Las Vegas Investment Masters Symposium. Folks truly enjoyed his presentation and his book moves in the same lively, clear manner as it lays out his six-step proprietary TROPHY formula: Timing, Risk, Operating Costs, Pay Careful Attention, High Occupancy Rate, and Yield. Rayat's Talia Jevan Properties generated 33% annualized equity growth in-house 2006–2015.

The Next Perfect Trade: A Magic Sword of Necessity, Alex Gurevich, eBookIt.com (self-published), $24.95. Alex came to us for help finding a publisher. While he was a star prop trader, he was not well known, so we advised he self-publish. Years on The Street taught Alex that what drives the market is less important than what drives successful trades. *The Next Perfect Trade* reveals his set of principles and his approach that has produced profits in all market climates.

Chart Patterns: After the Buy, Thomas N. Bulkowski, Wiley, $60.00. Prolific and astute, Mr. Bulkowski has outdone himself. His *Trading Classic Chart Patterns* was our 2003 Best Book. His *Encyclopedia of Chart Patterns* is invaluable! This latest masterpiece, *Chart Patterns: After the Buy*, tackles the toughest trading issue of all: What to do after you take a position. Buy and sell setups, price targets, common and lesser-known patterns. For both newbies and pros.

Technical Analysis and Chart Interpretations: A Comprehensive Guide to Understanding Established Trading Tactics for Ultimate Profit, Ed Ponsi, Wiley, $90.00. Ed Ponsi's years of experience trading and managing money, advising, analyzing, teaching, training, and consulting institutions and individuals alike come alive. He runs the gamut of TA and covers it all, including our favorite chapter, "Combining Technical and Fundamental Analysis."

Elliot Wave Techniques Simplified: How to Use the Probability Matrix to Profit on More Trades, Bennett A. McDowell, McGraw-Hill Education, $70.00. Our buddy Larry McMillan, the Option Strategist, says, "Ben McDowell does an excellent job of explaining a complicated subject," adding "a new dimension to the analysis with his Probability Matrix— taking some of the vagueness out of the analysis." As promised in the title, Elliott Wave analysis really is simplified in this book.

Bitcoin For Dummies, Prypto, For Dummies, $19.99. Everything you always wanted to know about Bitcoin, cryptocurrencies, and blockchain technology. The future of financial, banking, and monetary transactions may hang somewhere in the balance here. Authored by the outfit Prypto, which helps folks use Bitcoin and other cryptocurrencies.

The Industries of the Future, Alec Ross, Simon & Schuster, $28.00. Technology innovation thought leader Alec Ross, who traveled the planet at the behest of the State Department and the White House, imparts his observations and expectations of the fields that will shape our next *Super Boom*! Ross touches on two of our favs, robotics and genomics, but he omits one of our fancies: energy tech/personal power generation.

The Fourth Industrial Revolution, Klaus Schwab, World Economic Forum, $9.99. Professor Klaus Schwab, founder and executive chairman of the World Economic Forum, has been leading technology innovation from the front for over 45 years. We are clearly in the midst of the most profound technological revolution in human history. After a lively tour of The Fourth Industrial Revolution to date, Schwab discusses the state of affairs of 23 potential paradigm-shifting technologies.

Christmas Day *(Market Closed)*

Keep me away from the wisdom which does not cry, the philosophy which does not laugh and the greatness which does not bow before children.
— Kahlil Gibran (Lebanese-born American mystic, poet, and artist, 1883–1931)

TUESDAY

D 76.2
S 76.2
N 66.7
26

It's not that I am so smart; it's just that I stay with problems longer.
— Albert Einstein (German/American physicist, 1921 Nobel Prize, 1879–1955)

WEDNESDAY

D 52.4
S 61.9
N 52.4
27

The big guys are the status quo, not the innovators.
— Kenneth L. Fisher (*Forbes* columnist)

THURSDAY

D 42.9
S 52.4
N 38.1
28

There have been three great inventions since the beginning of time: Fire, the wheel, and central banking.
— Will Rogers (American humorist and showman, 1879–1935)

Last Trading Day of the Year, NASDAQ Down 14 of Last 16
NASDAQ Was Up 29 Years in a Row 1971–1999

FRIDAY

D 38.1
S 33.3
N 38.1
29

There is always plenty of capital for those who can create practical plans for using it.
— Napoleon Hill (Author, *Think and Grow Rich*, 1883–1970)

SATURDAY
30

January Almanac Investor Sector Seasonalities: See Pages 94, 96, and 98

SUNDAY
31

2018 STRATEGY CALENDAR

(Option expiration dates circled)

	MONDAY	TUESDAY	WEDNESDAY	THURSDAY	FRIDAY	SATURDAY	SUNDAY
JANUARY	1 JANUARY New Year's Day	2	3	4	5	6	7
	8	9	10	11	12	13	14
	15 Martin Luther King Day	16	17	18	(19)	20	21
	22	23	24	25	26	27	28
FEBRUARY	29	30	31	1 FEBRUARY	2	3	4
	5	6	7	8	9	10	11
	12	13	14 ♥ Ash Wednesday	15	(16)	17	18
	19 President's Day	20	21	22	23	24	25
MARCH	26	27	28	1 MARCH	2	3	4
	5	6	7	8	9	10	11 Daylight Saving Time Begins
	12	13	14	15	(16)	17 ♣ St. Patrick's Day	18
	19	20	21	22	23	24	25
APRIL	26	27	28	29	30 Good Friday	31 Passover	1 APRIL Easter
	2	3	4	5	6	7	8
	9	10	11	12	13	14	15
	16	17	18	19	(20)	21	22
MAY	23	24	25	26	27	28	29
	30	1 MAY	2	3	4	5	6
	7	8	9	10	11	12	13 Mother's Day
	14	15	16	17	(18)	19	20
JUNE	21	22	23	24	25	26	27
	28 Memorial Day	29	30	31	1 JUNE	2	3
	4	5	6	7	8	9	10
	11	12	13	14	(15)	16	17 Father's Day
	18	19	20	21	22	23	24
	25	26	27	28	29	30	1 JULY

Market closed on shaded weekdays; closes early when half-shaded.

2018 STRATEGY CALENDAR

(Option expiration dates circled)

MONDAY	TUESDAY	WEDNESDAY	THURSDAY	FRIDAY	SATURDAY	SUNDAY	
2	3	4 Independence Day	5	6	7	8	**JULY**
9	10	11	12	13	14	15	
16	17	18	19	(20)	21	22	
23	24	25	26	27	28	29	
30	31	1 AUGUST	2	3	4	5	
6	7	8	9	10	11	12	**AUGUST**
13	14	15	16	(17)	18	19	
20	21	22	23	24	25	26	
27	28	29	30	31	1 SEPTEMBER	2	
3 Labor Day	4	5	6	7	8	9	**SEPTEMBER**
10 Rosh Hashanah	11	12	13	14	15	16	
17	18	19 Yom Kippur	20	(21)	22	23	
24	25	26	27	28	29	30	
1 OCTOBER	2	3	4	5	6	7	**OCTOBER**
8 Columbus Day	9	10	11	12	13	14	
15	16	17	18	(19)	20	21	
22	23	24	25	26	27	28	
29	30	31	1 NOVEMBER	2	3	4 Daylight Saving Time Ends	**NOVEMBER**
5	6 Election Day	7	8	9	10	11 Veterans' Day	
12	13	14	15	(16)	17	18	
19	20	21	22 Thanksgiving Day	23	24	25	
26	27	28	29	30	1 DECEMBER	2	
3 Chanukah	4	5	6	7	8	9	**DECEMBER**
10	11	12	13	14	15	16	
17	18	19	20	(21)	22	23	
24	25 Christmas	26	27	28	29	30	
31	1 JANUARY New Year's Day	2	3	4	5	6	

DIRECTORY OF TRADING PATTERNS AND DATABANK

CONTENTS

DOW JONES INDUSTRIALS MARKET PROBABILITY CALENDAR 2017

THE % CHANCE OF THE MARKET RISING ON ANY TRADING DAY OF THE YEAR*
(Based on the number of times the DJIA rose on a particular trading day during January 1953–December 2015.)

Date	Jan	Feb	Mar	Apr	May	Jun	Jul	Aug	Sep	Oct	Nov	Dec
1	S	60.3	65.1	S	57.1	57.1	S	44.4	57.1	S	61.9	44.4
2	H	55.6	63.5	S	65.1	50.8	S	46.0	S	47.6	54.0	S
3	58.7	39.7	57.1	60.3	49.2	S	65.1	47.6	S	57.1	66.7	S
4	71.4	S	S	60.3	46.0	S	H	50.8	H	52.4	S	52.4
5	47.6	S	S	52.4	46.0	52.4	58.7	S	60.3	61.9	S	63.5
6	55.6	55.6	50.8	57.1	S	57.1	60.3	S	58.7	46.0	58.7	57.1
7	S	47.6	47.6	52.4	S	52.4	57.1	52.4	46.0	S	47.6	47.6
8	S	42.9	55.6	S	54.0	44.4	S	47.6	49.2	S	58.7	44.4
9	46.0	47.6	58.7	S	49.2	36.5	S	46.0	S	52.4	54.0	S
10	47.6	58.7	54.0	58.7	52.4	S	61.9	47.6	S	44.4	57.1	S
11	46.0	S	S	63.5	44.4	S	57.1	47.6	44.4	39.7	S	52.4
12	49.2	S	S	61.9	54.0	55.6	49.2	S	58.7	52.4	S	55.6
13	57.1	47.6	55.6	55.6	S	60.3	42.9	S	58.7	58.7	47.6	44.4
14	S	49.2	52.4	H	S	58.7	65.1	63.5	46.0	S	47.6	52.4
15	S	54.0	60.3	S	54.0	50.8	S	55.6	55.6	S	58.7	47.6
16	H	39.7	60.3	S	44.4	49.2	S	50.8	S	52.4	52.4	S
17	57.1	49.2	58.7	71.4	54.0	S	49.2	47.6	S	52.4	49.2	S
18	58.7	S	S	63.5	42.9	S	47.6	54.0	57.1	44.4	S	57.1
19	41.3	S	S	55.6	50.8	52.4	50.8	S	41.3	60.3	S	47.6
20	38.1	H	52.4	55.6	S	46.0	54.0	S	49.2	46.0	49.2	55.6
21	S	50.8	42.9	54.0	S	49.2	39.7	41.3	46.0	S	57.1	52.4
22	S	38.1	41.3	S	41.3	47.6	S	58.7	38.1	S	66.7	60.3
23	41.3	44.4	49.2	S	34.9	42.9	S	49.2	S	44.4	H	S
24	46.0	60.3	38.1	52.4	50.8	S	44.4	52.4	S	50.8	57.1	S
25	57.1	S	S	57.1	44.4	S	58.7	47.6	50.8	28.6	S	H
26	57.1	S	S	57.1	46.0	34.9	54.0	S	54.0	52.4	S	69.8
27	50.8	47.6	49.2	50.8	S	49.2	46.0	S	52.4	55.6	65.1	47.6
28	S	50.8	42.9	50.8	S	47.6	58.7	46.0	49.2	S	60.3	55.6
29	S		55.6	S	H	54.0	S	60.3	38.1	S	52.4	54.0
30	58.7		44.4	S	55.6	52.4	S	41.3	S	60.3	52.4	S
31	57.1		42.9		58.7		49.2	60.3		52.4		S

See new trends developing on pages 70, 92, 141–146.

RECENT DOW JONES INDUSTRIALS MARKET PROBABILITY CALENDAR 2017

THE % CHANCE OF THE MARKET RISING ON ANY TRADING DAY OF THE YEAR*
(Based on the number of times the DJIA rose on a particular trading day during January 1995–December 2015.**)

Date	Jan	Feb	Mar	Apr	May	Jun	Jul	Aug	Sep	Oct	Nov	Dec
1	S	76.2	61.9	S	66.7	66.7	S	33.3	57.1	S	57.1	47.6
2	H	47.6	42.9	S	66.7	47.6	S	57.1	S	47.6	61.9	S
3	66.7	47.6	57.1	76.2	33.3	S	81.0	47.6	S	52.4	66.7	S
4	66.7	S	S	71.4	33.3	S	H	52.4	H	52.4	S	42.9
5	47.6	S	S	42.9	47.6	52.4	38.1	S	71.4	71.4	S	66.7
6	52.4	57.1	47.6	61.9	S	57.1	52.4	S	52.4	38.1	76.2	52.4
7	S	52.4	61.9	42.9	S	61.9	57.1	52.4	42.9	S	57.1	47.6
8	S	47.6	52.4	S	71.4	52.4	S	47.6	66.7	S	47.6	47.6
9	38.1	57.1	57.1	S	52.4	33.3	S	42.9	S	38.1	47.6	S
10	47.6	57.1	61.9	52.4	71.4	S	57.1	42.9	S	47.6	42.9	S
11	47.6	S	S	57.1	42.9	S	52.4	38.1	52.4	42.9	S	52.4
12	57.1	S	S	61.9	57.1	47.6	57.1	S	66.7	47.6	S	42.9
13	52.4	66.7	52.4	52.4	S	57.1	66.7	S	61.9	71.4	66.7	47.6
14	S	47.6	61.9	H	S	66.7	61.9	66.7	52.4	S	57.1	52.4
15	S	66.7	66.7	S	57.1	61.9	S	47.6	52.4	S	71.4	52.4
16	H	42.9	52.4	S	47.6	57.1	S	57.1	S	47.6	47.6	S
17	57.1	38.1	66.7	71.4	57.1	S	47.6	66.7	S	57.1	52.4	S
18	52.4	S	S	66.7	38.1	S	57.1	42.9	71.4	47.6	S	57.1
19	42.9	S	S	61.9	52.4	61.9	52.4	S	38.1	66.7	S	42.9
20	33.3	H	57.1	57.1	S	52.4	71.4	S	57.1	38.1	52.4	47.6
21	S	52.4	33.3	66.7	S	38.1	19.0	33.3	52.4	S	52.4	76.2
22	S	52.4	47.6	S	28.6	42.9	S	61.9	28.6	S	66.7	47.6
23	33.3	38.1	42.9	S	42.9	38.1	S	47.6	S	57.1	H	S
24	33.3	47.6	42.9	47.6	47.6	S	42.9	52.4	S	52.4	61.9	S
25	61.9	S	S	52.4	47.6	S	61.9	47.6	38.1	38.1	S	H
26	57.1	S	S	66.7	47.6	33.3	52.4	S	52.4	57.1	S	76.2
27	57.1	47.6	61.9	71.4	S	42.9	42.9	S	57.1	66.7	66.7	52.4
28	S	42.9	23.8	38.1	S	57.1	42.9	42.9	61.9	S	61.9	42.9
29	S		52.4	S	H	52.4	S	71.4	33.3	S	57.1	38.1
30	47.6		57.1	S	61.9	38.1	S	23.8	S	61.9	47.6	S
31	52.4		38.1		47.6		33.3	52.4		57.1		S

* See new trends developing on pages 70, 92, 141–146. ** Based on most recent 21-year period.

S&P 500 MARKET PROBABILITY CALENDAR 2017

THE % CHANCE OF THE MARKET RISING ON ANY TRADING DAY OF THE YEAR*
(Based on the number of times the S&P 500 rose on a particular trading day during January 1953–December 2015.)

Date	Jan	Feb	Mar	Apr	May	Jun	Jul	Aug	Sep	Oct	Nov	Dec
1	S	61.9	61.9	S	57.1	55.6	S	47.6	60.3	S	61.9	47.6
2	H	58.7	58.7	S	68.3	60.3	S	44.4	S	49.2	57.1	S
3	47.6	46.0	60.3	63.5	55.6	S	71.4	49.2	S	66.7	68.3	S
4	68.3	S	S	60.3	42.9	S	H	50.8	H	54.0	S	52.4
5	52.4	S	S	54.0	44.4	52.4	55.6	S	54.0	60.3	S	61.9
6	50.8	50.8	49.2	54.0	S	55.6	55.6	S	58.7	47.6	55.6	57.1
7	S	50.8	49.2	54.0	S	46.0	60.3	52.4	47.6	S	47.6	42.9
8	S	44.4	57.1	S	52.4	42.9	S	47.6	50.8	S	57.1	49.2
9	44.4	41.3	58.7	S	47.6	41.3	S	52.4	S	50.8	60.3	S
10	50.8	61.9	50.8	60.3	52.4	S	60.3	47.6	S	42.9	57.1	S
11	52.4	S	S	63.5	44.4	S	55.6	46.0	52.4	44.4	S	54.0
12	54.0	S	S	54.0	50.8	55.6	50.8	S	58.7	52.4	S	49.2
13	58.7	55.6	63.5	50.8	S	63.5	50.8	S	63.5	54.0	47.6	47.6
14	S	46.0	46.0	H	S	58.7	69.8	63.5	50.8	S	49.2	44.4
15	S	54.0	61.9	S	54.0	57.1	S	61.9	54.0	S	50.8	47.6
16	H	36.5	61.9	S	49.2	47.6	S	54.0	S	52.4	50.8	S
17	63.5	52.4	57.1	61.9	54.0	S	52.4	54.0	S	57.1	54.0	S
18	55.6	S	S	61.9	39.7	S	44.4	50.8	57.1	44.4	S	58.7
19	50.8	S	S	58.7	47.6	57.1	47.6	S	47.6	66.7	S	44.4
20	47.6	H	49.2	54.0	S	41.3	54.0	S	50.8	49.2	52.4	47.6
21	S	44.4	42.9	54.0	S	49.2	39.7	44.4	47.6	S	55.6	49.2
22	S	42.9	44.4	S	49.2	52.4	S	60.3	36.5	S	65.1	60.3
23	47.6	39.7	42.9	S	44.4	44.4	S	47.6	S	44.4	H	S
24	58.7	57.1	52.4	49.2	50.8	S	44.4	50.8	S	46.0	57.1	S
25	54.0	S	S	57.1	49.2	S	55.6	46.0	49.2	31.7	S	H
26	52.4	S	S	50.8	47.6	34.9	54.0	S	49.2	58.7	S	71.4
27	47.6	52.4	44.4	47.6	S	42.9	49.2	S	58.7	58.7	66.7	52.4
28	S	57.1	44.4	57.1	S	50.8	65.1	46.0	50.8	S	60.3	61.9
29	S		55.6	S	H	57.1	S	60.3	41.3	S	60.3	61.9
30	61.9		38.1	S	55.6	49.2	S	44.4	S	60.3	50.8	S
31	61.9		41.3		60.3		60.3	63.5		54.0		S

* See new trends developing on pages 70, 92, 141–146.

123

RECENT S&P 500 MARKET PROBABILITY CALENDAR 2017

THE % CHANCE OF THE MARKET RISING ON ANY TRADING DAY OF THE YEAR*

(Based on the number of times the S&P 500 rose on a particular trading day during January 1995–December 2015.**)

Date	Jan	Feb	Mar	Apr	May	Jun	Jul	Aug	Sep	Oct	Nov	Dec
1	S	76.2	61.9	S	66.7	61.9	S	42.9	61.9	S	57.1	52.4
2	H	52.4	38.1	S	57.1	66.7	S	52.4	S	52.4	71.4	S
3	47.6	42.9	66.7	76.2	38.1	S	85.7	47.6	S	61.9	66.7	S
4	57.1	S	S	71.4	38.1	S	H	57.1	H	52.4	S	47.6
5	52.4	S	S	57.1	42.9	47.6	38.1	S	47.6	61.9	S	61.9
6	52.4	57.1	52.4	57.1	S	52.4	61.9	S	52.4	38.1	76.2	42.9
7	S	52.4	61.9	47.6	S	42.9	57.1	42.9	57.1	S	52.4	42.9
8	S	61.9	57.1	S	57.1	47.6	S	57.1	61.9	S	42.9	52.4
9	47.6	47.6	52.4	S	42.9	42.9	S	42.9	S	38.1	42.9	S
10	57.1	66.7	52.4	57.1	61.9	S	52.4	47.6	S	47.6	42.9	S
11	57.1	S	S	52.4	47.6	S	52.4	33.3	61.9	42.9	S	57.1
12	47.6	S	S	52.4	47.6	42.9	57.1	S	66.7	52.4	S	47.6
13	52.4	71.4	66.7	47.6	S	57.1	76.2	S	66.7	66.7	57.1	47.6
14	S	47.6	47.6	H	S	66.7	66.7	61.9	61.9	S	57.1	42.9
15	S	71.4	66.7	S	57.1	71.4	S	61.9	47.6	S	61.9	52.4
16	H	38.1	57.1	S	52.4	57.1	S	66.7	S	47.6	47.6	S
17	57.1	42.9	71.4	57.1	52.4	S	42.9	66.7	S	66.7	57.1	S
18	66.7	S	S	61.9	38.1	S	47.6	38.1	71.4	61.9	S	61.9
19	52.4	S	S	66.7	47.6	61.9	52.4	S	47.6	71.4	S	47.6
20	38.1	H	42.9	61.9	S	47.6	71.4	S	52.4	47.6	52.4	47.6
21	S	47.6	28.6	61.9	S	42.9	23.8	38.1	42.9	S	52.4	71.4
22	S	57.1	47.6	S	38.1	52.4	S	66.7	23.8	S	57.1	47.6
23	47.6	42.9	38.1	S	47.6	38.1	S	47.6	S	66.7	H	S
24	47.6	47.6	66.7	42.9	52.4	S	47.6	57.1	S	57.1	57.1	S
25	57.1	S	S	47.6	52.4	S	57.1	47.6	38.1	33.3	S	H
26	52.4	S	S	57.1	47.6	38.1	52.4	S	42.9	52.4	S	76.2
27	61.9	52.4	61.9	66.7	S	33.3	47.6	S	61.9	57.1	61.9	61.9
28	S	42.9	28.6	47.6	S	52.4	61.9	47.6	66.7	S	57.1	52.4
29	S		47.6	S	H	57.1	S	71.4	28.6	S	76.2	33.3
30	52.4		42.9	S	57.1	42.9	S	28.6	S	61.9	38.1	S
31	57.1		42.9		57.1		42.9	52.4		61.9		S

* See new trends developing on pages 70, 92, 141–146.   ** Based on most recent 21-year period.

NASDAQ COMPOSITE MARKET PROBABILITY CALENDAR 2017

THE % CHANCE OF THE MARKET RISING ON ANY TRADING DAY OF THE YEAR*

(Based on the number of times the NASDAQ rose on a particular trading day during January 1971–December 2015.)

Date	Jan	Feb	Mar	Apr	May	Jun	Jul	Aug	Sep	Oct	Nov	Dec
1	S	71.1	62.2	S	62.2	57.8	S	51.1	55.6	S	66.7	60.0
2	H	68.9	55.6	S	71.1	71.1	S	42.2	S	48.9	55.6	S
3	55.6	55.6	66.7	46.7	57.8	S	62.2	51.1	S	62.2	68.9	S
4	64.4	S	S	64.4	51.1	S	H	55.6	H	57.8	S	62.2
5	57.8	S	S	64.4	53.3	57.8	46.7	S	60.0	62.2	S	64.4
6	64.4	64.4	51.1	53.3	S	60.0	46.7	S	57.8	57.8	57.8	57.8
7	S	55.6	51.1	46.7	S	51.1	53.3	53.3	57.8	S	48.9	42.2
8	S	53.3	57.8	S	62.2	44.4	S	42.2	57.8	S	53.3	53.3
9	55.6	48.9	55.6	S	53.3	42.2	S	51.1	S	60.0	57.8	S
10	60.0	62.2	48.9	62.2	42.2	S	60.0	51.1	S	48.9	62.2	S
11	57.8	S	S	64.4	57.8	S	64.4	55.6	48.9	51.1	S	48.9
12	60.0	S	S	60.0	55.6	53.3	60.0	S	53.3	71.1	S	44.4
13	60.0	62.2	71.1	51.1	S	62.2	71.1	S	62.2	62.2	53.3	42.2
14	S	64.4	51.1	H	S	64.4	73.3	60.0	60.0	S	53.3	42.2
15	S	60.0	53.3	S	53.3	57.8	S	60.0	37.8	S	42.2	46.7
16	H	48.9	62.2	S	55.6	48.9	S	51.1	S	51.1	48.9	S
17	64.4	55.6	57.8	60.0	51.1	S	62.2	57.8	S	53.3	51.1	S
18	71.1	S	S	53.3	42.2	S	48.9	48.9	53.3	42.2	S	57.8
19	60.0	S	S	60.0	48.9	53.3	55.6	S	55.6	68.9	S	48.9
20	42.2	H	64.4	55.6	S	46.7	60.0	S	62.2	55.6	53.3	53.3
21	S	37.8	37.8	55.6	S	57.8	37.8	35.6	51.1	S	48.9	64.4
22	S	51.1	42.2	S	48.9	46.7	S	66.7	44.4	S	68.9	68.9
23	48.9	53.3	55.6	S	51.1	48.9	S	53.3	S	48.9	H	S
24	57.8	62.2	53.3	53.3	51.1	S	51.1	53.3	S	46.7	57.8	S
25	48.9	S	S	46.7	53.3	S	55.6	53.3	53.3	35.6	S	H
26	66.7	S	S	66.7	60.0	42.2	48.9	S	42.2	44.4	S	71.1
27	60.0	57.8	48.9	64.4	S	48.9	44.4	S	48.9	57.8	60.0	51.1
28	S	51.1	42.2	66.7	S	57.8	57.8	55.6	46.7	S	68.9	62.2
29	S		53.3	S	H	66.7	S	64.4	46.7	S	66.7	71.1
30	53.3		55.6	S	57.8	68.9	S	60.0	S	60.0	64.4	S
31	62.2		64.4		66.7		48.9	66.7		64.4		S

* See new trends developing on pages 70, 92, 141–146.
Based on NASDAQ composite, prior to Feb. 5, 1971; based on National Quotation Bureau indices.

RECENT NASDAQ COMPOSITE MARKET PROBABILITY CALENDAR 2017

THE % CHANCE OF THE MARKET RISING ON ANY TRADING DAY OF THE YEAR*
(Based on the number of times the NASDAQ rose on a particular trading day during January 1995–December 2015.**)

Date	Jan	Feb	Mar	Apr	May	Jun	Jul	Aug	Sep	Oct	Nov	Dec
1	S	81.0	57.1	S	71.4	52.4	S	42.9	61.9	S	71.4	61.9
2	H	57.1	38.1	S	61.9	66.7	S	42.9	S	42.9	66.7	S
3	66.7	42.9	66.7	66.7	47.6	S	76.2	47.6	S	61.9	71.4	S
4	52.4	S	S	61.9	42.9	S	H	52.4	H	61.9	S	57.1
5	47.6	S	S	71.4	38.1	52.4	38.1	S	52.4	61.9	S	57.1
6	57.1	57.1	38.1	52.4	S	52.4	57.1	S	47.6	47.6	66.7	57.1
7	S	57.1	42.9	38.1	S	47.6	61.9	38.1	57.1	S	57.1	38.1
8	S	61.9	52.4	S	76.2	42.9	S	38.1	66.7	S	52.4	57.1
9	57.1	47.6	42.9	S	42.9	42.9	S	42.9	S	52.4	42.9	S
10	61.9	57.1	47.6	66.7	47.6	S	57.1	47.6	S	52.4	52.4	S
11	61.9	S	S	52.4	57.1	S	61.9	47.6	61.9	52.4	S	61.9
12	52.4	S	S	61.9	47.6	42.9	57.1	S	57.1	61.9	S	42.9
13	47.6	66.7	66.7	42.9	S	52.4	71.4	S	71.4	71.4	61.9	42.9
14	S	66.7	47.6	H	S	57.1	71.4	61.9	76.2	S	52.4	42.9
15	S	57.1	47.6	S	52.4	71.4	S	66.7	33.3	S	47.6	47.6
16	H	42.9	57.1	S	57.1	57.1	S	66.7	S	47.6	52.4	S
17	42.9	47.6	61.9	52.4	61.9	S	57.1	61.9	S	57.1	52.4	S
18	76.2	S	S	47.6	33.3	S	52.4	38.1	76.2	47.6	S	57.1
19	66.7	S	S	57.1	61.9	66.7	61.9	S	57.1	71.4	S	38.1
20	33.3	H	61.9	57.1	S	47.6	71.4	S	61.9	42.9	57.1	47.6
21	S	38.1	33.3	61.9	S	52.4	19.0	33.3	47.6	S	47.6	66.7
22	S	66.7	42.9	S	42.9	38.1	S	76.2	38.1	S	66.7	61.9
23	38.1	57.1	52.4	S	52.4	38.1	S	52.4	S	61.9	H	S
24	57.1	52.4	61.9	57.1	38.1	S	42.9	47.6	S	47.6	61.9	S
25	47.6	S	S	42.9	47.6	S	61.9	52.4	42.9	42.9	S	H
26	71.4	S	S	57.1	57.1	38.1	57.1	S	42.9	47.6	S	66.7
27	66.7	52.4	66.7	76.2	S	42.9	42.9	S	42.9	57.1	57.1	52.4
28	S	28.6	33.3	61.9	S	66.7	66.7	42.9	47.6	S	61.9	38.1
29	S		47.6	S	H	66.7	S	71.4	28.6	S	71.4	38.1
30	47.6		52.4	S	66.7	66.7	S	52.4	S	61.9	47.6	S
31	52.4		57.1		52.4		38.1	57.1		61.9		S

* See new trends developing on pages 70, 92, 141–146. ** Based on most recent 21-year period.

RUSSELL 1000 INDEX MARKET PROBABILITY CALENDAR 2017

THE % CHANCE OF THE MARKET RISING ON ANY TRADING DAY OF THE YEAR*

(Based on the number of times the RUSSELL 1000 rose on a particular trading day during January 1979–December 2015.)

Date	Jan	Feb	Mar	Apr	May	Jun	Jul	Aug	Sep	Oct	Nov	Dec
1	S	67.6	59.5	S	56.8	59.5	S	45.9	51.4	S	73.0	51.4
2	H	59.5	48.6	S	64.9	56.8	S	43.2	S	54.1	56.8	S
3	43.2	54.1	59.5	59.5	54.1	S	73.0	48.6	S	59.5	59.5	S
4	56.8	S	S	64.9	37.8	S	H	45.9	H	54.1	S	54.1
5	59.5	S	S	54.1	43.2	51.4	40.5	S	48.6	59.5	S	62.2
6	54.1	54.1	43.2	54.1	S	56.8	45.9	S	54.1	43.2	59.5	43.2
7	S	59.5	45.9	45.9	S	35.1	59.5	51.4	43.2	S	45.9	43.2
8	S	51.4	59.5	S	56.8	40.5	S	59.5	51.4	S	54.1	48.6
9	51.4	43.2	54.1	S	56.8	43.2	S	45.9	S	54.1	51.4	S
10	62.2	70.3	45.9	64.9	51.4	S	56.8	48.6	S	37.8	56.8	S
11	54.1	S	S	59.5	54.1	S	51.4	43.2	54.1	40.5	S	51.4
12	56.8	S	S	51.4	51.4	51.4	56.8	S	64.9	62.2	S	45.9
13	56.8	67.6	62.2	45.9	S	56.8	67.6	S	67.6	64.9	56.8	45.9
14	S	45.9	43.2	H	S	59.5	78.4	62.2	59.5	S	54.1	45.9
15	S	62.2	59.5	S	56.8	62.2	S	64.9	51.4	S	51.4	54.1
16	H	37.8	59.5	S	56.8	51.4	S	59.5	S	56.8	45.9	S
17	70.3	45.9	59.5	56.8	56.8	S	48.6	64.9	S	54.1	62.2	S
18	64.9	S	S	64.9	45.9	S	51.4	62.2	51.4	45.9	S	59.5
19	43.2	S	S	59.5	51.4	64.9	48.6	S	45.9	73.0	S	48.6
20	37.8	H	48.6	48.6	S	40.5	62.2	S	48.6	51.4	48.6	45.9
21	S	40.5	37.8	54.1	S	48.6	37.8	48.6	40.5	S	51.4	59.5
22	S	45.9	45.9	S	48.6	54.1	S	70.3	35.1	S	64.9	62.2
23	48.6	43.2	45.9	S	43.2	43.2	S	48.6	S	48.6	H	S
24	48.6	56.8	45.9	48.6	59.5	S	40.5	56.8	S	43.2	59.5	S
25	54.1	S	S	54.1	62.2	S	73.0	43.2	40.5	32.4	S	H
26	62.2	S	S	56.8	56.8	32.4	54.1	S	45.9	56.8	S	70.3
27	56.8	56.8	54.1	54.1	S	40.5	45.9	S	64.9	56.8	64.9	59.5
28	S	56.8	35.1	56.8	S	51.4	67.6	54.1	56.8	S	73.0	64.9
29	S		48.6	S	H	59.5	S	56.8	45.9	S	67.6	51.4
30	56.8		43.2	S	54.1	51.4	S	48.6	S	64.9	45.9	S
31	56.8		48.6		56.8		56.8	59.5		62.2		S

* See new trends developing on pages 70, 92, 141–146.

RUSSELL 2000 INDEX MARKET PROBABILITY CALENDAR 2017

THE % CHANCE OF THE MARKET RISING ON ANY TRADING DAY OF THE YEAR*
(Based on the number of times the RUSSELL 2000 rose on a particular trading day during January 1979–December 2015.)

Date	Jan	Feb	Mar	Apr	May	Jun	Jul	Aug	Sep	Oct	Nov	Dec
1	S	67.6	64.9	S	59.5	62.2	S	48.6	51.4	S	62.2	51.4
2	H	64.9	59.5	S	67.6	67.6	S	45.9	S	48.6	70.3	S
3	45.9	51.4	64.9	48.6	59.5	S	64.9	51.4	S	51.4	64.9	S
4	62.2	S	S	62.2	56.8	S	H	48.6	H	51.4	S	62.2
5	59.5	S	S	48.6	54.1	54.1	48.6	S	59.5	67.6	S	64.9
6	62.2	67.6	54.1	51.4	S	56.8	43.2	S	54.1	43.2	59.5	62.2
7	S	62.2	59.5	43.2	S	56.8	54.1	45.9	64.9	S	54.1	45.9
8	S	62.2	54.1	S	54.1	37.8	S	48.6	56.8	S	54.1	54.1
9	56.8	45.9	54.1	S	62.2	45.9	S	56.8	S	48.6	54.1	S
10	64.9	70.3	43.2	56.8	48.6	S	51.4	48.6	S	45.9	67.6	S
11	54.1	S	S	62.2	54.1	S	59.5	45.9	56.8	51.4	S	48.6
12	67.6	S	S	62.2	48.6	54.1	51.4	S	62.2	67.6	S	48.6
13	62.2	64.9	62.2	48.6	S	59.5	62.2	S	67.6	62.2	48.6	40.5
14	S	64.9	54.1	H	S	64.9	64.9	73.0	56.8	S	48.6	43.2
15	S	56.8	51.4	S	45.9	59.5	S	62.2	35.1	S	48.6	40.5
16	H	54.1	59.5	S	56.8	51.4	S	59.5	S	59.5	21.6	S
17	67.6	43.2	67.6	56.8	54.1	S	54.1	59.5	S	43.2	59.5	S
18	70.3	S	S	59.5	54.1	S	48.6	48.6	51.4	48.6	S	56.8
19	67.6	S	S	56.8	54.1	43.2	48.6	S	45.9	70.3	S	59.5
20	35.1	H	56.8	48.6	S	43.2	51.4	S	43.2	51.4	45.9	59.5
21	S	37.8	48.6	59.5	S	51.4	37.8	48.6	45.9	S	32.4	67.6
22	S	54.1	51.4	S	48.6	45.9	S	64.9	40.5	S	64.9	78.4
23	51.4	54.1	59.5	S	54.1	48.6	S	48.6	S	48.6	H	S
24	54.1	59.5	48.6	51.4	56.8	S	45.9	59.5	S	45.9	62.2	S
25	48.6	S	S	59.5	54.1	S	62.2	56.8	45.9	32.4	S	H
26	67.6	S	S	62.2	67.6	37.8	62.2	S	29.7	40.5	S	67.6
27	59.5	64.9	51.4	59.5	S	48.6	48.6	S	54.1	56.8	62.2	56.8
28	S	56.8	40.5	67.6	S	56.8	59.5	59.5	56.8	S	64.9	59.5
29	S		51.4	S	H	70.3	S	64.9	59.5	S	70.3	67.6
30	54.1		54.1	S	64.9	67.6	S	62.2	S	56.8	67.6	S
31	73.0		81.1		64.9		64.9	70.3		70.3		S

* See new trends developing on pages 70, 92, 141–146.

DECENNIAL CYCLE: A MARKET PHENOMENON

By arranging each year's market gain or loss so that the first and succeeding years of each decade fall into the same column, certain interesting patterns emerge—strong fifth and eighth years; weak first, seventh, and zero years.

This fascinating phenomenon was first presented by Edgar Lawrence Smith in *Common Stocks and Business Cycles* (William-Frederick Press, 1959). Anthony Gaubis co-pioneered the decennial pattern with Smith.

When Smith first cut graphs of market prices into 10-year segments and placed them above one another, he observed that each decade tended to have three bull market cycles and that the longest and strongest bull markets seem to favor the middle years of a decade.

Don't place too much emphasis on the decennial cycle nowadays, other than the extraordinary fifth and zero years, as the stock market is more influenced by the quadrennial presidential election cycle, shown on page 130. Also, the last half-century, which has been the most prosperous in U.S. history, has distributed the returns among most years of the decade. Interestingly, NASDAQ suffered its worst bear market ever in a zero year.

Seventh years of decades have been the second worst of the cycle. 2017 is also a post-election year, the worst year of the four-year presidential election cycle. The market's prospects in 2017 will likely depend heavily on the outcome of November's elections and the Fed.

THE 10-YEAR STOCK MARKET CYCLE
Annual % Change in Dow Jones Industrial Average
Year of Decade

DECADES	1st	2nd	3rd	4th	5th	6th	7th	8th	9th	10th
1881–1890	3.0%	−2.9%	−8.5%	−18.8%	20.1%	12.4%	−8.4%	4.8%	5.5%	−14.1%
1891–1900	17.6	−6.6	−24.6	−0.6	2.3	−1.7	21.3	22.5	9.2	7.0
1901–1910	−8.7	−0.4	−23.6	41.7	38.2	−1.9	−37.7	46.6	15.0	−17.9
1911–1920	0.4	7.6	−10.3	−5.4	81.7	−4.2	−21.7	10.5	30.5	−32.9
1921–1930	12.7	21.7	−3.3	26.2	30.0	0.3	28.8	48.2	−17.2	−33.8
1931–1940	−52.7	−23.1	66.7	4.1	38.5	24.8	−32.8	28.1	−2.9	−12.7
1941–1950	−15.4	7.6	13.8	12.1	26.6	−8.1	2.2	−2.1	12.9	17.6
1951–1960	14.4	8.4	−3.8	44.0	20.8	2.3	−12.8	34.0	16.4	−9.3
1961–1970	18.7	−10.8	17.0	14.6	10.9	−18.9	15.2	4.3	−15.2	4.8
1971–1980	6.1	14.6	−16.6	−27.6	38.3	17.9	−17.3	−3.1	4.2	14.9
1981–1990	−9.2	19.6	20.3	−3.7	27.7	22.6	2.3	11.8	27.0	−4.3
1991–2000	20.3	4.2	13.7	2.1	33.5	26.0	22.6	16.1	25.2	−6.2
2001–2010	−7.1	−16.8	25.3	3.1	−0.6	16.3	6.4	−33.8	18.8	11.0
2011–2020	5.5	7.3	26.5	7.5	−2.2					
Total % Change	5.6%	30.4%	92.6%	99.3%	365.8%	87.3%	−31.9%	187.9%	129.4%	−75.9%
Avg % Change	0.4%	2.2%	6.6%	7.1%	26.1%	6.8%	−2.5%	14.5%	10.0%	−5.8%
Up Years	9	8	7	9	12	8	7	10	10	5
Down Years	5	6	7	5	2	5	6	3	3	8

Based on annual close; Cowles indices 1881–1885; 12 Mixed Stocks, 10 Rails, 2 Inds 1886–1889;
20 Mixed Stocks, 18 Rails, 2 Inds 1890–1896; Railroad average 1897 (First industrial average published May 26, 1896).

PRESIDENTIAL ELECTION/STOCK MARKET CYCLE: THE 183-YEAR SAGA CONTINUES

It is no mere coincidence that the last two years (pre-election year and election year) of the 45 administrations since 1833 produced a total net market gain of 729.1%, dwarfing the 307.1% gain of the first two years of these administrations.

Presidential elections every four years have a profound impact on the economy and the stock market. Wars, recessions, and bear markets tend to start or occur in the first half of the term; prosperous times and bull markets, in the latter half. After nine straight annual Dow gains during the millennial bull, the four-year election cycle reasserted its overarching domination of market behavior until 2008. Recovery from the worst recession since the Great Depression produced six straight annual gains, until 2015, when the Dow suffered its first pre-election year loss since 1939.

STOCK MARKET ACTION SINCE 1833
Annual % Change in Dow Jones Industrial Average[1]

4-Year Cycle Beginning	Elected President	Post-Election Year	Mid-Term Year	Pre-Election Year	Election Year
1833	Jackson (D)	−0.9	13.0	3.1	−11.7
1837	Van Buren (D)	−11.5	1.6	−12.3	5.5
1841*	W.H. Harrison (W)**	−13.3	−18.1	45.0	15.5
1845*	Polk (D)	8.1	−14.5	1.2	−3.6
1849*	Taylor (W)	N/C	18.7	−3.2	19.6
1853*	Pierce (D)	−12.7	−30.2	1.5	4.4
1857	Buchanan (D)	−31.0	14.3	−10.7	14.0
1861*	Lincoln (R)	−1.8	55.4	38.0	6.4
1865	Lincoln (R)**	−8.5	3.6	1.6	10.8
1869	Grant (R)	1.7	5.6	7.3	6.8
1873	Grant (R)	−12.7	2.8	−4.1	−17.9
1877	Hayes (R)	−9.4	6.1	43.0	18.7
1881	Garfield (R)**	3.0	−2.9	−8.5	−18.8
1885*	Cleveland (D)	20.1	12.4	−8.4	4.8
1889*	B. Harrison (R)	5.5	−14.1	17.6	−6.6
1893*	Cleveland (D)	−24.6	−0.6	2.3	−1.7
1897*	McKinley (R)	21.3	22.5	9.2	7.0
1901	McKinley (R)**	−8.7	−0.4	−23.6	41.7
1905	T. Roosevelt (R)	38.2	−1.9	−37.7	46.6
1909	Taft (R)	15.0	−17.9	0.4	7.6
1913*	Wilson (D)	−10.3	−5.4	81.7	−4.2
1917	Wilson (D)	−21.7	10.5	30.5	−32.9
1921*	Harding (R)**	12.7	21.7	−3.3	26.2
1925	Coolidge (R)	30.0	0.3	28.8	48.2
1929	Hoover (R)	−17.2	−33.8	−52.7	−23.1
1933*	F. Roosevelt (D)	66.7	4.1	38.5	24.8
1937	F. Roosevelt (D)	−32.8	28.1	−2.9	−12.7
1941	F. Roosevelt (D)	−15.4	7.6	13.8	12.1
1945	F. Roosevelt (D)**	26.6	−8.1	2.2	−2.1
1949	Truman (D)	12.9	17.6	14.4	8.4
1953*	Eisenhower (R)	−3.8	44.0	20.8	2.3
1957	Eisenhower (R)	−12.8	34.0	16.4	−9.3
1961*	Kennedy (D)**	18.7	−10.8	17.0	14.6
1965	Johnson (D)	10.9	−18.9	15.2	4.3
1969*	Nixon (R)	−15.2	4.8	6.1	14.6
1973	Nixon (R)***	−16.6	−27.6	38.3	17.9
1977*	Carter (D)	−17.3	−3.1	4.2	14.9
1981*	Reagan (R)	−9.2	19.6	20.3	−3.7
1985	Reagan (R)	27.7	22.6	2.3	11.8
1989	G. H. W. Bush (R)	27.0	−4.3	20.3	4.2
1993*	Clinton (D)	13.7	2.1	33.5	26.0
1997	Clinton (D)	22.6	16.1	25.2	−6.2
2001*	G. W. Bush (R)	−7.1	−16.8	25.3	3.1
2005	G. W. Bush (R)	−0.6	16.3	6.4	−33.8
2009*	Obama (D)	18.8	11.0	5.5	7.3
2013	Obama (D)	26.5	7.5	−2.2	
Total % Gain		**112.6%**	**194.5%**	**467.3%**	**261.8%**
Average % Gain		**2.5%**	**4.2%**	**10.2%**	**5.8%**
# Up		21	28	34	30
# Down		24	18	12	15

*Party in power ousted   **Death in office   ***Resigned   D–Democrat, W–Whig, R–Republican
[1] Based on annual close; prior to 1886 based on Cowles and other indices; 12 Mixed Stocks, 10 Rails, 2 Inds 1886–1889; 20 Mixed Stocks, 18 Rails, 2 Inds 1890–1896; Railroad average 1897 (First industrial average published May 26, 1896).

DOW JONES INDUSTRIALS BULL AND BEAR MARKETS SINCE 1900

Bear markets begin at the end of one bull market and end at the start of the next bull market (7/17/90 to 10/11/90 as an example). The high at Dow 3978.36 on 1/31/94, was followed by a 9.7 percent correction. A 10.3 percent correction occurred between the 5/22/96 closing high of 5778 and the intraday low on 7/16/96. The longest bull market on record ended on 7/17/98, and the shortest bear market on record ended on 8/31/98, when the new bull market began. The greatest bull super cycle in history that began 8/12/82 ended in 2000 after the Dow gained 1409% and NASDAQ climbed 3072%. The Dow gained only 497% in the eight-year super bull from 1921 to the top in 1929. NASDAQ suffered its worst loss ever from the 2000 top to the 2002 bottom, down 77.9%, nearly as much as the 89.2% drop in the Dow from the 1929 top to the 1932 bottom. The third-longest Dow bull since 1900 that began 10/9/02 ended on its fifth anniversary. The ensuing bear market was the second worst bear market since 1900, slashing the Dow 53.8%. European debt concerns in 2011 triggered a 16.8% Dow slide, ending the recovery bull shortly after its second anniversary. At press time, the Dow is struggling to break free from the mild bear market that began on May 19, 2015. (See page 132 for S&P 500 and NASDAQ bulls and bears.)

DOW JONES INDUSTRIALS BULL AND BEAR MARKETS SINCE 1900

— Beginning —		— Ending —		Bull		Bear	
Date	DJIA	Date	DJIA	% Gain	Days	% Change	Days
9/24/00	38.80	6/17/01	57.33	47.8%	266	−46.1%	875
11/9/03	30.88	1/19/06	75.45	144.3	802	−48.5	665
11/15/07	38.83	11/19/09	73.64	89.6	735	−27.4	675
9/25/11	53.43	9/30/12	68.97	29.1	371	−24.1	668
7/30/14	52.32	11/21/16	110.15	110.5	845	−40.1	393
12/19/17	65.95	11/3/19	119.62	81.4	684	−46.6	660
8/24/21	63.90	3/20/23	105.38	64.9	573	−18.6	221
10/27/23	85.76	9/3/29	381.17	344.5	2138	−47.9	71
11/13/29	198.69	4/17/30	294.07	48.0	155	−86.0	813
7/8/32	41.22	9/7/32	79.93	93.9	61	−37.2	173
2/27/33	50.16	2/5/34	110.74	120.8	343	−22.8	171
7/26/34	85.51	3/10/37	194.40	127.3	958	−49.1	386
3/31/38	98.95	11/12/38	158.41	60.1	226	−23.3	147
4/8/39	121.44	9/12/39	155.92	28.4	157	−40.4	959
4/28/42	92.92	5/29/46	212.50	128.7	1492	−23.2	353
5/17/47	163.21	6/15/48	193.16	18.4	395	−16.3	363
6/13/49	161.60	1/5/53	293.79	81.8	1302	−13.0	252
9/14/53	255.49	4/6/56	521.05	103.9	935	−19.4	564
10/22/57	419.79	1/5/60	685.47	63.3	805	−17.4	294
10/25/60	566.05	12/13/61	734.91	29.8	414	−27.1	195
6/26/62	535.76	2/9/66	995.15	85.7	1324	−25.2	240
10/7/66	744.32	12/3/68	985.21	32.4	788	−35.9	539
5/26/70	631.16	4/28/71	950.82	50.6	337	−16.1	209
11/23/71	797.97	1/11/73	1051.70	31.8	415	−45.1	694
12/6/74	577.60	9/21/76	1014.79	75.7	655	−26.9	525
2/28/78	742.12	9/8/78	907.74	22.3	192	−16.4	591
4/21/80	759.13	4/27/81	1024.05	34.9	371	−24.1	472
8/12/82	776.92	11/29/83	1287.20	65.7	474	−15.6	238
7/24/84	1086.57	8/25/87	2722.42	150.6	1127	−36.1	55
10/19/87	1738.74	7/17/90	2999.75	72.5	1002	−21.2	86
10/11/90	2365.10	7/17/98	9337.97	294.8	2836	−19.3	45
8/31/98	7539.07	1/14/00	11722.98	55.5	501	−29.7	616
9/21/01	8235.81	3/19/02	10635.25	29.1	179	−31.5	204
10/9/02	7286.27	10/9/07	14164.53	94.4	1826	−53.8	517
3/9/09	6547.05	4/29/11	12810.54	95.7	781	−16.8	157
10/3/11	10655.30	5/19/15	18312.39	71.9	1324*	−14.5*	351*
2/11/16	15660.18					*As of May 4, 2016—not in averages*	
		Average		**85.6%**	**772**	**−31.1%**	**402**

Based on Dow Jones Industrial Average.
The NYSE was closed from 7/31/1914 to 12/11/1914 due to World War I.
DJIA figures were then adjusted back to reflect the composition change from 12 to 20 stocks in September 1916.
1900–2000 Data: Ned Davis Research
131

STANDARD & POOR'S 500 BULL AND BEAR MARKETS SINCE 1929 NASDAQ COMPOSITE SINCE 1971

A constant debate of the definition and timing of bull and bear markets permeates Wall Street like the bell that signals the open and close of every trading day. We have relied on the Ned Davis Research parameters for years to track bulls and bears on the Dow (see page 131). Standard & Poor's 500 index has been a stalwart indicator for decades and at times marched to a different beat than the Dow. The moves of the S&P 500 and NASDAQ have been correlated to the bull and bear dates on page 131. Many dates line up for the three indices, but you will notice quite a lag or lead on several occasions, including NASDAQ's independent cadence from 1975 to 1980.

STANDARD & POOR'S 500 BULL AND BEAR MARKETS

— Beginning —		— Ending —		Bull		Bear	
Date	S&P 500	Date	S&P 500	% Gain	Days	% Change	Days
11/13/29	17.66	4/10/30	25.92	46.8%	148	−83.0%	783
6/1/32	4.40	9/7/32	9.31	111.6	98	−40.6	173
2/27/33	5.53	2/6/34	11.82	113.7	344	−31.8	401
3/14/35	8.06	3/6/37	18.68	131.8	723	−49.0	390
3/31/38	8.50	11/9/38	13.79	62.2	223	−26.2	150
4/8/39	10.18	10/25/39	13.21	29.8	200	−43.5	916
4/28/42	7.47	5/29/46	19.25	157.7	1492	−28.8	353
5/17/47	13.71	6/15/48	17.06	24.4	395	−20.6	363
6/13/49	13.55	1/5/53	26.66	96.8	1302	−14.8	252
9/14/53	22.71	8/2/56	49.74	119.0	1053	−21.6	446
10/22/57	38.98	8/3/59	60.71	55.7	650	−13.9	449
10/25/60	52.30	12/12/61	72.64	38.9	413	−28.0	196
6/26/62	52.32	2/9/66	94.06	79.8	1324	−22.2	240
10/7/66	73.20	11/29/68	108.37	48.0	784	−36.1	543
5/26/70	69.29	4/28/71	104.77	51.2	337	−13.9	209
11/23/71	90.16	1/11/73	120.24	33.4	415	−48.2	630
10/3/74	62.28	9/21/76	107.83	73.1	719	−19.4	531
3/6/78	86.90	9/12/78	106.99	23.1	190	−8.2	562
3/27/80	98.22	11/28/80	140.52	43.1	246	−27.1	622
8/12/82	102.42	10/10/83	172.65	68.6	424	−14.4	288
7/24/84	147.82	8/25/87	336.77	127.8	1127	−33.5	101
12/4/87	223.92	7/16/90	368.95	64.8	955	−19.9	87
10/11/90	295.46	7/17/98	1186.75	301.7	2836	−19.3	45
8/31/98	957.28	3/24/00	1527.46	59.6	571	−36.8	546
9/21/01	965.80	1/4/02	1172.51	21.4	105	−33.8	278
10/9/02	776.76	10/9/07	1565.15	101.5	1826	−56.8	517
3/9/09	676.53	4/29/11	1363.61	101.6	781	−19.4	157
10/3/11	1099.23	5/21/15	2130.82	93.8	1326	−14.2*	349*
2/11/16	1829.08*						

*As of May 4, 2016 — not in averages

		Average		**81.5%**	**750**	**−30.2%**	**379**

NASDAQ COMPOSITE BULL AND BEAR MARKETS

— Beginning —		— Ending —		Bull		Bear	
Date	NASDAQ	Date	NASDAQ	% Gain	Days	% Change	Days
11/23/71	100.31	1/11/73	136.84	36.4%	415	−59.9%	630
10/3/74	54.87	7/15/75	88.00	60.4	285	−16.2	63
9/16/75	73.78	9/13/78	139.25	88.7	1093	−20.4	62
11/14/78	110.88	2/8/80	165.25	49.0	451	−24.9	48
3/27/80	124.09	5/29/81	223.47	80.1	428	−28.8	441
8/13/82	159.14	6/24/83	328.91	106.7	315	−31.5	397
7/25/84	225.30	8/26/87	455.26	102.1	1127	−35.9	63
10/28/87	291.88	10/9/89	485.73	66.4	712	−33.0	372
10/16/90	325.44	7/20/98	2014.25	518.9	2834	−29.5	80
10/8/98	1419.12	3/10/00	5048.62	255.8	519	−71.8	560
9/21/01	1423.19	1/4/02	2059.38	44.7	105	−45.9	278
10/9/02	1114.11	10/31/07	2859.12	156.6	1848	−55.6	495
3/9/09	1268.64	4/29/11	2873.54	126.5	781	−18.7	157
10/3/11	2335.83	7/20/15	5218.86	123.4	1386	−18.2*	289*
2/11/16	4266.84*						

*As of May 4, 2016 — not in averages

		Average		**129.7%**	**878**	**−36.3%**	**280**

JANUARY DAILY POINT CHANGES DOW JONES INDUSTRIALS

Previous Month Close	2007	2008	2009	2010	2011	2012	2013	2014	2015	2016
	12463.15	13264.82	8776.39	10428.05	11577.51	12217.56	13104.14	16576.66	17823.07	17425.03
1	H	H	H	H	S	S	H	H	H	H
2	H*	−220.86	258.30	S	S	H	308.41	−135.31	9.92	S
3	11.37	12.76	S	S	93.24	179.82	−21.19	28.64	S	S
4	6.17	−256.54	S	155.91	20.43	21.04	43.85	S	S	−276.09
5	−82.68	S	−81.80	−11.94	31.71	−2.72	S	S	−331.34	9.72
6	S	S	62.21	1.66	−25.58	−55.78	S	−44.89	−130.01	−252.15
7	S	27.31	−245.40	33.18	−22.55	S	−50.92	105.84	212.88	−392.41
8	25.48	−238.42	−27.24	11.33	S	S	−55.44	−68.20	323.35	−167.65
9	−6.89	146.24	−143.28	S	S	32.77	61.66	−17.98	−170.50	S
10	25.56	117.78	S	S	−37.31	69.78	80.71	−7.71	S	S
11	72.82	−246.79	S	45.80	34.43	−13.02	17.21	S	S	52.12
12	41.10	S	−125.21	−36.73	83.56	21.57	S	S	−96.53	117.65
13	S	S	−25.41	53.51	−23.54	−48.96	S	−179.11	−27.16	−364.81
14	S	171.85	−248.42	29.78	55.48	S	18.89	115.92	−186.59	227.64
15	H	−277.04	12.35	−100.90	S	S	27.57	108.08	−106.38	−390.97
16	26.51	−34.95	68.73	S	S	H	−23.66	−64.93	190.86	S
17	−5.44	−306.95	S	S	H	60.01	84.79	41.55	S	S
18	−9.22	−59.91	S	H	50.55	96.88	53.68	S	S	H
19	−2.40	S	H	115.78	−12.64	45.03	S	S	H	27.94
20	S	S	−332.13	−122.28	−2.49	96.50	S	H	3.66	−249.28
21	S	H	279.01	−213.27	49.04	S	H	−44.12	39.05	115.94
22	−88.37	−128.11	−105.30	−216.90	S	S	62.51	−41.10	259.70	210.83
23	56.64	298.98	−45.24	S	S	108.68	67.12	−175.99	−141.38	S
24	87.97	108.44	S	S	108.68	−33.07	46.00	−318.24	S	S
25	−119.21	−171.44	S	23.88	−3.33	81.21	70.65	S	S	−208.29
26	−15.54	S	38.47	−2.57	8.25	−22.33	S	S	6.10	282.01
27	S	S	58.70	41.87	4.39	−74.17	S	−41.23	−291.49	−222.77
28	S	176.72	200.72	−115.70	−166.13	S	−14.05	90.68	−195.84	125.18
29	3.76	96.41	−226.44	−53.13	S	S	72.49	−189.77	225.48	396.66
30	32.53	−37.47	−148.15	S	S	−6.74	−44.00	109.82	−251.90	S
31	98.38	207.53	S	S	68.23	− 20.81	−49.84	−149.76	S	S
Close	12621.69	12650.36	8000.86	10067.33	11891.93	12632.91	13860.58	15698.85	17164.95	16466.30
Change	158.54	−614.46	−775.53	−360.72	314.42	415.35	756.44	−877.81	−658.12	−958.73

* Ford funeral

FEBRUARY DAILY POINT CHANGES DOW JONES INDUSTRIALS

Previous Month Close	2007	2008	2009	2010	2011	2012	2013	2014	2015	2016
	12621.69	12650.36	8000.86	10067.33	11891.93	12632.91	13860.58	15698.85	17164.95	16466.30
1	51.99	92.83	S	118.20	148.23	83.51	149.21	S	S	−17.12
2	−20.19	S	−64.03	111.32	1.81	−11.05	S	S	196.09	−295.64
3	S	S	141.53	−26.30	20.29	156.82	S	−326.05	305.36	183.12
4	S	−108.03	−121.70	−268.37	29.89	S	−129.71	72.44	6.62	79.92
5	8.25	−370.03	106.41	10.05	S	S	99.22	−5.01	211.86	− 211.61
6	4.57	−65.03	217.52	S	S	−17.10	7.22	188.30	−60.59	S
7	0.56	46.90	S	S	69.48	33.07	−42.47	165.55	S	S
8	−29.24	−64.87	S	−103.84	71.52	5.75	48.92	S	S	−177.92
9	−56.80	S	−9.72	150.25	6.74	6.51	S	S	−95.08	−12.67
10	S	S	−381.99	−20.26	−10.60	−89.23	S	7.71	139.55	−99.64
11	S	57.88	50.65	105.81	43.97	S	−21.73	192.98	−6.62	−254.56
12	−28.28	133.40	−6.77	−45.05	S	S	47.46	−30.83	110.24	313.66
13	102.30	178.83	−82.35	S	S	72.81	−35.79	63.65	46.97	S
14	87.01	−175.26	S	S	−5.07	4.24	−9.52	126.80	S	S
15	23.15	−28.77	S	H	−41.55	−97.33	8.37	S	S	H
16	2.56	S	H	169.67	61.53	123.13	S	S	H	222.57
17	S	S	−297.81	40.43	29.97	45.79	S	H	28.23	257.42
18	S	H	3.03	83.66	73.11	S	H	−23.99	−17.73	−40.40
19	H	−10.99	−89.68	9.45	S	S	53.91	−89.84	−44.08	−21.44
20	19.07	90.04	−100.28	S	S	H	−108.13	92.67	154.67	S
21	−48.23	−142.96	S	S	H	15.82	−46.92	−29.93	S	S
22	−52.39	96.72	S	−18.97	−178.46	−27.02	119.95	S	S	228.67
23	−38.54	S	−250.89	−100.97	−107.01	46.02	S	S	−23.60	−188.88
24	S	S	236.16	91.75	−37.28	−1.74	S	103.84	92.35	53.21
25	S	189.20	−80.05	−53.13	61.95	S	−216.40	−27.48	15.38	212.30
26	−15.22	114.70	−88.81	4.23	S	S	115.96	18.75	−10.15	−57.32
27	−416.02	9.36	−119.15	S	S	−1.44	175.24	74.24	−81.72	S
28	52.39	−112.10	S	S	95.89	23.61	−20.88	49.06	S	S
29	—	−315.79	—	—	—	−53.05	—	—	—	−123.47
Close	12268.63	12266.39	7062.93	10325.26	12226.34	12952.07	14054.49	16321.71	18132.70	16516.50
Change	−353.06	−383.97	−937.93	257.93	334.41	319.16	193.91	622.86	967.75	50.20

MARCH DAILY POINT CHANGES DOW JONES INDUSTRIALS

Previous Month	2007	2008	2009	2010	2011	2012	2013	2014	2015	2016
Close	12268.63	12266.39	7062.93	10325.26	12226.34	12952.07	14054.49	16321.71	18132.70	16516.50
1	−34.29	S	S	78.53	−168.32	28.23	35.17	S	S	348.58
2	−120.24	S	−299.64	2.19	8.78	−2.73	S	S	155.93	34.24
3	S	−7.49	−37.27	−9.22	191.40	S	S	−153.68	−85.26	44.58
4	S	−45.10	149.82	47.38	−88.32	S	38.16	227.85	−106.47	62.87
5	−63.69	41.19	−281.40	122.06	S	−14.76	125.95	−35.70	38.82	S
6	157.18	−214.60	32.50	S	S	−203.66	42.47	61.71	−278.94	S
7	−15.14	−146.70	S	S	−79.85	78.18	33.25	30.83	S	67.18
8	68.25	S	S	−13.68	124.35	70.61	67.58	S	S	−109.85
9	15.62	S	−79.89	11.86	−1.29	14.08	S	S	138.94	36.26
10	S	−153.54	379.44	2.95	−228.48	S	S	−34.04	−332.78	−5.23
11	S	416.66	3.91	44.51	59.79	S	50.22	−67.43	−27.55	218.18
12	42.30	−46.57	239.66	12.85	S	37.69	2.77	−11.17	259.83	S
13	−242.66	35.50	53.92	S	S	217.97	5.22	−231.19	−145.91	S
14	57.44	−194.65	S	S	−51.24	16.42	83.86	−43.22	S	15.82
15	26.28	S	S	17.46	−137.74	58.66	−25.03	S	S	22.40
16	−49.27	S	−7.01	43.83	−242.12	−20.14	S	S	228.11	74.23
17	S	21.16	178.73	47.69	161.29	S	S	181.55	−128.34	155.73
18	S	420.41	90.88	45.50	83.93	S	−62.05	88.97	227.11	120.81
19	115.76	−293.00	−85.78	−37.19	S	6.51	3.76	−114.02	−117.16	S
20	61.93	261.66	−122.42	S	S	−68.94	55.91	108.88	168.62	S
21	159.42	H	S	S	178.01	−45.57	−90.24	−28.28	S	21.57
22	13.62	S	S	43.91	−17.90	−78.48	90.54	S	S	−41.30
23	19.87	S	497.48	102.94	67.39	34.59	S	S	−11.61	−79.98
24	S	187.32	−115.89	−52.68	84.54	S	S	−26.08	−104.90	13.14
25	S	−16.04	89.84	5.06	50.03	S	−64.28	91.19	−292.60	H
26	−11.94	−109.74	174.75	9.15	S	160.90	111.90	−98.89	−40.31	S
27	−71.78	−120.40	−148.38	S	S	−43.90	−33.49	−4.76	34.43	S
28	−96.93	−86.06	S	S	−22.71	−71.52	52.38	58.83	S	19.66
29	48.39	S	S	45.50	81.13	19.61	H	S	S	97.72
30	5.60	S	−254.16	11.56	71.60	66.22	S	S	263.65	83.55
31	S	46.49	86.90	−50.79	−30.88	S	S	134.60	−200.19	−31.57
Close	12354.35	12262.89	7608.92	10856.63	12319.73	13212.04	14578.54	16457.66	17776.12	17685.09
Change	85.72	−3.50	545.99	531.37	93.39	259.97	524.05	135.95	−356.58	1168.59

APRIL DAILY POINT CHANGES DOW JONES INDUSTRIALS

Previous Month	2007	2008	2009	2010	2011	2012	2013	2014	2015	2016
Close	12354.35	12262.89	7608.92	10856.63	12319.73	13212.04	14578.54	16457.66	17776.12	17685.09
1	S	391.47	152.16	70.44	56.99	S	−5.69	74.95	−77.94	107.66
2	27.95	−48.53	216.48	H	S	52.45	89.16	40.39	65.06	S
3	128.00	20.20	39.51	S	S	−64.94	−111.66	−0.45	H	S
4	19.75	−16.61	S	S	23.31	−124.80	55.76	−159.84	S	−55.75
5	30.15	S	S	46.48	−6.13	−14.61	−40.86	S	S	−133.68
6	H	S	−41.74	−3.56	32.85	H	S	S	117.61	112.73
7	S	3.01	−186.29	−72.47	−17.26	S	S	−166.84	−5.43	−174.09
8	S	−35.99	47.55	29.55	−29.44	S	48.23	10.27	27.09	35.00
9	8.94	−49.18	246.27	70.28	S	−130.55	59.98	181.04	56.22	S
10	4.71	54.72	H	S	S	−213.66	128.78	−266.96	98.92	S
11	−89.23	−256.56	S	S	1.06	89.46	62.90	−143.47	S	−20.55
12	68.34	S	S	8.62	−117.53	181.19	−0.08	S	S	164.84
13	59.17	S	−25.57	13.45	7.41	−136.99	S	S	−80.61	187.03
14	S	−23.36	−137.63	103.69	14.16	S	S	146.49	59.66	18.15
15	S	60.41	109.44	21.46	56.68	S	−265.86	89.32	75.91	−28.97
16	108.33	256.80	95.81	−125.91	S	71.82	157.58	162.29	−6.84	S
17	52.58	1.22	5.90	S	S	194.13	−138.19	−16.31	−279.47	S
18	30.80	228.87	S	S	−140.24	−82.79	−81.45	H	S	106.70
19	4.79	S	S	73.39	65.16	−68.65	10.37	S	S	49.44
20	153.35	S	−289.60	25.01	186.79	65.16	S	S	208.63	42.67
21	S	−24.34	127.83	7.86	52.45	S	S	40.71	−85.34	−113.75
22	S	−104.79	−82.99	9.37	H	S	19.66	65.12	88.68	21.23
23	−42.58	42.99	70.49	69.99	S	−102.09	152.29	−12.72	20.42	S
24	34.54	85.73	119.23	S	S	74.39	−43.16	0.00	21.45	S
25	135.95	42.91	S	S	−26.11	89.16	24.50	−140.19	S	−26.51
26	15.61	S	S	0.75	115.49	113.90	11.75	S	S	13.08
27	15.44	S	−51.29	−213.04	95.59	23.69	S	S	−42.17	51.23
28	S	−20.11	−8.05	53.28	72.35	S	S	87.28	72.17	−210.79
29	S	−39.81	168.78	122.05	47.23	S	106.20	86.63	−74.61	−57.12
30	−58.03	−11.81	−17.61	−158.71	S	−14.68	21.05	45.47	−195.01	S
Close	13062.91	12820.13	8168.12	11008.61	12810.54	13213.63	14839.80	16580.84	17840.52	17773.64
Change	708.56	557.24	559.20	151.98	490.81	1.59	261.26	123.18	64.40	88.55

MAY DAILY POINT CHANGES DOW JONES INDUSTRIALS

Previous Month Close	2006	2007	2008	2009	2010	2011	2012	2013	2014	2015
	11367.14	13062.91	12820.13	8168.12	11008.61	12810.54	13213.63	14839.80	16580.84	17840.52
1	-23.85	73.23	189.87	44.29	S	S	65.69	-138.85	-21.97	183.54
2	73.16	75.74	48.20	S	S	-3.18	-10.75	130.63	-45.98	S
3	-16.17	29.50	S	S	143.22	0.15	-61.98	142.38	S	S
4	38.58	23.24	S	214.33	-225.06	-83.93	-168.32	S	S	46.34
5	138.88	S	-88.66	-16.09	-58.65	-139.41	S	S	17.66	-142.20
6	S	S	51.29	101.63	-347.80	54.57	S	-5.07	-129.53	-86.22
7	S	48.35	-206.48	-102.43	-139.89	S	-29.74	87.31	117.52	82.08
8	6.80	-3.90	52.43	164.80	S	S	-76.44	48.92	32.43	267.05
9	55.23	53.80	-120.90	S	S	45.94	-97.03	-22.50	32.37	S
10	2.88	-147.74	S	S	404.71	75.68	19.98	35.87	S	S
11	-141.92	111.09	S	-155.88	-36.88	-130.33	-34.44	S	S	-85.94
12	-119.74	S	130.43	50.34	148.65	65.89	S	S	112.13	-36.94
13	S	S	-44.13	-184.22	-113.96	-100.17	S	-26.81	19.97	-7.74
14	S	20.56	66.20	46.43	-162.79	S	-125.25	123.57	-101.47	191.75
15	47.78	37.06	94.28	-62.68	S	S	-63.35	60.44	-167.16	20.32
16	-8.88	103.69	-5.86	S	S	-47.38	-33.45	-42.47	44.50	S
17	-214.28	-10.81	S	S	5.67	-68.79	-156.06	121.18	S	S
18	-77.32	79.81	S	235.44	-114.88	80.60	-73.11	S	S	26.32
19	15.77	S	41.36	-29.23	-66.58	45.14	S	S	20.55	13.51
20	S	S	-199.48	-52.81	-376.36	-93.28	S	-19.12	-137.55	-26.99
21	S	-13.65	-227.49	-129.91	125.38	S	135.10	52.30	158.75	0.34
22	-18.73	-2.93	24.43	-14.81	S	S	-1.67	-80.41	10.02	-53.72
23	-26.98	-14.30	-145.99	S	S	-130.78	-6.66	-12.67	63.19	S
24	18.97	-84.52	S	S	-126.82	-25.05	33.60	8.60	S	S
25	93.73	66.15	S	H	-22.82	38.45	-74.92	S	S	H
26	67.56	S	H	196.17	-69.30	8.10	S	S	H	-190.48
27	S	S	68.72	-173.47	284.54	38.82	S	H	69.23	121.45
28	S	H	45.68	103.78	-122.36	S	H	106.29	-42.32	-36.87
29	H	14.06	52.19	96.53	S	S	125.86	-106.59	65.56	-115.44
30	-184.18	111.74	-7.90	S	S	H	-160.83	21.73	18.43	S
31	73.88	-5.44	S	S	H	128.21	-26.41	-208.96	S	S
Close	11168.31	13627.64	12638.32	8500.33	10136.63	12569.79	12393.45	15115.57	16717.17	18010.68
Change	-198.83	564.73	-181.81	332.21	-871.98	-240.75	-820.18	275.77	136.33	170.16

JUNE DAILY POINT CHANGES DOW JONES INDUSTRIALS

Previous Month Close	2006	2007	2008	2009	2010	2011	2012	2013	2014	2015
	11168.31	13627.64	12638.32	8500.33	10136.63	12569.79	12393.45	15115.57	16717.17	18010.68
1	91.97	40.47	S	221.11	-112.61	-279.65	-274.88	S	S	29.69
2	-12.41	S	-134.50	19.43	225.52	-41.59	S	S	26.46	-28.43
3	S	S	-100.97	-65.59	5.74	-97.29	S	138.46	-21.29	64.33
4	S	8.21	-12.37	74.96	-323.31	S	-17.11	-76.49	15.19	-170.69
5	-199.15	-80.86	213.97	12.89	S	S	26.49	-216.95	98.58	-56.12
6	-46.58	-129.79	-394.64	S	S	-61.30	286.84	80.03	88.17	S
7	-71.24	-198.94	S	S	-115.48	-19.15	46.17	207.50	S	S
8	7.92	157.66	S	1.36	123.49	-21.87	93.24	S	S	-82.91
9	-46.90	S	70.51	-1.43	-40.73	75.42	S	S	18.82	-2.51
10	S	S	9.44	-24.04	273.28	-172.45	S	-9.53	2.82	236.36
11	S	0.57	-205.99	31.90	38.54	S	-142.97	-116.57	-102.04	38.97
12	-99.34	-129.95	57.81	28.34	S	S	162.57	-126.79	-109.69	-140.53
13	-86.44	187.34	165.77	S	S	1.06	-77.42	180.85	41.55	S
14	110.78	71.37	S	S	-20.18	123.14	155.53	-105.90	S	S
15	198.27	85.76	S	-187.13	213.88	-178.84	115.26	S	S	-107.67
16	-0.64	S	-38.27	-107.46	4.69	64.25	S	S	5.27	113.31
17	S	S	-108.78	-7.49	24.71	42.84	S	109.67	27.48	31.26
18	S	-26.50	-131.24	58.42	16.47	S	-25.35	138.38	98.13	180.10
19	-72.44	22.44	34.03	-15.87	S	S	95.51	-206.04	14.84	-99.89
20	32.73	-146.00	-220.40	S	S	76.02	-12.94	-353.87	25.62	S
21	104.62	56.42	S	S	-8.23	109.63	-250.82	41.08	S	S
22	-60.35	-185.58	S	-200.72	-148.89	-80.34	67.21	S	S	103.83
23	-30.02	S	-0.33	-16.10	4.92	-59.67	S	S	-9.82	24.29
24	S	S	-34.93	-23.05	-145.64	-115.42	S	-139.84	-119.13	-178.00
25	S	-8.21	4.40	172.54	-8.99	S	-138.12	100.75	49.38	-75.71
26	56.19	-14.39	-358.41	-34.01	S	S	32.01	149.83	-21.38	56.32
27	-120.54	90.07	-106.91	S	S	108.98	92.34	114.35	5.71	S
28	48.82	-5.45	S	S	-5.29	145.13	-24.75	-114.89	S	S
29	217.24	-13.66	S	90.99	-268.22	72.73	277.83	S	S	-350.33
30	-40.58	S	3.50	-82.38	-96.28	152.92	S	S	-25.24	23.16
Close	11150.22	13408.62	11350.01	8447.00	9774.02	12414.34	12880.09	14909.60	16826.60	17619.51
Change	-18.09	-219.02	-1288.31	-53.33	-362.61	-155.45	486.64	-205.97	109.43	-391.17

JULY DAILY POINT CHANGES DOW JONES INDUSTRIALS

Previous Month Close	2006	2007	2008	2009	2010	2011	2012	2013	2014	2015
	11150.22	13408.62	11350.01	8447.00	9774.02	12414.34	12880.09	14909.60	16826.60	17619.51
1	S	S	32.25	57.06	−41.49	168.43	S	65.36	129.47	138.40
2	S	126.81	−166.75	−223.32	−46.05	S	−8.70	−42.55	20.17	−27.80
3	77.80*	41.87*	73.03*	H	S	S	72.43*	56.14*	92.02	H
4	H	H	H	S	S	H	H	H	H	S
5	−76.20	−11.46	S	S	H	−12.90	−47.15	147.29	S	S
6	73.48	45.84	S	44.13	57.14	56.15	−124.20	S	S	−46.53
7	−134.63	S	−56.58	−161.27	274.66	93.47	S	S	−44.05	93.33
8	S	S	152.25	14.81	120.71	−62.29	S	88.85	−117.59	−261.49
9	S	38.29	−236.77	4.76	59.04	S	−36.18	75.65	78.99	33.20
10	12.88	−148.27	81.58	−36.65	S	S	−83.17	−8.68	−70.54	211.79
11	31.22	76.17	−128.48	S	S	−151.44	−48.59	169.26	28.74	S
12	−121.59	283.86	S	S	18.24	−58.88	−31.26	3.38	S	S
13	−166.89	45.52	S	185.16	146.75	44.73	203.82	S	S	217.27
14	−106.94	S	−45.35	27.81	3.70	−54.49	S	S	111.61	75.90
15	S	S	−92.65	256.72	−7.41	42.61	S	19.96	5.26	−3.41
16	S	43.73	276.74	95.61	−261.41	S	−49.88	−32.41	77.52	70.08
17	8.01	20.57	207.38	32.12	S	S	78.33	18.67	−161.39	−33.80
18	51.87	−53.33	49.91	S	S	−94.57	103.16	78.02	123.37	S
19	212.19	82.19	S	S	56.53	202.26	34.66	−4.80	S	S
20	−83.32	−149.33	S	104.21	75.53	−15.51	−120.79	S	S	13.96
21	−59.72	S	−29.23	67.79	−109.43	152.50	S	S	−48.45	−181.12
22	S	S	135.16	−34.68	201.77	−43.25	S	1.81	61.81	−68.25
23	S	92.34	29.88	188.03	102.32	S	−101.11	22.19	−26.91	−119.12
24	182.67	−226.47	−283.10	23.95	S	S	−104.14	−25.50	−2.83	−163.39
25	52.66	68.12	21.41	S	S	−88.36	58.73	13.37	−123.23	S
26	−1.20	−311.50	S	S	100.81	−91.50	211.88	3.22	S	S
27	−2.08	−208.10	S	15.27	12.26	−198.75	187.73	S	S	−127.94
28	119.27	S	−239.61	−11.79	−39.81	−62.44	S	S	22.02	189.68
29	S	S	266.48	−26.00	−30.72	−96.87	S	−36.86	−70.48	121.12
30	S	92.84	186.13	83.74	−1.22	S	−2.65	−1.38	−31.75	−5.41
31	−34.02	−146.32	−205.67	17.15	S	S	−64.33	−21.05	−317.06	−56.12
Close	11185.68	13211.99	11378.02	9171.61	10465.94	12143.24	13008.68	15499.54	16563.30	17689.86
Change	35.46	−196.63	28.01	724.61	691.92	−271.10	128.59	589.94	−263.30	70.35

* Shortened trading day

AUGUST DAILY POINT CHANGES DOW JONES INDUSTRIALS

Previous Month Close	2006	2007	2008	2009	2010	2011	2012	2013	2014	2015
	11185.68	13211.99	11378.02	9171.61	10465.94	12143.24	13008.68	15499.54	16563.30	17689.86
1	−59.95	150.38	−51.70	S	S	−10.75	−37.62	128.48	−69.93	S
2	74.20	100.96	S	S	208.44	−265.87	−92.18	30.34	S	S
3	42.66	−281.42	S	114.95	−38.00	29.82	217.29	S	S	−91.66
4	−2.24	S	−42.17	33.63	44.05	−512.76	S	S	75.91	−47.51
5	S	S	331.62	−39.22	−5.45	60.93	S	−46.23	−139.81	−10.22
6	S	286.87	40.30	−24.71	−21.42	S	21.34	−93.39	13.87	−120.72
7	−20.97	35.52	−224.64	113.81	S	S	51.09	−48.07	−75.07	−46.37
8	−45.79	153.56	302.89	S	S	−634.76	7.04	27.65	185.66	S
9	−97.41	−387.18	S	S	45.19	429.92	−10.45	−72.81	S	S
10	48.19	−31.14	S	−32.12	−54.50	−519.83	42.76	S	S	241.79
11	−36.34	S	48.03	−96.50	−265.42	423.37	S	S	16.05	−212.33
12	S	S	−139.88	120.16	−58.88	125.71	S	−5.83	−9.44	−0.33
13	S	−3.01	−109.51	36.58	−16.80	S	−38.52	31.33	91.26	5.74
14	9.84	−207.61	82.97	−76.79	S	S	2.71	−113.35	61.78	69.15
15	132.39	−167.45	43.97	S	S	213.88	−7.36	−225.47	−50.67	S
16	96.86	−15.69	S	S	−1.14	−76.97	85.33	−30.72	S	S
17	7.84	233.30	S	−186.06	103.84	4.28	25.09	S	S	67.78
18	46.51	S	−180.51	82.60	9.69	−419.63	S	S	175.83	−33.84
19	S	S	−130.84	61.22	−144.33	−172.93	S	−70.73	80.85	−162.61
20	S	42.27	68.88	70.89	−57.59	S	−3.56	−7.75	59.54	−358.04
21	−36.42	−30.49	12.78	155.91	S	S	−68.06	−105.44	60.36	−530.94
22	−5.21	145.27	197.85	S	S	37.00	−30.82	66.19	−38.27	S
23	−41.94	−0.25	S	S	−39.21	322.11	−115.30	46.77	S	S
24	6.56	142.99	S	3.32	−133.96	143.95	100.51	S	S	−588.40
25	−20.41	S	−241.81	30.01	19.61	−170.89	S	S	75.65	−204.91
26	S	S	26.62	4.23	−74.25	134.72	S	−64.05	29.83	619.07
27	S	−56.74	89.64	37.11	164.84	S	−33.30	−170.33	15.31	369.26
28	67.96	−280.28	212.67	−36.43	S	S	−21.68	48.38	−42.44	−11.76
29	17.93	247.44	−171.63	S	S	254.71	4.49	16.44	18.88	S
30	12.97	−50.56	S	S	−140.92	20.70	−106.77	−30.64	S	S
31	−1.76	119.01	S	−47.92	4.99	53.58	90.13	S	S	−114.98
Close	11381.15	13357.74	11543.55	9496.28	10014.72	11613.53	13090.84	14810.31	17098.45	16528.03
Change	195.47	145.75	165.53	324.67	−451.22	−529.71	82.16	−689.23	535.15	−1161.83

SEPTEMBER DAILY POINT CHANGES DOW JONES INDUSTRIALS

Previous Month Close	2006	2007	2008	2009	2010	2011	2012	2013	2014	2015
	11381.15	13357.74	11543.55	9496.28	10014.72	11613.53	13090.84	14810.31	17098.45	16528.03
1	83.00	S	H	−185.68	254.75	−119.96	S	S	H	−469.68
2	S	S	−26.63	−29.93	50.63	−253.31	S	H	−30.89	293.03
3	S	H	15.96	63.94	157.83	S	H	23.65	10.72	23.38
4	H	91.12	−344.65	96.66	S	S	−54.90	96.91	−8.70	−272.38
5	5.13	−143.39	32.73	S	S	H	11.54	6.61	67.78	S
6	−63.08	57.88	S	S	H	−100.96	244.52	−14.98	S	S
7	−74.76	−249.97	S	H	−137.24	275.56	14.64	S	S	H
8	60.67	S	289.78	56.07	46.32	−119.05	S	S	−25.94	390.30
9	S	S	−280.01	49.88	28.23	−303.68	S	140.62	−97.55	−239.11
10	S	14.47	38.19	80.26	47.53	S	−52.35	127.94	54.84	76.83
11	4.73	180.54	164.79	−22.07	S	S	69.07	135.54	−19.71	102.69
12	101.25	−16.74	−11.72	S	S	68.99	9.99	−25.96	−61.49	S
13	45.23	133.23	S	S	81.36	44.73	206.51	75.42	S	S
14	−15.93	17.64	S	21.39	−17.64	140.88	53.51	S	S	−62.13
15	33.38	S	−504.48	56.61	46.24	186.45	S	S	43.63	228.89
16	S	S	141.51	108.30	22.10	75.91	S	118.72	100.83	140.10
17	S	−39.10	−449.36	−7.79	13.02	S	−40.27	34.95	24.88	−65.21
18	−5.77	335.97	410.03	36.28	S	S	11.54	147.21	109.14	−290.16
19	−14.09	76.17	368.75	S	S	−108.08	13.32	−40.39	13.75	S
20	72.28	−48.86	S	S	145.77	7.65	18.97	−185.46	S	S
21	−79.96	53.49	S	−41.34	7.41	−283.82	−17.46	S	S	125.61
22	−25.13	S	−372.75	51.01	−21.72	−391.01	S	S	−107.06	−179.72
23	S	S	−161.52	−81.32	−76.89	37.65	S	−49.71	−116.81	−50.58
24	S	−61.13	−29.00	−41.11	197.84	S	−20.55	−66.79	154.19	−78.57
25	67.71	19.59	196.89	−42.25	S	S	−101.37	−61.33	−264.26	113.35
26	93.58	99.50	121.07	S	S	272.38	−44.04	55.04	167.35	S
27	19.85	34.79	S	S	−48.22	146.83	72.46	−70.06	S	S
28	29.21	−17.31	S	124.17	46.10	−179.79	−48.84	S	S	−312.78
29	−39.38	S	−777.68	−47.16	−22.86	143.08	S	S	−41.93	47.24
30	S	S	485.32	−29.92	−47.23	−240.60	S	−128.57	−28.32	234.87
Close	11679.07	13895.63	10850.66	9712.28	10788.05	10913.38	13437.13	15129.67	17042.90	16284.00
Change	297.92	537.89	−692.89	216.00	773.33	−700.15	346.29	319.36	−55.55	−244.03

OCTOBER DAILY POINT CHANGES DOW JONES INDUSTRIALS

Previous Month Close	2006	2007	2008	2009	2010	2011	2012	2013	2014	2015
	11679.07	13895.63	10850.66	9712.28	10788.05	10913.38	13437.13	15129.67	17042.90	16284.00
1	S	191.92	−19.59	−203.00	41.63	S	77.98	62.03	−238.19	−11.99
2	−8.72	−40.24	−348.22	−21.61	S	S	−32.75	−58.56	−3.66	200.36
3	56.99	−79.26	−157.47	S	S	−258.00	12.25	−136.66	208.64	S
4	123.27	6.26	S	S	−78.41	153.41	80.75	76.10	S	S
5	16.08	91.70	S	112.08	193.45	131.24	34.79	S	S	304.06
6	−16.48	S	−369.88	131.50	22.93	183.38	S	S	−17.78	13.76
7	S	S	−508.39	−5.67	−19.07	−20.21	S	−136.34	−272.52	122.10
8	S	−22.28	−189.01	61.29	57.90	S	−26.50	−159.71	274.83	138.46
9	7.60	120.80	−678.91	78.07	S	S	−110.12	26.45	−334.97	33.74
10	9.36	−85.84	−128.00	S	S	330.06	−128.56	323.09	−115.15	S
11	−15.04	−63.57	S	S	3.86	−16.88	−18.58	111.04	S	S
12	95.57	77.96	S	20.86	10.06	102.55	2.46	S	S	47.37
13	12.81	S	936.42	−14.74	75.68	−40.72	S	S	−223.03	−49.97
14	S	S	−76.62	144.80	−1.51	166.36	S	64.15	−5.88	−157.14
15	S	−108.28	−733.08	47.08	−31.79	S	95.38	−133.25	−173.45	217.00
16	20.09	−71.86	401.35	−67.03	S	S	127.55	205.82	−24.50	74.22
17	−30.58	−20.40	−127.04	S	S	−247.49	5.22	−2.18	263.17	S
18	42.66	−3.58	S	S	80.91	180.05	−8.06	28.00	S	S
19	19.05	−366.94	S	96.28	−165.07	−72.43	−205.43	S	S	14.57
20	−9.36	S	413.21	−50.71	129.35	37.16	S	S	19.26	−13.43
21	S	S	−231.77	−92.12	38.60	267.01	S	−7.45	215.14	−48.50
22	S	44.95	−514.45	131.95	−14.01	S	2.38	75.46	−153.49	320.55
23	114.54	109.26	172.04	−109.13	S	S	−243.36	−54.33	216.58	157.54
24	10.97	−0.98	−312.30	S	S	104.83	−25.19	95.88	127.51	S
25	6.80	−3.33	S	S	31.49	−207.00	26.34	61.07	S	S
26	28.98	134.78	S	−104.22	5.41	162.42	3.53	S	S	−23.65
27	−73.40	S	−203.18	14.21	−43.18	339.51	S	S	12.53	−41.62
28	S	S	889.35	−119.48	−12.33	22.56	S	−1.35	187.81	198.09
29	S	63.56	−74.16	199.89	4.54	S	H*	111.42	−31.44	−23.72
30	−3.76	−77.79	189.73	−249.85	S	S	H*	−61.59	221.11	−92.26
31	−5.77	137.54	144.32	S	S	−276.10	−10.75	−73.01	195.10	S
Close	12080.73	13930.01	9325.01	9712.73	11118.49	11955.01	13096.46	15545.75	17390.52	17663.54
Change	401.66	34.38	−1525.65	0.45	330.44	1041.63	−340.67	416.08	347.62	1379.54

* Hurricane Sandy

NOVEMBER DAILY POINT CHANGES DOW JONES INDUSTRIALS

Previous Month	2006	2007	2008	2009	2010	2011	2012	2013	2014	2015
Close	12080.73	13930.01	9325.01	9712.73	11118.49	11955.01	13096.46	15545.75	17390.52	17663.54
1	−49.71	−362.14	S	S	6.13	−297.05	136.16	69.80	S	S
2	−12.48	27.23	S	76.71	64.10	178.08	−139.46	S	S	165.22
3	−32.50	S	−5.18	−17.53	26.41	208.43	S	S	−24.28	89.39
4	S	S	305.45	30.23	219.71	−61.23	S	23.57	17.60	−50.57
5	S	−51.70	−486.01	203.82	9.24	S	19.28	−20.90	100.69	−4.15
6	119.51	117.54	−443.48	17.46	S	S	133.24	128.66	69.94	46.90
7	51.22	−360.92	248.02	S	S	85.15	−312.95	−152.90	19.46	S
8	19.77	−33.73	S	S	−37.24	101.79	−121.41	167.80	S	S
9	−73.24	−223.55	S	203.52	−60.09	−389.24	4.07	S	S	−179.85
10	5.13	S	−73.27	20.03	10.29	112.85	S	S	39.81	27.73
11	S	S	−176.58	44.29	−73.94	259.89	S	21.32	1.16	−55.99
12	S	−55.19	−411.30	−93.79	−90.52	S	−0.31	−32.43	−2.70	−254.15
13	23.45	319.54	552.59	73.00	S	S	−58.90	70.96	40.59	−202.83
14	86.13	−76.08	−337.94	S	S	−74.70	−185.23	54.59	−18.05	S
15	33.70	−120.96	S	S	9.39	17.18	−28.57	85.48	S	S
16	54.11	66.74	S	136.49	−178.47	−190.57	45.93	S	S	237.77
17	36.74	S	−223.73	30.46	−15.62	−134.86	S	S	13.01	6.49
18	S	S	151.17	−11.11	173.35	25.43	S	14.32	40.07	247.66
19	S	−218.35	−427.47	−93.87	22.32	S	207.65	−8.99	−2.09	−4.41
20	−26.02	51.70	−444.99	−14.28	S	S	−7.45	−66.21	33.27	91.06
21	5.05	−211.10	494.13	S	S	−248.85	48.38	109.17	91.06	S
22	5.36	H	S	S	−24.97	−53.59	S	54.78	S	S
23	H	181.84*	S	132.79	−142.21	−236.17	172.79*	S	S	−31.13
24	−46.78*	S	396.97	−17.24	150.91	H	S	S	7.84	19.51
25	S	S	36.08	30.69	H	−25.77*	S	7.77	−2.96	1.20
26	S	−237.44	247.14	H	−95.28*	S	−42.31	0.26	−2.69	H
27	−158.46	215.00	H	−154.48*	S	S	−89.24	24.53	H	−14.90*
28	14.74	331.01	102.43*	S	S	291.23	106.98	H	15.99*	S
29	90.28	22.28	S	S	−39.51	32.62	36.71	−10.92*	S	S
30	−4.80	59.99	S	34.92	−46.47	490.05	3.76	S	S	−78.57
Close	12221.93	13371.72	8829.04	10344.84	11006.02	12045.68	13025.58	16086.41	17828.24	17719.92
Change	141.20	−558.29	−495.97	632.11	−112.47	90.67	−70.88	540.66	437.72	56.38

* Shortened trading day

DECEMBER DAILY POINT CHANGES DOW JONES INDUSTRIALS

Previous Month	2006	2007	2008	2009	2010	2011	2012	2013	2014	2015
Close	12221.93	13371.72	8829.04	10344.84	11006.02	12045.68	13025.58	16086.41	17828.24	17719.92
1	−27.80	S	−679.95	126.74	249.76	−25.65	S	S	−51.44	168.43
2	S	S	270.00	−18.90	106.63	−0.61	S	−77.64	102.75	−158.67
3	S	−57.15	172.60	−86.53	19.68	S	−59.98	−94.15	33.07	−252.01
4	89.72	−65.84	−215.45	22.75	S	S	−13.82	−24.85	−12.52	369.96
5	47.75	196.23	259.18	S	S	78.41	82.71	−68.26	58.69	S
6	−22.35	174.93	S	S	−19.90	52.30	39.55	198.69	S	S
7	−30.84	5.69	S	1.21	−3.03	46.24	81.09	S	S	−117.12
8	29.08	S	298.76	−104.14	13.32	−198.67	S	S	−106.31	−162.51
9	S	S	−242.85	51.08	−2.42	186.56	S	5.33	−51.28	−75.70
10	S	101.45	70.09	68.78	40.26	S	14.75	−52.40	−268.05	82.45
11	20.99	−294.26	−196.33	65.67	S	S	78.56	−129.60	63.19	−309.54
12	−12.90	41.13	64.59	S	S	−162.87	−2.99	−104.10	−315.51	S
13	1.92	44.06	S	S	18.24	−66.45	−74.73	15.93	S	S
14	99.26	−178.11	S	29.55	47.98	−131.46	−35.71	S	S	103.29
15	28.76	S	−65.15	−49.05	−19.07	45.33	S	S	−99.99	156.41
16	S	S	359.61	−10.88	41.78	−2.42	S	129.21	−111.97	224.18
17	S	−172.65	−99.80	−132.86	−7.34	S	100.38	−9.31	288.00	−253.25
18	−4.25	65.27	−219.35	20.63	S	S	115.57	292.71	421.28	−367.29
19	30.05	−25.20	−25.88	S	S	−100.13	−98.99	11.11	26.65	S
20	−7.45	38.37	S	S	−13.78	337.32	59.75	42.06	S	S
21	−42.62	205.01	S	85.25	55.03	4.16	−120.88	S	S	123.07
22	−78.03	S	−59.34	50.79	26.33	61.91	S	S	154.64	165.65
23	S	S	−100.28	1.51	14.00	124.35	S	73.47	64.73	185.34
24	S	98.68*	48.99*	53.66*	H	S	−51.76*	62.94*	6.04*	−50.44*
25	H	H	H	H	S	S	H	H	H	H
26	64.41	2.36	47.07	S	S	H	−24.49	122.33	23.50	S
27	102.94	−192.08	S	S	−18.46	−2.65	−18.28	−1.47	S	S
28	−9.05	6.26	S	26.98	20.51	−139.94	−158.20	S	S	−23.90
29	−38.37	S	−31.62	−1.67	9.84	135.63	S	S	−15.48	192.71
30	S	S	184.46	3.10	−15.67	−69.48	S	25.88	−55.16	−117.11
31	S	−101.05	108.00	−120.46	7.80	S	166.03	72.37	−160.00	−178.84
Close	12463.15	13264.82	8776.39	10428.05	11577.51	12217.56	13104.14	16576.66	17823.07	17425.03
Change	241.22	−106.90	−52.65	83.21	571.49	171.88	78.56	490.25	−5.17	−294.89

* Shortened trading day

A TYPICAL DAY IN THE MARKET

Half-hourly data became available for the Dow Jones Industrial Average starting in January 1987. The NYSE switched 10:00 a.m. openings to 9:30 a.m. in October 1985. Below is the comparison between half-hourly performance from January 1987 to April 15, 2016, and hourly performance from November 1963 to June 1985. Stronger openings and closings in a more bullish climate are evident. Morning and afternoon weaknesses appear an hour earlier.

MARKET % PERFORMANCE EACH HALF-HOUR OF THE DAY
(January 1987–April 15, 2016)

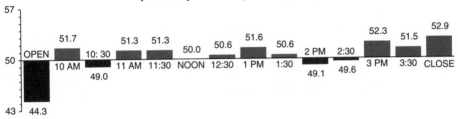

Based on the number of times the Dow Jones Industrial Average increased over previous half-hour.

MARKET % PERFORMANCE EACH HOUR OF THE DAY
(November 1963–June 1985)

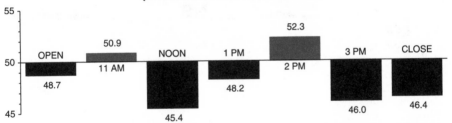

Based on the number of times the Dow Jones Industrial Average increased over previous hour.

On the next page, half-hourly movements since January 1987 are separated by day of the week. From 1953 to 1989, Monday was the worst day of the week, especially during long bear markets, but times changed. Monday reversed positions and became the best day of the week and on the plus side eleven years in a row from 1990 to 2000.

During the last 15 years (2001–April 15, 2016) Monday and Friday are net losers. Tuesday through Thursday are solid gainers, Tuesday the best (page 70). On all days, stocks do tend to firm up near the close with weakness in the early morning and from 1:30 to 2:30 frequently.

THROUGH THE WEEK ON A HALF-HOURLY BASIS

From the chart showing the percentage of times the Dow Jones Industrial Average rose over the preceding half-hour (January 1987 to April 15, 2016*), the typical week unfolds.

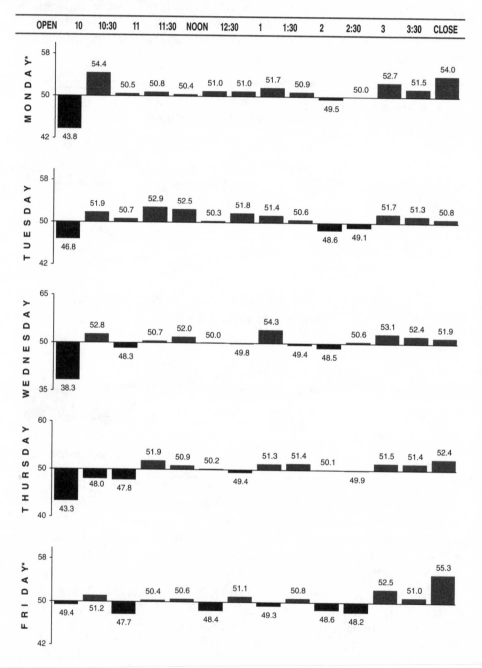

*Monday denotes first trading day of the week, Friday denotes last trading day of the week.

TUESDAY MOST PROFITABLE DAY OF WEEK

Between 1952 and 1989, Monday was the worst trading day of the week. The first trading day of the week (including Tuesday, when Monday is a holiday) rose only 44.3% of the time, while the other trading days closed higher 54.8% of the time. (NYSE Saturday trading was discontinued June 1952.)

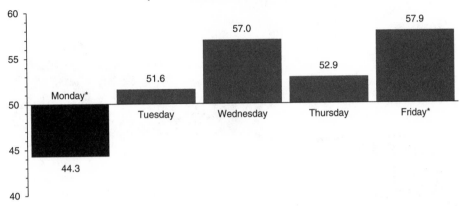

MARKET % PERFORMANCE EACH DAY OF THE WEEK
(June 1952–December 1989)

A dramatic reversal occurred in 1990—Monday became the most powerful day of the week. However, during the last 15 and a third years, Tuesday has produced the most gains. Since the top in 2000, traders have not been inclined to stay long over the weekend nor buy up equities at the outset of the week. This is not uncommon during uncertain market times. Monday was the worst day during the 2007–2009 bear, and only Tuesday was a net gainer. Since the March 2009 bottom, Tuesday and Thursday are best. See pages 70 and 143.

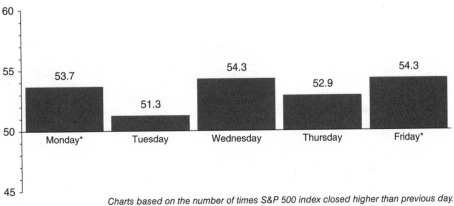

MARKET % PERFORMANCE EACH DAY OF THE WEEK
(January 1990–April 29, 2016)

Charts based on the number of times S&P 500 index closed higher than previous day.
*Monday denotes first trading day of the week, Friday denotes last trading day of the week.

NASDAQ STRONGEST LAST 3 DAYS OF WEEK

Despite 20 years less data, daily trading patterns on NASDAQ through 1989 appear to be fairly similar to the S&P on page 141, except for more bullishness on Thursdays. During the mostly flat markets of the 1970s and early 1980s, it would appear that apprehensive investors decided to throw in the towel over weekends and sell on Mondays and Tuesdays.

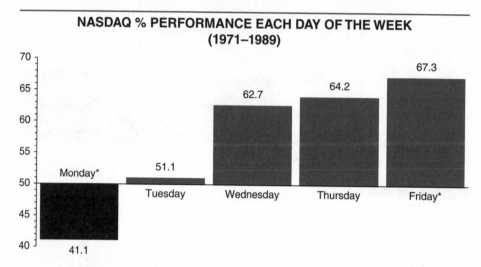

NASDAQ % PERFORMANCE EACH DAY OF THE WEEK (1971–1989)

Notice the vast difference in the daily trading pattern between NASDAQ and S&P from January 1, 1990, to recent times. The reason for so much more bullishness is that NASDAQ moved up 1010%, over three times as much during the 1990 to 2000 period. The gain for the S&P was 332% and for the Dow Jones industrials, 326%. NASDAQ's weekly patterns are beginning to move in step with the rest of the market. Notice the similarities to the S&P since 2001 on pages 143 and 144—Monday and Friday weakness, midweek strength.

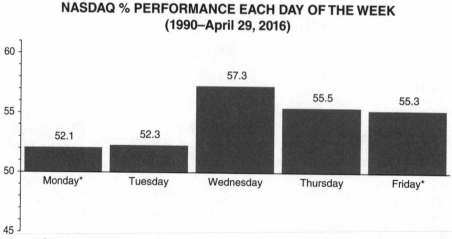

NASDAQ % PERFORMANCE EACH DAY OF THE WEEK (1990–April 29, 2016)

Based on NASDAQ composite, prior to February 5, 1971, based on National Quotation Bureau indices.
*Monday denotes first trading day of the week, Friday denotes last trading day of the week.

S&P DAILY PERFORMANCE EACH YEAR SINCE 1952

To determine if market trend alters performance of different days of the week, we separated 23 bear years—1953, '56, '57, '60, '62, '66, '69, '70, '73, '74, '77, '78, '81, '84, '87, '90, '94, 2000, 2001, 2002, 2008, 2011, and 2015—from 41 bull market years. While Tuesday and Thursday did not vary much between bull and bear years, Mondays and Fridays were sharply affected. There was a swing of 10.2 percentage points in Monday's performance and 9.8 in Friday's. Tuesday is the best day of the week based upon total points gained. See page 70.

PERCENTAGE OF TIMES MARKET CLOSED HIGHER THAN PREVIOUS DAY
(JUNE 1952–APRIL 29, 2016)

	Monday*	Tuesday	Wednesday	Thursday	Friday*
1952	48.4%	55.6%	58.1%	51.9%	66.7%
1953	32.7	50.0	54.9	57.5	56.6
1954	50.0	57.5	63.5	59.2	73.1
1955	50.0	45.7	63.5	60.0	78.9
1956	36.5	39.6	46.9	50.0	59.6
1957	25.0	54.0	66.7	48.9	44.2
1958	59.6	52.0	59.6	68.1	72.6
1959	42.3	53.1	55.8	48.9	69.8
1960	34.6	50.0	44.2	54.0	59.6
1961	52.9	54.4	64.7	56.0	67.3
1962	28.3	52.1	54.0	51.0	50.0
1963	46.2	63.3	51.0	57.5	69.2
1964	40.4	48.0	61.5	58.7	77.4
1965	44.2	57.5	55.8	51.0	71.2
1966	36.5	47.8	53.9	42.0	57.7
1967	38.5	50.0	60.8	64.0	69.2
1968†	49.1	57.5	64.3	42.6	54.9
1969	30.8	45.8	50.0	67.4	50.0
1970	38.5	46.0	63.5	48.9	52.8
1971	44.2	64.6	57.7	55.1	51.9
1972	38.5	60.9	57.7	51.0	67.3
1973	32.1	51.1	52.9	44.9	44.2
1974	32.7	57.1	51.0	36.7	30.8
1975	53.9	38.8	61.5	56.3	55.8
1976	55.8	55.3	55.8	40.8	58.5
1977	40.4	40.4	46.2	53.1	53.9
1978	51.9	43.5	59.6	54.0	48.1
1979	54.7	53.2	58.8	66.0	44.2
1980	55.8	54.2	71.7	35.4	59.6
1981	44.2	38.8	55.8	53.2	47.2
1982	46.2	39.6	44.2	44.9	50.0
1983	55.8	46.8	61.5	52.0	55.8
1984	39.6	63.8	31.4	46.0	44.2
1985	44.2	61.2	54.9	56.3	53.9
1986	51.9	44.9	67.3	58.3	55.8
1987	51.9	57.1	63.5	61.7	49.1
1988	51.9	61.7	51.9	48.0	59.6
1989	51.9	47.8	69.2	58.0	69.2
1990	67.9	53.2	52.9	40.0	51.9
1991	44.2	46.9	52.9	49.0	51.9
1992	51.9	49.0	53.9	56.3	45.3
1993	65.4	41.7	55.8	44.9	48.1
1994	55.8	46.8	52.9	48.0	59.6
1995	63.5	56.5	63.5	62.0	63.5
1996	54.7	44.9	51.0	57.1	63.5
1997	67.3	67.4	42.3	41.7	57.7
1998	57.7	62.5	57.7	38.3	60.4
1999	46.2	29.8	67.3	53.1	46.2
2000	51.9	43.5	40.4	56.0	43.1
2001	45.3	51.1	44.0	59.2	48.1
2002	40.4	37.5	56.9	38.8	50.0
2003	59.6	62.5	42.3	58.3	52.8
2004	51.9	61.7	59.6	52.1	55.8
2005	59.6	47.8	59.6	56.0	48.1
2006	55.8	55.6	67.3	52.0	61.5
2007	47.2	50.0	64.0	50.0	55.8
2008	42.3	50.0	41.5	60.4	52.8
2009	53.9	50.0	57.7	63.8	57.7
2010	61.5	57.5	55.8	53.1	57.7
2011	48.1	56.5	55.8	56.0	57.7
2012	52.8	48.9	50.0	58.0	53.9
2013	51.9	60.4	54.9	59.2	65.4
2014	53.9	56.3	57.7	56.3	61.5
2015	51.9	43.8	44.2	53.2	43.4
2016‡	47.1	53.3	64.7	56.3	52.9
Average	**48.2%**	**51.4%**	**55.7%**	**52.8%**	**56.5%**
41 Bull Years	**51.8%**	**53.0%**	**58.1%**	**53.7%**	**60.0%**
23 Bear Years	**41.7%**	**48.7%**	**51.4%**	**51.3%**	**50.2%**

Based on S&P 500

† Most Wednesdays closed last 7 months of 1968. ‡ Through 4/29/2016 only, not included in averages.
*Monday denotes first trading day of the week, Friday denotes last trading day of the week.

NASDAQ DAILY PERFORMANCE EACH YEAR SINCE 1971

After dropping a hefty 77.9% from its 2000 high (versus −37.8% on the Dow and −49.1% on the S&P 500), NASDAQ tech stocks still outpace the blue chips and big caps—but not by nearly as much as they did. From January 1, 1971 through April 29, 2016, NASDAQ, moved up an impressive 5229%. The Dow (up 2019%) and the S&P (up 2141%) gained less than half as much.

Monday's performance on NASDAQ was lackluster during the three-year bear market of 2000–2002. As NASDAQ rebounded (up 50% in 2003), strength returned to Monday during 2003–2006. During the bear market from late 2007 to early 2009, weakness was most consistent on Monday and Friday. At press time, Mondays and Tuesdays have been treacherous.

PERCENTAGE OF TIMES NASDAQ CLOSED HIGHER THAN PREVIOUS DAY (1971–APRIL 29, 2016)

	Monday*	Tuesday	Wednesday	Thursday	Friday*
1971	51.9%	52.1%	59.6%	65.3%	71.2%
1972	30.8	60.9	63.5	57.1	78.9
1973	34.0	48.9	52.9	53.1	48.1
1974	30.8	44.9	52.9	51.0	42.3
1975	44.2	42.9	63.5	64.6	63.5
1976	50.0	63.8	67.3	59.2	58.5
1977	51.9	40.4	53.9	63.3	73.1
1978	48.1	47.8	73.1	72.0	84.6
1979	45.3	53.2	64.7	86.0	82.7
1980	46.2	64.6	84.9	52.1	73.1
1981	42.3	32.7	67.3	76.6	69.8
1982	34.6	47.9	59.6	51.0	63.5
1983	42.3	44.7	67.3	68.0	73.1
1984	22.6	53.2	35.3	52.0	51.9
1985	36.5	59.2	62.8	68.8	66.0
1986	38.5	55.1	65.4	72.9	75.0
1987	42.3	49.0	65.4	68.1	66.0
1988	50.0	55.3	61.5	66.0	63.5
1989	38.5	54.4	71.2	72.0	75.0
1990	54.7	42.6	60.8	46.0	55.8
1991	51.9	59.2	66.7	65.3	51.9
1992	44.2	53.1	59.6	60.4	45.3
1993	55.8	56.3	69.2	57.1	67.3
1994	51.9	46.8	54.9	52.0	55.8
1995	50.0	52.2	63.5	64.0	63.5
1996	50.9	57.1	64.7	61.2	63.5
1997	65.4	59.2	53.9	52.1	55.8
1998	59.6	58.3	65.4	44.7	58.5
1999	61.5	40.4	63.5	57.1	65.4
2000	40.4	41.3	42.3	60.0	57.7
2001	41.5	57.8	52.0	55.1	47.1
2002	44.2	37.5	56.9	46.9	46.2
2003	57.7	60.4	40.4	60.4	46.2
2004	57.7	59.6	53.9	50.0	50.9
2005	61.5	47.8	51.9	48.0	59.6
2006	55.8	51.1	65.4	50.0	44.2
2007	47.2	63.0	66.0	56.0	57.7
2008	34.6	52.1	49.1	54.2	42.3
2009	51.9	54.2	63.5	63.8	50.9
2010	61.5	53.2	61.5	55.1	61.5
2011	50.0	56.5	50.0	64.0	53.9
2012	49.1	53.3	50.0	54.0	51.9
2013	57.7	60.4	52.9	59.2	67.3
2014	57.7	58.3	57.7	52.1	59.6
2015	55.8	39.6	53.9	59.6	49.1
2016†	35.3	40.0	58.8	50.0	64.7
Average	**47.8%**	**52.0%**	**59.6%**	**59.3%**	**60.2%**
32 Bull Years	**49.9%**	**53.5%**	**61.8%**	**60.0%**	**62.8%**
12 Bear Years	**41.9%**	**46.4%**	**53.4%**	**56.8%**	**52.8%**

Based on NASDAQ composite; prior to February 5, 1971, based on National Quotation Bureau indices.
† Through 4/29/2016 only, not included in averages.
*Monday denotes first trading day of the week, Friday denotes last trading day of the week.

MONTHLY CASH INFLOWS INTO S&P STOCKS

For many years, the last trading day of the month, plus the first four of the following month, were the best market days of the month. This pattern is quite clear in the first chart, showing these five consecutive trading days towering above the other 16 trading days of the average month in the 1953–1981 period. The rationale was that individuals and institutions tended to operate similarly, causing a massive flow of cash into stocks near beginnings of months.

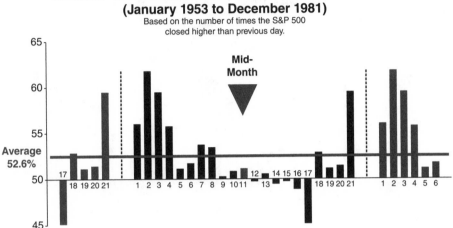

MARKET % PERFORMANCE EACH DAY OF THE MONTH
(January 1953 to December 1981)
Based on the number of times the S&P 500
closed higher than previous day.

Clearly, "front-running" traders took advantage of this phenomenon, drastically altering the previous pattern. The second chart from 1982 onward shows the trading shift caused by these "anticipators" to the last three trading days of the month, plus the first two. Another astonishing development shows the ninth, tenth, and eleventh trading days rising strongly as well. Growth of 401(k) retirement plans, IRAs, and similar plans (participants' salaries are usually paid twice monthly) is responsible for this mid-month bulge. First trading days of the month have produced the greatest gains in recent years (see page 86).

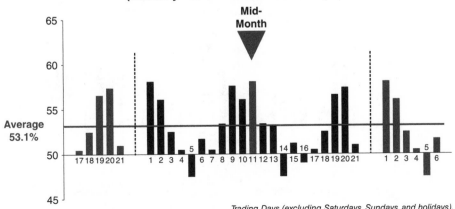

MARKET % PERFORMANCE EACH DAY OF THE MONTH
(January 1982 to December 2015)

Trading Days (excluding Saturdays, Sundays, and holidays).

145

MONTHLY CASH INFLOWS INTO NASDAQ STOCKS

NASDAQ stocks moved up 58.1% of the time through 1981 compared to 52.6% for the S&P on page 145. Ends and beginnings of the month are fairly similar, specifically the last plus the first four trading days. But notice how investors piled into NASDAQ stocks until mid-month. NASDAQ rose 118.6% from January 1, 1971, to December 31, 1981, compared to 33.0% for the S&P.

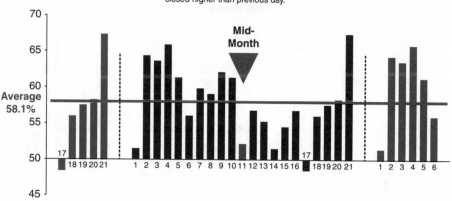

NASDAQ % PERFORMANCE EACH DAY OF THE MONTH
(January 1971 to December 1981)
Based on the number of times the NASDAQ composite
closed higher than previous day.

After the air was let out of the tech market 2000–2002, S&P's 1568% gain over the last 34 years is more evenly matched with NASDAQ's 2457% gain. Last three, first four, and middle ninth and tenth days rose the most. Where the S&P has three days of the month that go down more often than up, NASDAQ has none. NASDAQ exhibits the most strength on the last trading day of the month; however, over the past 18 years, last days have weakened considerably, down more often than not.

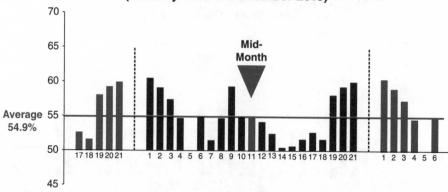

NASDAQ % PERFORMANCE EACH DAY OF THE MONTH
(January 1982 to December 2015)

Trading Days (excluding Saturdays, Sundays, and holidays).
Based on NASDAQ composite, prior to February 5, 1971, based on National Quotation Bureau indices.

146

NOVEMBER, DECEMBER, AND JANUARY: YEAR'S BEST THREE-MONTH SPAN

The most important observation to be made from a chart showing the average monthly percent change in market prices since 1950 is that institutions (mutual funds, pension funds, banks, etc.) determine the trading patterns in today's market.

The "investment calendar" reflects the annual, semi-annual, and quarterly operations of institutions during January, April, and July. October, besides being the last campaign month before elections, is also the time when most bear markets seem to end, as in 1946, 1957, 1960, 1966, 1974, 1987, 1990, 1998, and 2002. (August and September tend to combine to make the worst consecutive two-month period.)

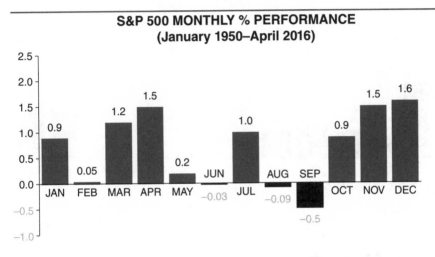

S&P 500 MONTHLY % PERFORMANCE
(January 1950–April 2016)

Average month-to-month % change in S&P 500.
(Based on monthly closing prices.)

Unusual year-end strength comes from corporate and private pension funds, producing a 4.0% gain on average between November 1 and January 31. In 2007–2008, these three months were all down for the fourth time since 1930; previously in 1931–1932, 1940–1941, and 1969–1970, also bear markets. September's dismal performance makes it the worst month of the year. However, in the last 12 years, it has been up 8 times after being down five in a row 1999–2003.

In post-election years since 1953, July is the best month, +2.2% (10–6). November and May tie for runner-up with a 1.7% average gain. January, March, April, and October are also positive. February is worst, –1.8% (7–9), while June, August, and September are net losers as well.

See page 50 for monthly performance tables for the S&P 500 and the Dow Jones industrials. See pages 52, 54, and 62 for unique switching strategies.

On page 66, you can see how the first month of the first three quarters far outperforms the second and the third months since 1950, and note the improvement in May's and October's performance since 1991.

NOVEMBER THROUGH JUNE: NASDAQ'S EIGHT-MONTH RUN

The two-and-a-half-year plunge of 77.9% in NASDAQ stocks, between March 10, 2000, and October 9, 2002, brought several horrendous monthly losses (the two greatest were November 2000, −22.9%, and February 2001, −22.4%), which trimmed average monthly performance over the $45^1/_3$-year period. Ample Octobers in 13 of the last 18 years, including three huge turnarounds in 2001 (+12.8%), 2002 (+13.5%), and 2011 (+11.1%) have put bear-killing October in the number one spot since 1998. January's 2.5% average gain is still awesome, and more than twice S&P's 1.1% January average since 1971.

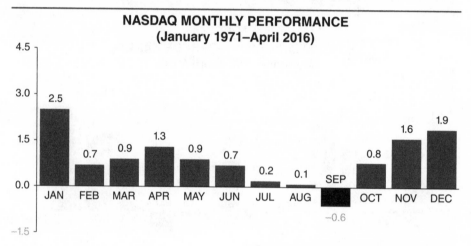

NASDAQ MONTHLY PERFORMANCE
(January 1971–April 2016)

*Average month-to-month % change in NASDAQ composite,
prior to February 5, 1971, based on National Quotation Bureau indices.
(Based on monthly closing prices.)*

Bear in mind, when comparing NASDAQ to the S&P on page 147, that there are 22 fewer years of data here. During this $45^1/_3$-year (1971–April 2016) period, NASDAQ gained 5229%, while the S&P and the Dow rose only 2141% and 2019%, respectively. On page 58, you can see a statistical monthly comparison between NASDAQ and the Dow.

Year-end strength is even more pronounced in NASDAQ, producing a 6.0% gain on average between November 1 and January 31—1.5 times greater than that of the S&P 500 on page 147. September is the worst month of the year for the over-the-counter index as well, posting an average loss of −0.6%. These extremes underscore NASDAQ's higher volatility—and moves of greater magnitude.

In post-election years since 1973, May and July are tied for the top spot with an average gain of 3.4% with identical records (9–2). January, April, June, October, November, and December also produce average gains. February is the worst month, off 3.9% (3–8). March, August, and September are net losers as well.

DOW JONES INDUSTRIALS ANNUAL HIGHS, LOWS, & CLOSES SINCE 1901

YEAR	HIGH DATE	HIGH CLOSE	LOW DATE	LOW CLOSE	YEAR CLOSE	YEAR	HIGH DATE	HIGH CLOSE	LOW DATE	LOW CLOSE	YEAR CLOSE
1901	6/17	57.33	12/24	45.07	47.29	1959	12/31	679.36	2/9	574.46	679.36
1902	4/24	50.14	12/15	43.64	47.10	1960	1/5	685.47	10/25	566.05	615.89
1903	2/16	49.59	11/9	30.88	35.98	1961	12/13	734.91	1/3	610.25	731.14
1904	12/5	53.65	3/12	34.00	50.99	1962	1/3	726.01	6/26	535.76	652.10
1905	12/29	70.74	1/25	50.37	70.47	1963	12/18	767.21	1/2	646.79	762.95
1906	1/19	75.45	7/13	62.40	69.12	1964	11/18	891.71	1/2	766.08	874.13
1907	1/7	70.60	11/15	38.83	43.04	1965	12/31	969.26	6/28	840.59	969.26
1908	11/13	64.74	2/13	42.94	63.11	1966	2/9	995.15	10/7	744.32	785.69
1909	11/19	73.64	2/23	58.54	72.56	1967	9/25	943.08	1/3	786.41	905.11
1910	1/3	72.04	7/26	53.93	59.60	1968	12/3	985.21	3/21	825.13	943.75
1911	6/19	63.78	9/25	53.43	59.84	1969	5/14	968.85	12/17	769.93	800.36
1912	9/30	68.97	2/10	58.72	64.37	1970	12/29	842.00	5/26	631.16	838.92
1913	1/9	64.88	6/11	52.83	57.71	1971	4/28	950.82	11/23	797.97	890.20
1914	3/20	61.12	7/30	52.32	54.58	1972	12/11	1036.27	1/26	889.15	1020.02
1915	12/27	99.21	2/24	54.22	99.15	1973	1/11	1051.70	12/5	788.31	850.86
1916	11/21	110.15	4/22	84.96	95.00	1974	3/13	891.66	12/6	577.60	616.24
1917	1/3	99.18	12/19	65.95	74.38	1975	7/15	881.81	1/2	632.04	852.41
1918	10/18	89.07	1/15	73.38	82.20	1976	9/21	1014.79	1/2	858.71	1004.65
1919	11/3	119.62	2/8	79.15	107.23	1977	1/3	999.75	11/2	800.85	831.17
1920	1/3	109.88	12/21	66.75	71.95	1978	9/8	907.74	2/28	742.12	805.01
1921	12/15	81.50	8/24	63.90	81.10	1979	10/5	897.61	11/7	796.67	838.74
1922	10/14	103.43	1/10	78.59	98.73	1980	11/20	1000.17	4/21	759.13	963.99
1923	3/20	105.38	10/27	85.76	95.52	1981	4/27	1024.05	9/25	824.01	875.00
1924	12/31	120.51	5/20	88.33	120.51	1982	12/27	1070.55	8/12	776.92	1046.54
1925	11/6	159.39	3/30	115.00	156.66	1983	11/29	1287.20	1/3	1027.04	1258.64
1926	8/14	166.64	3/30	135.20	157.20	1984	1/6	1286.64	7/24	1086.57	1211.57
1927	12/31	202.40	1/25	152.73	202.40	1985	12/16	1553.10	1/4	1184.96	1546.67
1928	12/31	300.00	2/20	191.33	300.00	1986	12/2	1955.57	1/22	1502.29	1895.95
1929	9/3	381.17	11/13	198.69	248.48	1987	8/25	2722.42	10/19	1738.74	1938.83
1930	4/17	294.07	12/16	157.51	164.58	1988	10/21	2183.50	1/20	1879.14	2168.57
1931	2/24	194.36	12/17	73.79	77.90	1989	10/9	2791.41	1/3	2144.64	2753.20
1932	3/8	88.78	7/8	41.22	59.93	1990	7/17	2999.75	10/11	2365.10	2633.66
1933	7/18	108.67	2/27	50.16	99.90	1991	12/31	3168.83	1/9	2470.30	3168.83
1934	2/5	110.74	7/26	85.51	104.04	1992	6/1	3413.21	10/9	3136.58	3301.11
1935	11/19	148.44	3/14	96.71	144.13	1993	12/29	3794.33	1/20	3241.95	3754.09
1936	11/17	184.90	1/6	143.11	179.90	1994	1/31	3978.36	4/4	3593.35	3834.44
1937	3/10	194.40	11/24	113.64	120.85	1995	12/13	5216.47	1/30	3832.08	5117.12
1938	11/12	158.41	3/31	98.95	154.76	1996	12/27	6560.91	1/10	5032.94	6448.27
1939	9/12	155.92	4/8	121.44	150.24	1997	8/6	8259.31	4/11	6391.69	7908.25
1940	1/3	152.80	6/10	111.84	131.13	1998	11/23	9374.27	8/31	7539.07	9181.43
1941	1/10	133.59	12/23	106.34	110.96	1999	12/31	11497.12	1/22	9120.67	11497.12
1942	12/26	119.71	4/28	92.92	119.40	2000	1/14	11722.98	3/7	9796.03	10786.85
1943	7/14	145.82	1/8	119.26	135.89	2001	5/21	11337.92	9/21	8235.81	10021.50
1944	12/16	152.53	2/7	134.22	152.32	2002	3/19	10635.25	10/9	7286.27	8341.63
1945	12/11	195.82	1/24	151.35	192.91	2003	12/31	10453.92	3/11	7524.06	10453.92
1946	5/29	212.50	10/9	163.12	177.20	2004	12/28	10854.54	10/25	9749.99	10783.01
1947	7/24	186.85	5/17	163.21	181.16	2005	3/4	10940.55	4/20	10012.36	10717.50
1948	6/15	193.16	3/16	165.39	177.30	2006	12/27	12510.57	1/20	10667.39	12463.15
1949	12/30	200.52	6/13	161.60	200.13	2007	10/9	14164.53	3/5	12050.41	13264.82
1950	11/24	235.47	1/13	196.81	235.41	2008	5/2	13058.20	11/20	7552.29	8776.39
1951	9/13	276.37	1/3	238.99	269.23	2009	12/30	10548.51	3/9	6547.05	10428.05
1952	12/30	292.00	5/1	256.35	291.90	2010	12/29	11585.38	7/2	9686.48	11577.51
1953	1/5	293.79	9/14	255.49	280.90	2011	4/29	12810.54	10/3	10655.30	12217.56
1954	12/31	404.39	1/11	279.87	404.39	2012	10/5	13610.15	6/4	12101.46	13104.14
1955	12/30	488.40	1/17	388.20	488.40	2013	12/31	16576.66	1/8	13328.85	16576.66
1956	4/6	521.05	1/23	462.35	499.47	2014	12/26	18053.71	2/3	15372.80	17823.07
1957	7/12	520.77	10/22	419.79	435.69	2015	5/19	18312.39	8/25	15666.44	17425.03
1958	12/31	583.65	2/25	436.89	583.65	2016*	4/20	18096.27	2/11	15660.18	*At Press-time*

*Through April 29, 2016

S&P 500 ANNUAL HIGHS, LOWS, & CLOSES SINCE 1930

YEAR	HIGH DATE	HIGH CLOSE	LOW DATE	LOW CLOSE	YEAR CLOSE	YEAR	HIGH DATE	HIGH CLOSE	LOW DATE	LOW CLOSE	YEAR CLOSE
1930	4/10	25.92	12/16	14.44	15.34	1974	1/3	99.80	10/3	62.28	68.56
1931	2/24	18.17	12/17	7.72	8.12	1975	7/15	95.61	1/8	70.04	90.19
1932	9/7	9.31	6/1	4.40	6.89	1976	9/21	107.83	1/2	90.90	107.46
1933	7/18	12.20	2/27	5.53	10.10	1977	1/3	107.00	11/2	90.71	95.10
1934	2/6	11.82	7/26	8.36	9.50	1978	9/12	106.99	3/6	86.90	96.11
1935	11/19	13.46	3/14	8.06	13.43	1979	10/5	111.27	2/27	96.13	107.94
1936	11/9	17.69	1/2	13.40	17.18	1980	11/28	140.52	3/27	98.22	135.76
1937	3/6	18.68	11/24	10.17	10.55	1981	1/6	138.12	9/25	112.77	122.55
1938	11/9	13.79	3/31	8.50	13.21	1982	11/9	143.02	8/12	102.42	140.64
1939	1/4	13.23	4/8	10.18	12.49	1983	10/10	172.65	1/3	138.34	164.93
1940	1/3	12.77	6/10	8.99	10.58	1984	11/6	170.41	7/24	147.82	167.24
1941	1/10	10.86	12/29	8.37	8.69	1985	12/16	212.02	1/4	163.68	211.28
1942	12/31	9.77	4/28	7.47	9.77	1986	12/2	254.00	1/22	203.49	242.17
1943	7/14	12.64	1/2	9.84	11.67	1987	8/25	336.77	12/4	223.92	247.08
1944	12/16	13.29	2/7	11.56	13.28	1988	10/21	283.66	1/20	242.63	277.72
1945	12/10	17.68	1/23	13.21	17.36	1989	10/9	359.80	1/3	275.31	353.40
1946	5/29	19.25	10/9	14.12	15.30	1990	7/16	368.95	10/11	295.46	330.22
1947	2/8	16.20	5/17	13.71	15.30	1991	12/31	417.09	1/9	311.49	417.09
1948	6/15	17.06	2/14	13.84	15.20	1992	12/18	441.28	4/8	394.50	435.71
1949	12/30	16.79	6/13	13.55	16.76	1993	12/28	470.94	1/8	429.05	466.45
1950	12/29	20.43	1/14	16.65	20.41	1994	2/2	482.00	4/4	438.92	459.27
1951	10/15	23.85	1/3	20.69	23.77	1995	12/13	621.69	1/3	459.11	615.93
1952	12/30	26.59	2/20	23.09	26.57	1996	11/25	757.03	1/10	598.48	740.74
1953	1/5	26.66	9/14	22.71	24.81	1997	12/5	983.79	1/2	737.01	970.43
1954	12/31	35.98	1/11	24.80	35.98	1998	12/29	1241.81	1/9	927.69	1229.23
1955	11/14	46.41	1/17	34.58	45.48	1999	12/31	1469.25	1/14	1212.19	1469.25
1956	8/2	49.74	1/23	43.11	46.67	2000	3/24	1527.46	12/20	1264.74	1320.28
1957	7/15	49.13	10/22	38.98	39.99	2001	2/1	1373.47	9/21	965.80	1148.08
1958	12/31	55.21	1/2	40.33	55.21	2002	1/4	1172.51	10/9	776.76	879.82
1959	8/3	60.71	2/9	53.58	59.89	2003	12/31	1111.92	3/11	800.73	1111.92
1960	1/5	60.39	10/25	52.30	58.11	2004	12/30	1213.55	8/12	1063.23	1211.92
1961	12/12	72.64	1/3	57.57	71.55	2005	12/14	1272.74	4/20	1137.50	1248.29
1962	1/3	71.13	6/26	52.32	63.10	2006	12/15	1427.09	6/13	1223.69	1418.30
1963	12/31	75.02	1/2	62.69	75.02	2007	10/9	1565.15	3/5	1374.12	1468.36
1964	11/20	86.28	1/2	75.43	84.75	2008	1/2	1447.16	11/20	752.44	903.25
1965	11/15	92.63	6/28	81.60	92.43	2009	12/28	1127.78	3/9	676.53	1115.10
1966	2/9	94.06	10/7	73.20	80.33	2010	12/29	1259.78	7/2	1022.58	1257.64
1967	9/25	97.59	1/3	80.38	96.47	2011	4/29	1363.61	10/3	1099.23	1257.60
1968	11/29	108.37	3/5	87.72	103.86	2012	9/14	1465.77	1/3	1277.06	1426.19
1969	5/14	106.16	12/17	89.20	92.06	2013	12/31	1848.36	1/8	1457.15	1848.36
1970	1/5	93.46	5/26	69.29	92.15	2014	12/29	2090.57	2/3	1741.89	2058.90
1971	4/28	104.77	11/23	90.16	102.09	2015	5/21	2130.82	8/25	1867.61	2043.94
1972	12/11	119.12	1/3	101.67	118.05	2016*	4/20	2102.40	2/11	1829.08	At Press-time
1973	1/11	120.24	12/5	92.16	97.55						

*Through April 29, 2016

NASDAQ ANNUAL HIGHS, LOWS, & CLOSES SINCE 1971

YEAR	HIGH DATE	HIGH CLOSE	LOW DATE	LOW CLOSE	YEAR CLOSE	YEAR	HIGH DATE	HIGH CLOSE	LOW DATE	LOW CLOSE	YEAR CLOSE
1971	12/31	114.12	1/5	89.06	114.12	1994	3/18	803.93	6/24	693.79	751.96
1972	12/8	135.15	1/3	113.65	133.73	1995	12/4	1069.79	1/3	743.58	1052.13
1973	1/11	136.84	12/24	88.67	92.19	1996	12/9	1316.27	1/15	988.57	1291.03
1974	3/15	96.53	10/3	54.87	59.82	1997	10/9	1745.85	4/2	1201.00	1570.35
1975	7/15	88.00	1/2	60.70	77.62	1998	12/31	2192.69	10/8	1419.12	2192.69
1976	12/31	97.88	1/2	78.06	97.88	1999	12/31	4069.31	1/4	2208.05	4069.31
1977	12/30	105.05	4/5	93.66	105.05	2000	3/10	5048.62	12/20	2332.78	2470.52
1978	9/13	139.25	1/11	99.09	117.98	2001	1/24	2859.15	9/21	1423.19	1950.40
1979	10/5	152.29	1/2	117.84	151.14	2002	1/4	2059.38	10/9	1114.11	1335.51
1980	11/28	208.15	3/27	124.09	202.34	2003	12/30	2009.88	3/11	1271.47	2003.37
1981	5/29	223.47	9/28	175.03	195.84	2004	12/30	2178.34	8/12	1752.49	2175.44
1982	12/8	240.70	8/13	159.14	232.41	2005	12/2	2273.37	4/28	1904.18	2205.32
1983	6/24	328.91	1/3	230.59	278.60	2006	11/22	2465.98	7/21	2020.39	2415.29
1984	1/6	287.90	7/25	225.30	247.35	2007	10/31	2859.12	3/5	2340.68	2652.28
1985	12/16	325.16	1/2	245.91	324.93	2008	1/2	2609.63	11/20	1316.12	1577.03
1986	7/3	411.16	1/9	323.01	349.33	2009	12/30	2291.28	3/9	1268.64	2269.15
1987	8/26	455.26	10/28	291.88	330.47	2010	12/22	2671.48	7/2	2091.79	2652.87
1988	7/5	396.11	1/12	331.97	381.38	2011	4/29	2873.54	10/3	2335.83	2605.15
1989	10/9	485.73	1/3	378.56	454.82	2012	9/14	3183.95	1/4	2648.36	3019.51
1990	7/16	469.60	10/16	325.44	373.84	2013	12/31	4176.59	1/8	3091.81	4176.59
1991	12/31	586.34	1/14	355.75	586.34	2014	12/29	4806.91	2/3	3996.96	4736.05
1992	12/31	676.95	6/26	547.84	676.95	2015	7/20	5218.86	8/25	4506.49	5007.41
1993	10/15	787.42	4/26	645.87	776.80	2016*	4/18	4960.02	2/11	4266.84	At Press-time

RUSSELL 1000 ANNUAL HIGHS, LOWS, & CLOSES SINCE 1979

YEAR	HIGH DATE	HIGH CLOSE	LOW DATE	LOW CLOSE	YEAR CLOSE	YEAR	HIGH DATE	HIGH CLOSE	LOW DATE	LOW CLOSE	YEAR CLOSE
1979	10/5	61.18	2/27	51.83	59.87	1998	12/29	645.36	1/9	490.26	642.87
1980	11/28	78.26	3/27	53.68	75.20	1999	12/31	767.97	2/9	632.53	767.97
1981	1/6	76.34	9/25	62.03	67.93	2000	9/1	813.71	12/20	668.75	700.09
1982	11/9	78.47	8/12	55.98	77.24	2001	1/30	727.35	9/21	507.98	604.94
1983	10/10	95.07	1/3	76.04	90.38	2002	3/19	618.74	10/9	410.52	466.18
1984	1/6	92.80	7/24	79.49	90.31	2003	12/31	594.56	3/11	425.31	594.56
1985	12/16	114.97	1/4	88.61	114.39	2004	12/30	651.76	8/13	566.06	650.99
1986	7/2	137.87	1/22	111.14	130.00	2005	12/14	692.09	4/20	613.37	679.42
1987	8/25	176.22	12/4	117.65	130.02	2006	12/15	775.08	6/13	665.81	770.08
1988	10/21	149.94	1/20	128.35	146.99	2007	10/9	852.32	3/5	749.85	799.82
1989	10/9	189.93	1/3	145.78	185.11	2008	1/2	788.62	11/20	402.91	487.77
1990	7/16	191.56	10/11	152.36	171.22	2009	12/28	619.22	3/9	367.55	612.01
1991	12/31	220.61	1/9	161.94	220.61	2010	12/29	698.11	7/2	562.58	696.90
1992	12/18	235.06	4/8	208.87	233.59	2011	4/29	758.45	10/3	604.42	693.36
1993	10/15	252.77	1/8	229.91	250.71	2012	9/14	809.01	1/4	703.72	789.90
1994	2/1	258.31	4/4	235.38	244.65	2013	12/31	1030.36	1/8	807.95	1030.36
1995	12/13	331.18	1/3	244.41	328.89	2014	12/29	1161.45	2/3	972.95	1144.37
1996	12/2	401.21	1/10	318.24	393.75	2015	5/21	1189.55	8/25	1042.77	1131.88
1997	12/5	519.72	4/11	389.03	513.79	2016*	4/20	1163.23	2/11	1008.89	At Press-time

RUSSELL 2000 ANNUAL HIGHS, LOWS, & CLOSES SINCE 1979

YEAR	HIGH DATE	HIGH CLOSE	LOW DATE	LOW CLOSE	YEAR CLOSE	YEAR	HIGH DATE	HIGH CLOSE	LOW DATE	LOW CLOSE	YEAR CLOSE
1979	12/31	55.91	1/2	40.81	55.91	1998	4/21	491.41	10/8	310.28	421.96
1980	11/28	77.70	3/27	45.36	74.80	1999	12/31	504.75	3/23	383.37	504.75
1981	6/15	85.16	9/25	65.37	73.67	2000	3/9	606.05	12/20	443.80	483.53
1982	12/8	91.01	8/12	60.33	88.90	2001	5/22	517.23	9/21	378.89	488.50
1983	6/24	126.99	1/3	88.29	112.27	2002	4/16	522.95	10/9	327.04	383.09
1984	1/12	116.69	7/25	93.95	101.49	2003	12/30	565.47	3/12	345.94	556.91
1985	12/31	129.87	1/2	101.21	129.87	2004	12/28	654.57	8/12	517.10	651.57
1986	7/3	155.30	1/9	128.23	135.00	2005	12/2	690.57	4/28	575.02	673.22
1987	8/25	174.44	10/28	106.08	120.42	2006	12/27	797.73	7/21	671.94	787.66
1988	7/15	151.42	1/12	121.23	147.37	2007	7/13	855.77	11/26	735.07	766.03
1989	10/9	180.78	1/3	146.79	168.30	2008	6/5	763.27	11/20	385.31	499.45
1990	6/15	170.90	10/30	118.82	132.16	2009	12/24	634.07	3/9	343.26	625.39
1991	12/31	189.94	1/15	125.25	189.94	2010	12/27	792.35	2/8	586.49	783.65
1992	12/31	221.01	7/8	185.81	221.01	2011	4/29	865.29	10/3	609.49	740.92
1993	11/2	260.17	2/23	217.55	258.59	2012	9/14	864.70	6/4	737.24	849.35
1994	3/18	271.08	12/9	235.16	250.36	2013	12/31	1163.64	1/3	872.60	1163.64
1995	9/14	316.12	1/30	246.56	315.97	2014	12/29	1219.11	10/13	1049.30	1204.70
1996	5/22	364.61	1/16	301.75	362.61	2015	6/23	1295.80	9/29	1083.91	1135.89
1997	10/13	465.21	4/25	335.85	437.02	2016*	4/27	1154.15	2/11	953.72	At Press-time

*Through April 29, 2016

151

DOW JONES INDUSTRIALS MONTHLY PERCENT CHANGES SINCE 1950

	Jan	Feb	Mar	Apr	May	Jun	Jul	Aug	Sep	Oct	Nov	Dec	Year's Change
1950	0.8	0.8	1.3	4.0	4.2	-6.4	0.1	3.6	4.4	-0.6	1.2	3.4	17.6
1951	5.7	1.3	-1.6	4.5	-3.7	-2.8	6.3	4.8	0.3	-3.2	-0.4	3.0	14.4
1952	0.5	-3.9	3.6	-4.4	2.1	4.3	1.9	-1.6	-1.6	-0.5	5.4	2.9	8.4
1953	-0.7	-1.9	-1.5	-1.8	-0.9	-1.5	2.7	-5.1	1.1	4.5	2.0	-0.2	-3.8
1954	4.1	0.7	3.0	5.2	2.6	1.8	4.3	-3.5	7.3	-2.3	9.8	4.6	44.0
1955	1.1	0.7	-0.5	3.9	-0.2	6.2	3.2	0.5	-0.3	-2.5	6.2	1.1	20.8
1956	-3.6	2.7	5.8	0.8	-7.4	3.1	5.1	-3.0	-5.3	1.0	-1.5	5.6	2.3
1957	-4.1	-3.0	2.2	4.1	2.1	-0.3	1.0	-4.8	-5.8	-3.3	2.0	-3.2	-12.8
1958	3.3	-2.2	1.6	2.0	1.5	3.3	5.2	1.1	4.6	2.1	2.6	4.7	34.0
1959	1.8	1.6	-0.3	3.7	3.2	-0.03	4.9	-1.6	-4.9	2.4	1.9	3.1	16.4
1960	-8.4	1.2	-2.1	-2.4	4.0	2.4	-3.7	1.5	-7.3	0.04	2.9	3.1	-9.3
1961	5.2	2.1	2.2	0.3	2.7	-1.8	3.1	2.1	-2.6	0.4	2.5	1.3	18.7
1962	-4.3	1.1	-0.2	-5.9	-7.8	-8.5	6.5	1.9	-5.0	1.9	10.1	0.4	-10.8
1963	4.7	-2.9	3.0	5.2	1.3	-2.8	-1.6	4.9	0.5	3.1	-0.6	1.7	17.0
1964	2.9	1.9	1.6	-0.3	1.2	1.3	1.2	-0.3	4.4	-0.3	0.3	-0.1	14.6
1965	3.3	0.1	-1.6	3.7	-0.5	-5.4	1.6	1.3	4.2	3.2	-1.5	2.4	10.9
1966	1.5	-3.2	-2.8	1.0	-5.3	-1.6	-2.6	-7.0	-1.8	4.2	-1.9	-0.7	-18.9
1967	8.2	-1.2	3.2	3.6	-5.0	0.9	5.1	-0.3	2.8	-5.1	-0.4	3.3	15.2
1968	-5.5	-1.7	0.02	8.5	-1.4	-0.1	-1.6	1.5	4.4	1.8	3.4	-4.2	4.3
1969	0.2	-4.3	3.3	1.6	-1.3	-6.9	-6.6	2.6	-2.8	5.3	-5.1	-1.5	-15.2
1970	-7.0	4.5	1.0	-6.3	-4.8	-2.4	7.4	4.1	-0.5	-0.7	5.1	5.6	4.8
1971	3.5	1.2	2.9	4.1	-3.6	-1.8	-3.7	4.6	-1.2	-5.4	-0.9	7.1	6.1
1972	1.3	2.9	1.4	1.4	0.7	-3.3	-0.5	4.2	-1.1	0.2	6.6	0.2	14.6
1973	-2.1	-4.4	-0.4	-3.1	-2.2	-1.1	3.9	-4.2	6.7	1.0	-14.0	3.5	-16.6
1974	0.6	0.6	-1.6	-1.2	-4.1	0.03	-5.6	-10.4	-10.4	9.5	-7.0	-0.4	-27.6
1975	14.2	5.0	3.9	6.9	1.3	5.6	-5.4	0.5	-5.0	5.3	2.9	-1.0	38.3
1976	14.4	-0.3	2.8	-0.3	-2.2	2.8	-1.8	-1.1	1.7	-2.6	-1.8	6.1	17.9
1977	-5.0	-1.9	-1.8	0.8	-3.0	2.0	-2.9	-3.2	-1.7	-3.4	1.4	0.2	-17.3
1978	-7.4	-3.6	2.1	10.6	0.4	-2.6	5.3	1.7	-1.3	-8.5	0.8	0.7	-3.1
1979	4.2	-3.6	6.6	-0.8	-3.8	2.4	0.5	4.9	-1.0	-7.2	0.8	2.0	4.2
1980	4.4	-1.5	-9.0	4.0	4.1	2.0	7.8	-0.3	-0.02	-0.9	7.4	-3.0	14.9
1981	-1.7	2.9	3.0	-0.6	-0.6	-1.5	-2.5	-7.4	-3.6	0.3	4.3	-1.6	-9.2
1982	-0.4	-5.4	-0.2	3.1	-3.4	-0.9	-0.4	11.5	-0.6	10.7	4.8	0.7	19.6
1983	2.8	3.4	1.6	8.5	-2.1	1.8	-1.9	1.4	1.4	-0.6	4.1	-1.4	20.3
1984	-3.0	-5.4	0.9	0.5	-5.6	2.5	-1.5	9.8	-1.4	0.1	-1.5	1.9	-3.7
1985	6.2	-0.2	-1.3	-0.7	4.6	1.5	0.9	-1.0	-0.4	3.4	7.1	5.1	27.7
1986	1.6	8.8	6.4	-1.9	5.2	0.9	-6.2	6.9	-6.9	6.2	1.9	-1.0	22.6
1987	13.8	3.1	3.6	-0.8	0.2	5.5	6.3	3.5	-2.5	-23.2	-8.0	5.7	2.3
1988	1.0	5.8	-4.0	2.2	-0.1	5.4	-0.6	-4.6	4.0	1.7	-1.6	2.6	11.8
1989	8.0	-3.6	1.6	5.5	2.5	-1.6	9.0	2.9	-1.6	-1.8	2.3	1.7	27.0
1990	-5.9	1.4	3.0	-1.9	8.3	0.1	0.9	-10.0	-6.2	-0.4	4.8	2.9	-4.3
1991	3.9	5.3	1.1	-0.9	4.8	-4.0	4.1	0.6	-0.9	1.7	-5.7	9.5	20.3
1992	1.7	1.4	-1.0	3.8	1.1	-2.3	2.3	-4.0	0.4	-1.4	2.4	-0.1	4.2
1993	0.3	1.8	1.9	-0.2	2.9	-0.3	0.7	3.2	-2.6	3.5	0.1	1.9	13.7
1994	6.0	-3.7	-5.1	1.3	2.1	-3.5	3.8	4.0	-1.8	1.7	-4.3	2.5	2.1
1995	0.2	4.3	3.7	3.9	3.3	2.0	3.3	-2.1	3.9	-0.7	6.7	0.8	33.5
1996	5.4	1.7	1.9	-0.3	1.3	0.2	-2.2	1.6	4.7	2.5	8.2	-1.1	26.0
1997	5.7	0.9	-4.3	6.5	4.6	4.7	7.2	-7.3	4.2	-6.3	5.1	1.1	22.6
1998	-0.02	8.1	3.0	3.0	-1.8	0.6	-0.8	-15.1	4.0	9.6	6.1	0.7	16.1
1999	1.9	-0.6	5.2	10.2	-2.1	3.9	-2.9	1.6	-4.5	3.8	1.4	5.7	25.2
2000	-4.8	-7.4	7.8	-1.7	-2.0	-0.7	0.7	6.6	-5.0	3.0	-5.1	3.6	-6.2
2001	0.9	-3.6	-5.9	8.7	1.6	-3.8	0.2	-5.4	-11.1	2.6	8.6	1.7	-7.1
2002	-1.0	1.9	2.9	-4.4	-0.2	-6.9	-5.5	-0.8	-12.4	10.6	5.9	-6.2	-16.8
2003	-3.5	-2.0	1.3	6.1	4.4	1.5	2.8	2.0	-1.5	5.7	-0.2	6.9	25.3
2004	0.3	0.9	-2.1	-1.3	-0.4	2.4	-2.8	0.3	-0.9	-0.5	4.0	3.4	3.1
2005	-2.7	2.6	-2.4	-3.0	2.7	-1.8	3.6	-1.5	0.8	-1.2	3.5	-0.8	-0.6
2006	1.4	1.2	1.1	2.3	-1.7	-0.2	0.3	1.7	2.6	3.4	1.2	2.0	16.3
2007	1.3	-2.8	0.7	5.7	4.3	-1.6	-1.5	1.1	4.0	0.2	-4.0	-0.8	6.4
2008	-4.6	-3.0	-0.03	4.5	-1.4	-10.2	0.2	1.5	-6.0	-14.1	-5.3	-0.6	-33.8
2009	-8.8	-11.7	7.7	7.3	4.1	-0.6	8.6	3.5	2.3	0.005	6.5	0.8	18.8
2010	-3.5	2.6	5.1	1.4	-7.9	-3.6	7.1	-4.3	7.7	3.1	-1.0	5.2	11.0
2011	2.7	2.8	0.8	4.0	-1.9	-1.2	-2.2	-4.4	-6.0	9.5	0.8	1.4	5.5
2012	3.4	2.5	2.0	0.01	-6.2	3.9	1.0	0.6	2.6	-2.5	-0.5	0.6	7.3
2013	5.8	1.4	3.7	1.8	1.9	-1.4	4.0	-4.4	2.2	2.8	3.5	3.0	26.5
2014	-5.3	4.0	0.8	0.7	0.8	0.7	-1.6	3.2	-0.3	2.0	2.5	-0.03	7.5
2015	-3.7	5.6	-2.0	0.4	1.0	-2.2	0.4	-6.6	-1.5	8.5	0.3	-1.7	-2.2
2016	-5.5	0.3	7.1	0.5									
TOTALS	57.7	14.1	77.7	127.6	-1.5	-21.9	75.9	-12.0	-50.1	43.3	99.1	107.8	
AVG.	0.9	0.2	1.2	1.9	-0.02	-0.3	1.2	-0.2	-0.8	0.7	1.5	1.6	
# Up	42	40	44	45	34	30	41	37	26	40	44	46	
# Down	25	27	23	22	32	36	25	29	40	26	22	20	

152

DOW JONES INDUSTRIALS MONTHLY POINT CHANGES SINCE 1950

	Jan	Feb	Mar	Apr	May	Jun	Jul	Aug	Sep	Oct	Nov	Dec	Year's Close
1950	1.66	1.65	2.61	8.28	9.09	−14.31	0.29	7.47	9.49	−1.35	2.59	7.81	235.41
1951	13.42	3.22	−4.11	11.19	−9.48	−7.01	15.22	12.39	0.91	−8.81	−1.08	7.96	269.23
1952	1.46	−10.61	9.38	−11.83	5.31	11.32	5.30	−4.52	−4.43	−1.38	14.43	8.24	291.90
1953	−2.13	−5.50	−4.40	−5.12	−2.47	−4.02	7.12	−14.16	2.82	11.77	5.56	−0.47	280.90
1954	11.49	2.15	8.97	15.82	8.16	6.04	14.39	−12.12	24.66	−8.32	34.63	17.62	404.39
1955	4.44	3.04	−2.17	15.95	−0.79	26.52	14.47	2.33	−1.56	−11.75	28.39	5.14	488.40
1956	−17.66	12.91	28.14	4.33	−38.07	14.73	25.03	−15.77	−26.79	4.60	−7.07	26.69	499.47
1957	−20.31	−14.54	10.19	19.55	10.57	−1.64	5.23	−24.17	−28.05	−15.26	8.83	−14.18	435.69
1958	14.33	−10.10	6.84	9.10	6.84	15.48	24.81	5.64	23.46	11.13	14.24	26.19	583.65
1959	10.31	9.54	−1.79	22.04	20.04	−0.19	31.28	−10.47	−32.73	14.92	12.58	20.18	679.36
1960	−56.74	7.50	−13.53	−14.89	23.80	15.12	−23.89	9.26	−45.85	0.22	16.86	18.67	615.89
1961	32.31	13.88	14.55	2.08	18.01	−12.76	21.41	14.57	−18.73	2.71	17.68	9.54	731.14
1962	−31.14	8.05	−1.10	−41.62	−51.97	−52.08	36.65	11.25	−30.20	10.79	59.53	2.80	652.10
1963	30.75	−19.91	19.58	35.18	9.26	−20.08	−11.45	33.89	3.47	22.44	−4.71	12.43	762.95
1964	22.39	14.80	13.15	−2.52	9.79	10.94	9.60	−2.62	36.89	−2.29	2.35	−1.30	874.13
1965	28.73	0.62	−14.43	33.26	−4.27	−50.01	13.71	11.36	37.48	30.24	−14.11	22.55	969.26
1966	14.25	−31.62	−27.12	8.91	−49.61	−13.97	−22.72	−58.97	−14.19	32.85	−15.48	−5.90	785.69
1967	64.20	−10.52	26.61	31.07	−44.49	7.70	43.98	−2.95	25.37	−46.92	−3.93	29.30	905.11
1968	−49.64	−14.97	0.17	71.55	−13.22	−1.20	−14.80	13.01	39.78	16.60	32.69	−41.33	943.75
1969	2.30	−40.84	30.27	14.70	−12.62	−64.37	−57.72	21.25	−23.63	42.90	−43.69	−11.94	800.36
1970	−56.30	33.53	7.98	−49.50	−35.63	−16.91	50.59	30.46	−3.90	−5.07	38.48	44.83	838.92
1971	29.58	10.33	25.54	37.38	−33.94	−16.67	−32.71	39.64	−10.88	−48.19	−7.66	58.86	890.20
1972	11.97	25.96	12.57	13.47	6.55	−31.69	−4.29	38.99	−10.46	2.25	62.69	1.81	1020.02
1973	−21.00	−43.95	−4.06	−29.58	−20.02	−9.70	34.69	−38.83	59.53	9.48	−134.33	28.61	850.86
1974	4.69	4.98	−13.85	−9.93	−34.58	0.24	−44.98	−78.85	−70.71	57.65	−46.86	−2.42	616.24
1975	87.45	35.36	29.10	53.19	10.95	46.70	−47.48	3.83	−41.46	42.16	24.63	−8.26	852.41
1976	122.87	−2.67	26.84	−2.60	−21.62	27.55	−18.14	−10.90	16.45	−25.26	−17.71	57.43	1004.65
1977	−50.28	−17.95	−17.29	7.77	−28.24	17.64	−26.23	−28.58	−14.38	−28.76	11.35	1.47	831.17
1978	−61.25	−27.80	15.24	79.96	3.29	−21.66	43.32	14.55	−11.00	−73.37	6.58	5.98	805.01
1979	34.21	−30.40	53.36	−7.28	−32.57	19.65	4.44	41.21	−9.05	−62.88	6.65	16.39	838.74
1980	37.11	−12.71	−77.39	31.31	33.79	17.07	67.40	−2.73	−0.17	−7.93	68.85	−29.35	963.99
1981	−16.72	27.31	29.29	−6.12	−6.00	−14.87	−24.54	−70.87	−31.49	2.57	36.43	−13.98	875.00
1982	−3.90	−46.71	−1.62	25.59	−28.82	−7.61	−3.33	92.71	−5.06	95.47	47.56	7.26	1046.54
1983	29.16	36.92	17.41	96.17	−26.22	21.98	−22.74	16.94	16.97	−7.93	50.82	−17.38	1258.64
1984	−38.06	−65.95	10.26	5.86	−65.90	27.55	−17.12	109.10	−17.67	0.67	−18.44	22.63	1211.57
1985	75.20	−2.76	−17.23	−8.72	57.35	20.05	11.99	−13.44	−5.38	45.68	97.82	74.54	1546.67
1986	24.32	138.07	109.55	−34.63	92.73	16.01	−117.41	123.03	−130.76	110.23	36.42	−18.28	1895.95
1987	262.09	65.95	80.70	−18.33	5.21	126.96	153.54	90.88	−66.67	−602.75	−159.98	105.28	1938.83
1988	19.39	113.40	−83.56	44.27	−1.21	110.59	−12.98	−97.08	81.26	35.74	−34.14	54.06	2168.57
1989	173.75	−83.93	35.23	125.18	61.35	−40.09	220.60	76.61	−44.45	−47.74	61.19	46.93	2753.20
1990	−162.66	36.71	79.96	−50.45	219.90	4.03	24.51	−290.84	−161.88	−10.15	117.32	74.01	2633.66
1991	102.73	145.79	31.68	−25.99	139.63	−120.75	118.07	18.78	−26.83	52.33	−174.42	274.15	3168.83
1992	54.56	44.28	−32.20	123.65	37.76	−78.36	75.26	−136.43	14.31	−45.38	78.88	−4.05	3301.11
1993	8.92	60.78	64.30	−7.56	99.88	−11.35	23.39	111.78	−96.13	125.47	3.36	70.14	3754.09
1994	224.27	−146.34	−196.06	45.73	76.68	−133.41	139.54	148.92	−70.23	64.93	−168.89	95.21	3834.44
1995	9.42	167.19	146.64	163.58	143.87	90.96	152.37	−97.91	178.52	−33.60	319.01	42.63	5117.12
1996	278.18	90.32	101.52	−18.06	74.10	11.45	−125.72	87.30	265.96	147.21	492.32	−73.43	6448.27
1997	364.82	64.65	−294.26	425.51	322.05	341.75	549.82	−600.19	322.84	−503.18	381.05	85.12	7908.25
1998	−1.75	639.22	254.09	263.56	−163.42	52.07	−68.73	−1344.22	303.55	749.48	524.45	64.88	9181.43
1999	177.40	−52.25	479.58	1002.88	−229.30	411.06	−315.65	174.13	−492.33	392.91	147.95	619.31	11497.12
2000	−556.59	−812.22	793.61	−188.01	−211.58	−74.44	74.09	693.12	−564.18	320.22	−556.65	372.36	10786.85
2001	100.51	−392.08	−616.50	856.19	176.97	−409.54	20.41	−573.06	−1102.19	227.58	776.42	169.94	10021.50
2002	−101.50	186.13	297.81	−457.72	−20.97	−681.99	−506.67	−73.09	−1071.57	805.10	499.06	−554.46	8341.63
2003	−287.82	−162.73	101.05	487.96	370.17	135.18	248.36	182.02	−140.76	526.06	−18.66	671.46	10453.92
2004	34.15	95.85	−226.22	−132.13	−37.12	247.03	−295.77	34.21	−93.65	−52.80	400.55	354.99	10783.01
2005	−293.07	276.29	−262.47	−311.25	274.97	−192.51	365.94	−159.31	87.10	−128.63	365.80	−88.37	10717.50
2006	147.36	128.55	115.91	257.82	−198.83	−18.09	35.46	195.47	297.92	401.66	141.20	241.22	12463.15
2007	158.54	−353.06	85.72	708.56	564.73	−219.02	−196.63	145.75	537.89	34.38	−558.29	−106.90	13264.82
2008	−614.46	−383.97	−3.50	557.24	−181.81	−1288.31	28.01	165.53	−692.89	−1525.65	−495.97	−52.65	8776.39
2009	−775.53	−937.93	545.99	559.20	332.21	−53.33	724.61	324.67	216.00	0.45	632.11	83.21	10428.05
2010	−360.72	257.93	531.37	151.98	−871.98	−362.61	691.92	−451.22	773.33	330.44	−112.47	571.49	11577.51
2011	314.42	334.41	93.39	490.81	−240.75	−155.45	−271.10	−529.71	−700.15	1041.63	90.67	171.88	12217.56
2012	415.35	319.16	259.97	1.59	−820.18	486.64	128.59	82.16	346.29	−340.67	−70.88	78.56	13104.14
2013	756.44	193.91	524.05	261.26	275.77	−205.97	589.94	−689.23	319.36	416.08	540.66	490.25	16576.66
2014	−877.81	622.86	135.95	123.18	136.33	109.43	−263.30	535.15	−55.55	347.62	437.72	−5.17	17823.07
2015	−658.12	967.75	−356.58	64.40	170.16	−391.01	70.35	−1161.83	−244.03	1379.54	56.38	−294.89	17425.03
2016	−958.73	50.20	1168.59	88.55									
TOTALS	−1762.99	1517.13	4163.27	6022.97	269.59	−2347.70	2369.60	−2874.71	−2170.41	4320.14	4139.32	3927.30	
# Up	42	40	44	45	34	30	41	37	26	40	44	46	
# Down	25	27	23	22	32	36	25	29	40	26	22	20	

153

	Jan	Feb	Mar	Apr	May	Jun	Jul	Aug	Sep	Oct	Nov	Dec
1950	201.79	203.44	206.05	214.33	223.42	209.11	209.40	216.87	226.36	225.01	227.60	235.41
1951	248.83	252.05	247.94	259.13	249.65	242.64	257.86	270.25	271.16	262.35	261.27	269.23
1952	270.69	260.08	269.46	257.63	262.94	274.26	279.56	275.04	270.61	269.23	283.66	291.90
1953	289.77	284.27	279.87	274.75	272.28	268.26	275.38	261.22	264.04	275.81	281.37	280.90
1954	292.39	294.54	303.51	319.33	327.49	333.53	347.92	335.80	360.46	352.14	386.77	404.39
1955	408.83	411.87	409.70	425.65	424.86	451.38	465.85	468.18	466.62	454.87	483.26	488.40
1956	470.84	483.65	511.79	516.12	478.05	492.78	517.81	502.04	475.25	479.85	472.78	499.47
1957	479.16	464.62	474.81	494.36	504.93	503.29	508.52	484.35	456.30	441.04	449.87	435.69
1958	450.02	439.92	446.76	455.86	462.70	478.18	502.99	508.63	532.09	543.22	557.46	583.65
1959	593.96	603.50	601.71	623.75	643.79	643.60	674.88	664.41	631.68	646.60	659.18	679.36
1960	622.62	630.12	616.59	601.70	625.50	640.62	616.73	625.99	580.14	580.36	597.22	615.89
1961	648.20	662.08	676.63	678.71	696.72	683.96	705.37	719.94	701.21	703.92	721.60	731.14
1962	700.00	708.05	706.95	665.33	613.36	561.28	597.93	609.18	578.98	589.77	649.30	652.10
1963	682.85	662.94	682.52	717.70	726.96	706.88	695.43	729.32	732.79	755.23	750.52	762.95
1964	785.34	800.14	813.29	810.77	820.56	831.50	841.10	838.48	875.37	873.08	875.43	874.13
1965	902.86	903.48	889.05	922.31	918.04	868.03	881.74	893.10	930.58	960.82	946.71	969.26
1966	983.51	951.89	924.77	933.68	884.07	870.10	847.38	788.41	774.22	807.07	791.59	785.69
1967	849.89	839.37	865.98	897.05	852.56	860.26	904.24	901.29	926.66	879.74	875.81	905.11
1968	855.47	840.50	840.67	912.22	899.00	897.80	883.00	896.01	935.79	952.39	985.08	943.75
1969	946.05	905.21	935.48	950.18	937.56	873.19	815.47	836.72	813.09	855.99	812.30	800.36
1970	744.06	777.59	785.57	736.07	700.44	683.53	734.12	764.58	760.68	755.61	794.09	838.92
1971	868.50	878.83	904.37	941.75	907.81	891.14	858.43	898.07	887.19	839.00	831.34	890.20
1972	902.17	928.13	940.70	954.17	960.72	929.03	924.74	963.73	953.27	955.52	1018.21	1020.02
1973	999.02	955.07	951.01	921.43	901.41	891.71	926.40	887.57	947.10	956.58	822.25	850.86
1974	855.55	860.53	846.68	836.75	802.17	802.41	757.43	678.58	607.87	665.52	618.66	616.24
1975	703.69	739.05	768.15	821.34	832.29	878.99	831.51	835.34	793.88	836.04	860.67	852.41
1976	975.28	972.61	999.45	996.85	975.23	1002.78	984.64	973.74	990.19	964.93	947.22	1004.65
1977	954.37	936.42	919.13	926.90	898.66	916.30	890.07	861.49	847.11	818.35	829.70	831.17
1978	769.92	742.12	757.36	837.32	840.61	818.95	862.27	876.82	865.82	792.45	799.03	805.01
1979	839.22	808.82	862.18	854.90	822.33	841.98	846.42	887.63	878.58	815.70	822.35	838.74
1980	875.85	863.14	785.75	817.06	850.85	867.92	935.32	932.59	932.42	924.49	993.34	963.99
1981	947.27	974.58	1003.87	997.75	991.75	976.88	952.34	881.47	849.98	852.55	888.98	875.00
1982	871.10	824.39	822.77	848.36	819.54	811.93	808.60	901.31	896.25	991.72	1039.28	1046.54
1983	1075.70	1112.62	1130.03	1226.20	1199.98	1221.96	1199.22	1216.16	1233.13	1225.20	1276.02	1258.64
1984	1220.58	1154.63	1164.89	1170.75	1104.85	1132.40	1115.28	1224.38	1206.71	1207.38	1188.94	1211.57
1985	1286.77	1284.01	1266.78	1258.06	1315.41	1335.46	1347.45	1334.01	1328.63	1374.31	1472.13	1546.67
1986	1570.99	1709.06	1818.61	1783.98	1876.71	1892.72	1775.31	1898.34	1767.58	1877.81	1914.23	1895.95
1987	2158.04	2223.99	2304.69	2286.36	2291.57	2418.53	2572.07	2662.95	2596.28	1993.53	1833.55	1938.83
1988	1958.22	2071.62	1988.06	2032.33	2031.12	2141.71	2128.73	2031.65	2112.91	2148.65	2114.51	2168.57
1989	2342.32	2258.39	2293.62	2418.80	2480.15	2440.06	2660.66	2737.27	2692.82	2645.08	2706.27	2753.20
1990	2590.54	2627.25	2707.21	2656.76	2876.66	2880.69	2905.20	2614.36	2452.48	2442.33	2559.65	2633.66
1991	2736.39	2882.18	2913.86	2887.87	3027.50	2906.75	3024.82	3043.60	3016.77	3069.10	2894.68	3168.83
1992	3223.39	3267.67	3235.47	3359.12	3396.88	3318.52	3393.78	3257.35	3271.66	3226.28	3305.16	3301.11
1993	3310.03	3370.81	3435.11	3427.55	3527.43	3516.08	3539.47	3651.25	3555.12	3680.59	3683.95	3754.09
1994	3978.36	3832.02	3635.96	3681.69	3758.37	3624.96	3764.50	3913.42	3843.19	3908.12	3739.23	3834.44
1995	3843.86	4011.05	4157.69	4321.27	4465.14	4556.10	4708.47	4610.56	4789.08	4755.48	5074.49	5117.12
1996	5395.30	5485.62	5587.14	5569.08	5643.18	5654.63	5528.91	5616.21	5882.17	6029.38	6521.70	6448.27
1997	6813.09	6877.74	6583.48	7008.99	7331.04	7672.79	8222.61	7622.42	7945.26	7442.08	7823.13	7908.25
1998	7906.50	8545.72	8799.81	9063.37	8899.95	8952.02	8883.29	7539.07	7842.62	8592.10	9116.55	9181.43
1999	9358.83	9306.58	9786.16	10789.04	10559.74	10970.80	10655.15	10829.28	10336.95	10729.86	10877.81	11497.12
2000	10940.53	10128.31	10921.92	10733.91	10522.33	10447.89	10521.98	11215.10	10650.92	10971.14	10414.49	10786.85
2001	10887.36	10495.28	9878.78	10734.97	10911.94	10502.40	10522.81	9949.75	8847.56	9075.14	9851.56	10021.50
2002	9920.00	10106.13	10403.94	9946.22	9925.25	9243.26	8736.59	8663.50	7591.93	8397.03	8896.09	8341.63
2003	8053.81	7891.08	7992.13	8480.09	8850.26	8985.44	9233.80	9415.82	9275.06	9801.12	9782.46	10453.92
2004	10488.07	10583.92	10357.70	10225.57	10188.45	10435.48	10139.71	10173.92	10080.27	10027.47	10428.02	10783.01
2005	10489.94	10766.23	10503.76	10192.51	10467.48	10274.97	10640.91	10481.60	10568.70	10440.07	10805.87	10717.50
2006	10864.86	10993.41	11109.32	11367.14	11168.31	11150.22	11185.68	11381.15	11679.07	12080.73	12221.93	12463.15
2007	12621.69	12268.63	12354.35	13062.91	13627.64	13408.62	13211.99	13357.74	13895.63	13930.01	13371.72	13264.82
2008	12650.36	12266.39	12262.89	12820.13	12638.32	11350.01	11378.02	11543.55	10850.66	9325.01	8829.04	8776.39
2009	8000.86	7062.93	7608.92	8168.12	8500.33	8447.00	9171.61	9496.28	9712.28	9712.73	10344.84	10428.05
2010	10067.33	10325.26	10856.63	11008.61	10136.63	9774.02	10465.94	10014.72	10788.05	11118.49	11006.02	11577.51
2011	11891.93	12226.34	12319.73	12810.54	12569.79	12414.34	12143.24	11613.53	10913.38	11955.01	12045.68	12217.56
2012	12632.91	12952.07	13212.04	13213.63	12393.45	12880.09	13008.68	13090.84	13437.13	13096.46	13025.58	13104.14
2013	13860.58	14054.49	14578.54	14839.80	15115.57	14909.60	15499.54	14810.31	15129.67	15545.75	16086.41	16576.66
2014	15698.85	16321.71	16457.66	16580.84	16717.17	16826.60	16563.30	17098.45	17042.90	17390.52	17828.24	17823.07
2015	17164.95	18132.70	17776.12	17840.52	18010.68	17619.51	17689.86	16528.03	16284.00	17663.54	17719.92	17425.03
2016	16466.30	16516.50	17685.09	17773.64								

154

STANDARD & POOR'S 500 MONTHLY PERCENT CHANGES SINCE 1950

	Jan	Feb	Mar	Apr	May	Jun	Jul	Aug	Sep	Oct	Nov	Dec	Year's Change
1950	1.7	1.0	0.4	4.5	3.9	-5.8	0.8	3.3	5.6	0.4	-0.1	4.6	21.8
1951	6.1	0.6	-1.8	4.8	-4.1	-2.6	6.9	3.9	-0.1	-1.4	-0.3	3.9	16.5
1952	1.6	-3.6	4.8	-4.3	2.3	4.6	1.8	-1.5	-2.0	-0.1	4.6	3.5	11.8
1953	-0.7	-1.8	-2.4	-2.6	-0.3	-1.6	2.5	-5.8	0.1	5.1	0.9	0.2	-6.6
1954	5.1	0.3	3.0	4.9	3.3	0.1	5.7	-3.4	8.3	-1.9	8.1	5.1	45.0
1955	1.8	0.4	-0.5	3.8	-0.1	8.2	6.1	-0.8	1.1	-3.0	7.5	-0.1	26.4
1956	-3.6	3.5	6.9	-0.2	-6.6	3.9	5.2	-3.8	-4.5	0.5	-1.1	3.5	2.6
1957	-4.2	-3.3	2.0	3.7	3.7	-0.1	1.1	-5.6	-6.2	-3.2	1.6	-4.1	-14.3
1958	4.3	-2.1	3.1	3.2	1.5	2.6	4.3	1.2	4.8	2.5	2.2	5.2	38.1
1959	0.4	-0.02	0.1	3.9	1.9	-0.4	3.5	-1.5	-4.6	1.1	1.3	2.8	8.5
1960	-7.1	0.9	-1.4	-1.8	2.7	2.0	-2.5	2.6	-6.0	-0.2	4.0	4.6	-3.0
1961	6.3	2.7	2.6	0.4	1.9	-2.9	3.3	2.0	-2.0	2.8	3.9	0.3	23.1
1962	-3.8	1.6	-0.6	-6.2	-8.6	-8.2	6.4	1.5	-4.8	0.4	10.2	1.3	-11.8
1963	4.9	-2.9	3.5	4.9	1.4	-2.0	-0.3	4.9	-1.1	3.2	-1.1	2.4	18.9
1964	2.7	1.0	1.5	0.6	1.1	1.6	1.8	-1.6	2.9	0.8	-0.5	0.4	13.0
1965	3.3	-0.1	-1.5	3.4	-0.8	-4.9	1.3	2.3	3.2	2.7	-0.9	0.9	9.1
1966	0.5	-1.8	-2.2	2.1	-5.4	-1.6	-1.3	-7.8	-0.7	4.8	0.3	-0.1	-13.1
1967	7.8	0.2	3.9	4.2	-5.2	1.8	4.5	-1.2	3.3	-2.9	0.1	2.6	20.1
1968	-4.4	-3.1	0.9	8.2	1.1	0.9	-1.8	1.1	3.9	0.7	4.8	-4.2	7.7
1969	-0.8	-4.7	3.4	2.1	-0.2	-5.6	-6.0	4.0	-2.5	4.4	-3.5	-1.9	-11.4
1970	-7.6	5.3	0.1	-9.0	-6.1	-5.0	7.3	4.4	3.3	-1.1	4.7	5.7	0.1
1971	4.0	0.9	3.7	3.6	-4.2	0.1	-4.1	3.6	-0.7	-4.2	-0.3	8.6	10.8
1972	1.8	2.5	0.6	0.4	1.7	-2.2	0.2	3.4	-0.5	0.9	4.6	1.2	15.6
1973	-1.7	-3.7	-0.1	-4.1	-1.9	-0.7	3.8	-3.7	4.0	-0.1	-11.4	1.7	-17.4
1974	-1.0	-0.4	-2.3	-3.9	-3.4	-1.5	-7.8	-9.0	-11.9	16.3	-5.3	-2.0	-29.7
1975	12.3	6.0	2.2	4.7	4.4	4.4	-6.8	-2.1	-3.5	6.2	2.5	-1.2	31.5
1976	11.8	-1.1	3.1	-1.1	-1.4	4.1	-0.8	-0.5	2.3	-2.2	-0.8	5.2	19.1
1977	-5.1	-2.2	-1.4	0.02	-2.4	4.5	-1.6	-2.1	-0.2	-4.3	2.7	0.3	-11.5
1978	-6.2	-2.5	2.5	8.5	0.4	-1.8	5.4	2.6	-0.7	-9.2	1.7	1.5	1.1
1979	4.0	-3.7	5.5	0.2	-2.6	3.9	0.9	5.3	N/C	-6.9	4.3	1.7	12.3
1980	5.8	-0.4	-10.2	4.1	4.7	2.7	6.5	0.6	2.5	1.6	10.2	-3.4	25.8
1981	-4.6	1.3	3.6	-2.3	-0.2	-1.0	-0.2	-6.2	-5.4	4.9	3.7	-3.0	-9.7
1982	-1.8	-6.1	-1.0	4.0	-3.9	-2.0	-2.3	11.6	0.8	11.0	3.6	1.5	14.8
1983	3.3	1.9	3.3	7.5	-1.2	3.5	-3.3	1.1	1.0	-1.5	1.7	-0.9	17.3
1984	-0.9	-3.9	1.3	0.5	-5.9	1.7	-1.6	10.6	-0.3	-0.01	-1.5	2.2	1.4
1985	7.4	0.9	-0.3	-0.5	5.4	1.2	-0.5	-1.2	-3.5	4.3	6.5	4.5	26.3
1986	0.2	7.1	5.3	-1.4	5.0	1.4	-5.9	7.1	-8.5	5.5	2.1	-2.8	14.6
1987	13.2	3.7	2.6	-1.1	0.6	4.8	4.8	3.5	-2.4	-21.8	-8.5	7.3	2.0
1988	4.0	4.2	-3.3	0.9	0.3	4.3	-0.5	-3.9	4.0	2.6	-1.9	1.5	12.4
1989	7.1	-2.9	2.1	5.0	3.5	-0.8	8.8	1.6	-0.7	-2.5	1.7	2.1	27.3
1990	-6.9	0.9	2.4	-2.7	9.2	-0.9	-0.5	-9.4	-5.1	-0.7	6.0	2.5	-6.6
1991	4.2	6.7	2.2	0.03	3.9	-4.8	4.5	2.0	-1.9	1.2	-4.4	11.2	26.3
1992	-2.0	1.0	-2.2	2.8	0.1	-1.7	3.9	-2.4	0.9	0.2	3.0	1.0	4.5
1993	0.7	1.0	1.9	-2.5	2.3	0.1	-0.5	3.4	-1.0	1.9	-1.3	1.0	7.1
1994	3.3	-3.0	-4.6	1.2	1.2	-2.7	3.1	3.8	-2.7	2.1	-4.0	1.2	-1.5
1995	2.4	3.6	2.7	2.8	3.6	2.1	3.2	-0.03	4.0	-0.5	4.1	1.7	34.1
1996	3.3	0.7	0.8	1.3	2.3	0.2	-4.6	1.9	5.4	2.6	7.3	-2.2	20.3
1997	6.1	0.6	-4.3	5.8	5.9	4.3	7.8	-5.7	5.3	-3.4	4.5	1.6	31.0
1998	1.0	7.0	5.0	0.9	-1.9	3.9	-1.2	-14.6	6.2	8.0	5.9	5.6	26.7
1999	4.1	-3.2	3.9	3.8	-2.5	5.4	-3.2	-0.6	-2.9	6.3	1.9	5.8	19.5
2000	-5.1	-2.0	9.7	-3.1	-2.2	2.4	-1.6	6.1	-5.3	-0.5	-8.0	0.4	-10.1
2001	3.5	-9.2	-6.4	7.7	0.5	-2.5	-1.1	-6.4	-8.2	1.8	7.5	0.8	-13.0
2002	-1.6	-2.1	3.7	-6.1	-0.9	-7.2	-7.9	0.5	-11.0	8.6	5.7	-6.0	-23.4
2003	-2.7	-1.7	1.0	8.0	5.1	1.1	1.6	1.8	-1.2	5.5	0.7	5.1	26.4
2004	1.7	1.2	-1.6	-1.7	1.2	1.8	-3.4	0.2	0.9	1.4	3.9	3.2	9.0
2005	-2.5	1.9	-1.9	-2.0	3.0	-0.01	3.6	-1.1	0.7	-1.8	3.5	-0.1	3.0
2006	2.5	0.05	1.1	1.2	-3.1	0.01	0.5	2.1	2.5	3.2	1.6	1.3	13.6
2007	1.4	-2.2	1.0	4.3	3.3	-1.8	-3.2	1.3	3.6	1.5	-4.4	-0.9	3.5
2008	-6.1	-3.5	-0.6	4.8	1.1	-8.6	-1.0	1.2	-9.1	-16.9	-7.5	0.8	-38.5
2009	-8.6	-11.0	8.5	9.4	5.3	0.02	7.4	3.4	3.6	-2.0	5.7	1.8	23.5
2010	-3.7	2.9	5.9	1.5	-8.2	-5.4	6.9	-4.7	8.8	3.7	-0.2	6.5	12.8
2011	2.3	3.2	-0.1	2.8	-1.4	-1.8	-2.1	-5.7	-7.2	10.8	-0.5	0.9	-0.003
2012	4.4	4.1	3.1	-0.7	-6.3	4.0	1.3	2.0	2.4	-2.0	0.3	0.7	13.4
2013	5.0	1.1	3.6	1.8	2.1	-1.5	4.9	-3.1	3.0	4.5	2.8	2.4	29.6
2014	-3.6	4.3	0.7	0.6	2.1	1.9	-1.5	3.8	-1.6	2.3	2.5	-0.4	11.4
2015	-3.1	5.5	-1.7	0.9	1.0	-2.1	2.0	-6.3	-2.6	8.3	0.1	-1.8	-0.7
2016	-5.1	-0.4	6.6	0.3									
TOTALS	62.8	3.1	83.4	98.8	13.0	-2.2	64.5	-6.0	-34.2	62.3	99.0	106.7	
AVG.	0.9	0.05	1.2	1.5	0.2	-0.03	1.0	-0.09	-0.5	0.9	1.5	1.6	
# Up	40	37	44	47	38	34	36	36	29	40	44	49	
# Down	27	30	23	20	28	32	30	30	36	26	22	17	

STANDARD & POOR'S 500 MONTHLY CLOSING PRICES SINCE 1950

	Jan	Feb	Mar	Apr	May	Jun	Jul	Aug	Sep	Oct	Nov	Dec
1950	17.05	17.22	17.29	18.07	18.78	17.69	17.84	18.42	19.45	19.53	19.51	20.41
1951	21.66	21.80	21.40	22.43	21.52	20.96	22.40	23.28	23.26	22.94	22.88	23.77
1952	24.14	23.26	24.37	23.32	23.86	24.96	25.40	25.03	24.54	24.52	25.66	26.57
1953	26.38	25.90	25.29	24.62	24.54	24.14	24.75	23.32	23.35	24.54	24.76	24.81
1954	26.08	26.15	26.94	28.26	29.19	29.21	30.88	29.83	32.31	31.68	34.24	35.98
1955	36.63	36.76	36.58	37.96	37.91	41.03	43.52	43.18	43.67	42.34	45.51	45.48
1956	43.82	45.34	48.48	48.38	45.20	46.97	49.39	47.51	45.35	45.58	45.08	46.67
1957	44.72	43.26	44.11	45.74	47.43	47.37	47.91	45.22	42.42	41.06	41.72	39.99
1958	41.70	40.84	42.10	43.44	44.09	45.24	47.19	47.75	50.06	51.33	52.48	55.21
1959	55.42	55.41	55.44	57.59	58.68	58.47	60.51	59.60	56.88	57.52	58.28	59.89
1960	55.61	56.12	55.34	54.37	55.83	56.92	55.51	56.96	53.52	53.39	55.54	58.11
1961	61.78	63.44	65.06	65.31	66.56	64.64	66.76	68.07	66.73	68.62	71.32	71.55
1962	68.84	69.96	69.55	65.24	59.63	54.75	58.23	59.12	56.27	56.52	62.26	63.10
1963	66.20	64.29	66.57	69.80	70.80	69.37	69.13	72.50	71.70	74.01	73.23	75.02
1964	77.04	77.80	78.98	79.46	80.37	81.69	83.18	81.83	84.18	84.86	84.42	84.75
1965	87.56	87.43	86.16	89.11	88.42	84.12	85.25	87.17	89.96	92.42	91.61	92.43
1966	92.88	91.22	89.23	91.06	86.13	84.74	83.60	77.10	76.56	80.20	80.45	80.33
1967	86.61	86.78	90.20	94.01	89.08	90.64	94.75	93.64	96.71	93.90	94.00	96.47
1968	92.24	89.36	90.20	97.59	98.68	99.58	97.74	98.86	102.67	103.41	108.37	103.86
1969	103.01	98.13	101.51	103.69	103.46	97.71	91.83	95.51	93.12	97.24	93.81	92.06
1970	85.02	89.50	89.63	81.52	76.55	72.72	78.05	81.52	84.21	83.25	87.20	92.15
1971	95.88	96.75	100.31	103.95	99.63	99.70	95.58	99.03	98.34	94.23	93.99	102.09
1972	103.94	106.57	107.20	107.67	109.53	107.14	107.39	111.09	110.55	111.58	116.67	118.05
1973	116.03	111.68	111.52	106.97	104.95	104.26	108.22	104.25	108.43	108.29	95.96	97.55
1974	96.57	96.22	93.98	90.31	87.28	86.00	79.31	72.15	63.54	73.90	69.97	68.56
1975	76.98	81.59	83.36	87.30	91.15	95.19	88.75	86.88	83.87	89.04	91.24	90.19
1976	100.86	99.71	102.77	101.64	100.18	104.28	103.44	102.91	105.24	102.90	102.10	107.46
1977	102.03	99.82	98.42	98.44	96.12	100.48	98.85	96.77	96.53	92.34	94.83	95.10
1978	89.25	87.04	89.21	96.83	97.24	95.53	100.68	103.29	102.54	93.15	94.70	96.11
1979	99.93	96.28	101.59	101.76	99.08	102.91	103.81	109.32	109.32	101.82	106.16	107.94
1980	114.16	113.66	102.09	106.29	111.24	114.24	121.67	122.38	125.46	127.47	140.52	135.76
1981	129.55	131.27	136.00	132.81	132.59	131.21	130.92	122.79	116.18	121.89	126.35	122.55
1982	120.40	113.11	111.96	116.44	111.88	109.61	107.09	119.51	120.42	133.71	138.54	140.64
1983	145.30	148.06	152.96	164.42	162.39	168.11	162.56	164.40	166.07	163.55	166.40	164.93
1984	163.41	157.06	159.18	160.05	150.55	153.18	150.66	166.68	166.10	166.09	163.58	167.24
1985	179.63	181.18	180.66	179.83	189.55	191.85	190.92	188.63	182.08	189.82	202.17	211.28
1986	211.78	226.92	238.90	235.52	247.35	250.84	236.12	252.93	231.32	243.98	249.22	242.17
1987	274.08	284.20	291.70	288.36	290.10	304.00	318.66	329.80	321.83	251.79	230.30	247.08
1988	257.07	267.82	258.89	261.33	262.16	273.50	272.02	261.52	271.91	278.97	273.70	277.72
1989	297.47	288.86	294.87	309.64	320.52	317.98	346.08	351.45	349.15	340.36	345.99	353.40
1990	329.08	331.89	339.94	330.80	361.23	358.02	356.15	322.56	306.05	304.00	322.22	330.22
1991	343.93	367.07	375.22	375.35	389.83	371.16	387.81	395.43	387.86	392.46	375.22	417.09
1992	408.79	412.70	403.69	414.95	415.35	408.14	424.21	414.03	417.80	418.68	431.35	435.71
1993	438.78	443.38	451.67	440.19	450.19	450.53	448.13	463.56	458.93	467.83	461.79	466.45
1994	481.61	467.14	445.77	450.91	456.50	444.27	458.26	475.49	462.69	472.35	453.69	459.27
1995	470.42	487.39	500.71	514.71	533.40	544.75	562.06	561.88	584.41	581.50	605.37	615.93
1996	636.02	640.43	645.50	654.17	669.12	670.63	639.95	651.99	687.31	705.27	757.02	740.74
1997	786.16	790.82	757.12	801.34	848.28	885.14	954.29	899.47	947.28	914.62	955.40	970.43
1998	980.28	1049.34	1101.75	1111.75	1090.82	1133.84	1120.67	957.28	1017.01	1098.67	1163.63	1229.23
1999	1279.64	1238.33	1286.37	1335.18	1301.84	1372.71	1328.72	1320.41	1282.71	1362.93	1388.91	1469.25
2000	1394.46	1366.42	1498.58	1452.43	1420.60	1454.60	1430.83	1517.68	1436.51	1429.40	1314.95	1320.28
2001	1366.01	1239.94	1160.33	1249.46	1255.82	1224.42	1211.23	1133.58	1040.94	1059.78	1139.45	1148.08
2002	1130.20	1106.73	1147.39	1076.92	1067.14	989.82	911.62	916.07	815.28	885.76	936.31	879.82
2003	855.70	841.15	849.18	916.92	963.59	974.50	990.31	1008.01	995.97	1050.71	1058.20	1111.92
2004	1131.13	1144.94	1126.21	1107.30	1120.68	1140.84	1101.72	1104.24	1114.58	1130.20	1173.82	1211.92
2005	1181.27	1203.60	1180.59	1156.85	1191.50	1191.33	1234.18	1220.33	1228.81	1207.01	1249.48	1248.29
2006	1280.08	1280.66	1294.83	1310.61	1270.09	1270.20	1276.66	1303.82	1335.85	1377.94	1400.63	1418.30
2007	1438.24	1406.82	1420.86	1482.37	1530.62	1503.35	1455.27	1473.99	1526.75	1549.38	1481.14	1468.36
2008	1378.55	1330.63	1322.70	1385.59	1400.38	1280.00	1267.38	1282.83	1166.36	968.75	896.24	903.25
2009	825.88	735.09	797.87	872.81	919.14	919.32	987.48	1020.62	1057.08	1036.19	1095.63	1115.10
2010	1073.87	1104.49	1169.43	1186.69	1089.41	1030.71	1101.60	1049.33	1141.20	1183.26	1180.55	1257.64
2011	1286.12	1327.22	1325.83	1363.61	1345.20	1320.64	1292.28	1218.89	1131.42	1253.30	1246.96	1257.60
2012	1312.41	1365.68	1408.47	1397.91	1310.33	1362.16	1379.32	1406.58	1440.67	1412.16	1416.18	1426.19
2013	1498.11	1514.68	1569.19	1597.57	1630.74	1606.28	1685.73	1632.97	1681.55	1756.54	1805.81	1848.36
2014	1782.59	1859.45	1872.34	1883.95	1923.57	1960.23	1930.67	2003.37	1972.29	2018.05	2067.56	2058.90
2015	1994.99	2104.50	2067.89	2085.51	2107.39	2063.11	2103.84	1972.18	1920.03	2079.36	2080.41	2043.94
2016	1940.24	1932.23	2059.74	2065.30								

	Jan	Feb	Mar	Apr	May	Jun	Jul	Aug	Sep	Oct	Nov	Dec	Year's Change
1971	10.2	2.6	4.6	6.0	-3.6	-0.4	-2.3	3.0	0.6	-3.6	-1.1	9.8	27.4
1972	4.2	5.5	2.2	2.5	0.9	-1.8	-1.8	1.7	-0.3	0.5	2.1	0.6	17.2
1973	-4.0	-6.2	-2.4	-8.2	-4.8	-1.6	7.6	-3.5	6.0	-0.9	-15.1	-1.4	-31.1
1974	3.0	-0.6	-2.2	-5.9	-7.7	-5.3	-7.9	-10.9	-10.7	17.2	-3.5	-5.0	-35.1
1975	16.6	4.6	3.6	3.8	5.8	4.7	-4.4	-5.0	-5.9	3.6	2.4	-1.5	29.8
1976	12.1	3.7	0.4	-0.6	-2.3	2.6	1.1	-1.7	1.7	-1.0	0.9	7.4	26.1
1977	-2.4	-1.0	-0.5	1.4	0.1	4.3	0.9	-0.5	0.7	-3.3	5.8	1.8	7.3
1978	-4.0	0.6	4.7	8.5	4.4	0.05	5.0	6.9	-1.6	-16.4	3.2	2.9	12.3
1979	6.6	-2.6	7.5	1.6	-1.8	5.1	2.3	6.4	-0.3	-9.6	6.4	4.8	28.1
1980	7.0	-2.3	-17.1	6.9	7.5	4.9	8.9	5.7	3.4	2.7	8.0	-2.8	33.9
1981	-2.2	0.1	6.1	3.1	3.1	-3.5	-1.9	-7.5	-8.0	8.4	3.1	-2.7	-3.2
1982	-3.8	-4.8	-2.1	5.2	-3.3	-4.1	-2.3	6.2	5.6	13.3	9.3	0.04	18.7
1983	6.9	5.0	3.9	8.2	5.3	3.2	-4.6	-3.8	1.4	-7.4	4.1	-2.5	19.9
1984	-3.7	-5.9	-0.7	-1.3	-5.9	2.9	-4.2	10.9	-1.8	-1.2	-1.8	2.0	-11.2
1985	12.7	2.0	-1.7	0.5	3.6	1.9	1.7	-1.2	-5.8	4.4	7.3	3.5	31.4
1986	3.3	7.1	4.2	2.3	4.4	1.3	-8.4	3.1	-8.4	2.9	-0.3	-2.8	7.5
1987	12.2	8.4	1.2	-2.8	-0.3	2.0	2.4	4.6	-2.3	-27.2	-5.6	8.3	-5.4
1988	4.3	6.5	2.1	1.2	-2.3	6.6	-1.9	-2.8	3.0	-1.4	-2.9	2.7	15.4
1989	5.2	-0.4	1.8	5.1	4.4	-2.4	4.3	3.4	0.8	-3.7	0.1	-0.3	19.3
1990	-8.6	2.4	2.3	-3.6	9.3	0.7	-5.2	-13.0	-9.6	-4.3	8.9	4.1	-17.8
1991	10.8	9.4	6.5	0.5	4.4	-6.0	5.5	4.7	0.2	3.1	-3.5	11.9	56.8
1992	5.8	2.1	-4.7	-4.2	1.1	-3.7	3.1	-3.0	3.6	3.8	7.9	3.7	15.5
1993	2.9	-3.7	2.9	-4.2	5.9	0.5	0.1	5.4	2.7	2.2	-3.2	3.0	14.7
1994	3.0	-1.0	-6.2	-1.3	0.2	-4.0	2.3	6.0	-0.2	1.7	-3.5	0.2	-3.2
1995	0.4	5.1	3.0	3.3	2.4	8.0	7.3	1.9	2.3	-0.7	2.2	-0.7	39.9
1996	0.7	3.8	0.1	8.1	4.4	-4.7	-8.8	5.6	7.5	-0.4	5.8	-0.1	22.7
1997	6.9	-5.1	-6.7	3.2	11.1	3.0	10.5	-0.4	6.2	-5.5	0.4	-1.9	21.6
1998	3.1	9.3	3.7	1.8	-4.8	6.5	-1.2	-19.9	13.0	4.6	10.1	12.5	39.6
1999	14.3	-8.7	7.6	3.3	-2.8	8.7	-1.8	3.8	0.2	8.0	12.5	22.0	85.6
2000	-3.2	19.2	-2.6	-15.6	-11.9	16.6	-5.0	11.7	-12.7	-8.3	-22.9	-4.9	-39.3
2001	12.2	-22.4	-14.5	15.0	-0.3	2.4	-6.2	-10.9	-17.0	12.8	14.2	1.0	-21.1
2002	-0.8	-10.5	6.6	-8.5	-4.3	-9.4	-9.2	-1.0	-10.9	13.5	11.2	-9.7	-31.5
2003	-1.1	1.3	0.3	9.2	9.0	1.7	6.9	4.3	-1.3	8.1	1.5	2.2	50.0
2004	3.1	-1.8	-1.8	-3.7	3.5	3.1	-7.8	-2.6	3.2	4.1	6.2	3.7	8.6
2005	-5.2	-0.5	-2.6	-3.9	7.6	-0.5	6.2	-1.5	-0.02	-1.5	5.3	-1.2	1.4
2006	4.6	-1.1	2.6	-0.7	-6.2	-0.3	-3.7	4.4	3.4	4.8	2.7	-0.7	9.5
2007	2.0	-1.9	0.2	4.3	3.1	-0.05	-2.2	2.0	4.0	5.8	-6.9	-0.3	9.8
2008	-9.9	-5.0	0.3	5.9	4.6	-9.1	1.4	1.8	-11.6	-17.7	-10.8	2.7	-40.5
2009	-6.4	-6.7	10.9	12.3	3.3	3.4	7.8	1.5	5.6	-3.6	4.9	5.8	43.9
2010	-5.4	4.2	7.1	2.6	-8.3	-6.5	6.9	-6.2	12.0	5.9	-0.4	6.2	16.9
2011	1.8	3.0	-0.04	3.3	-1.3	-2.2	-0.6	-6.4	-6.4	11.1	-2.4	-0.6	-1.8
2012	8.0	5.4	4.2	-1.5	-7.2	3.8	0.2	4.3	1.6	-4.5	1.1	0.3	15.9
2013	4.1	0.6	3.4	1.9	3.8	-1.5	6.6	-1.0	5.1	3.9	3.6	2.9	38.3
2014	-1.7	5.0	-2.5	-2.0	3.1	3.9	-0.9	4.8	-1.9	3.1	3.5	-1.2	13.4
2015	-2.1	7.1	-1.3	0.8	2.6	-1.6	2.8	-6.9	-3.3	9.4	1.1	-2.0	5.7
2016	-7.9	-1.2	6.8	-1.9									
TOTALS	115.6	30.6	41.2	61.9	39.8	33.2	9.5	4.4	-26.2	36.7	71.9	83.7	
AVG.	2.5	0.7	0.9	1.3	0.9	0.7	0.2	0.1	-0.6	0.8	1.6	1.9	
# Up	29	25	29	29	27	25	23	24	24	25	30	26	
# Down	17	21	17	17	18	20	22	21	21	20	15	19	

Based on NASDAQ composite; prior to February 5, 1971, based on National Quotation Bureau indices.

NASDAQ COMPOSITE MONTHLY CLOSING PRICES SINCE 1971

	Jan	Feb	Mar	Apr	May	Jun	Jul	Aug	Sep	Oct	Nov	Dec
1971	98.77	101.34	105.97	112.30	108.25	107.80	105.27	108.42	109.03	105.10	103.97	114.12
1972	118.87	125.38	128.14	131.33	132.53	130.08	127.75	129.95	129.61	130.24	132.96	133.73
1973	128.40	120.41	117.46	107.85	102.64	100.98	108.64	104.87	111.20	110.17	93.51	92.19
1974	94.93	94.35	92.27	86.86	80.20	75.96	69.99	62.37	55.67	65.23	62.95	59.82
1975	69.78	73.00	75.66	78.54	83.10	87.02	83.19	79.01	74.33	76.99	78.80	77.62
1976	87.05	90.26	90.62	90.08	88.04	90.32	91.29	89.70	91.26	90.35	91.12	97.88
1977	95.54	94.57	94.13	95.48	95.59	99.73	100.65	100.10	100.85	97.52	103.15	105.05
1978	100.84	101.47	106.20	115.18	120.24	120.30	126.32	135.01	132.89	111.12	114.69	117.98
1979	125.82	122.56	131.76	133.82	131.42	138.13	141.33	150.44	149.98	135.53	144.26	151.14
1980	161.75	158.03	131.00	139.99	150.45	157.78	171.81	181.52	187.76	192.78	208.15	202.34
1981	197.81	198.01	210.18	216.74	223.47	215.75	211.63	195.75	180.03	195.24	201.37	195.84
1982	188.39	179.43	175.65	184.70	178.54	171.30	167.35	177.71	187.65	212.63	232.31	232.41
1983	248.35	260.67	270.80	293.06	308.73	318.70	303.96	292.42	296.65	274.55	285.67	278.60
1984	268.43	252.57	250.78	247.44	232.82	239.65	229.70	254.64	249.94	247.03	242.53	247.35
1985	278.70	284.17	279.20	280.56	290.80	296.20	301.29	297.71	280.33	292.54	313.95	324.93
1986	335.77	359.53	374.72	383.24	400.16	405.51	371.37	382.86	350.67	360.77	359.57	349.33
1987	392.06	424.97	430.05	417.81	416.54	424.67	434.93	454.97	444.29	323.30	305.16	330.47
1988	344.66	366.95	374.64	379.23	370.34	394.66	387.33	376.55	387.71	382.46	371.45	381.38
1989	401.30	399.71	406.73	427.55	446.17	435.29	453.84	469.33	472.92	455.63	456.09	454.82
1990	415.81	425.83	435.54	420.07	458.97	462.29	438.24	381.21	344.51	329.84	359.06	373.84
1991	414.20	453.05	482.30	484.72	506.11	475.92	502.04	525.68	526.88	542.98	523.90	586.34
1992	620.21	633.47	603.77	578.68	585.31	563.60	580.83	563.12	583.27	605.17	652.73	676.95
1993	696.34	670.77	690.13	661.42	700.53	703.95	704.70	742.84	762.78	779.26	754.39	776.80
1994	800.47	792.50	743.46	733.84	735.19	705.96	722.16	765.62	764.29	777.49	750.32	751.96
1995	755.20	793.73	817.21	843.98	864.58	933.45	1001.21	1020.11	1043.54	1036.06	1059.20	1052.13
1996	1059.79	1100.05	1101.40	1190.52	1243.43	1185.02	1080.59	1141.50	1226.92	1221.51	1292.61	1291.03
1997	1379.85	1309.00	1221.70	1260.76	1400.32	1442.07	1593.81	1587.32	1685.69	1593.61	1600.55	1570.35
1998	1619.36	1770.51	1835.68	1868.41	1778.87	1894.74	1872.39	1499.25	1693.84	1771.39	1949.54	2192.69
1999	2505.89	2288.03	2461.40	2542.85	2470.52	2686.12	2638.49	2739.35	2746.16	2966.43	3336.16	4069.31
2000	3940.35	4696.69	4572.83	3860.66	3400.91	3966.11	3766.99	4206.35	3672.82	3369.63	2597.93	2470.52
2001	2772.73	2151.83	1840.26	2116.24	2110.49	2160.54	2027.13	1805.43	1498.80	1690.20	1930.58	1950.40
2002	1934.03	1731.49	1845.35	1688.23	1615.73	1463.21	1328.26	1314.85	1172.06	1329.75	1478.78	1335.51
2003	1320.91	1337.52	1341.17	1464.31	1595.91	1622.80	1735.02	1810.45	1786.94	1932.21	1960.26	2003.37
2004	2066.15	2029.82	1994.22	1920.15	1986.74	2047.79	1887.36	1838.10	1896.84	1974.99	2096.81	2175.44
2005	2062.41	2051.72	1999.23	1921.65	2068.22	2056.96	2184.83	2152.09	2151.69	2120.30	2232.82	2205.32
2006	2305.82	2281.39	2339.79	2322.57	2178.88	2172.09	2091.47	2183.75	2258.43	2366.71	2431.77	2415.29
2007	2463.93	2416.15	2421.64	2525.09	2604.52	2603.23	2545.57	2596.36	2701.50	2859.12	2660.96	2652.28
2008	2389.86	2271.48	2279.10	2412.80	2522.66	2292.98	2325.55	2367.52	2091.88	1720.95	1535.57	1577.03
2009	1476.42	1377.84	1528.59	1717.30	1774.33	1835.04	1978.50	2009.06	2122.42	2045.11	2144.60	2269.15
2010	2147.35	2238.26	2397.96	2461.19	2257.04	2109.24	2254.70	2114.03	2368.62	2507.41	2498.23	2652.87
2011	2700.08	2782.27	2781.07	2873.54	2835.30	2773.52	2756.38	2579.46	2415.40	2684.41	2620.34	2605.15
2012	2813.84	2966.89	3091.57	3046.36	2827.34	2935.05	2939.52	3066.96	3116.23	2977.23	3010.24	3019.51
2013	3142.13	3160.19	3267.52	3328.79	3455.91	3403.25	3626.37	3589.87	3771.48	3919.71	4059.89	4176.59
2014	4103.88	4308.12	4198.99	4114.56	4242.62	4408.18	4369.77	4580.27	4493.39	4630.74	4791.63	4736.05
2015	4635.24	4963.53	4900.88	4941.42	5070.03	4986.87	5128.28	4776.51	4620.16	5053.75	5108.67	5007.41
2016	4613.95	4557.95	4869.85	4775.36								

Based on NASDAQ composite; prior to February 5, 1971, based on National Quotation Bureau indices.

RUSSELL 1000 INDEX MONTHLY PERCENT CHANGES SINCE 1979

	Jan	Feb	Mar	Apr	May	Jun	Jul	Aug	Sep	Oct	Nov	Dec	Year's Change
1979	4.2	-3.5	6.0	0.3	-2.2	4.3	1.1	5.6	0.02	-7.1	5.1	2.1	16.1
1980	5.9	-0.5	-11.5	4.6	5.0	3.2	6.4	1.1	2.6	1.8	10.1	-3.9	25.6
1981	-4.6	1.0	3.8	-1.9	0.2	-1.2	-0.1	-6.2	-6.4	5.4	4.0	-3.3	-9.7
1982	-2.7	-5.9	-1.3	3.9	-3.6	-2.6	-2.3	11.3	1.2	11.3	4.0	1.3	13.7
1983	3.2	2.1	3.2	7.1	-0.2	3.7	-3.2	0.5	1.3	-2.4	2.0	-1.2	17.0
1984	-1.9	-4.4	1.1	0.3	-5.9	2.1	-1.8	10.8	-0.2	-0.1	-1.4	2.2	-0.1
1985	7.8	1.1	-0.4	-0.3	5.4	1.6	-0.8	-1.0	-3.9	4.5	6.5	4.1	26.7
1986	0.9	7.2	5.1	-1.3	5.0	1.4	-5.9	6.8	-8.5	5.1	1.4	-3.0	13.6
1987	12.7	4.0	1.9	-1.8	0.4	4.5	4.2	3.8	-2.4	-21.9	-8.0	7.2	0.02
1988	4.3	4.4	-2.9	0.7	0.2	4.8	-0.9	-3.3	3.9	2.0	-2.0	1.7	13.1
1989	6.8	-2.5	2.0	4.9	3.8	-0.8	8.2	1.7	-0.5	-2.8	1.5	1.8	25.9
1990	-7.4	1.2	2.2	-2.8	8.9	-0.7	-1.1	-9.6	-5.3	-0.8	6.4	2.7	-7.5
1991	4.5	6.9	2.5	-0.1	3.8	-4.7	4.6	2.2	-1.5	1.4	-4.1	11.2	28.8
1992	-1.4	0.9	-2.4	2.3	0.3	-1.9	4.1	-2.5	1.0	0.7	3.5	1.4	5.9
1993	0.7	0.6	2.2	-2.8	2.4	0.4	-0.4	3.5	-0.5	1.2	-1.7	1.6	7.3
1994	2.9	-2.9	-4.5	1.1	1.0	-2.9	3.1	3.9	-2.6	1.7	-3.9	1.2	-2.4
1995	2.4	3.8	2.3	2.5	3.5	2.4	3.7	0.5	3.9	-0.6	4.2	1.4	34.4
1996	3.1	1.1	0.7	1.4	2.1	-0.1	-4.9	2.5	5.5	2.1	7.1	-1.8	19.7
1997	5.8	0.2	-4.6	5.3	6.2	4.0	8.0	-4.9	5.4	-3.4	4.2	1.9	30.5
1998	0.6	7.0	4.9	0.9	-2.3	3.6	-1.3	-15.1	6.5	7.8	6.1	6.2	25.1
1999	3.5	-3.3	3.7	4.2	-2.3	5.1	-3.2	-1.0	-2.8	6.5	2.5	6.0	19.5
2000	-4.2	-0.4	8.9	-3.3	-2.7	2.5	-1.8	7.4	-4.8	-1.2	-9.3	1.1	-8.8
2001	3.2	-9.5	-6.7	8.0	0.5	-2.4	-1.4	-6.2	-8.6	2.0	7.5	0.9	-13.6
2002	-1.4	-2.1	4.0	-5.8	-1.0	-7.5	-7.5	0.3	-10.9	8.1	5.7	-5.8	-22.9
2003	-2.5	-1.7	0.9	7.9	5.5	1.2	1.8	1.9	-1.2	5.7	1.0	4.6	27.5
2004	1.8	1.2	-1.5	-1.9	1.3	1.7	-3.6	0.3	1.1	1.5	4.1	3.5	9.5
2005	-2.6	2.0	-1.7	-2.0	3.4	0.3	3.8	-1.1	0.8	-1.9	3.5	0.01	4.4
2006	2.7	0.01	1.3	1.1	-3.2	0.003	0.1	2.2	2.3	3.3	1.9	1.1	13.3
2007	1.8	-1.9	0.9	4.1	3.4	-2.0	-3.2	1.2	3.7	1.6	-4.5	-0.8	3.9
2008	-6.1	-3.3	-0.8	5.0	1.6	-8.5	-1.3	1.2	-9.7	-17.6	-7.9	1.3	-39.0
2009	-8.3	-10.7	8.5	10.0	5.3	0.1	7.5	3.4	3.9	-2.3	5.6	2.3	25.5
2010	-3.7	3.1	6.0	1.8	-8.1	-5.7	6.8	-4.7	9.0	3.8	0.1	6.5	13.9
2011	2.3	3.3	0.1	2.9	-1.3	-1.9	-2.3	-6.0	-7.6	11.1	-0.5	0.7	-0.5
2012	4.8	4.1	3.0	-0.7	-6.4	3.7	1.1	2.2	2.4	-1.8	0.5	0.8	13.9
2013	5.3	1.1	3.7	1.7	2.0	-1.5	5.2	-3.0	3.3	4.3	2.6	2.5	30.4
2014	-3.3	4.5	0.5	0.4	2.1	2.1	-1.7	3.9	-1.9	2.3	2.4	-0.4	11.1
2015	-2.8	5.5	-1.4	0.6	1.1	-2.0	1.8	-6.2	-2.9	8.0	0.1	-2.0	-1.1
2016	-5.5	-0.3	6.8	0.4									
TOTALS	32.8	13.4	46.5	58.7	35.2	6.3	22.8	7.4	-24.4	39.3	60.3	57.1	
AVG.	0.9	0.4	1.2	1.5	1.0	0.2	0.6	0.2	-0.7	1.1	1.6	1.5	
# Up	23	23	26	26	25	21	17	23	18	24	27	28	
# Down	15	15	12	12	12	16	20	14	19	13	10	9	

RUSSELL 1000 INDEX MONTHLY CLOSING PRICES SINCE 1979

	Jan	Feb	Mar	Apr	May	Jun	Jul	Aug	Sep	Oct	Nov	Dec
1979	53.76	51.88	54.97	55.15	53.92	56.25	56.86	60.04	60.05	55.78	58.65	59.87
1980	63.40	63.07	55.79	58.38	61.31	63.27	67.30	68.05	69.84	71.08	78.26	75.20
1981	71.75	72.49	75.21	73.77	73.90	73.01	72.92	68.42	64.06	67.54	70.23	67.93
1982	66.12	62.21	61.43	63.85	61.53	59.92	58.54	65.14	65.89	73.34	76.28	77.24
1983	79.75	81.45	84.06	90.04	89.89	93.18	90.18	90.65	91.85	89.69	91.50	90.38
1984	88.69	84.76	85.73	86.00	80.94	82.61	81.13	89.87	89.67	89.62	88.36	90.31
1985	97.31	98.38	98.03	97.72	103.02	104.65	103.78	102.76	98.75	103.16	109.91	114.39
1986	115.39	123.71	130.07	128.44	134.82	136.75	128.74	137.43	125.70	132.11	133.97	130.00
1987	146.48	152.29	155.20	152.39	152.94	159.84	166.57	172.95	168.83	131.89	121.28	130.02
1988	135.55	141.54	137.45	138.37	138.66	145.31	143.99	139.26	144.68	147.55	144.59	146.99
1989	156.93	152.98	155.99	163.63	169.85	168.49	182.27	185.33	184.40	179.17	181.85	185.11
1990	171.44	173.43	177.28	172.32	187.66	186.29	184.32	166.69	157.83	156.62	166.69	171.22
1991	179.00	191.34	196.15	195.94	203.32	193.78	202.67	207.18	204.02	206.96	198.46	220.61
1992	217.52	219.50	214.29	219.13	219.71	215.60	224.37	218.86	221.15	222.65	230.44	233.59
1993	235.25	236.67	241.80	235.13	240.80	241.78	240.78	249.20	247.95	250.97	246.70	250.71
1994	258.00	250.52	239.19	241.71	244.13	237.11	244.44	254.04	247.49	251.62	241.82	244.65
1995	250.52	260.08	266.11	272.81	282.48	289.29	299.98	301.40	313.28	311.37	324.36	328.89
1996	338.97	342.56	345.01	349.84	357.35	357.10	339.44	347.79	366.77	374.38	401.05	393.75
1997	416.71	417.46	398.19	419.15	445.06	462.95	499.89	475.33	500.78	483.86	504.25	513.79
1998	517.02	553.14	580.31	585.46	572.16	592.57	584.97	496.66	529.11	570.63	605.31	642.87
1999	665.64	643.67	667.49	695.25	679.10	713.61	690.51	683.27	663.83	707.19	724.66	767.97
2000	736.08	733.04	797.99	771.58	750.98	769.68	755.57	811.17	772.60	763.06	692.40	700.09
2001	722.55	654.25	610.36	658.90	662.39	646.64	637.43	597.67	546.46	557.29	599.32	604.94
2002	596.66	583.88	607.55	572.04	566.18	523.72	484.39	486.08	433.22	468.51	495.00	466.18
2003	454.30	446.37	450.35	486.09	512.92	518.94	528.53	538.40	532.15	562.51	568.32	594.56
2004	605.21	612.58	603.42	591.83	599.40	609.31	587.21	589.09	595.66	604.51	629.26	650.99
2005	633.99	646.93	635.78	623.32	644.28	645.92	670.26	663.13	668.53	656.09	679.35	679.42
2006	697.79	697.83	706.74	714.37	691.78	691.80	692.59	707.55	723.48	747.30	761.43	770.08
2007	784.11	768.92	775.97	807.82	835.14	818.17	792.11	801.22	830.59	844.20	806.44	799.82
2008	750.97	726.42	720.32	756.03	768.28	703.22	694.07	702.17	634.08	522.47	481.43	487.77
2009	447.32	399.61	433.67	476.84	501.95	502.27	539.88	558.21	579.97	566.50	598.41	612.01
2010	589.41	607.45	643.79	655.06	601.79	567.37	606.09	577.68	629.78	653.57	654.24	696.90
2011	712.97	736.24	737.07	758.45	748.75	734.48	717.77	674.79	623.45	692.41	688.77	693.36
2012	726.33	756.42	778.92	773.50	724.12	750.61	758.60	775.07	793.74	779.35	783.37	789.90
2013	831.74	840.97	872.11	886.89	904.44	890.67	937.16	909.28	939.50	979.68	1004.97	1030.36
2014	996.48	1041.36	1046.42	1050.20	1071.96	1094.59	1075.60	1117.71	1096.43	1121.98	1148.90	1144.37
2015	1111.85	1173.46	1156.95	1164.03	1176.67	1152.64	1173.55	1100.51	1068.46	1153.55	1154.66	1131.88
2016	1069.78	1066.58	1138.84	1143.76								

RUSSELL 2000 INDEX MONTHLY PERCENT CHANGES SINCE 1979

	Jan	Feb	Mar	Apr	May	Jun	Jul	Aug	Sep	Oct	Nov	Dec	Year's Change
1979	9.0	-3.2	9.7	2.3	-1.8	5.3	2.9	7.8	-0.7	-11.3	8.1	6.6	38.0
1980	8.2	-2.1	-18.5	6.0	8.0	4.0	11.0	6.5	2.9	3.9	7.0	-3.7	33.8
1981	-0.6	0.3	7.7	2.5	3.0	-2.5	-2.6	-8.0	-8.6	8.2	2.8	-2.0	-1.5
1982	-3.7	-5.3	-1.5	5.1	-3.2	-4.0	-1.7	7.5	3.6	14.1	8.8	1.1	20.7
1983	7.5	6.0	2.5	7.2	7.0	4.4	-3.0	-4.0	1.6	-7.0	5.0	-2.1	26.3
1984	-1.8	-5.9	0.4	-0.7	-5.4	2.6	-5.0	11.5	-1.0	-2.0	-2.9	1.4	-9.6
1985	13.1	2.4	-2.2	-1.4	3.4	1.0	2.7	-1.2	-6.2	3.6	6.8	4.2	28.0
1986	1.5	7.0	4.7	1.4	3.3	-0.2	-9.5	3.0	-6.3	3.9	-0.5	-3.1	4.0
1987	11.5	8.2	2.4	-3.0	-0.5	2.3	2.8	2.9	-2.0	-30.8	-5.5	7.8	-10.8
1988	4.0	8.7	4.4	2.0	-2.5	7.0	-0.9	-2.8	2.3	-1.2	-3.6	3.8	22.4
1989	4.4	0.5	2.2	4.3	4.2	-2.4	4.2	2.1	0.01	-6.0	0.4	0.1	14.2
1990	-8.9	2.9	3.7	-3.4	6.8	0.1	-4.5	-13.6	-9.2	-6.2	7.3	3.7	-21.5
1991	9.1	11.0	6.9	-0.2	4.5	-6.0	3.1	3.7	0.6	2.7	-4.7	7.7	43.7
1992	8.0	2.9	-3.5	-3.7	1.2	-5.0	3.2	-3.1	2.2	3.1	7.5	3.4	16.4
1993	3.2	-2.5	3.1	-2.8	4.3	0.5	1.3	4.1	2.7	2.5	-3.4	3.3	17.0
1994	3.1	-0.4	-5.4	0.6	-1.3	-3.6	1.6	5.4	-0.5	-0.4	-4.2	2.5	-3.2
1995	-1.4	3.9	1.6	2.1	1.5	5.0	5.7	1.9	1.7	-4.6	4.2	2.4	26.2
1996	-0.2	3.0	1.8	5.3	3.9	-4.2	-8.8	5.7	3.7	-1.7	4.0	2.4	14.8
1997	1.9	-2.5	-4.9	0.1	11.0	4.1	4.6	2.2	7.2	-4.5	-0.8	1.7	20.5
1998	-1.6	7.4	4.1	0.5	-5.4	0.2	-8.2	-19.5	7.6	4.0	5.2	6.1	-3.4
1999	1.2	-8.2	1.4	8.8	1.4	4.3	-2.8	-3.8	-0.1	0.3	5.9	11.2	19.6
2000	-1.7	16.4	-6.7	-6.1	-5.9	8.6	-3.2	7.4	-3.1	-4.5	-10.4	8.4	-4.2
2001	5.1	-6.7	-5.0	7.7	2.3	3.3	-5.4	-3.3	-13.6	5.8	7.6	6.0	1.0
2002	-1.1	-2.8	7.9	0.8	-4.5	-5.1	-15.2	-0.4	-7.3	3.1	8.8	-5.7	-21.6
2003	-2.9	-3.1	1.1	9.4	10.6	1.7	6.2	4.5	-2.0	8.3	3.5	1.9	45.4
2004	4.3	0.8	0.8	-5.2	1.5	4.1	-6.8	-0.6	4.6	1.9	8.6	2.8	17.0
2005	-4.2	1.6	-3.0	-5.8	6.4	3.7	6.3	-1.9	0.2	-3.2	4.7	-0.6	3.3
2006	8.9	-0.3	4.7	-0.1	-5.7	0.5	-3.3	2.9	0.7	5.7	2.5	0.2	17.0
2007	1.6	-0.9	0.9	1.7	4.0	-1.6	-6.9	2.2	1.6	2.8	-7.3	-0.2	-2.7
2008	-6.9	-3.8	0.3	4.1	4.5	-7.8	3.6	3.5	-8.1	-20.9	-12.0	5.6	-34.8
2009	-11.2	-12.3	8.7	15.3	2.9	1.3	9.5	2.8	5.6	-6.9	3.0	7.9	25.2
2010	-3.7	4.4	8.0	5.6	-7.7	-7.9	6.8	-7.5	12.3	4.0	3.4	7.8	25.3
2011	-0.3	5.4	2.4	2.6	-2.0	-2.5	-3.7	-8.8	-11.4	15.0	-0.5	0.5	-5.5
2012	7.0	2.3	2.4	-1.6	-6.7	4.8	-1.4	3.2	3.1	-2.2	0.4	3.3	14.6
2013	6.2	1.0	4.4	-0.4	3.9	-0.7	6.9	-3.3	6.2	2.5	3.9	1.8	37.0
2014	-2.8	4.6	-0.8	-3.9	0.7	5.2	-6.1	4.8	-6.2	6.5	-0.02	2.7	3.5
2015	-3.3	5.8	1.6	-2.6	2.2	0.6	-1.2	-6.4	-5.1	5.6	3.1	-5.2	-5.7
2016	-8.8	-0.1	7.8	1.5									
TOTALS	53.7	46.4	56.1	56.0	49.9	21.1	-17.8	7.4	-21.0	-5.9	66.7	95.7	
AVG.	1.4	1.2	1.5	1.5	1.3	0.6	-0.5	0.2	-0.6	-0.2	1.8	2.6	
# Up	20	22	28	23	24	23	17	21	20	21	24	29	
# Down	18	16	10	15	13	14	20	16	17	16	13	8	

RUSSELL 2000 INDEX MONTHLY CLOSING PRICES SINCE 1979

	Jan	Feb	Mar	Apr	May	Jun	Jul	Aug	Sep	Oct	Nov	Dec
1979	44.18	42.78	46.94	48.00	47.13	49.62	51.08	55.05	54.68	48.51	52.43	55.91
1980	60.50	59.22	48.27	51.18	55.26	57.47	63.81	67.97	69.94	72.64	77.70	74.80
1981	74.33	74.52	80.25	82.25	84.72	82.56	80.41	73.94	67.55	73.06	75.14	73.67
1982	70.96	67.21	66.21	69.59	67.39	64.67	63.59	68.38	70.84	80.86	87.96	88.90
1983	95.53	101.23	103.77	111.20	118.94	124.17	120.43	115.60	117.43	109.17	114.66	112.27
1984	110.21	103.72	104.10	103.34	97.75	100.30	95.25	106.21	105.17	103.07	100.11	100.49
1985	114.77	117.54	114.92	113.35	117.26	118.38	121.56	120.10	112.65	116.73	124.62	129.87
1986	131.78	141.00	147.63	149.66	154.61	154.23	139.65	143.83	134.73	139.95	139.26	135.00
1987	150.48	162.84	166.79	161.82	161.02	164.75	169.42	174.25	170.81	118.26	111.70	120.42
1988	125.24	136.10	142.15	145.01	141.37	151.30	149.89	145.74	149.08	147.25	142.01	147.37
1989	153.84	154.56	157.89	164.68	171.53	167.42	174.50	178.20	178.21	167.47	168.17	168.30
1990	153.27	157.72	163.63	158.09	168.91	169.04	161.51	139.52	126.70	118.83	127.50	132.16
1991	144.17	160.00	171.01	170.61	178.34	167.61	172.76	179.11	180.16	185.00	176.37	189.94
1992	205.16	211.15	203.69	196.25	198.52	188.64	194.74	188.79	192.92	198.90	213.81	221.01
1993	228.10	222.41	229.21	222.68	232.19	233.35	236.46	246.19	252.95	259.18	250.41	258.59
1994	266.52	265.53	251.06	252.55	249.28	240.29	244.06	257.32	256.12	255.02	244.25	250.36
1995	246.85	256.57	260.77	266.17	270.25	283.63	299.72	305.31	310.38	296.25	308.58	315.97
1996	315.38	324.93	330.77	348.28	361.85	346.61	316.00	333.88	346.39	340.57	354.11	362.61
1997	369.45	360.05	342.56	343.00	380.76	396.37	414.48	423.43	453.82	433.26	429.92	437.02
1998	430.05	461.83	480.68	482.89	456.62	457.39	419.75	337.95	363.59	378.16	397.75	421.96
1999	427.22	392.26	397.63	432.81	438.68	457.68	444.77	427.83	427.30	428.64	454.08	504.75
2000	496.23	577.71	539.09	506.25	476.18	517.23	500.64	537.89	521.37	497.68	445.94	483.53
2001	508.34	474.37	450.53	485.32	496.50	512.64	484.78	468.56	404.87	428.17	460.78	488.50
2002	483.10	469.36	506.46	510.67	487.47	462.64	392.42	390.96	362.27	373.50	406.35	383.09
2003	372.17	360.52	364.54	398.68	441.00	448.37	476.02	497.42	487.68	528.22	546.51	556.91
2004	580.76	585.56	590.31	559.80	568.28	591.52	551.29	547.93	572.94	583.79	633.77	651.57
2005	624.02	634.06	615.07	579.38	616.71	639.66	679.75	666.51	667.80	646.61	677.29	673.22
2006	733.20	730.64	765.14	764.54	721.01	724.67	700.56	720.53	725.59	766.84	786.12	787.66
2007	800.34	793.30	800.71	814.57	847.19	833.69	776.13	792.86	805.45	828.02	767.77	766.03
2008	713.30	686.18	687.97	716.18	748.28	689.66	714.52	739.50	679.58	537.52	473.14	499.45
2009	443.53	389.02	422.75	487.56	501.58	508.28	556.71	572.07	604.28	562.77	579.73	625.39
2010	602.04	628.56	678.64	716.60	661.61	609.49	650.89	602.06	676.14	703.35	727.01	783.65
2011	781.25	823.45	843.55	865.29	848.30	827.43	797.03	726.81	644.16	741.06	737.42	740.92
2012	792.82	810.94	830.30	816.88	761.82	798.49	786.94	812.09	837.45	818.73	821.92	849.35
2013	902.09	911.11	951.54	947.46	984.14	977.48	1045.26	1010.90	1073.79	1100.15	1142.89	1163.64
2014	1130.88	1183.03	1173.04	1126.86	1134.50	1192.96	1120.07	1174.35	1101.68	1173.51	1173.23	1204.70
2015	1165.39	1233.37	1252.77	1220.13	1246.53	1253.95	1238.68	1159.45	1100.69	1161.86	1198.11	1135.89
2016	1035.38	1033.90	1114.03	1130.84								

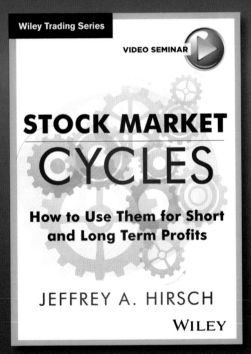

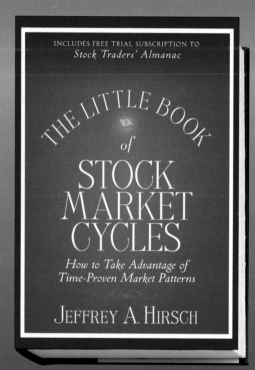

10 **BEST** DAYS BY PERCENT AND POINT

	BY PERCENT CHANGE				BY POINT CHANGE		
DAY	CLOSE	PNT CHANGE	% CHANGE	DAY	CLOSE	PNT CHANGE	% CHANGE
DJIA 1901 to 1949							
3/15/33	62.10	8.26	15.3	10/30/29	258.47	28.40	12.3
10/6/31	99.34	12.86	14.9	11/14/29	217.28	18.59	9.4
10/30/29	258.47	28.40	12.3	10/5/29	341.36	16.19	5.0
9/21/32	75.16	7.67	11.4	10/31/29	273.51	15.04	5.8
8/3/32	58.22	5.06	9.5	10/6/31	99.34	12.86	14.9
2/11/32	78.60	6.80	9.5	11/15/29	228.73	11.45	5.3
11/14/29	217.28	18.59	9.4	6/19/30	228.97	10.13	4.6
12/18/31	80.69	6.90	9.4	9/5/39	148.12	10.03	7.3
2/13/32	85.82	7.22	9.2	11/22/28	290.34	9.81	3.5
5/6/32	59.01	4.91	9.1	10/1/30	214.14	9.24	4.5
DJIA 1950 to APRIL 2016							
10/13/08	9387.61	936.42	11.1	10/13/08	9387.61	936.42	11.1
10/28/08	9065.12	889.35	10.9	10/28/08	9065.12	889.35	10.9
10/21/87	2027.85	186.84	10.2	8/26/15	16285.51	619.07	4.0
3/23/09	7775.86	497.48	6.8	11/13/08	8835.25	552.59	6.7
11/13/08	8835.25	552.59	6.7	3/16/00	10630.60	499.19	4.9
11/21/08	8046.42	494.13	6.5	3/23/09	7775.86	497.48	6.8
7/24/02	8191.29	488.95	6.4	11/21/08	8046.42	494.13	6.5
10/20/87	1841.01	102.27	5.9	11/30/11	12045.68	490.05	4.2
3/10/09	6926.49	379.44	5.8	7/24/02	8191.29	488.95	6.4
7/29/02	8711.88	447.49	5.4	9/30/08	10850.66	485.21	4.7
S&P 500 1930 to APRIL 2016							
3/15/33	6.81	0.97	16.6	10/13/08	1003.35	104.13	11.6
10/6/31	9.91	1.09	12.4	10/28/08	940.51	91.59	10.8
9/21/32	8.52	0.90	11.8	8/26/15	1940.51	72.90	3.9
10/13/08	1003.35	104.13	11.6	3/16/00	1458.47	66.32	4.8
10/28/08	940.51	91.59	10.8	1/3/01	1347.56	64.29	5.0
2/16/35	10.00	0.94	10.4	9/30/08	1166.36	59.97	5.4
8/17/35	11.70	1.08	10.2	11/13/08	911.29	58.99	6.9
3/16/35	9.05	0.82	10.0	3/23/09	822.92	54.38	7.1
9/12/38	12.06	1.06	9.6	3/18/08	1330.74	54.14	4.2
9/5/39	12.64	1.11	9.6	8/9/11	1172.53	53.07	4.7
NASDAQ 1971 to APRIL 2016							
1/3/01	2616.69	324.83	14.2	1/3/01	2616.69	324.83	14.2
10/13/08	1844.25	194.74	11.8	12/5/00	2889.80	274.05	10.5
12/5/00	2889.80	274.05	10.5	4/18/00	3793.57	254.41	7.2
10/28/08	1649.47	143.57	9.5	5/30/00	3459.48	254.37	7.9
4/5/01	1785.00	146.20	8.9	10/19/00	3418.60	247.04	7.8
4/18/01	2079.44	156.22	8.1	10/13/00	3316.77	242.09	7.9
5/30/00	3459.48	254.37	7.9	6/2/00	3813.38	230.88	6.4
10/13/00	3316.77	242.09	7.9	4/25/00	3711.23	228.75	6.6
10/19/00	3418.60	247.04	7.8	4/17/00	3539.16	217.87	6.6
5/8/02	1696.29	122.47	7.8	10/13/08	1844.25	194.74	11.8
RUSSELL 1000 1979 to APRIL 2016							
10/13/08	542.98	56.75	11.7	10/13/08	542.98	56.75	11.7
10/28/08	503.74	47.68	10.5	10/28/08	503.74	47.68	10.5
10/21/87	135.85	11.15	8.9	8/26/15	1081.77	39.00	3.7
3/23/09	446.90	29.36	7.0	3/16/00	777.86	36.60	4.9
11/13/08	489.83	31.99	7.0	1/3/01	712.63	35.74	5.3
11/24/08	456.14	28.26	6.6	11/13/08	489.83	31.99	7.0
3/10/09	391.01	23.46	6.4	9/30/08	634.08	31.74	5.3
11/21/08	427.88	24.97	6.2	8/9/11	647.85	30.57	5.0
7/24/02	448.05	23.87	5.6	12/5/00	728.44	30.36	4.4
7/29/02	477.61	24.69	5.5	3/23/09	446.90	29.36	7.0
RUSSELL 2000 1979 to APRIL 2016							
10/13/08	570.89	48.41	9.3	10/13/08	570.89	48.41	9.3
11/13/08	491.23	38.43	8.5	9/18/08	723.68	47.30	7.0
3/23/09	433.72	33.61	8.4	8/9/11	696.16	45.20	6.9
10/21/87	130.65	9.26	7.6	11/30/11	737.42	41.32	5.9
10/28/08	482.55	34.15	7.6	10/4/11	648.64	39.15	6.4
11/24/08	436.80	30.26	7.4	11/13/08	491.23	38.43	8.5
3/10/09	367.75	24.49	7.1	10/27/11	765.43	38.28	5.3
9/18/08	723.68	47.30	7.0	5/10/10	689.61	36.61	5.6
8/9/11	696.16	45.20	6.9	8/11/11	695.89	35.68	5.4
10/16/08	536.57	34.46	6.9	12/17/14	1174.83	35.45	3.1

10 <u>WORST</u> DAYS BY PERCENT AND POINT

	BY PERCENT CHANGE				BY POINT CHANGE		
DAY	CLOSE	PNT CHANGE	% CHANGE	DAY	CLOSE	PNT CHANGE	% CHANGE
DJIA 1901 to 1949							
10/28/29	260.64	−38.33	−12.8	10/28/29	260.64	−38.33	−12.8
10/29/29	230.07	−30.57	−11.7	10/29/29	230.07	−30.57	−11.7
11/6/29	232.13	−25.55	−9.9	11/6/29	232.13	−25.55	−9.9
8/12/32	63.11	−5.79	−8.4	10/23/29	305.85	−20.66	−6.3
3/14/07	55.84	−5.05	−8.3	11/11/29	220.39	−16.14	−6.8
7/21/33	88.71	−7.55	−7.8	11/4/29	257.68	−15.83	−5.8
10/18/37	125.73	−10.57	−7.8	12/12/29	243.14	−15.30	−5.9
2/1/17	88.52	−6.91	−7.2	10/3/29	329.95	−14.55	−4.2
10/5/32	66.07	−5.09	−7.2	6/16/30	230.05	−14.20	−5.8
9/24/31	107.79	−8.20	−7.1	8/9/29	337.99	−14.11	−4.0
DJIA 1950 to APRIL 2016							
10/19/87	1738.74	−508.00	−22.6	9/29/08	10365.45	−777.68	−7.0
10/26/87	1793.93	−156.83	−8.0	10/15/08	8577.91	−733.08	−7.9
10/15/08	8577.91	−733.08	−7.9	9/17/01	8920.70	−684.81	−7.1
12/1/08	8149.09	−679.95	−7.7	12/1/08	8149.09	−679.95	−7.7
10/9/08	8579.19	−678.91	−7.3	10/9/08	8579.19	−678.91	−7.3
10/27/97	7161.15	−554.26	−7.2	8/8/11	10809.85	−634.76	−5.6
9/17/01	8920.70	−684.81	−7.1	4/14/00	10305.77	−617.78	−5.7
9/29/08	10365.45	−777.68	−7.0	8/24/15	15871.35	−588.40	−3.6
10/13/89	2569.26	−190.58	−6.9	10/27/97	7161.15	−554.26	−7.2
1/8/88	1911.31	−140.58	−6.9	8/21/15	16459.75	−530.94	−3.1
S&P 500 1930 to APRIL 2016							
10/19/87	224.84	−57.86	−20.5	9/29/08	1106.39	−106.62	−8.8
3/18/35	8.14	−0.91	−10.1	10/15/08	907.84	−90.17	−9.0
4/16/35	8.22	−0.91	−10.0	4/14/00	1356.56	−83.95	−5.8
9/3/46	15.00	−1.65	−9.9	12/1/08	816.21	−80.03	−8.9
10/18/37	10.76	−1.10	−9.3	8/8/11	1119.46	−79.92	−6.7
10/15/08	907.84	−90.17	−9.0	8/24/15	1893.21	−77.68	−3.9
12/1/08	816.21	−80.03	−8.9	10/9/08	909.92	−75.02	−7.6
7/20/33	10.57	−1.03	−8.9	8/31/98	957.28	−69.86	−6.8
9/29/08	1106.39	−106.62	−8.8	8/21/15	1970.89	−64.84	−3.2
7/21/33	9.65	−0.92	−8.7	10/27/97	876.99	−64.65	−6.9
NASDAQ 1971 to APRIL 2016							
10/19/87	360.21	−46.12	−11.4	4/14/00	3321.29	−355.49	−9.7
4/14/00	3321.29	−355.49	−9.7	4/3/00	4223.68	−349.15	−7.6
9/29/08	1983.73	−199.61	−9.1	4/12/00	3769.63	−286.27	−7.1
10/26/87	298.90	−29.55	−9.0	4/10/00	4188.20	−258.25	−5.8
10/20/87	327.79	−32.42	−9.0	1/4/00	3901.69	−229.46	−5.6
12/1/08	1398.07	−137.50	−9.0	3/14/00	4706.63	−200.61	−4.1
8/31/98	1499.25	−140.43	−8.6	5/10/00	3384.73	−200.28	−5.6
10/15/08	1628.33	−150.68	−8.5	5/23/00	3164.55	−199.66	−5.9
4/3/00	4223.68	−349.15	−7.6	9/29/08	1983.73	−199.61	−9.1
1/2/01	2291.86	−178.66	−7.2	10/25/00	3229.57	−190.22	−5.6
RUSSELL 1000 1979 to APRIL 2016							
10/19/87	121.04	−28.40	−19.0	9/29/08	602.34	−57.35	−8.7
10/15/08	489.71	−49.11	−9.1	10/15/08	489.71	−49.11	−9.1
12/1/08	437.75	−43.68	−9.1	4/14/00	715.20	−45.74	−6.0
9/29/08	602.34	−57.35	−8.7	8/8/11	617.28	−45.56	−6.9
10/26/87	119.45	−10.74	−8.3	12/1/08	437.75	−43.68	−9.1
10/9/08	492.13	−40.05	−7.5	8/24/15	1056.36	−43.45	−4.0
8/8/11	617.28	−45.56	−6.9	10/9/08	492.13	−40.05	−7.5
11/20/08	402.91	−29.62	−6.9	8/31/98	496.66	−35.77	−6.7
8/31/98	496.66	−35.77	−6.7	8/21/15	1099.81	−35.07	−3.1
10/27/97	465.44	−32.96	−6.6	8/4/11	664.65	−34.92	−5.0
RUSSELL 2000 1979 to APRIL 2016							
10/19/87	133.60	−19.14	−12.5	8/8/11	650.96	−63.67	−8.9
12/1/08	417.07	−56.07	−11.9	12/1/08	417.07	−56.07	−11.9
10/15/08	502.11	−52.54	−9.5	10/15/08	502.11	−52.54	−9.5
10/26/87	110.33	−11.26	−9.3	10/9/08	499.20	−47.37	−8.7
10/20/87	121.39	−12.21	−9.1	9/29/08	657.72	−47.00	−6.7
8/8/11	650.96	−63.67	−8.9	8/4/11	726.80	−45.98	−6.0
10/9/08	499.20	−47.37	−8.7	8/24/15	1111.69	−45.10	−3.9
11/19/08	412.38	−35.13	−7.9	8/18/11	662.51	−41.52	−5.9
4/14/00	453.72	−35.50	−7.3	10/7/08	558.95	−36.96	−6.2
11/14/08	456.52	−34.71	−7.1	11/9/11	718.86	−36.41	−4.8

162

10 BEST WEEKS BY PERCENT AND POINT

	BY PERCENT CHANGE				BY POINT CHANGE		
WEEK ENDS	CLOSE	PNT CHANGE	% CHANGE	WEEK ENDS	CLOSE	PNT CHANGE	% CHANGE
DJIA 1901 to 1949							
8/6/32	66.56	12.30	22.7	12/7/29	263.46	24.51	10.3
6/25/38	131.94	18.71	16.5	6/25/38	131.94	18.71	16.5
2/13/32	85.82	11.37	15.3	6/27/31	156.93	17.97	12.9
4/22/33	72.24	9.36	14.9	11/22/29	245.74	17.01	7.4
10/10/31	105.61	12.84	13.8	8/17/29	360.70	15.86	4.6
7/30/32	54.26	6.42	13.4	12/22/28	285.94	15.22	5.6
6/27/31	156.93	17.97	12.9	8/24/29	375.44	14.74	4.1
9/24/32	74.83	8.39	12.6	2/21/29	310.06	14.21	4.8
8/27/32	75.61	8.43	12.6	5/10/30	272.01	13.70	5.3
3/18/33	60.56	6.72	12.5	11/15/30	186.68	13.54	7.8
DJIA 1950 to APRIL 2016							
10/11/74	658.17	73.61	12.6	10/31/08	9325.01	946.06	11.3
10/31/08	9325.01	946.06	11.3	12/2/11	12019.42	787.64	7.0
8/20/82	869.29	81.24	10.3	11/28/08	8829.04	782.62	9.7
11/28/08	8829.04	782.62	9.7	3/17/00	10595.23	666.41	6.7
3/13/09	7223.98	597.04	9.0	3/21/03	8521.97	662.26	8.4
10/8/82	986.85	79.11	8.7	2/6/15	17824.29	659.34	3.8
3/21/03	8521.97	662.26	8.4	7/1/11	12582.77	648.19	5.4
8/3/84	1202.08	87.46	7.9	10/9/15	17084.49	612.12	3.7
9/28/01	8847.56	611.75	7.4	9/28/01	8847.56	611.75	7.4
7/17/09	8743.94	597.42	7.3	7/17/09	8743.94	597.42	7.3
S&P 500 1930 to APRIL 2016							
8/6/32	7.22	1.12	18.4	6/2/00	1477.26	99.24	7.2
6/25/38	11.39	1.72	17.8	11/28/08	896.24	96.21	12.0
7/30/32	6.10	0.89	17.1	10/31/08	968.75	91.98	10.5
4/22/33	7.75	1.09	16.4	12/2/11	1244.28	85.61	7.4
10/11/74	71.14	8.80	14.1	4/20/00	1434.54	77.98	5.8
2/13/32	8.80	1.08	14.0	10/24/14	1964.58	77.82	4.1
9/24/32	8.52	1.02	13.6	7/2/99	1391.22	75.91	5.8
10/10/31	10.64	1.27	13.6	3/3/00	1409.17	75.81	5.7
8/27/32	8.57	1.01	13.4	9/28/01	1040.94	75.14	7.8
3/18/33	6.61	0.77	13.2	3/13/09	756.55	73.17	10.7
NASDAQ 1971 to APRIL 2016							
6/2/00	3813.38	608.27	19.0	6/2/00	3813.38	608.27	19.0
4/12/01	1961.43	241.07	14.0	2/4/00	4244.14	357.07	9.2
11/28/08	1535.57	151.22	10.9	3/3/00	4914.79	324.29	7.1
10/31/08	1720.95	168.92	10.9	4/20/00	3643.88	322.59	9.7
3/13/09	1431.50	137.65	10.6	12/8/00	2917.43	272.14	10.3
4/20/01	2163.41	201.98	10.3	4/12/01	1961.43	241.07	14.0
12/8/00	2917.43	272.14	10.3	10/24/14	4483.72	225.28	5.3
4/20/00	3643.88	322.59	9.7	7/14/00	4246.18	222.98	5.5
10/11/74	60.42	5.26	9.5	1/12/01	2626.50	218.85	9.1
2/4/00	4244.14	357.07	9.0	4/28/00	3860.66	216.78	6.0
RUSSELL 1000 1979 to APRIL 2016							
11/28/08	481.43	53.55	12.5	6/2/00	785.02	57.93	8.0
10/31/08	522.47	50.94	10.8	11/28/08	481.43	53.55	12.5
3/13/09	411.10	39.88	10.7	10/31/08	522.47	50.94	10.8
8/20/82	61.51	4.83	8.5	12/2/11	687.44	47.63	7.4
6/2/00	785.02	57.93	8.0	10/24/14	1092.59	43.55	4.2
9/28/01	546.46	38.48	7.6	4/20/00	757.32	42.12	5.9
10/16/98	546.09	38.45	7.6	3/3/00	756.41	41.55	5.8
8/3/84	87.43	6.13	7.5	3/13/09	411.10	39.88	10.7
12/2/11	687.44	47.63	7.4	7/1/11	745.21	39.46	5.6
3/21/03	474.58	32.69	7.4	10/14/11	675.52	38.87	6.1
RUSSELL 2000 1979 to APRIL 2016							
11/28/08	473.14	66.60	16.4	12/2/11	735.02	68.86	10.3
10/31/08	537.52	66.40	14.1	11/28/08	473.14	66.60	16.4
6/2/00	513.03	55.66	12.2	10/31/08	537.52	66.40	14.1
3/13/09	393.09	42.04	12.0	10/14/11	712.46	56.25	8.6
12/2/11	735.02	68.86	10.3	6/2/00	513.03	55.66	12.2
10/14/11	712.46	56.25	8.6	10/31/14	1173.51	54.69	4.9
7/17/09	519.22	38.24	8.0	10/9/15	1165.36	51.24	4.6
10/16/98	342.87	24.47	7.7	10/28/11	761.00	48.58	6.8
12/18/87	116.94	8.31	7.7	1/4/13	879.15	47.05	5.7
3/3/00	597.88	41.14	7.4	3/4/16	1081.93	44.75	4.3

10 WORST WEEKS BY PERCENT AND POINT

	BY PERCENT CHANGE				BY POINT CHANGE		
WEEK ENDS	CLOSE	PNT CHANGE	% CHANGE	WEEK ENDS	CLOSE	PNT CHANGE	% CHANGE
DJIA 1901 to 1949							
7/22/33	88.42	−17.68	−16.7	11/8/29	236.53	−36.98	−13.5
5/18/40	122.43	−22.42	−15.5	12/8/28	257.33	−33.47	−11.5
10/8/32	61.17	−10.92	−15.2	6/21/30	215.30	−28.95	−11.9
10/3/31	92.77	−14.59	−13.6	10/19/29	323.87	−28.82	−8.2
11/8/29	236.53	−36.98	−13.5	5/3/30	258.31	−27.15	−9.5
9/17/32	66.44	−10.10	−13.2	10/31/29	273.51	−25.46	−8.5
10/21/33	83.64	−11.95	−12.5	10/26/29	298.97	−24.90	−7.7
12/12/31	78.93	−11.21	−12.4	5/18/40	122.43	−22.42	−15.5
5/8/15	62.77	−8.74	−12.2	2/8/29	301.53	−18.23	−5.7
6/21/30	215.30	−28.95	−11.9	10/11/30	193.05	−18.05	−8.6
DJIA 1950 to APRIL 2016							
10/10/08	8451.19	−1874.19	−18.2	10/10/08	8451.19	−1874.19	−18.2
9/21/01	8235.81	−1369.70	−14.3	9/21/01	8235.81	−1369.70	−14.3
10/23/87	1950.76	−295.98	−13.2	1/8/16	16346.45	−1078.58	−6.2
10/16/87	2246.74	−235.47	−9.5	8/21/15	16459.75	−1017.65	−5.8
10/13/89	2569.26	−216.26	−7.8	3/16/01	9823.41	−821.21	−7.7
3/16/01	9823.41	−821.21	−7.7	10/3/08	10325.38	−817.75	−7.3
7/19/02	8019.26	−665.27	−7.7	4/14/00	10305.77	−805.71	−7.3
12/4/87	1766.74	−143.74	−7.5	9/23/11	10771.48	−737.61	−6.4
9/13/74	627.19	−50.69	−7.5	8/5/11	11444.61	−698.63	−5.8
9/12/86	1758.72	−141.03	−7.4	7/12/02	8684.53	−694.97	−7.4
S&P 500 1930 to APRIL 2016							
7/22/33	9.71	−2.20	−18.5	10/10/08	899.22	−200.01	−18.2
10/10/08	899.22	−200.01	−18.2	4/14/00	1356.56	−159.79	−10.5
5/18/40	9.75	−2.05	−17.4	9/21/01	965.80	−126.74	−11.6
10/8/32	6.77	−1.38	−16.9	1/8/16	1922.03	−121.91	−6.0
9/17/32	7.50	−1.28	−14.6	8/21/15	1970.89	−120.65	−5.8
10/21/33	8.57	−1.31	−13.3	10/3/08	1099.23	−113.78	−9.4
10/3/31	9.37	−1.36	−12.7	8/5/11	1199.38	−92.90	−7.2
10/23/87	248.22	−34.48	−12.2	10/15/99	1247.41	−88.61	−6.6
12/12/31	8.20	−1.13	−12.1	3/16/01	1150.53	−82.89	−6.7
3/26/38	9.20	−1.21	−11.6	1/28/00	1360.16	−81.20	−5.6
NASDAQ 1971 to APRIL 2016							
4/14/00	3321.29	−1125.16	−25.3	4/14/00	3321.29	−1125.16	−25.3
10/23/87	328.45	−77.88	−19.2	7/28/00	3663.00	−431.45	−10.5
9/21/01	1423.19	−272.19	−16.1	11/10/00	3028.99	−422.59	−12.2
10/10/08	1649.51	−297.88	−15.3	3/31/00	4572.83	−390.20	−7.9
11/10/00	3028.99	−422.59	−12.2	1/8/16	4643.63	−363.78	−7.3
10/3/08	1947.39	−235.95	−10.8	1/28/00	3887.07	−348.33	−8.2
7/28/00	3663.00	−431.45	−10.5	8/21/15	4706.04	−342.20	−6.8
10/24/08	1552.03	−159.26	−9.3	10/6/00	3361.01	−311.81	−8.5
12/15/00	2653.27	−264.16	−9.1	10/10/08	1649.51	−297.88	−15.3
12/1/00	2645.29	−259.09	−8.9	5/12/00	3529.06	−287.76	−7.5
RUSSELL 1000 1979 to APRIL 2016							
10/10/08	486.23	−108.31	−18.2	10/10/08	486.23	−108.31	−18.2
10/23/87	130.19	−19.25	−12.9	4/14/00	715.20	−90.39	−11.2
9/21/01	507.98	−67.59	−11.7	1/8/16	1063.55	−68.33	−6.0
4/14/00	715.20	−90.39	−11.2	9/21/01	507.98	−67.59	−11.7
10/3/08	594.54	−65.15	−9.9	8/21/15	1099.81	−66.86	−5.7
10/16/87	149.44	−14.42	−8.8	10/3/08	594.54	−65.15	−9.9
11/21/08	427.88	−41.15	−8.8	8/5/11	662.84	−54.93	−7.7
9/12/86	124.95	−10.87	−8.0	9/23/11	627.56	−45.42	−6.8
8/5/11	662.84	−54.93	−7.7	12/11/15	1114.63	−44.64	−3.9
7/19/02	450.64	−36.13	−7.4	10/15/99	646.79	−43.89	−6.4
RUSSELL 2000 1979 to APRIL 2016							
10/23/87	121.59	−31.15	−20.4	10/10/08	522.48	−96.92	−15.7
4/14/00	453.72	−89.27	−16.4	1/8/16	1046.20	−89.69	−7.9
10/10/08	522.48	−96.92	−15.7	4/14/00	453.72	−89.27	−16.4
9/21/01	378.89	−61.84	−14.0	10/3/08	619.40	−85.39	−12.1
10/3/08	619.40	−85.39	−12.1	8/5/11	714.63	−82.40	−10.3
11/21/08	406.54	−49.98	−11.0	5/7/10	653.00	−63.60	−8.9
10/24/08	471.12	−55.31	−10.5	9/23/11	652.43	−61.88	−8.7
8/5/11	714.63	−82.40	−10.3	9/21/01	378.89	−61.84	−14.0
3/6/09	351.05	−37.97	−9.8	12/11/15	1123.61	−59.79	−5.1
11/14/08	456.52	−49.27	−9.7	7/27/07	777.83	−58.61	−7.0

10 **BEST** MONTHS BY PERCENT AND POINT

	BY PERCENT CHANGE				BY POINT CHANGE		
MONTH	CLOSE	PNT CHANGE	% CHANGE	MONTH	CLOSE	PNT CHANGE	% CHANGE
			DJIA 1901 to 1949				
APR-1933	77.66	22.26	40.2	NOV-1928	293.38	41.22	16.3
AUG-1932	73.16	18.90	34.8	JUN-1929	333.79	36.38	12.2
JUL-1932	54.26	11.42	26.7	AUG-1929	380.33	32.63	9.4
JUN-1938	133.88	26.14	24.3	JUN-1938	133.88	26.14	24.3
APR-1915	71.78	10.95	18.0	AUG-1928	240.41	24.41	11.3
JUN-1931	150.18	21.72	16.9	APR-1933	77.66	22.26	40.2
NOV-1928	293.38	41.22	16.3	FEB-1931	189.66	22.11	13.2
NOV-1904	52.76	6.59	14.3	JUN-1931	150.18	21.72	16.9
MAY-1919	105.50	12.62	13.6	AUG-1932	73.16	18.90	34.8
SEP-1939	152.54	18.13	13.5	JAN-1930	267.14	18.66	7.5
			DJIA 1950 to APRIL 2016				
JAN-1976	975.28	122.87	14.4	OCT-2015	17663.54	1379.54	8.5
JAN-1975	703.69	87.45	14.2	MAR-2016	17685.09	1168.59	7.1
JAN-1987	2158.04	262.09	13.8	OCT-2011	11955.01	1041.63	9.5
AUG-1982	901.31	92.71	11.5	APR-1999	10789.04	1002.88	10.2
OCT-1982	991.72	95.47	10.7	FEB-2015	18132.70	967.75	5.6
OCT-2002	8397.03	805.10	10.6	APR-2001	10734.97	856.19	8.7
APR-1978	837.32	79.96	10.6	OCT-2002	8397.03	805.10	10.6
APR-1999	10789.04	1002.88	10.2	MAR-2000	10921.92	793.61	7.8
NOV-1962	649.30	59.53	10.1	NOV-2001	9851.56	776.42	8.6
NOV-1954	386.77	34.63	9.8	SEP-2010	10788.05	773.33	7.7
			S&P 500 1930 to APRIL 2016				
APR-1933	8.32	2.47	42.2	OCT-2015	2079.36	159.33	8.3
JUL-1932	6.10	1.67	37.7	MAR-2000	1498.58	132.16	9.7
AUG-1932	8.39	2.29	37.5	MAR-2016	2059.74	127.51	6.6
JUN-1938	11.56	2.29	24.7	OCT-2011	1253.30	121.88	10.8
SEP-1939	13.02	1.84	16.5	FEB-2015	2104.50	109.51	5.5
OCT-1974	73.90	10.36	16.3	SEP-2010	1141.20	91.87	8.8
MAY-1933	9.64	1.32	15.9	APR-2001	1249.46	89.13	7.7
APR-1938	9.70	1.20	14.1	AUG-2000	1517.68	86.85	6.1
JUN-1931	14.83	1.81	13.9	OCT-1998	1098.67	81.66	8.0
JAN-1987	274.08	31.91	13.2	DEC-1999	1469.25	80.34	5.8
			NASDAQ 1971 to APRIL 2016				
DEC-1999	4069.31	733.15	22.0	FEB-2000	4696.69	756.34	19.2
FEB-2000	4696.69	756.34	19.2	DEC-1999	4069.31	733.15	22.0
OCT-1974	65.23	9.56	17.2	JUN-2000	3966.11	565.20	16.6
JAN-1975	69.78	9.96	16.6	AUG-2000	4206.35	439.36	11.7
JUN-2000	3966.11	565.20	16.6	OCT-2015	5053.75	433.59	9.4
APR-2001	2116.24	275.98	15.0	NOV-1999	3336.16	369.73	12.5
JAN-1999	2505.89	313.20	14.3	FEB-2015	4963.53	328.29	7.1
NOV-2001	1930.58	240.38	14.2	JAN-1999	2505.89	313.20	14.3
OCT-2002	1329.75	157.69	13.5	MAR-2016	4869.85	311.90	6.8
OCT-1982	212.63	24.98	13.3	JAN-2001	2772.73	302.21	12.2
			RUSSELL 1000 1979 to APRIL 2016				
JAN-1987	146.48	16.48	12.7	OCT-2015	1153.55	85.09	8.0
OCT-1982	73.34	7.45	11.3	MAR-2016	1138.84	72.26	6.8
AUG-1982	65.14	6.60	11.3	OCT-2011	692.41	68.96	11.1
DEC-1991	220.61	22.15	11.2	MAR-2000	797.99	64.95	8.9
OCT-2011	692.41	68.96	11.1	FEB-2015	1173.46	61.61	5.5
AUG-1984	89.87	8.74	10.8	AUG-2000	811.17	55.60	7.4
NOV-1980	78.26	7.18	10.1	SEP-2010	629.78	52.10	9.0
APR-2009	476.84	43.17	10.0	APR-2001	658.90	48.54	8.0
SEP-2010	629.78	52.10	9.0	JUL-2013	937.16	46.49	5.2
MAY-1990	187.66	15.34	8.0	FEB-2014	1041.36	44.88	4.5
			RUSSELL 2000 1979 to APRIL 2016				
FEB-2000	577.71	81.48	16.4	OCT-2011	741.06	96.90	15.0
APR-2009	487.56	64.81	15.3	FEB-2000	577.71	81.48	16.4
OCT-2011	741.06	96.90	15.0	MAR-2016	1114.03	80.13	7.8
OCT-1982	80.86	10.02	14.1	SEP-2010	676.14	74.08	12.3
JAN-1985	114.77	13.28	13.1	OCT-2014	1173.51	71.83	6.5
SEP-2010	676.14	74.08	12.3	FEB-2015	1233.37	67.98	5.8
AUG-1984	106.21	10.96	11.5	JUL-2013	1045.26	67.78	6.9
JAN-1987	150.48	15.48	11.5	APR-2009	487.56	64.81	15.3
DEC-1999	504.75	50.67	11.2	SEP-2013	1073.79	62.89	6.2
JUL-1980	63.81	6.34	11.0	OCT-2015	1161.86	61.17	5.6

10 <u>WORST</u> MONTHS BY PERCENT AND POINT

	BY PERCENT CHANGE				BY POINT CHANGE		
MONTH	CLOSE	PNT CHANGE	% CHANGE	MONTH	CLOSE	PNT CHANGE	% CHANGE
DJIA 1901 to 1949							
SEP-1931	96.61	−42.80	−30.7	OCT-1929	273.51	−69.94	−20.4
MAR-1938	98.95	−30.69	−23.7	JUN-1930	226.34	−48.73	−17.7
APR-1932	56.11	−17.17	−23.4	SEP-1931	96.61	−42.80	−30.7
MAY-1940	116.22	−32.21	−21.7	SEP-1929	343.45	−36.88	−9.7
OCT-1929	273.51	−69.94	−20.4	SEP-1930	204.90	−35.52	−14.8
MAY-1932	44.74	−11.37	−20.3	NOV-1929	238.95	−34.56	−12.6
JUN-1930	226.34	−48.73	−17.7	MAY-1940	116.22	−32.21	−21.7
DEC-1931	77.90	−15.97	−17.0	MAR-1938	98.95	−30.69	−23.7
FEB-1933	51.39	−9.51	−15.6	SEP-1937	154.57	−22.84	−12.9
MAY-1931	128.46	−22.73	−15.0	MAY-1931	128.46	−22.73	−15.0
DJIA 1950 to APRIL 2016							
OCT-1987	1993.53	−602.75	−23.2	OCT-2008	9325.01	−1525.65	−14.1
AUG-1998	7539.07	−1344.22	−15.1	AUG-1998	7539.07	−1344.22	−15.1
OCT-2008	9325.01	−1525.65	−14.1	JUN-2008	11350.01	−1288.31	−10.2
NOV-1973	822.25	−134.33	−14.0	AUG-2015	16528.03	−1161.83	−6.6
SEP-2002	7591.93	−1071.57	−12.4	SEP-2001	8847.56	−1102.19	−11.1
FEB-2009	7062.93	−937.93	−11.7	SEP-2002	7591.93	−1071.57	−12.4
SEP-2001	8847.56	−1102.19	−11.1	JAN-2016	16466.30	−958.73	−5.5
SEP-1974	607.87	−70.71	−10.4	FEB-2009	7062.93	−937.93	−11.7
AUG-1974	678.58	−78.85	−10.4	JAN-2014	15698.85	−877.81	−5.3
JUN-2008	11350.01	−1288.31	−10.2	MAY-2010	10136.63	−871.98	−7.9
S&P 500 1930 to APRIL 2016							
SEP-1931	9.71	−4.15	−29.9	OCT-2008	968.75	−197.61	−16.9
MAR-1938	8.50	−2.84	−25.0	AUG-1998	957.28	−163.39	−14.6
MAY-1940	9.27	−2.92	−24.0	AUG-2015	1972.18	−131.66	−6.3
MAY-1932	4.47	−1.36	−23.3	FEB-2001	1239.94	−126.07	−9.2
OCT-1987	251.79	−70.04	−21.8	JUN-2008	1280.00	−120.38	−8.6
APR-1932	5.83	−1.48	−20.2	SEP-2008	1166.36	−116.47	−9.1
FEB-1933	5.66	−1.28	−18.4	NOV-2000	1314.95	−114.45	−8.0
OCT-2008	968.75	−197.61	−16.9	JAN-2016	1940.24	−103.70	−5.1
JUN-1930	20.46	−4.03	−16.5	SEP-2002	815.28	−100.79	−11.0
AUG-1998	957.28	−163.39	−14.6	MAY-2010	1089.41	−97.28	−8.2
NASDAQ 1971 to APRIL 2016							
OCT-1987	323.30	−120.99	−27.2	NOV-2000	2597.93	−771.70	−22.9
NOV-2000	2597.93	−771.70	−22.9	APR-2000	3860.66	−712.17	−15.6
FEB-2001	2151.83	−620.90	−22.4	FEB-2001	2151.83	−620.90	−22.4
AUG-1998	1499.25	−373.14	−19.9	SEP-2000	3672.82	−533.53	−12.7
OCT-2008	1720.95	−370.93	−17.7	MAY-2000	3400.91	−459.75	−11.9
MAR-1980	131.00	−27.03	−17.1	JAN-2016	4613.95	−393.46	−7.9
SEP-2001	1498.80	−306.63	−17.0	AUG-1998	1499.25	−373.14	−19.9
OCT-1978	111.12	−21.77	−16.4	OCT-2008	1720.95	−370.93	−17.7
APR-2000	3860.66	−712.17	−15.6	AUG-2015	4776.51	−351.77	−6.9
NOV-1973	93.51	−16.66	−15.1	MAR-2001	1840.26	−311.57	−14.5
RUSSELL 1000 1979 to APRIL 2016							
OCT-1987	131.89	−36.94	−21.9	OCT-2008	522.47	−111.61	−17.6
OCT-2008	522.47	−111.61	−17.6	AUG-1998	496.66	−88.31	−15.1
AUG-1998	496.66	−88.31	−15.1	AUG-2015	1100.51	−73.04	−6.2
MAR-1980	55.79	−7.28	−11.5	NOV-2000	692.40	−70.66	−9.3
SEP-2002	433.22	−52.86	−10.9	FEB-2001	654.25	−68.30	−9.5
FEB-2009	399.61	−47.71	−10.7	SEP-2008	634.08	−68.09	−9.7
SEP-2008	634.08	−68.09	−9.7	JUN-2008	703.22	−65.06	−8.5
AUG-1990	166.69	−17.63	−9.6	JAN-2016	1069.78	−62.10	−5.5
FEB-2001	654.25	−68.30	−9.5	MAY-2010	601.79	−53.27	−8.1
NOV-2000	692.40	−70.66	−9.3	SEP-2002	433.22	−52.86	−10.9
RUSSELL 2000 1979 to APRIL 2016							
OCT-1987	118.26	−52.55	−30.8	OCT-2008	537.52	−142.06	−20.9
OCT-2008	537.52	−142.06	−20.9	JAN-2016	1035.38	−100.51	−8.8
AUG-1998	337.95	−81.80	−19.5	SEP-2011	644.16	−82.65	−11.4
MAR-1980	48.27	−10.95	−18.5	AUG-1998	337.95	−81.80	−19.5
JUL-2002	392.42	−70.22	−15.2	AUG-2015	1159.45	−79.23	−6.4
AUG-1990	139.52	−21.99	−13.6	JUL-2014	1120.07	−72.89	−6.1
SEP-2001	404.87	−63.69	−13.6	SEP-2014	1101.68	−72.67	−6.2
FEB-2009	389.02	−54.51	−12.3	JUL-2002	392.42	−70.22	−15.2
NOV-2008	473.14	−64.38	−12.0	AUG-2011	726.81	−70.22	−8.8
SEP-2011	644.16	−82.65	−11.4	NOV-2008	473.14	−64.38	−12.0

10 **BEST** QUARTERS BY PERCENT AND POINT

	BY PERCENT CHANGE				BY POINT CHANGE		
QUARTER	CLOSE	PNT CHANGE	% CHANGE	QUARTER	CLOSE	PNT CHANGE	% CHANGE
DJIA 1901 to 1949							
JUN-1933	98.14	42.74	77.1	DEC-1928	300.00	60.57	25.3
SEP-1932	71.56	28.72	67.0	JUN-1933	98.14	42.74	77.1
JUN-1938	133.88	34.93	35.3	MAR-1930	286.10	37.62	15.1
SEP-1915	90.58	20.52	29.3	JUN-1938	133.88	34.93	35.3
DEC-1928	300.00	60.57	25.3	SEP-1927	197.59	31.36	18.9
DEC-1904	50.99	8.80	20.9	SEP-1928	239.43	28.88	13.7
JUN-1919	106.98	18.13	20.4	SEP-1932	71.56	28.72	67.0
SEP-1927	197.59	31.36	18.9	JUN-1929	333.79	24.94	8.1
DEC-1905	70.47	10.47	17.4	SEP-1939	152.54	21.91	16.8
JUN-1935	118.21	17.40	17.3	SEP-1915	90.58	20.52	29.3
DJIA 1950 to APRIL 2016							
MAR-1975	768.15	151.91	24.7	MAR-2013	14578.54	1474.40	11.3
MAR-1987	2304.69	408.74	21.6	DEC-2013	16576.66	1446.99	9.6
MAR-1986	1818.61	271.94	17.6	DEC-1998	9181.43	1338.81	17.1
MAR-1976	999.45	147.04	17.2	DEC-2011	12217.56	1304.18	12.0
DEC-1998	9181.43	1338.81	17.1	SEP-2009	9712.28	1265.28	15.0
DEC-1982	1046.54	150.29	16.8	JUN-1999	10970.80	1184.64	12.1
JUN-1997	7672.79	1089.31	16.5	DEC-2003	10453.92	1178.86	12.7
DEC-1985	1546.67	218.04	16.4	DEC-2001	10021.50	1173.94	13.3
SEP-2009	9712.28	1265.28	15.0	DEC-1999	11497.12	1160.17	11.2
JUN-1975	878.99	110.84	14.4	DEC-2015	17425.03	1141.03	7.0
S&P 500 1930 to APRIL 2016							
JUN-1933	10.91	5.06	86.5	DEC-1998	1229.23	212.22	20.9
SEP-1932	8.08	3.65	82.4	DEC-1999	1469.25	186.54	14.5
JUN-1938	11.56	3.06	36.0	DEC-2013	1848.36	166.81	9.9
MAR-1975	83.36	14.80	21.6	MAR-2012	1408.47	150.87	12.0
DEC-1998	1229.23	212.22	20.9	MAR-2013	1569.19	143.00	10.0
JUN-1935	10.23	1.76	20.8	SEP-2009	1057.08	137.76	15.0
MAR-1987	291.70	49.53	20.5	MAR-1998	1101.75	131.32	13.5
SEP-1939	13.02	2.16	19.9	JUN-1997	885.14	128.02	16.9
MAR-1943	11.58	1.81	18.5	DEC-2011	1257.60	126.18	11.2
MAR-1930	25.14	3.69	17.2	JUN-2003	974.50	125.32	14.8
NASDAQ 1971 to APRIL 2016							
DEC-1999	4069.31	1323.15	48.2	DEC-1999	4069.31	1323.15	48.2
DEC-2001	1950.40	451.60	30.1	MAR-2000	4572.83	503.52	12.4
DEC-1998	2192.69	498.85	29.5	DEC-1998	2192.69	498.85	29.5
MAR-1991	482.30	108.46	29.0	MAR-2012	3091.57	486.42	18.7
MAR-1975	75.66	15.84	26.5	DEC-2001	1950.40	451.60	30.1
DEC-1982	232.41	44.76	23.9	DEC-2013	4176.59	405.11	10.7
MAR-1987	430.05	80.72	23.1	DEC-2015	5007.41	387.25	8.4
JUN-2003	1622.80	281.63	21.0	SEP-2013	3771.48	368.23	10.8
JUN-1980	157.78	26.78	20.4	JUN-2001	2160.54	320.28	17.4
JUN-2009	1835.04	306.45	20.0	JUN-2009	1835.04	306.45	20.0
RUSSELL 1000 1979 to APRIL 2016							
DEC-1998	642.87	113.76	21.5	DEC-1998	642.87	113.76	21.5
MAR-1987	155.20	25.20	19.4	DEC-1999	767.97	104.14	15.7
DEC-1982	77.24	11.35	17.2	DEC-2013	1030.36	90.86	9.7
JUN-1997	462.95	64.76	16.3	MAR-2012	778.92	85.56	12.3
DEC-1985	114.39	15.64	15.8	MAR-2013	872.11	82.21	10.4
JUN-2009	502.27	68.60	15.8	SEP-2009	579.97	77.70	15.5
DEC-1999	767.97	104.14	15.7	DEC-2011	693.36	69.91	11.2
SEP-2009	579.97	77.70	15.5	JUN-2009	502.27	68.60	15.8
JUN-2003	518.94	68.59	15.2	JUN-2003	518.94	68.59	15.2
MAR-1991	196.15	24.93	14.6	DEC-2010	696.90	67.12	10.7
RUSSELL 2000 1979 to APRIL 2016							
MAR-1991	171.01	38.85	29.4	DEC-2010	783.65	107.51	15.9
DEC-1982	88.90	18.06	25.5	DEC-2014	1204.70	103.02	9.4
MAR-1987	166.79	31.79	23.5	MAR-2013	951.54	102.19	12.0
JUN-2003	448.37	83.83	23.0	DEC-2011	740.92	96.76	15.0
SEP-1980	69.94	12.47	21.7	SEP-2013	1073.79	96.31	9.9
DEC-2001	488.50	83.63	20.7	SEP-2009	604.28	96.00	18.9
JUN-1983	124.17	20.40	19.7	MAR-2006	765.14	91.92	13.7
JUN-1980	57.47	9.20	19.1	DEC-2013	1163.64	89.85	8.4
DEC-1999	504.75	77.45	18.1	MAR-2012	830.30	89.38	12.1
SEP-2009	604.28	96.00	18.9	JUN-2009	508.28	85.53	20.2

10 WORST QUARTERS BY PERCENT AND POINT

	BY PERCENT CHANGE				BY POINT CHANGE		
QUARTER	CLOSE	PNT CHANGE	% CHANGE	QUARTER	CLOSE	PNT CHANGE	% CHANGE
DJIA 1901 to 1949							
JUN-1932	42.84	−30.44	−41.5	DEC-1929	248.48	−94.97	−27.7
SEP-1931	96.61	−53.57	−35.7	JUN-1930	226.34	−59.76	−20.9
DEC-1929	248.48	−94.97	−27.7	SEP-1931	96.61	−53.57	−35.7
SEP-1903	33.55	−9.73	−22.5	DEC-1930	164.58	−40.32	−19.7
DEC-1937	120.85	−33.72	−21.8	DEC-1937	120.85	−33.72	−21.8
JUN-1930	226.34	−59.76	−20.9	SEP-1946	172.42	−33.20	−16.1
DEC-1930	164.58	−40.32	−19.7	JUN-1932	42.84	−30.44	−41.5
DEC-1931	77.90	−18.71	−19.4	JUN-1940	121.87	−26.08	−17.6
MAR-1938	98.95	−21.90	−18.1	MAR-1939	131.84	−22.92	−14.8
JUN-1940	121.87	−26.08	−17.6	JUN-1931	150.18	−22.18	−12.9
DJIA 1950 to APRIL 2016							
DEC-1987	1938.83	−657.45	−25.3	DEC-2008	8776.39	−2074.27	−19.1
SEP-1974	607.87	−194.54	−24.2	SEP-2001	8847.56	−1654.84	−15.8
JUN-1962	561.28	−145.67	−20.6	SEP-2002	7591.93	−1651.33	−17.9
DEC-2008	8776.39	−2074.27	−19.1	SEP-2011	10913.38	−1500.96	−12.1
SEP-2002	7591.93	−1651.33	−17.9	SEP-2015	16284.00	−1335.51	−7.6
SEP-2001	8847.56	−1654.84	−15.8	MAR-2009	7608.92	−1167.47	−13.3
SEP-1990	2452.48	−428.21	−14.9	JUN-2002	9243.26	−1160.68	−11.2
MAR-2009	7608.92	−1167.47	−13.3	SEP-1998	7842.62	−1109.40	−12.4
SEP-1981	849.98	−126.90	−13.0	JUN-2010	9774.02	−1082.61	−10.0
JUN-1970	683.53	−102.04	−13.0	MAR-2008	12262.89	−1001.93	−7.6
S&P 500 1930 to APRIL 2016							
JUN-1932	4.43	−2.88	−39.4	DEC-2008	903.25	−263.11	−22.6
SEP-1931	9.71	−5.12	−34.5	SEP-2011	1131.42	−189.22	−14.3
SEP-1974	63.54	−22.46	−26.1	SEP-2001	1040.94	−183.48	−15.0
DEC-1937	10.55	−3.21	−23.3	SEP-2002	815.28	−174.54	−17.6
DEC-1987	247.08	−74.75	−23.2	MAR-2001	1160.33	−159.95	−12.1
DEC-2008	903.25	−263.11	−22.6	JUN-2002	989.82	−157.57	−13.7
JUN-1962	54.75	−14.80	−21.3	MAR-2008	1322.70	−145.66	−9.9
MAR-1938	8.50	−2.05	−19.4	SEP-2015	1920.03	−143.08	−6.9
JUN-1970	72.72	−16.91	−18.9	JUN-2010	1030.71	−138.72	−11.9
SEP-1946	14.96	−3.47	−18.8	SEP-1998	1017.01	−116.83	−10.3
NASDAQ 1971 to APRIL 2016							
DEC-2000	2470.52	−1202.30	−32.7	DEC-2000	2470.52	−1202.30	−32.7
SEP-2001	1498.80	−661.74	−30.6	SEP-2001	1498.80	−661.74	−30.6
SEP-1974	55.67	−20.29	−26.7	MAR-2001	1840.26	−630.26	−25.5
DEC-1987	330.47	−113.82	−25.6	JUN-2000	3966.11	−606.72	−13.3
MAR-2001	1840.26	−630.26	−25.5	DEC-2008	1577.03	−514.85	−24.6
SEP-1990	344.51	−117.78	−25.5	JUN-2002	1463.21	−382.14	−20.7
DEC-2008	1577.03	−514.85	−24.6	MAR-2008	2279.10	−373.18	−14.1
JUN-2002	1463.21	−382.14	−20.7	SEP-2015	4620.16	−366.71	−7.4
SEP-2002	1172.06	−291.15	−19.9	SEP-2011	2415.40	−358.12	−12.9
JUN-1974	75.96	−16.31	−17.7	SEP-2000	3672.82	−293.29	−7.4
RUSSELL 1000 1979 to APRIL 2016							
DEC-2008	487.77	−146.31	−23.1	DEC-2008	487.77	−146.31	−23.1
DEC-1987	130.02	−38.81	−23.0	SEP-2011	623.45	−111.03	−15.1
SEP-2002	433.22	−90.50	−17.3	SEP-2001	546.46	−100.18	−15.5
SEP-2001	546.46	−100.18	−15.5	SEP-2002	433.22	−90.50	−17.3
SEP-1990	157.83	−28.46	−15.3	MAR-2001	610.36	−89.73	−12.8
SEP-2011	623.45	−111.03	−15.1	SEP-2015	1068.46	−84.18	−7.3
JUN-2002	523.72	−83.63	−13.8	JUN-2002	523.72	−83.63	−13.8
MAR-2001	610.36	−89.73	−12.8	MAR-2008	720.32	−79.50	−9.9
SEP-1981	64.06	−8.95	−12.3	JUN-2010	567.37	−76.42	−11.9
JUN-2010	567.37	−76.42	−11.9	DEC-2000	700.09	−72.51	−9.4
RUSSELL 2000 1979 to APRIL 2016							
DEC-1987	120.42	−50.39	−29.5	SEP-2011	644.16	−183.27	−22.1
DEC-2008	499.45	−180.13	−26.5	DEC-2008	499.45	−180.13	−26.5
SEP-1990	126.70	−42.34	−25.0	SEP-2015	1100.69	−153.26	−12.2
SEP-2011	644.16	−183.27	−22.1	SEP-2001	404.87	−107.77	−21.0
SEP-2002	362.27	−100.37	−21.7	SEP-2002	362.27	−100.37	−21.7
SEP-2001	404.87	−107.77	−21.0	SEP-1998	363.59	−93.80	−20.5
SEP-1998	363.59	−93.80	−20.5	SEP-2014	1101.68	−91.28	−7.7
SEP-1981	67.55	−15.01	−18.2	MAR-2008	687.97	−78.06	−10.2
MAR-2009	422.75	−76.70	−15.4	MAR-2009	422.75	−76.70	−15.4
MAR-1980	48.27	−7.64	−13.7	JUN-2010	609.49	−69.15	−10.2

10 <u>BEST</u> YEARS BY PERCENT AND POINT

	BY PERCENT CHANGE				BY POINT CHANGE		
YEAR	CLOSE	PNT CHANGE	% CHANGE	YEAR	CLOSE	PNT CHANGE	% CHANGE
DJIA 1901 to 1949							
1915	99.15	44.57	81.7	1928	300.00	97.60	48.2
1933	99.90	39.97	66.7	1927	202.40	45.20	28.8
1928	300.00	97.60	48.2	1915	99.15	44.57	81.7
1908	63.11	20.07	46.6	1945	192.91	40.59	26.6
1904	50.99	15.01	41.7	1935	144.13	40.09	38.5
1935	144.13	40.09	38.5	1933	99.90	39.97	66.7
1905	70.47	19.48	38.2	1925	156.66	36.15	30.0
1919	107.23	25.03	30.5	1936	179.90	35.77	24.8
1925	156.66	36.15	30.0	1938	154.76	33.91	28.1
1927	202.40	45.20	28.8	1919	107.23	25.03	30.5
DJIA 1950 to APRIL 2016							
1954	404.39	123.49	44.0	2013	16576.66	3472.52	26.5
1975	852.41	236.17	38.3	1999	11497.12	2315.69	25.2
1958	583.65	147.96	34.0	2003	10453.92	2112.29	25.3
1995	5117.12	1282.68	33.5	2006	12463.15	1745.65	16.3
1985	1546.67	335.10	27.7	2009	10428.05	1651.66	18.8
1989	2753.20	584.63	27.0	1997	7908.25	1459.98	22.6
2013	16576.66	3472.52	26.5	1996	6448.27	1331.15	26.0
1996	6448.27	1331.15	26.0	1995	5117.12	1282.68	33.5
2003	10453.92	2112.29	25.3	1998	9181.43	1273.18	16.1
1999	11497.12	2315.69	25.2	2014	17823.07	1246.41	7.5
S&P 500 1930 to APRIL 2016							
1933	10.10	3.21	46.6	2013	1848.36	422.17	29.6
1954	35.98	11.17	45.0	1998	1229.23	258.80	26.7
1935	13.43	3.93	41.4	1999	1469.25	240.02	19.5
1958	55.21	15.22	38.1	2003	1111.92	232.10	26.4
1995	615.93	156.66	34.1	1997	970.43	229.69	31.0
1975	90.19	21.63	31.5	2009	1115.10	211.85	23.5
1997	970.43	229.69	31.0	2014	2058.90	210.54	11.4
1945	17.36	4.08	30.7	2006	1418.30	170.01	13.6
2013	1848.36	422.17	29.6	2012	1426.19	168.59	13.4
1936	17.18	3.75	27.9	1995	615.93	156.66	34.1
NASDAQ 1971 to APRIL 2016							
1999	4069.31	1876.62	85.6	1999	4069.31	1876.62	85.6
1991	586.34	212.50	56.8	2013	4176.59	1157.08	38.3
2003	2003.37	667.86	50.0	2009	2269.15	692.12	43.9
2009	2269.15	692.12	43.9	2003	2003.37	667.86	50.0
1995	1052.13	300.17	39.9	1998	2192.69	622.34	39.6
1998	2192.69	622.34	39.6	2014	4736.05	559.46	13.4
2013	4176.59	1157.08	38.3	2012	3019.51	414.36	15.9
1980	202.34	51.20	33.9	2010	2652.87	383.72	16.9
1985	324.93	77.58	31.4	1995	1052.13	300.17	39.9
1975	77.62	17.80	29.8	1997	1570.35	279.32	21.6
RUSSELL 1000 1979 to APRIL 2016							
1995	328.89	84.24	34.4	2013	1030.36	240.46	30.4
1997	513.79	120.04	30.5	1998	642.87	129.08	25.1
2013	1030.36	240.46	30.4	2003	594.56	128.38	27.5
1991	220.61	49.39	28.8	1999	767.97	125.10	19.5
2003	594.56	128.38	27.5	2009	612.01	124.24	25.5
1985	114.39	24.08	26.7	1997	513.79	120.04	30.5
1989	185.11	38.12	25.9	2014	1144.37	114.01	11.1
1980	75.20	15.33	25.6	2012	789.90	96.54	13.9
2009	612.01	124.24	25.5	2006	770.08	90.66	13.3
1998	642.87	129.08	25.1	2010	696.90	84.89	13.9
RUSSELL 2000 1979 to APRIL 2016							
2003	556.91	173.82	45.4	2013	1163.64	314.29	37.0
1991	189.94	57.78	43.7	2003	556.91	173.82	45.4
1979	55.91	15.39	38.0	2010	783.65	158.26	25.3
2013	1163.64	314.29	37.0	2009	625.39	125.94	25.2
1980	74.80	18.89	33.8	2006	787.66	114.44	17.0
1985	129.87	28.38	28.0	2012	849.35	108.43	14.6
1983	112.27	23.37	26.3	2004	651.57	94.66	17.0
1995	315.97	65.61	26.2	1999	504.75	82.79	19.6
2010	783.65	158.26	25.3	1997	437.02	74.41	20.5
2009	625.39	125.94	25.2	1995	315.97	65.61	26.2

10 <u>WORST</u> YEARS BY PERCENT AND POINT

	BY PERCENT CHANGE				BY POINT CHANGE		
YEAR	CLOSE	PNT CHANGE	% CHANGE	YEAR	CLOSE	PNT CHANGE	% CHANGE
			DJIA 1901 to 1949				
1931	77.90	−86.68	−52.7	1931	77.90	−86.68	−52.7
1907	43.04	−26.08	−37.7	1930	164.58	−83.90	−33.8
1930	164.58	−83.90	−33.8	1937	120.85	−59.05	−32.8
1920	71.95	−35.28	−32.9	1929	248.48	−51.52	−17.2
1937	120.85	−59.05	−32.8	1920	71.95	−35.28	−32.9
1903	35.98	−11.12	−23.6	1907	43.04	−26.08	−37.7
1932	59.93	−17.97	−23.1	1917	74.38	−20.62	−21.7
1917	74.38	−20.62	−21.7	1941	110.96	−20.17	−15.4
1910	59.60	−12.96	−17.9	1940	131.13	−19.11	−12.7
1929	248.48	−51.52	−17.2	1932	59.93	−17.97	−23.1
			DJIA 1950 to APRIL 2016				
2008	8776.39	−4488.43	−33.8	2008	8776.39	−4488.43	−33.8
1974	616.24	−234.62	−27.6	2002	8341.63	−1679.87	−16.8
1966	785.69	−183.57	−18.9	2001	10021.50	−765.35	−7.1
1977	831.17	−173.48	−17.3	2000	10786.85	−710.27	−6.2
2002	8341.63	−1679.87	−16.8	2015	17425.03	−398.04	−2.2
1973	850.86	−169.16	−16.6	1974	616.24	−234.62	−27.6
1969	800.36	−143.39	−15.2	1966	785.69	−183.57	−18.9
1957	435.69	−63.78	−12.8	1977	831.17	−173.48	−17.3
1962	652.10	−79.04	−10.8	1973	850.86	−169.16	−16.6
1960	615.89	−63.47	−9.3	1969	800.36	−143.39	−15.2
			S&P 500 1930 to APRIL 2016				
1931	8.12	−7.22	−47.1	2008	903.25	−565.11	−38.5
1937	10.55	−6.63	−38.6	2002	879.82	−268.26	−23.4
2008	903.25	−565.11	−38.5	2001	1148.08	−172.20	−13.0
1974	68.56	−28.99	−29.7	2000	1320.28	−148.97	−10.1
1930	15.34	−6.11	−28.5	1974	68.56	−28.99	−29.7
2002	879.82	−268.26	−23.4	1990	330.22	−23.18	−6.6
1941	8.69	−1.89	−17.9	1973	97.55	−20.50	−17.4
1973	97.55	−20.50	−17.4	2015	2043.94	−14.96	−0.7
1940	10.58	−1.91	−15.3	1981	122.55	−13.21	−9.7
1932	6.89	−1.23	−15.1	1977	95.10	−12.36	−11.5
			NASDAQ 1971 to APRIL 2016				
2008	1577.03	−1075.25	−40.5	2000	2470.52	−1598.79	−39.3
2000	2470.52	−1598.79	−39.3	2008	1577.03	−1075.25	−40.5
1974	59.82	−32.37	−35.1	2002	1335.51	−614.89	−31.5
2002	1335.51	−614.89	−31.5	2001	1950.40	−520.12	−21.1
1973	92.19	−41.54	−31.1	1990	373.84	−80.98	−17.8
2001	1950.40	−520.12	−21.1	2011	2605.15	−47.72	−1.8
1990	373.84	−80.98	−17.8	1973	92.19	−41.54	−31.1
1984	247.35	−31.25	−11.2	1974	59.82	−32.37	−35.1
1987	330.47	−18.86	−5.4	1984	247.35	−31.25	−11.2
1981	195.84	−6.50	−3.2	1994	751.96	−24.84	−3.2
			RUSSELL 1000 1979 to APRIL 2016				
2008	487.77	−312.05	−39.0	2008	487.77	−312.05	−39.0
2002	466.18	−138.76	−22.9	2002	466.18	−138.76	−22.9
2001	604.94	−95.15	−13.6	2001	604.94	−95.15	−13.6
1981	67.93	−7.27	−9.7	2000	700.09	−67.88	−8.8
2000	700.09	−67.88	−8.8	1990	171.22	−13.89	−7.5
1990	171.22	−13.89	−7.5	2015	1131.88	−12.49	−1.1
1994	244.65	−6.06	−2.4	1981	67.93	−7.27	−9.7
2015	1131.88	−12.49	−1.1	1994	244.65	−6.06	−2.4
2011	693.36	−3.54	−0.5	2011	693.36	−3.54	−0.5
1984	90.31	−0.07	−0.1	1984	90.31	−0.07	−0.10
			RUSSELL 2000 1979 to APRIL 2016				
2008	499.45	−266.58	−34.8	2008	499.45	−266.58	−34.8
2002	383.09	−105.41	−21.6	2002	383.09	−105.41	−21.6
1990	132.16	−36.14	−21.5	2015	1135.89	−68.81	−5.7
1987	120.42	−14.58	−10.8	2011	740.92	−42.73	−5.5
1984	101.49	−10.78	−9.6	1990	132.16	−36.14	−21.5
2015	1135.89	−68.81	−5.7	2007	766.03	−21.63	−2.7
2011	740.92	−42.73	−5.5	2000	483.53	−21.22	−4.2
2000	483.53	−21.22	−4.2	1998	421.96	−15.06	−3.4
1998	421.96	−15.06	−3.4	1987	120.42	−14.58	−10.8
1994	250.36	−8.23	−3.2	1984	101.49	−10.78	−9.6

DOW JONES INDUSTRIALS ONE-YEAR SEASONAL PATTERN CHARTS SINCE 1901

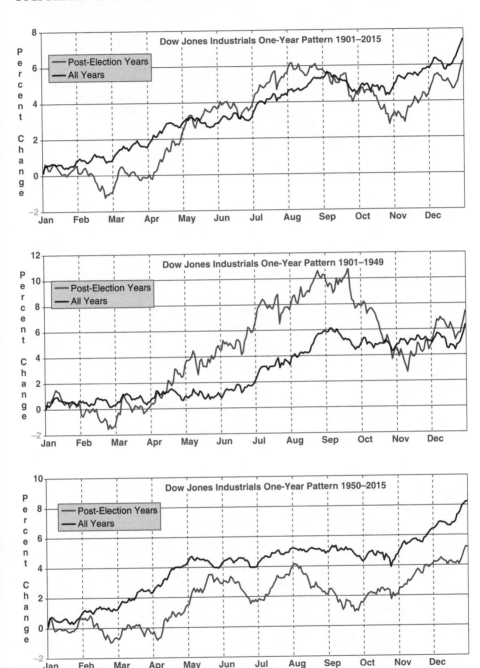

S&P 500 ONE-YEAR SEASONAL PATTERN CHARTS SINCE 1930

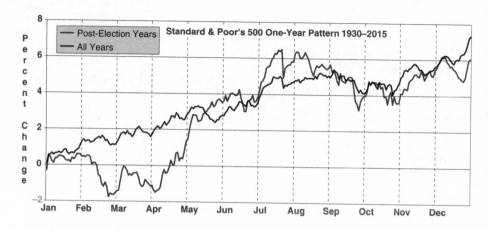

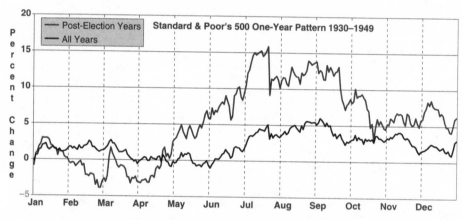

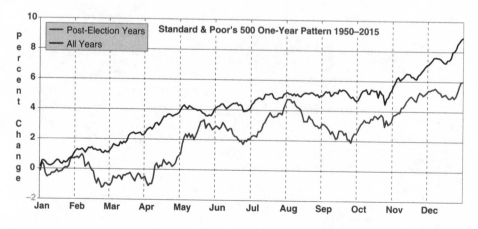

NASDAQ, RUSSELL 1000 & 2000 ONE-YEAR SEASONAL PATTERN CHARTS SINCE 1971

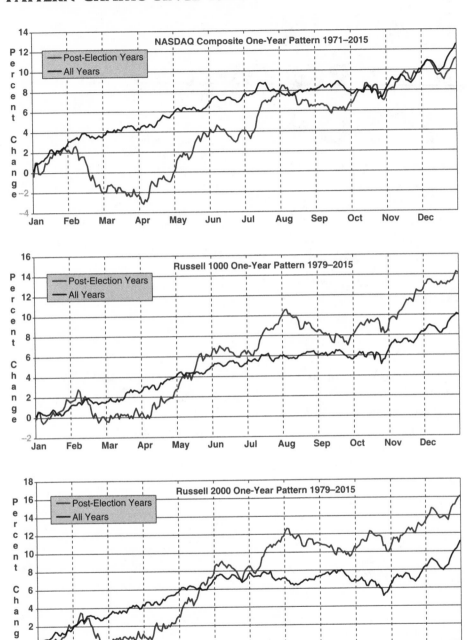

STRATEGY PLANNING AND RECORD SECTION

CONTENTS

These forms are available at our website www.stocktradersalmanac.com.

PORTFOLIO AT START OF 2017

DATE ACQUIRED	NO. OF SHARES	SECURITY	PRICE	TOTAL COST	PAPER PROFITS	PAPER LOSSES

ADDITIONAL PURCHASES

DATE ACQUIRED	NO. OF SHARES	SECURITY	PRICE	TOTAL COST	REASON FOR PURCHASE PRIME OBJECTIVE, ETC.

ADDITIONAL PURCHASES

DATE ACQUIRED	NO. OF SHARES	SECURITY	PRICE	TOTAL COST	REASON FOR PURCHASE PRIME OBJECTIVE, ETC.

SHORT-TERM TRANSACTIONS

Pages 178–181 can accompany next year's income tax return (Schedule D). Enter transactions as completed to avoid last-minute pressures.

NO. OF SHARES	SECURITY	DATE ACQUIRED	DATE SOLD	SALE PRICE	COST	LOSS	GAIN

TOTALS:
Carry over to next page

SHORT-TERM TRANSACTIONS (continued)

NO. OF SHARES	SECURITY	DATE ACQUIRED	DATE SOLD	SALE PRICE	COST	LOSS	GAIN
TOTALS:							

LONG-TERM TRANSACTIONS

Pages 178–181 can accompany next year's income tax return (Schedule D). Enter transactions as completed to avoid last-minute pressures.

NO. OF SHARES	SECURITY	DATE ACQUIRED	DATE SOLD	SALE PRICE	COST	LOSS	GAIN

TOTALS:
Carry over to next page

LONG-TERM TRANSACTIONS (continued)

NO. OF SHARES	SECURITY	DATE ACQUIRED	DATE SOLD	SALE PRICE	COST	LOSS	GAIN

TOTALS:

INTEREST/DIVIDENDS RECEIVED DURING 2017

SHARES	STOCK/BOND	FIRST QUARTER		SECOND QUARTER		THIRD QUARTER		FOURTH QUARTER	
		$		$		$		$	

BROKERAGE ACCOUNT DATA 2017

	MARGIN INTEREST	TRANSFER TAXES	CAPITAL ADDED	CAPITAL WITHDRAWN
JAN				
FEB				
MAR				
APR				
MAY				
JUN				
JUL				
AUG				
SEP				
OCT				
NOV				
DEC				

WEEKLY PORTFOLIO PRICE RECORD 2017 (FIRST HALF)

Place purchase price above stock name and weekly closes below.

STOCKS Week Ending	1	2	3	4	5	6	7	8	9	10
JANUARY 6										
13										
20										
27										
FEBRUARY 3										
10										
17										
24										
MARCH 3										
10										
17										
24										
31										
APRIL 7										
14										
21										
28										
MAY 5										
12										
19										
26										
JUNE 2										
9										
16										
23										
30										

WEEKLY PORTFOLIO PRICE RECORD 2017 (SECOND HALF)

Place purchase price above stock name and weekly closes below.

STOCKS Week Ending	1	2	3	4	5	6	7	8	9	10
JULY										
7										
14										
21										
28										
AUGUST										
4										
11										
18										
25										
SEPTEMBER										
1										
8										
15										
22										
29										
OCTOBER										
6										
13										
20										
27										
NOVEMBER										
3										
10										
17										
24										
DECEMBER										
1										
8										
15										
22										
29										

WEEKLY INDICATOR DATA 2017 (FIRST HALF)

	Dow Jones Industrial Average	Net Change for Week	Net Change on Friday	Net Change Next Monday	S&P or NASDAQ	NYSE Ad-vances	NYSE De-clines	New Highs	New Lows	CBOE Put/Call Ratio	90-Day Treas. Rate	Moody's AAA Rate
JANUARY 6												
13												
20												
27												
FEBRUARY 3												
10												
17												
24												
MARCH 3												
10												
17												
24												
31												
APRIL 7												
14												
21												
28												
MAY 5												
12												
19												
26												
JUNE 2												
9												
16												
23												
30												

WEEKLY INDICATOR DATA 2017 (SECOND HALF)

	Week Ending	Dow Jones Industrial Average	Net Change for Week	Net Change on Friday	Net Change Next Monday	S&P or NASDAQ	NYSE Advances	NYSE Declines	New Highs	New Lows	CBOE Put/Call Ratio	90-Day Treas. Rate	Moody's AAA Rate
JULY	7												
	14												
	21												
	28												
AUGUST	4												
	11												
	18												
	25												
SEPTEMBER	1												
	8												
	15												
	22												
	29												
OCTOBER	6												
	13												
	20												
	27												
NOVEMBER	3												
	10												
	17												
	24												
DECEMBER	1												
	8												
	15												
	22												
	29												

MONTHLY INDICATOR DATA 2017

	DJIA% Last 3 + 1st 2 Days	DJIA% 9th to 11th Trading Days	DJIA% Change Rest of Month	DJIA% Change Whole Month	% Change Your Stocks	Gross Domestic Product	Prime Rate	Trade Deficit $ Billion	CPI % Change	% Unem- ployment Rate
JAN										
FEB										
MAR										
APR										
MAY										
JUN										
JUL										
AUG										
SEP										
OCT										
NOV										
DEC										

INSTRUCTIONS:

Weekly Indicator Data (pages 185–186). Keeping data on several indicators may give you a better feel of the market. In addition to the closing DJIA and its net change for the week, post the net change for Friday's Dow and also the following Monday's. A series of "down Fridays" followed by "down Mondays" often precedes a downswing (see page 80). Tracking either the S&P or NASDAQ composite, and advances and declines, will help prevent the Dow from misleading you. New highs and lows and put/call ratios (www. cboe.com) are also useful indicators. All these weekly figures appear in weekend papers or *Barron's*. Data for 90-day Treasury Rate and Moody's AAA Bond Rate are quite important for tracking short- and long-term interest rates. These figures are available from:

> Weekly U.S. Financial Data
> Federal Reserve Bank of St. Louis
> P.O. Box 442
> St. Louis MO 63166
> **http://research.stlouisfed.org**

Monthly Indicator Data. The purpose of the first three columns is to enable you to track the market's bullish bias near the end, beginning, and middle of the month, which has been shifting lately (see pages 92, 145, and 146). Market direction, performance of your stocks, gross domestic product, prime rate, trade deficit, Consumer Price Index, and unemployment rate are worthwhile indicators to follow. Or, readers may wish to gauge other data.

PORTFOLIO AT END OF 2017

DATE ACQUIRED	NO. OF SHARES	SECURITY	PRICE	TOTAL COST	PAPER PROFITS	PAPER LOSSES

IF YOU DON'T PROFIT FROM YOUR INVESTMENT MISTAKES, SOMEONE ELSE WILL

No matter how much we may deny it, almost every successful person in Wall Street pays a great deal of attention to trading suggestions—especially when they come from "the right sources."

One of the hardest things to learn is to distinguish between good tips and bad ones. Usually, the best tips have a logical reason in back of them, which accompanies the tip. Poor tips usually have no reason to support them.

The important thing to remember is that the market discounts. It does not review, it does not reflect. The Street's real interest in "tips," inside information, buying and selling suggestions, and everything else of this kind emanates from a desire to find out just what the market has on hand to discount. The process of finding out involves separating the wheat from the chaff—and there is plenty of chaff.

HOW TO MAKE USE OF STOCK "TIPS"

- The source should be **reliable**. (By listing all "tips" and suggestions on a Performance Record of Recommendations, such as the form below, and then periodically evaluating the outcomes, you will soon know the "batting average" of your sources.)

- The story should make sense. Would the merger violate antitrust laws? Are there too many computers on the market already? How many years will it take to become profitable?

- The stock should not have had a recent sharp run-up. Otherwise, the story may already be discounted, and confirmation or denial in the press would most likely be accompanied by a sell-off in the stock.

PERFORMANCE RECORD OF RECOMMENDATIONS

STOCK RECOMMENDED	BY WHOM	DATE	PRICE	REASON FOR RECOMMENDATION	SUBSEQUENT ACTION OF STOCK

INDIVIDUAL RETIREMENT ACCOUNT (IRA): MOST AWESOME MASS INVESTMENT INCENTIVE EVER DEVISED

MAX IRA INVESTMENTS OF $5,500* A YEAR COMPOUNDED AT VARIOUS INTEREST RATES OF RETURN FOR DIFFERENT PERIODS

Annual Rate	5 Yrs	10 Yrs	15 Yrs	20 Yrs	25 Yrs	30 Yrs	35 Yrs	40 Yrs	45 Yrs	50 Yrs
1%	$28,336	$58,118	$89,418	$122,316	$156,891	$193,230	$231,423	$271,564	$313,752	$358,093
2%	29,195	61,428	97,016	136,308	179,690	227,587	280,469	338,855	403,318	474,490
3%	30,076	64,943	105,363	152,221	206,542	269,515	342,518	427,148	525,258	638,994
4%	30,981	68,675	114,535	170,331	238,215	320,806	421,291	543,546	692,288	873,256
5%	31,911	72,637	124,616	190,956	275,624	383,684	521,600	697,619	922,268	1,208,985
6%	32,864	76,844	135,699	214,460	319,860	460,909	649,665	902,262	1,240,295	1,692,658
7%	33,843	81,310	147,884	241,258	372,221	555,902	813,524	1,174,853	1,681,635	2,392,423
8%	34,848	86,050	161,284	271,826	434,249	672,902	1,023,562	1,538,796	2,295,843	3,408,195
9%	35,878	91,082	176,019	306,705	507,782	817,164	1,293,186	2,025,605	3,152,523	4,886,426
10%	36,936	96,421	192,224	346,514	595,000	995,189	1,639,697	2,677,685	4,349,374	7,041,647
11%	38,021	102,088	210,045	391,958	698,493	1,215,022	2,085,404	3,552,048	6,023,428	10,187,848
12%	39,134	108,100	229,643	443,843	821,337	1,486,609	2,659,047	4,725,283	8,366,697	14,784,112
13%	40,275	114,479	251,195	503,085	967,176	1,822,233	3,397,621	6,300,172	11,647,933	21,500,837
14%	41,445	121,245	274,892	570,726	1,140,330	2,237,054	4,348,701	8,414,497	16,242,841	31,315,649
15%	42,646	128,421	300,946	647,956	1,345,916	2,749,763	5,573,401	11,252,746	22,675,938	45,652,055
16%	43,876	136,031	329,588	736,123	1,589,985	3,383,389	7,150,149	15,061,631	31,678,448	66,579,439
17%	45,138	144,100	361,069	836,762	1,879,695	4,166,271	9,179,470	20,170,648	44,268,235	97,100,943
18%	46,431	152,653	395,665	951,616	2,223,497	5,133,252	11,790,069	27,019,253	61,859,935	141,566,978
19%	47,756	161,720	433,676	1,082,661	2,631,368	6,327,131	15,146,529	36,192,731	86,416,412	206,267,876
20%	49,115	171,327	475,432	1,232,141	3,115,075	7,800,418	19,459,052	48,469,462	120,656,646	300,281,459

* At Press Time—2017 Contribution Limit will be indexed to inflation.

G. M. LOEB'S "BATTLE PLAN" FOR INVESTMENT SURVIVAL

LIFE IS CHANGE: Nothing can ever be the same a minute from now as it was a minute ago. Everything you own is changing in price and value. You can find that last price of an active security on the stock ticker, but you cannot find the next price anywhere. The value of your money is changing. Even the value of your home is changing, though no one walks in front of it with a sandwich board consistently posting the changes.

RECOGNIZE CHANGE: Your basic objective should be to profit from change. The art of investing is being able to recognize change and to adjust investment goals accordingly.

WRITE THINGS DOWN: You will score more investment success and avoid more investment failures if you write things down. Very few investors have the drive and inclination to do this.

KEEP A CHECKLIST: If you aim to improve your investment results, get into the habit of keeping a checklist on every issue you consider buying. Before making a commitment, it will pay you to write down the answers to at least some of the basic questions—How much am I investing in this company? How much do I think I can make? How much do I have to risk? How long do I expect to take to reach my goal?

HAVE A SINGLE RULING REASON: Above all, writing things down is the best way to find "the ruling reason." When all is said and done, there is invariably a single reason that stands out above all others, why a particular security transaction can be expected to show a profit. All too often, many relatively unimportant statistics are allowed to obscure this single important point.

Any one of a dozen factors may be the point of a particular purchase or sale. It could be a technical reason—an increase in earnings or dividend not yet discounted in the market price—a change of management—a promising new product—an expected improvement in the market's valuation of earnings—or many others. But, in any given case, one of these factors will almost certainly be more important than all the rest put together.

CLOSING OUT A COMMITMENT: If you have a loss, the solution is automatic, provided you decide what to do at the time you buy. Otherwise, the question divides itself into two parts. Are we in a bull or bear market? Few of us really know until it is too late. For the sake of the record, if you think it is a bear market, just put that consideration first and sell as much as your conviction suggests and your nature allows.

If you think it is a bull market, or at least a market where some stocks move up, some mark time, and only a few decline, do not sell unless:

✓ You see a bear market ahead.

✓ You see trouble for a particular company in which you own shares.

✓ Time and circumstances have turned up a new and seemingly far better buy than the issue you like least in your list.

✓ Your shares stop going up and start going down.

A subsidiary question is, which stock to sell first? Two further observations may help:

✓ Do not sell solely because you think a stock is "overvalued."

✓ If you want to sell some of your stocks and not all, in most cases it is better to go against your emotional inclinations and sell first the issues with losses, small profits, or none at all, the weakest, the most disappointing, etc.

Mr. Loeb is the author of *The Battle for Investment Survival*, John Wiley & Sons.

G. M. LOEB'S INVESTMENT SURVIVAL CHECKLIST

OBJECTIVES AND RISKS

Security		Price	Shares	Date

"Ruling reason" for commitment	Amount of commitment
	$_____
	% of my investment capital
	_____%

Price objective	Est. time to achieve it	I will risk _____ points	Which would be $_____

TECHNICAL POSITION

Price action of stock:	Dow Jones Industrial Average
❏ Hitting new highs ❏ In a trading range	
❏ Pausing in an uptrend ❏ Moving up from low ground	Trend of market
❏ Acting stronger than market ❏ _____	

SELECTED YARDSTICKS

	Price Range		Earnings Per Share Actual or Projected	Price/Earnings Ratio Actual or Projected
	High	Low		
Current year Previous year				
Merger possibilities			Years for earnings to double in past	
Comment on future			Years for market price to double in past	

PERIODIC RE-CHECKS

Date	Stock Price	DJIA	Comment	Action taken, if any

COMPLETED TRANSACTIONS

Date closed	Period of time held	Profit or loss
Reason for profit or loss		

192